Hamburger AMERICA

A STATE-BY-STATE GUIDE TO 200 GREAT BURGER JOINTS

George Motz

Running Press
PHILADELPHIA

Running Press
Hachette Book Group
1290 Avenue of the Americas, New York, NY 10104
www.runningpress.com
@Running_Press

Printed in China

First Edition: May 2008
Second Edition: May 2011
Third Edition: May 2018

Published by Running Press, an imprint of Perseus Books, LLC, a subsidiary of
Hachette Book Group, Inc. The Running Press name and logo is a trademark
of the Hachette Book Group.

The publisher is not responsible for websites (or their content) that are not owned
by the publisher.

Print book cover and interior design by Jason Kayser
All color photography by George Motz, with the exception of: pg 198, 296,
and 380 Kristoffer Brearton
Historical photos courtesy of the respective restaurants
Back cover photo credit: Douglas Young

Library of Congress Control Number: 2017964363

ISBNs: 978-0-7624-6206-3 (paperback); 978-0-7624-9222-0 (ebook)

RRD-S

10 9 8 7 6 5 4 3 2 1

This book is dedicated to my Hamburger Heroes—
the men and women who wake up every morning,
open the doors of their iconic, multigenerational
restaurants and thanklessly make hamburger magic.
You truly are the heartbeat of America.

For Ruby and Mac—I love you both.

CONTENTS

FOREWORD

By Nick Solares, Food Writer–at–Large
Host, The Meat Show

George Motz is a man on a mission: the preservation of the great American hamburger. And given his particular talents—part food writer, part anthropologist, part raconteur, part photographer, part filmmaker—he is the right man for the job. George's mission might seem quixotic at first blush. After all, hamburgers are everywhere, aren't they? Not exactly. At least not in the sense that George sees them.

To George, the hamburger and the people who serve them, and, indeed, the restaurants, bars, and joints where they are served, are an indispensable part of our heritage. There is arguably no more universal symbol of America than the hamburger. It is as close to a national dish as we have, and just like the American project itself, the burger is reflective of both our regional uniqueness and our national unity.

George understands this better than anyone. Over the last two decades he has crisscrossed the nation, seeking out and documenting unique and captivating visions of the hamburger, each telling its own tale, and at once painting a larger picture of America. Long before Instagram and Twitter reduced discourse to a single image or 160 characters, long before Yelp and Facebook, long before the food blogs even, there was George traveling America and amassing an encyclopedic knowledge of the subject.

And unlike social media posts designed to garner likes, or pay-for-play reviews, George does not beat around the bush, nor suffer fools gladly. And he most certainly does not, as he will often say, "play favorites"—every burger in this book is worthy of your time. And collectively, they are worthy of preservation. Just don't expect George to rank them. Because what is important to George is not that one particular style of burger becomes ubiquitous, but rather that the local nuances are maintained. He stands as a bulwark to the commoditization of the national chains.

I first met George as one of his students—he was presenting his film, *Hamburger America*, that spawned this very book—at a continuing education course at New York University, replete with a practical lesson—burgers where served! I was a budding food writer at the time, focusing on steakhouses. But George's mission inspired me to broaden my scope, and led to my job as a professional hamburger reviewer for Serious Eats.

It's true that what you hold in your hands is a book. You can certainly use it as travel guide. But it can also be a call to arms. You should absolutely visit as many of the places here as possible. But you should also seek out similar, undiscovered places. Just make sure you let George know when you do so he can include it the next edition.

So go forth into Hamburger America. Seek out and devour the delicious, evocative, compelling, life-affirming hamburgers you will find. And don't forget to thank George—the Patron Saint of Hamburgers.

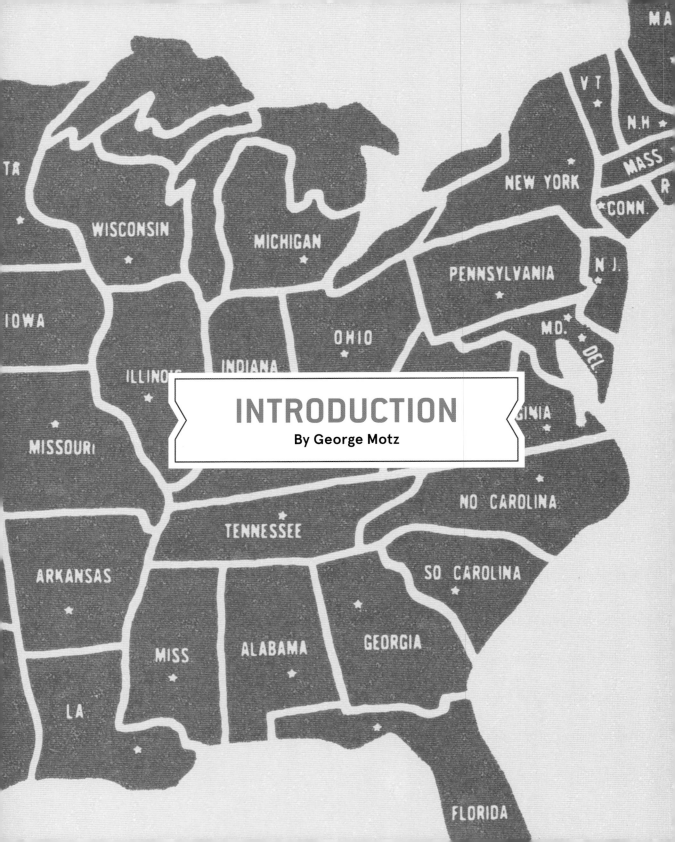

INTRODUCTION

By George Motz

The American burger joint is far more than just a place to eat. It's a community center, and even the ones that don't serve alcohol act as a sort of bar without booze. It's a place for people to catch up and get news whether it's local or global, and every burger joint has its characters, its regulars, and its lifers. For all of the burger counters, shacks, and dives I've fallen in love with over the years, it's the ones with the deepest souls I find myself returning to for my fix of community. And the best ones out there are those that make me feel like a regular after being a complete stranger but a few minutes earlier. This book is full of such places.

It has been one hell of an 18-year mission rambling through America eating burgers and meeting my true burger heroes. As time goes by I've had the good fortune to be able to retrace my steps and check in with old friends at burger joints. I've been pleasantly surprised to find sons, daughters, nephews, cousins . . . all jumping in to help and in many cases take over the restaurants in which they've grown up. These brave souls are the future of Hamburger America.

When I'm on the road, I always find it amusing when people blurt out "This is your job?! You just drive around eating burgers?" That as we know is only part of the story. I do get to travel for burgers, often, but it's taxing on the body and mind. Good health is important, and I exercise and eat well when not on the road. You should, too.

Putting things in perspective—when I started compiling information on America's greatest burger destinations, the Internet was downright ridiculously disorganized, I used paper maps to get around, and Instagram did not exist (how is this possible?). I jumped on the first Garmin GPS system, but traveling with it required a separate case.

Today, my life is much easier. Research is a snap with the amount of information out there and every news source archiving their entire print output. But life is also easier because my name and burger reputation seem to precede me. It's amazing to walk into a classic burger joint for the first time and be greeted with, "We have your book!"

The part of my job that's not easy is hearing about a place that has closed, which happens all too often. Between this version and the last, we lost an astonishing 14 classic burger joints. Most closed for financial reasons, a few the victims of highway expansion, development, and one (Cotham's Mercantile) sadly burned to the ground. Two of them closed as I was buttoning up this revision.

But the new crop is good! I went deep and we discovered classic places open for decades that could easily have been in the first edition of this book. Many of the new discoveries came from a dedicated legion of fans that understand exactly what belongs in Hamburger America. Anyone that takes the time to reach out to me with a hot burger tip is my hero, and I take every piece of information very seriously. It is, understandably, one of the reasons I've been able to do what I do.

Get out there and eat burgers that are, according to this book, some of the best in America. But as you enjoy your heavenly handful of greasy goodness, take a moment to ponder the history of the place you are eating in. It's the reason that burger tastes so damn good. And when you leave, please don't forget to tell them what a great job they are doing. Your appreciation makes them the historically significant burger destinations that they have become.

ARKANSAS

HAMBURGER STATION

110 East Main St | Paragould, AR 72450
870-239-9956 | Mon–Fri 10 am–8 pm | Sat 10 am–7 pm | Closed Sun

You'll smell Hamburger Station before you see it. That's because the unmistakable aroma of onions commingling with beef grease fills this neighborhood just across the tracks from downtown working-class Paragould, Arkansas. "Blue collar are my bread and butter," the friendly Bert Daggett told me in his tiny, clean, short-order kitchen with two young girls helping out. "But we get all types: from the bottom of the ladder to the top come here." Just then a large diesel locomotive pulling thirty-plus grain cars slowly lumbered past only a few feet from the burger stand. The entire stand shook, the engineer let out a few blasts of the horn, and Bert said, "We don't even hear it anymore."

The burger to get at Hamburger Station is the Hum-Burger, also sometimes called the "Hum." It starts as a five-ounce patty of fresh ground 73/27 chuck from a local butcher and is cooked on a tiny flattop that has been in operation since opening day. The patty gets a generous sprinkle of salt and pepper after it hits the griddle. "It's just one of those things,"

Bert explained of the single-sided seasoning approach, "some science someone figured out before me. Pepper on the bottom burns and gives it a harsh taste." A regular cheeseburger comes with mustard, onion, and pickles on a toasted bun, but the Hum adds sweet Texas onions that are thinly sliced and cooked into the patty, much like the style of the Fried Onion Burgers of El Reno, OK (page 273).

The Hum-Burger is an incredible burger. I've only had one to date but its simple perfection knocked me over. The paper wrapping, even for only a few minutes from window to picnic table, warms the finished product perfectly. The pepper is not overwhelming, the dill pickle gives a vinegar bite, and the onions create a deeply satisfying, savory hamburger experience.

Seating is limited to a handful of picnic tables outside (there's no seating inside). Place your order at the window and wait patiently for heaven to arrive. Everything gets wrapped in paper to go, so you'll be eating out of a paper bag outside. It's the way a hamburger stand should be.

looking to retire. They were tired of running the business and only wanted to sell it to someone who wouldn't change a thing. It has been twenty years since he bought Hamburger Station and as he put it, "It must be working!"

He did make one change though in the past twenty years, and it became his one mistake. "I switched from Kraft to Hellmann's mayonnaise." He got a call soon after from the ladies at Lucille's Beauty Salon only a few blocks away. "They let me have it!" Bert remembers, and he switched back to Kraft mayo right away.

It was a life lesson that has helped Bert and his crew crank out consistently great burgers over the past two decades at Hamburger Station. People in the area refer to the Hum-Burger as an "undiscovered gem," and Bert has customers who travel from as far away as Memphis for his under-the-radar burgers. "When someone tells you 'that's the best burger' it just recharges your batteries."

Bert is not the sort of person you'd think to find in a place like this. He has three college degrees and had a successful career but when he was in between jobs the opportunity to purchase Hamburger Station came up. The burger stand was owned by two women, Marky Callum and Dottie Bittick, who converted a closed gas station into a burger stand in 1985. The station was already on the National Historic Register, which means the structure can never be torn down. Bert came along in 1998 and found the women, golf buddies of his mother's, were

Bert is one hard-working guy. The tiny stand is open all winter and, as he explained, "If my girls can't get to work because of snow, I'll go pick them up." Bert himself is at the stand daily and has only taken one break since buying the place. "I was out once for surgery, for a whole week!"

THE APPLE PAN

10801 West Pico Blvd | Los Angeles, CA 90064 | 310-475-3585
Tues–Thurs & Sun 11 am–12 am | Fri & Sat 11 am–1 am | Closed Mon

The Apple Pan serves up one of the best burger experiences in America. The synthesis of flavors and textures in their burgers is second to none, and the presentation is entirely Californian with its waxed paper wrapping. The atmosphere of the place is pure nostalgia, not the kind that is manufactured, but real and enduring. In the twenty years that I have been going there, nothing has changed—the burger I ate in the early '90s is exactly the same as the one I ate last week.

The Apple Pan looks completely out of place on Pico Boulevard in the neighborhood of West Los Angeles. The small white-shingled burger cottage is directly across the street from the towering behemoth Westside Pavilion Mall. All of Westside has built up around the tiny burger spot but the Apple Pan remains. Where the four-story mall stands was once a pony ride field. If you look directly at the Apple Pan and block out all of the surrounding urban chaos, you will be transported to a burger shack on a quiet country road somewhere in rural America.

Clark Gable used to visit regularly when he was working down the street at Paramount. Jack Nicholson and Barbra Streisand are regulars, as are many other Hollywood stars looking for a late-night burger fix.

formed into quarter-pound patties in the restaurant daily. "We'll patty up to a thousand a day," Sunny Sherman, the owner and granddaughter of the man who started the restaurant told me. The most popular burger at the Apple Pan is the Hickoryburger. What separates this burger from most is a proprietary, tangy hickory sauce that goes on the burger along with pickles, mayo, and a sizable wedge of crisp iceberg lettuce (no tomato). All of this (and a slice of Tillamook cheddar if desired) is placed on a toasted white squishy bun and served the way most burgers are in Southern California—wrapped in waxed paper, no plate. The Steakburger replaces the hickory sauce with a sweet relish.

Iceberg lettuce on a burger is an LA tradition, but no burger I've met takes this condiment so seriously. "We only use the middle layers of the head, not the core or outside," grillman Lupe told me. "Just the crisp part." A prep chef slices perfect chunks of the crisp lettuce—one head of iceberg can yield only seven to eight chunks. That's a lot of heads of lettuce when you are cranking out up to a thousand burgers a day.

The result of biting into this pile of textures and flavors is pure bliss. The softness of the bun, the tang of the sauce, the warmth of the griddled beef, and the snap of the lettuce and pickle synthesize in that first bite like no other. It's nearly a perfect burger experience.

Walking into the Apple Pan at peak times can be daunting. There's no real order to who sits where. The trick is to position yourself behind someone who looks like they are finishing (look

The interior looks the same as it did on opening day in 1947 with its scotch plaid wallpaper and now worn terrazzo floor. A horseshoe counter with twenty-six red leather stools and two clunky old mechanical cash registers surround an efficient short-order kitchen. The counter and grillmen all wear crisp white shirts and paper hats and take your order the minute your pants hit the stool. If you ask for fries, out comes a paper plate and the *thwock-thwock* of a counterman pouring ketchup for you. Ask for milk and you'll receive a metal cup holder with a paper insert. It's almost as if someone forgot to tell them the '50s were over. I hope no one does.

The burger menu consists of only two choices—the "Steakburger" and the "Hickoryburger." Both start as fresh ground beef that is for half-eaten pie). If you are alone, the wait is minimal. For groups of ten—forget it.

Ellen and Allan Baker opened the Apple Pan in 1947. Allan had succeeded with another venture across town called King's Kitchen. From King's he brought the Steakburger. With the Apple Pan he introduced the Hickoryburger.

Allan built the Apple Pan as a business to retire on and had not planned to work there but did anyway. He hired Joe Kelly, his caddy from his golf days in Chicago, to be the general manager. In 1973, when Joe fell ill, Charles Collins took his job. Charles celebrated his fiftieth year of employment at the Apple Pan in 2007 (and retired after fifty-two years in 2009), but he is not alone. Many of the countermen have been donning paper caps and serving up burgers and pie for decades. Today, the Bakers' daughter and granddaughter, Martha Gamble and Sunny Sherman, own the Apple Pan. They are committed to keeping the Los Angeles landmark as vibrant as it has been for seventy years.

The timeless quality of old Los Angeles is a draw that is hard to ignore. The Apple Pan does its part to remind us of what can endure in this town of disposable careers and an ever-changing cityscape. There's no need to rush down to the Apple Pan. It'll be there forever.

CAPITOL BURGERS

4301 West Pico Blvd | Los Angeles, CA 90019
323-936-0366 | Mon–Sun 7 am–7 pm

John Stamouvlasis is one of the greatest characters in this book. He is hardboiled and gruff with a striking, deadpan sense of humor and piercing green eyes. He's also extraordinarily passionate about simple cooking and food. It may be the perfect combination for a burger joint operator.

"My dad used to say, 'Don't let anyone take advantage of you.'" When I asked John a question about the history of Capitol Burgers that he couldn't answer, he would respond with a straight face, "Ask my dad." His father, who built the stand in 1965, has been dead for some time. The humor was not lost on me.

patties are cooked quickly on the flattop and married to a heap of waiting fresh veggies on a big toasted bun. A burger with everything comes with chopped onion, crisp iceberg lettuce, a few slices of tomato, pickles, and mustard, held together by the classic SoCal waxed paper wrap. Lean on the counter near the order window and take in the vibe of urban South Central LA.

John started working for his dad in 1972 when he was eight and takes the business of burgers very seriously. "If you don't put your heart and soul into it," he imparted, "you're not going to make it." His day starts as most others are ending—at midnight. That's when John heads to the produce market to buy veggies for the day. He does all the prep himself, opens by 7 a.m., and sometimes has the help of a few nephews to run the place. They offer relief, but John pointed out, "There's more to the business than opening and closing." I asked John when he sleeps, and he simply shook his head.

John's dad, George, arrived in America from Greece in the late 1950s by way of Mobile, Alabama. By 1961 he ventured out to Los Angeles looking for work. His first move was to visit a Greek church and ask where other Greeks were. A Greek bus driver gave him a lead on a Greek burger joint called Jim's Burgers. He worked there for three years, saved his money, and hand-built the stand that is still with us over fifty years later on West Pico.

Show up hungry because the double cheeseburger at Capitol is no joke. Fresh, thin, pre-formed

The quiet, urban neighborhood went into decline during the 1970s and '80s, but came around after the Rodney King riots of 1992 (the epicenter of the violence was only a few blocks away). "Now there's traffic," John pointed out, almost in disbelief. And through it all, the burgers have never changed.

CASSELL'S HAMBURGERS

3600 West 6th St | Los Angeles, CA 90020 | 213-387-5502
Sun–Thurs 7 am–11 pm | Fri & Sat 7 am–2 am | www.cassellshamburgers.com

Sometimes when a good burger joint fails or begins to slip into obscurity, I feel helpless but know that its demise was predestined and possibly necessary. In the case of Cassell's Hamburgers, by the time Al Cassell sold his award-winning burger joint, things in the neighborhood had transformed dramatically.

In 1948, Cassell opened a burger spot across from the Bullock's Department store on Wilshire Boulevard in what is now part of Los Angeles's Koreatown. He successfully ran the restaurant until 1984 when he sold the business to Hakbae Kim. Mr. Kim, as he was affectionately known, was smart enough not to change anything, but in 1986 he moved the restaurant just a few blocks from its original location and out of the slipstream of Wilshire Boulevard. Mr. Kim's son, Jon Kim, became the next owner and while he tried to stay true to Cassell's vision, the writing was on the wall. Although the burgers were fantastic every time I visited the Koreatown burger outpost, I was always in the place alone; never another customer in sight. The joint was out of place in a rapidly changing neighborhood and Cassell's felt like a burger museum that was only open for me. The end was imminent.

Cassell's closed, but then something extraordinary happened—it came back to life. Many great burger legends have faded into history and I've unfortunately witnessed too many of them. Very rarely does an icon become not only resurrected but handled with respect to its former life.

"I'm not really a foodie guy," new owner, Jingbo Lou, told me recently sitting at the bar at the new Cassell's. Jingbo, a Korean American architect, purchased the dilapidated Hotel Normandie and turned it into an amazing boutique hotel. The ground-floor space with huge windows

overlooking Normandie Avenue and 6th Street was screaming for a restaurant and Jingbo told me, "I was looking for a classic American place to come to this corner." He had heard from a preservationist friend that Cassell's was for sale and he jumped at the opportunity. In December 2014, it became a reality. Everything from the original Cassell's was moved to the new location six blocks away, including the grilling apparatus that made the burger famous.

Al Cassell made a name for himself by employing a unique method for cooking burgers on equipment that was given to him by his uncle-in-law. The large, high flattop griddle contains two smaller flattops that slide out from underneath. These smaller, sliding flattops are actually the bottom half of a double broiler called a "crossfire." When the patty is placed on this flattop and slid back in, the burger cooks simultaneously from the top as well as the bottom. I'm guessing that Al's griddle was designed for speed but he inadvertently created a method for keeping the burger very moist. When a burger is placed in this contraption, it is not touched until it is placed on a bun. No flipping or pressing is necessary. Legend has it that only two of these grills were made and came from San Francisco.

Cassell's brought in veteran chef Christian Page, who had previously worked with Nancy Silverton to open the newish LA burger spot Short Order. His ideas about preservation were in line with Jingbo's, right down to grinding the beef daily for the burgers, just like Al had done for decades. "Most importantly, for us, is keeping the soul of the place," Christian told me. They did, however, add a "vegan" patty to the menu to, as Christian put it, "cover all of the Angelenos." The burger, thanks to grinding in-house and cooking on the original equipment, tastes pretty much the same.

In the old days, you took your undressed burger to a limited toppings bar. Health codes prevented this in the new space so Christian serves those toppings on the side now. He also worked hard to get the famous horseradish potato salad right and nailed it. "It wasn't easy!" he told me. "His recipe called for 'handfuls' as a measurement, so we tested with different sized hands to get it right." Now that is dedication to the craft with a deep appreciation for history.

All of the original signage made the trek to Hotel Normandie as did the tables and chairs. It's not exactly like the original Cassell's, of course, but if anyone were to revive and gently update a burger joint it would be these guys. And hey, it's probably the only burger you can get in this book with valet parking!

GEORGE'S BAR & GRILL

68885 Ramon Rd | Cathedral City, CA 92234 | 760-328-9991
Mon–Sat 11 am-3 pm | Closed Sun

You were warned by the sign outside, written as clear as day, for all to see: "World Famous Burgers and Insults." This is no joke. You have been warned.

Obviously, I would never send you into a dangerous place or a joint that serves bad burgers. But I have to tell you that this is one of those places where if you are even the slightest bit of an asshole you are NOT getting a burger. Period. True story: A good friend of mine went in, made a wisecrack about ketchup, and was shown the door. All that travel for nothing.

That said, assuming you are having a great day and are playing by the very simple rules at George's you will be rewarded with a burger that I dream about constantly. Even the man behind all of those insults can become a friend if you see things his way, in his bar.

That man is Ed Marinko, second-generation owner of this desert watering hole surrounded by strip malls near Palm Springs, California. Ed is tough, grouchy, and sparsely covered in simple dark blue tattoos. He also sports a thick white beard giving him the look of Santa's badass younger brother. Ed is married to his craft, and anyone who knows anything about burgers knows that this man is a burger savant.

Here's how it works at George's: Ed is ever-present, at the griddle or prep station behind the bar. He will make small talk and say hello to just about everyone that walks into the dark bar out of the blazing desert sun. He's actually a really nice guy, that is, until you cross him. He has a rule about ketchup on burgers—it's a big no-no. However, he does provide ketchup for his fries. If he catches you putting ketchup on your burger, you'll be dining on the hood of your car. But there are other ways to get into trouble with Ed. Being too drunk makes him angry. Dumping your bowl of chili on your burger is indefensible. Even general narcissism will set him off. I once heard a woman that he knew say, "Aren't you going to wish me a happy birthday??" Ed's loud response, "*My* birthday doesn't mean anything to me, yours means *less*." Under the old TV, mounted high in the corner of the bar, is a plaque that reads, "SCREW THE CUSTOMERS." Just be happy you followed my advice and are eating a burger.

George Marinko was a middleweight boxer in Pennsylvania before moving to the California desert to open a bar in 1969. His impressive collection of vintage baseball bats is still on the wall behind the bar, in the care of George's son, Ed, who became the owner of the place over two decades ago.

Plain and simple, the burger at George's is one where you will begin to make plans for

a return visit while still holding an unfinished burger in your hands. Unquestionably, get the double cheeseburger. Ed uses fresh ground, fatty chuck and makes four-ounce patties by hand every morning. He cooks the patties slowly on a very seasoned griddle, sprinkles them with a secret seasoned salt, then transfers the patties to buns that have been set up with condiments, by Ed, while the burgers are cooking. When you finally get your cheeseburger, with shredded lettuce, fresh tomato, and slice of raw onion, wrapped in waxed paper, you'll understand from the perfect construction just what Ed was doing back there.

Every burger that leaves the tiny, efficient bar kitchen is made by Ed from beginning to end, from open to close. Ed takes his time, too, because he has a pace that seems to work (and that's that). I've waited as little as twenty minutes and up to one hour and forty-five minutes on busy days.

The crowd is a funny mix of old-timers in pastel polo shirts (it's the Land of the Retiree) and tattooed bikers in leather and do-rags, and they seem to mix well.

George's is closed in the summer because it's just too damn hot in the Coachella Valley. (It can reach 115 degrees in August, yuck.) So Ed and Linda hit the road for Hawaii every year.

GOTT'S ROADSIDE

933 Main St | St Helena, CA 94574 | 707-963-3486 | Open Daily 10 am–9 pm (Winter)
10 am–10 pm (Summer) | (Six Other Locations) | www.gotts.com

The drive to Gott's takes you right through the heart of the Napa Valley. You'll pass rows and rows of vineyards and welcoming wineries with products to sample. Take a deep breath and smell the dense, pungent odor of freshly pressed grapes. It seems like the last place you'd find a good hamburger joint. That is, of course, until you pull into Gott's Roadside.

Gott's is in the center of it all. Most of the patrons of this updated classic '40s burger drive-in seem to be the buttoned-down wine-tasting types, but the stand does get its fair share of working-class locals as well. A bit of an anomaly in this part of the Napa Valley, Gott's has endured the influx of luxury hotels, inns, and spas as well as a number of high-end restaurants.

The burger stand opened in 1949 as Taylor's Refresher. In the late '90s, two brothers with a long family history in winemaking, Duncan and Joel Gott, bought the ailing stand. The structure received a first-class face-lift, but they made sure to maintain the integrity of the original stand. The city of St. Helena allowed the Gott brothers to expand only slightly, as Duncan put it, "for health reasons." He explained, "Before we bought the place, the refrigerators used to be outside, out back." Today's Gott's is a superclean, contemporary version of the former stand with an upgraded kitchen and menu full of gourmet road food. In 2010, the Gott brothers, proud of the burger stand they had resurrected, decided to change the name from Taylor's to Gott's Roadside. The change became the subject of local news and debate.

The hamburgers at Gott's are well thought out, tasty, and like so many quality hamburgers of the Pacific Northwest, socially conscious. Duncan explained, "We spent weeks of testing to come up with the right blend for the burgers." The one-third-pound fresh patties come from naturally raised, hormone-free cattle of Niman Ranch. They are cooked on an open-flame grill and served on locally made, soft, pillowy buns. A "secret sauce" also goes on all of the burgers at Gott's. It's a creamy, tangy, mayo-based sauce similar to "Goop," (see page 380) the standard condiment on some old-school burgers of the Northwest. "The spices in the sauce we keep secret," manager at the time, Dave, told me. All of the burgers are served with lettuce, pickle, and presented in fry boats on a small metal sheet pan (which helps perpetuate the drive-in aesthetic).

The burger selection at Gott's ranges from the traditional with american cheese to gourmet creations topped with guacamole or blue cheese. New to the menu is a kimchi burger and Gott's now has a tasty green chile cheeseburger, too. The extensive menu also includes healthy options like ahi poke tacos and Cobb salad but no meal at Gott's would be complete without one of their extraordinary milkshakes. Gott's now uses organic Three Twins premium ice cream and organic milk, which means their milkshake game is strong.

There is no indoor seating and the carhops are long gone, so find a spot at one of the many large red picnic tables in front, or on the spacious back lawn. Save your wine tasting for Gott's, too. There's a separate "bar" here that serves a rotating selection of over twenty local wines and twenty different beers on tap, in bottles and cans. I'm not too confident about the pairing of a cheeseburger and a good Cabernet, but I can tell you there's nothing like a great burger and a cold beer. Or maybe kombucha is your thing—they have that, too.

I asked Duncan why the offspring of a wine family (his brother is a fifth-generation winemaker in the region) decided to buy a hamburger stand and he told me, "We have a family love affair with food." They weren't even sure the venture would work. "The day we opened five hundred people showed up, and we thought, 'We could do this . . . we could be successful!'"

HINANO CAFE

15 Washington Blvd | Venice, CA 90292
310-822-3902 | Mon–Sun 8 am–2 am | www.hinanocafevenice.com

Saturday morning is special at Hinano Cafe. "This whole bar is full of people with pitchers in front of them," manager of twenty-five years, Mary Alice, told me. I can see myself indulging in this activity as well because Hinano is one of those places you dream about melting into. It's the perfect, broken-in tiki-themed bar only steps from the sands of Venice Beach. Outside, surfers are pulling on wet suits in the street and pumping the parking meters. Inside, the air is filled with the saltiness of the Pacific and the aroma of burgers. What else could you ask for?

The moment also makes you hum that famous line sung by the Doors in 1970, "*I woke up this morning and I got myself a beer. . . .*" It's very fitting for this bar but even more so since the legendary lead singer Jim Morrison lived nearby and apparently frequented the place. "Ahhhh, it could be an exaggeration, but it's a good story," Mary Alice admitted, but added, "Dennis Wilson [Beach Boys drummer] was here often for sure."

The burgers are available all day, starting at 8 a.m. The short-order kitchen is just inside the front door, connected to the long bar. Everything comes to Hinano fresh daily. The chef cooks fresh 80/20 one-third-pound chuck patties on the flat-top and toasts the seeded buns, both sides, on the flattop, too. The griddling of sesame seeds "wakes up" the seeds and brings out an almost nutty flavor. Ask for everything and you'll get red onion, shredded lettuce, tomato, pickle relish, mustard, and mayonnaise. Your cheese choices are limited to cheddar or swiss.

The only thing frozen at Hinano are the veggie burgers. "So many of them go out with bacon on them," Mary Alice pointed out, "I don't get it."

The tiki theme is not random. As the story goes, former owner Joe Larson opened the bar on Christmas Eve in 1961. "He spent a whole bunch of time in Tahiti," Mary Alice told me, and he was an extra in the film *Mutiny on the Bounty*. The bar's name comes from a white flower that grows in Tahiti. The old-school bar has thick leather-topped stools for your drinking comfort and sawdust on the floor. For the last twenty-two years Hinano has been owned and run by Andy Schelich and Mark Van Gessel, only the third owners in the bar's long history.

Finding old, comfortable things like Hinano Cafe in Los Angeles is a treat. It tends to be a town of new, flashy things. It's good to see LA hold on to a bit of its past.

HODAD'S

5010 Newport Ave | Ocean Beach, CA 92107 | 619-224-4623
Open Daily 11 am–10 pm | (Two Other Locations in San Diego) | www.hodadies.com

Hodad's is exactly what you're looking for in a Southern California burger destination—an open-air restaurant serving enormous, tasty, no-frills burgers wrapped in waxed paper just steps from the beach. The atmosphere is inviting, with its license plate–covered walls, the front end of a '66 VW Microbus that serves as a two-person booth, a public water bowl for dogs outside, and a sign reading "No shoes, no shirt . . . no problem!"

There are basically three burgers to order here: the Mini, the Single, and the Double. Single burgers start as a one-third-pound patty. A Double involves two patties, and after adding cheese, lettuce, tomato, onion, mayo, bacon, and so on, becomes very large.

The bacon served at Hodad's is out of this world. An employee once invited me into the kitchen to show me how the bacon is prepared. Fortunately, for the sake of keeping proprietary secrets safe, I didn't really follow the process. It involved large amounts of special, uncooked bacon in a sieve sitting over a pot of boiling water. At some point this bacon boil is transferred to the grill, cooked until crispy, and married to your burger. The taste is truly unique and adds an intense smokiness to the burger experience. I also got a glimpse of the decades-old cast-iron grill. Needless to say, I can see where a Hodad burger gets its flavor.

The restaurant doesn't grind their own beef anymore, though they get a delivery of fresh

patties every morning. Don't miss the fries! They are enormous, battered slices of potato that resemble the popular "Jo-Jo," a deep-fried, midwestern truck-stop spud specialty.

Like a surprising number of hamburger stands in America, Hodad's has moved locations three times, but all within a few blocks. The first Hodad's, built in the sand right next to the lifeguard tower, opened in 1969 by Byron and Virginia Hardin. Their son, Michael, moved the business one block inland to its current location. Michael was a beloved character and the unofficial "Mayor of Ocean Beach," but passed away suddenly in 2015. He was a tattoo-covered surfer who drove a customized VW Microbus with about six feet missing from its center. Michael was known to drive it into the O.B. parades unregistered and employees would throw fries out the window.

Soon after his passing, his two children, Shane and Lexi, assumed ownership of the restaurant. Shane is ultra-laid-back, confident, and friendly and runs the day-to-day at Hodad's. He clearly sets the vibe in the place and knows everyone. He has kept the legacy that his father built intact but is adding to it, and is set to open a brewery that will supply the restaurant with its very own craft brew.

Hodad's still accepts license-plate donations, and if you submit a custom plate your meal is free. You really have never seen a collection of plates quite this extensive.

What is a "hodad"? A person who hangs out at the beach and pretends to be a surfer. Hodad or not, I would suggesting eating here after surfing, not before.

THE SECRET MENU AT IN-N-OUT: SOME INSIGHT

The first time I visited an In-N-Out I ordered the Double-Double and was underwhelmed. In an effort to understand the hype, I visited a few more times but decided that In-N-Out was clearly the most overrated burger chain in America. A few weeks later, Oprah's gal pal, Gayle King, had me on her radio show and the first thing out of her mouth was, "I have a bone to pick with you. . . . How can you NOT LOVE In-N-Out??" The backlash that followed was real. More research was necessary.

Years earlier I had heard rumor of a "secret menu" but didn't have the guts to try it out because I didn't believe it actually existed (we are talking pre-Internet here). Then one day as I was giving the SoCal fresh beef burger chain one more shot I overheard someone in front of me order a Double-Double "Animal Style." There it was, right off the secret menu and the smiling girl at the register seemed completely unfazed. I followed with a similar order (my default for over a decade now at In-N-Out, a Triple-Triple Animal Style and a Neapolitan shake) and was knocked over by how good it was. My opinion about In-N-Out had been altered.

The menu at In-N-Out contains only four items (not including drinks), a spartan collection of fast-food standards. The *real* menu is a "secret" that contains well over eighty items, mostly modifications using elements of the printed menu. And it turns out that the staff is fully prepared and well versed on the options available, and eager to please. It's an institutionalized secret that has been around for decades at In-N-Out, one that is part of employee training at every one of their 313 units in six states. Just about all of the fast-food chains out there have some sort of a secret menu but nothing rivals the size and depth of In-N-Out's. Secret menu items at other chains, regardless of their popularity (like the Rodeo Burger at Burger King, or poutine at KFC), are *not* available at every location. You can walk confidently into any In-N-Out, ask for a Flying Dutchman Animal Style and receive the same two-patty, bunless cheeseburger available across the chain.

The company has listed a few of the more popular items on their website under the heading "The Not-So-Secret Menu" (I have a hunch it's for legal reasons and trademarked burger concoctions) but we all know the list of options is much larger. A call to In-N-Out headquarters in an effort to learn more about the secret menu's origins led to nothing. A friendly associate told me that there was no way to assess the actual number of available secret menu items (even though many of them are in the database and appear on your receipt). Add to the list a handful of menu hacks by fans (like Monkey Style, where fries are shoved into the burger—In-N-Out associates will respectfully deny this request) and the list expands. The gentle pushback by In-N-Out for certain requests shows that the company takes the integrity of their cult menu very seriously. And they should; by carefully controlling the entire menu, fostering mystique, and standardizing it across the entire chain, they've vastly improved the quality of offerings and built a sizable fan base.

Animal Style is arguably the most popular secret menu choice, and the origins of its name are a bit murky. Stacy Perman, who wrote the definitive story of the cult burger chain (*In-N-Out Burger*, HarperCollins, 2009) offered this explanation: In-N-Out was a popular hang for surfers and hippies in the 1960s. It's very likely that one of them asked for a custom order, which stuck, and was so named by an associate because its progenitor was dirty, long-haired and "animal-like." And for all of its hype, the Double-Double Animal Style is a pretty straight-forward burger: two thin patties made from fresh ground beef on a toasted white squishy bun served with two slices of american cheese, crisp iceberg lettuce, tomato, and a dollop of

Thousand Island dressing. It is presented California-style, wrapped in wax paper, to facilitate one-handed driving.

For those that love In-N-Out, and for those that have gone far past love into the fanatic stage, there is a sound basis as to how a standard burger joint can reach such status—integrity. The company has proved the age-old tenet that real customer service and an actual connection to the people that consume your product means everything. The secret menu at In-N-Out is a big part of their success but the company's gentle touch with how a menu can be perceived speaks volumes.

IRV'S BURGERS

7998 Santa Monica Blvd | West Hollywood, CA 90046 | 323-650-2456
Mon–Fri 7:30 am–8 pm | Sat 8 am–7 pm | Closed Sun | www.irvsburgers.com

Sonia tried as hard as she could to save her tiny burger stand but the forces around her were too great. Korean American Sonia and her brother, Sean, bought the business with every penny they had in 2000 from Irving Gendis, who had flipped burgers there from 1978 to 2000. Before it was Irv's, the tiny stand on old Route 66 opened as Queen's Burgers in 1948. Almost from the day she bought the place, she was dogged by the threat of corporate coffee (Peet's) taking over the property and a crazy landlord that wanted to throw her out and tear the historic burger stand down. The regulars were appalled, the neighborhood was empowered, and cute, little Sonia was not going down without a fight. At some point, she and a very generous customer took the fight to city hall and after a year, Los Angeles County declared Irv's an historical monument. Take that!

But unfortunately, it still wasn't enough, and in 2013 the landlord raised her rent to an unreasonable sum. The family was forced to move out. But now that the stand was landmarked it could not be torn down. See if you can guess what happened to the business that moved into Irv's old stand and the adjoining property? You guessed it—already closed. Nice work, guys.

Irv's did not move very far. You can now find the beloved burger joint in arguably better digs only four blocks east of the old location. Indoor seating eliminates the need to shout over the traffic to tell your lunch mates a story. But if you miss the thrill of dining only a few feet from lovely LA traffic, grab one of the outdoor tables.

Irv's is blessed with a very rich history of colorful customers. Over the decades, many Hollywood stars and musicians became regulars including Jim Morrison and Janis Joplin, cementing the popularity of this burger destination. Irv's also made a great backdrop for the inner sleeve of Linda Ronstadt's *Living in the USA*. Open the record album and you'll see a nighttime snapshot, two feet wide, taken in 1978 at Irv's with Linda and her band posing. It's great to see the vintage stand immortalized through music.

The move did not change the menu one bit, in fact, the Hongs took the griddle with them to ensure continuity. The burger at Irv's is still a California classic: tucked into waxed paper, on a soft, toasted white bun, and served on a paper plate. A wad of fresh ground beef is slapped on the tiny griddle and smashed HARD with a bacon weight once. Somehow Sonia, or whoever is at the grill, manages to whack the ball of meat with just the right amount of force to create the perfect-sized patty.

Usually, three people are hard at work at Irv's including Mama, Sonia's mother. In all of the craziness that goes on at Irv's during lunch Sonia still has time to write personalized messages on everyone's paper plate. On my last visit she drew, down to the color, the shirt I was wearing and included the message, "Just for George." She positions the burger on the plate so that both the burger and the art can be admired simultaneously. I believe the shirt drawings are her way of matching the burger to the customer—one of the more unique methods of order management.

Opt for a double with cheese because a single thin patty will not sate your appetite. Available condiments are the standard lettuce, tomato, onion, and pickle. Mayo, ketchup, and mustard are also available, and the menu lists a burger that comes with "special sauce." When I asked Sonia what the sauce was, she replied, without pause, "Love! Love is the special sauce."

The next time you visit Irv's, meet Sonia and Mama and feel proud to be an American. Eat your waxed paper–wrapped burger, take in the vibe of old Route 66, and remember the fight that Sonia, her family, and dedicated customers fought to save the American Hamburger—each bite will taste that much better. A soulless corporation and unscrupulous landlord may have won the battle over real estate, but they were powerless to the mighty cheeseburger.

JIM-DENNY'S

816 12th St | Sacramento, CA 95814 | 916-443-9655
Wed–Sun 7 am–2 pm | Closed Mon & Tues | www.jimdennys.net

For its first forty years Jim-Denny's never closed. From 1934 to the late '70s the tiny ten-stool hamburger stand in downtown Sacramento was open twenty-four hours. Most of those odd late-night/early-morning hours fed bus drivers from the Trailways depot just across the parking lot and late-night revelers at the long-gone dance hall across the street. The bus depot is no longer active and the restaurant's hours have been reduced, but Jim-Denny's survives thanks to its fifth owners Leada Flowers and her son, James McCuen.

behind the counter remain intact, labeled with features of the old menu (Fancy Cheeseburgers and a Fancy Cube Steak Sandwich for twenty-five cents). The ten original red leather swivel stools are still anchored at their spots facing the worn, Formica counter. The griddle continues to occupy the same spot just inside the front window.

Jim and a friend, Denny, started Jim-Denny's just before World War II. After the war, Jim and Denny parted ways and Jim opened a new restaurant with the same name around the corner. That location (also known as number two) is the only one that remains, and thanks to the efforts of Jim in 1988, this classic American burger stand has been designated as an historic landmark by the city of Sacramento.

The burgers at Jim-Denny's come in two sizes—a three-ounce patty and a six-ounce. Both arrive at Jim-Denny's daily as fresh, pre-formed patties.

The burger menu is extensive. You can order a Megaburger (two-and-a-half-pound patties), a Superburger (one-and-a-half-pound patty), or the Five Cent Burger, the original price for the quarter-pound burger. Each is served on locally made fluffy white rolls with lettuce, tomato, onion, pickle, mayo, and mustard—standard.

A tradition that disappeared with Jim along with his "my way or no way" attitude was one

Prior to Leada and Jimmy, Patsy Lane owned the cozy burger joint for five years and was responsible for removing decades of grease and grime that had almost rendered the place unusable. "The ceiling had almost caved in, it was caked with so much grease," Patsy told me years ago. "If you put your hand on the wall it would just stick there!"

Regardless of the rebuild and deep cleansing that the restaurant went through, Jim-Denny's still serves beautifully greasy, griddled burgers that are slightly larger than those that Jim Van Nort and subsequent owners served for the first eighty years. And with the exception of new curtains on the windows, everything else is pretty much the same. The wooden candy and cigarette shelves of the restaurant's most endearing qualities—if you sat at the last seat at the counter you had to answer the phone and take the orders. The rule was created based on the seat's proximity to the phone. Fortunately for lovers of tradition like myself, I was glad to see that Jim's original note to diners at the seat remains, right next to the nonfunctioning pay phone. "If you sit near the phone you must answer it. Take the order, or ask them to hold." This was followed by sample greetings: "Jim-Denny's may I help you?" or "Jim-Denny's, please hold."

Leada and Jimmy plan to own the landmarked business for a while and did a very smart thing—they bought the land underneath Jim-Denny's. When it came up for sale from Jim Van Nort's daughter they jumped at the chance. General manager and family member Crystal Coronel proudly pointed out to me, "That's how this place will survive."

MARTY'S HAMBURGER STAND

10558 West Pico Blvd | Los Angeles, CA 90064 | 310-836-6944
Mon–Sat 8 am–6 pm | Sun 10 am–6 pm

In a town where finding old, established anything is getting harder and harder look for this tiny burger stand in West LA for a genuine blast from LA's past. What's more, Marty's has been serving up quality fast food made with fresh ingredients and has never succumbed to the temptation to serve processed frozen food. For nearly five decades almost nothing has changed. "Nothing," Vicki Bassman told me. "Never will." Vicki is the daughter-in-law of Marty himself. She told me without pause, "There's nothing like fresh meat."

Marty's is the "Home of the Combo" and this fact is proudly displayed on a sign on the roof of the stand (but is slightly obscured by new exhaust housing so the old sign now reads "Home of the Comb"). The combo is so basic you'll wonder why more restaurants have not followed suit. Invented in the 1950s, the combo at Marty's is a hamburger with a hot dog on top. It's a great-tasting way to be indecisive and order both fast-food icons together.

Both meats for the combo come from high-quality ingredients; the hot dogs are Vienna Beef foot-longs and the burgers are pattied on the premises daily from fresh ground chuck. Longtime grillman, Geraldo, told me, "We take a three-and-a-half ounce measured scoop of fresh ground beef and press each patty by hand." They use a single press that produces an almost paper-thin patty, one at a time. On the original, perfectly seasoned griddle, the combo is cooked separately, then wed. The foot-long is halved lengthwise, flattened, and then halved again, resembling a small, square red raft. The burger is cooked for less than a minute on each side before the hot dog raft is

placed on top. The stack of America's two favorite fast foods piggybacked on the griddle and separated by a square of yellow american cheese is a sight both absurd and beautiful; a sight that makes you proud to be an American.

Burgers come standard with mayonnaise, ketchup, lettuce, onion, and a tomato slice (which Angel slices as your burger comes off the griddle). Mustard and pickles need to be requested. One time a guy on line in front of me asked for his combo "my way," and told me, "That just means extra mustard, extra mayo."

Marty Bassman opened the roadside stand in 1958 and worked the griddle until the late 1960s when operations were handed over to his son, Howard. When Howard assumed the business he was only seventeen years old. Today, Howard and his wife run the stand as well as a successful

catering business that focuses on supplying local schools with high-quality lunches and private barbecues around Los Angeles.

The tiny blue-and-orange burger stand is a blur to most as they speed down Pico. Wedged between a gas station and a fire department, and down the street from popular Rancho Park, the stand is a daily lunch spot for firefighters. "They have a gym upstairs," former manager Angel, told me, "they have nothing to worry about." The hard-working crew at Marty's takes orders without writing a single thing down. "I can remember up to twenty-five orders at a time, in my head," Angel told me once, tapping his temple.

A throwback to simpler times, the stand offers walk-up service, a few outdoor stools, and narrow counters along the sides of the structure. A patio behind the stand (that I only discovered recently) has enough seating for fifty.

Howard told me, "When I was a kid, there were mom-and-pop hamburger stands like Marty's all over Los Angeles. They've all disappeared." Across the street from Marty's stands the ubiquitous golden arches of a popular American burger chain. Its garish presence, though, doesn't seem to affect the brisk business being conducted at Marty's. It seems that the waiting customers are smarter than that. They know where to find a real burger.

PIE 'N BURGER

913 East California Blvd | Pasadena, CA 91106 | 626-795-1123
Sun–Thurs 7 am–9 pm | Fri & Sat 7 am–10 pm | www.pienburger.com

"That was the last slice of butterscotch pie. Hope you didn't want one," the waitress said to me on my first visit to this fifty-five-year-old burger counter. The customer I had just been speaking to, who had told me he was visiting from London, said he was not leaving California without a slice of butterscotch pie from Pie 'n Burger. No big deal. I didn't know what I was missing. Then I visited two more times and ran into the same problem (one time I showed up on a day they were not even offering the fabled pie). Finally, on my fourth visit, I got my slice. This pie is not to be missed. Their pie motto (written on the pie safe): "Take home one of our famous homemade pies for that special occasion or just when you want to live it up."

But the obvious reason to visit Pie 'n Burger is for their incredible hamburgers. Since 1963, the long, faux-wood-grain Formica countertop has seen its share of burger perfection. The burger they made in the '60s is the same one that is served today. Even the local retail butcher that supplies the ground chuck has not changed in over forty years. Longtime employee and owner Michael Osborn told me, "The beef we use is top quality and ground coarse. That's why they taste so good."

Two other important factors that go into the great-tasting burgers are the original, well-seasoned, flattop griddle, and the homemade Thousand Island dressing. "We go through about one hundred pounds of dressing a week," Michael told me. The recipe came directly from Kraft in the '30s. Original owners Benny and Florence Foote were in the restaurant business long before opening Pie 'n Burger. According to Michael, Benny contacted Kraft and they gave him the recipe. "We still make it the same exact way, using Kraft mayonnaise."

A burger with Thousand Island dressing may sound familiar. California's own burger phenomenon, In-N-Out, also uses the dressing on their burgers but the burger at Pie 'n Burger

smashed flat with a huge can of tomato juice.

The system for cooking and assembling the burgers is all about efficiency. One person flips the burgers while another preps buns with a wedge of lettuce and dressing. The grillmen are seasoned professionals—one, Franciso, told me enthusiastically, "I've been here for forty-two years!"

Michael started working at the restaurant in 1972, flipping burgers and going to USC full-time. When he graduated, he continued to work at the restaurant, gradually helping out with managerial duties. In the late '70s, Michael bought a piece of the business and in 1992 the Foote family, in search of retirement, sold the remainder of the shares to him.

Pie 'n Burger looks exactly as it did in 1963 (with some obvious wear). The wood-paneled walls and plaid wallpaper look beautifully out of date, as does the hand-painted wall menu. A cup of buttermilk is still offered with the usual diner fare of tuna sandwiches and chicken pot pie.

I asked Michael why he had stuck with the burger counter for so long and he told me, "I took the job because it was fun working here. To me, life is about having fun." Michael also feels like he has been entrusted to Pie 'n Burger's survival. "I feel like a caretaker to the business for the community."

is far superior. For years, a double cheeseburger was an off-menu item and I never knew this. The first time I visited back in 2005, I ordered what a friend ordered and never even looked at the menu. Fast-forward to 2014 when we put Pie 'n Burger on my Travel Channel show, *Burger Land*, and again ordered the double cheeseburger. "We definitely had a double cheeseburger bump after the show aired," Michael confessed, "So we added it to the menu." Yours truly, accidentally affecting burger change.

The burgers at Pie 'n Burger are made from fresh ground beef, griddled, served on toasted white buns with iceberg lettuce and Thousand Island dressing and presented wrapped in waxed paper. The patties at Pie 'n Burger are also somewhat hand-formed. Quarter-pound balls of fresh beef are measured with an ice-cream scoop then

ROCKY'S CROWN PUB

3786 Ingraham St | San Diego, CA 92109 | 858-273-9140
Open Daily 11 am–12 am | www.rockyburgers.com

Step into Rocky's Crown Pub and into darkness. As your eyes adjust, you'll find a very clean bar with tiny windows that are just large enough to let in a bit of California sunshine. The clientele is a mixed bag of locals in Hawaiian shirts and beach blondes sipping beer and watching sports on a few television screens. The first time I visited, I arrived at 11:30 a.m. on a weekday and the place was at capacity. There was plenty of parking outside, which told me that most of the customers arrived on foot, read: very local. They are all there for one thing: Rocky's famous burgers.

"It's the greatest business in the world!" A longtime regular sitting at the bar named Billy Graham told me. "Two kinds of burgers, beer and wine only, and *cash*." He's absolutely correct. Anyone that can pull off this business model and be a success is a genius.

The menu at Rocky's is limited to five things: hamburger or cheeseburger, either one-third- or half-pound, and fries. That's it, and that's the way it has always been. What the bar lacks in hard booze is made up for in the excellent selection of local beers on tap. It is San Diego, after all, where there is no shortage of great craft beer.

The burgers are cooked in a minuscule kitchen by the back door of Rocky's. They hand-form patties from fresh 80/20 chuck and have two different-sized buns depending on which burger you

order. Do the right thing and get the half-pound burger. Your cheese choices are american or swiss (the bartender will ask, "yellow" or "white"?) and the burger is served with green-leaf lettuce, red onion, tomato, and mayonnaise with a few pickle slices speared to the top of the bun. "People complain often that we only have burgers on the menu," bartender Joe told me. For those oddballs, Joe said, "we have a cheese sandwich." I'm going to guess that a cheese sandwich is a burger without the meat, cold. Please don't order this.

Rocky's is all about zero pretense. The place is ordinary by design and not trying to be anything but good. Orders are taken on yellow Post-it notes, and the burgers are served in red plastic boats. Condiments line the bar in their branded containers, and don't miss out on the crock filled with hot, pickled California chiles.

A regular named Billy told me, "I used to ride my bike by here when I was a kid in the late 1940s. It was a bar with no windows and I always wondered what went on in there." In 1977, the bar became Rocky's Crown Pub when a woman named Rocky bought the place and started serving burgers.

Don't show up with a huge group; you'll only be miserable. And don't do what I did and stand by the kitchen door (temporarily blocking access to burger delivery). The best way to truly enjoy Rocky's is to show up solo. If you are lucky, grab a stool at the bar, get a beer, and take in the Crown Point neighborhood vibe. For under ten bucks you can walk out into the SoCal sunlight with a full belly and a smile on your face.

THE SPOT

389 Linden Ave | Carpinteria, CA 93013 | 805-684-6311
Tues–Thurs & Sun 10 am–7 pm | Fri & Sat 10 am–8 pm | Mon 10 am–4 pm

True to its SoCal roots, the Spot is about as accurate as it gets in terms of the classic, wax paper–wrapped double cheeseburger. It's been making burger lovers happy for decades, and there's no question that this is a great burger. In a way, there's something at the Spot that transcends the burger itself—the owner Jesse Bustillos. Jesse is not like other restaurateurs. To date, Jesse owns and operates five similar burger stands from Carpinteria to Oxnard. He's a sort of "collector" of fading but historically significant hamburger joints. This makes Jesse a hamburger hero on a level that even I had not considered.

Jesse grew up in the business working at his grandparents' Mexican restaurants in Milwaukee.

When he moved to California, he began to eye the classic SoCal burger stand. "I like to clean them up and restore them," Jesse told me, "I have nothing against corporate chains, I just like to keep old Mom 'n' Pops going I guess."

The Spot has been around in name since 1948, but the structure itself dates back to 1914. Originally, the property was an oceanside campground and the stand was the food shack for the campers. Today, the campground is a dusty parking lot, and beachfront camping is limited to a highly coveted state site nearby. Julia Child, who retired to nearby Montecito later in life, apparently loved the Spot and would visit often.

The tiny stand with the ancient, overpainted sign on top has no indoor seating, just a walk-up window. When Jesse bought the Spot, there were just a few chairs next to the structure so he built an enclosed patio (which is larger than the burger stand itself). If you arrive at peak times, in warmer months, expect to stand on a line that can stretch all the way to the train tracks, about two hundred feet away. The line moves fast, don't worry. If you can't find a seat at the Spot, head to the beach, only one block to the west.

The menu is varied but stick to the basics. The burger to get is the double cheeseburger with everything, which includes a healthy portion of crisp iceberg lettuce, fresh tomato, raw onion, pickles, and some Thousand Island dressing. It's a curious build, which I've never seen before—both sides of the bun get a swipe of dressing, then the two burger patties are separated by the veggies, not stacked together. It's actually well-thought-out burger architecture. The veggies are fresh daily because, as Jesse explained, "we are so busy, especially in summer."

Jesse bought the Spot in 1999 after discovering that the owner of twenty-six years Ted Barajas was in his seventies and wanted to sell. That type of owner has become Jesse's target because, like me, he hates to see these places close and disappear. Jesse also liked the stand's proximity to the beach and the fact that there are no other food options nearby for beachgoers.

It's good to know that someone with the preservation bug like Jesse exists. He plans to keep buying and restoring burger stands and most of his leads on real estate come from friends. He told me, "A lot of people know I'm looking."

VAL'S BURGERS

2115 Kelly St | Hayward, CA 94541 | 510-889-8257
Tues–Sat 6:30 am–10 pm | Closed Mon & Sun

Many diners across America attempt to re-create the '50s malt shop experience but few offer an authentic experience. It's not easy to bottle that feeling unless you happen to have been able to survive the last five decades with your values intact. Val's was created to be exactly what it is today—a perfect example of a midcentury West Coast hangout that still cranks out some of the best shakes and burgers in America.

Val's is always busy. At dinnertime, every red leather booth is taken, and you'd be hard-pressed to find a stool at the long counter that runs the entire length of the diner. There is a constant stream of take-out orders leaving through a side door and the wide indoor flame grill is loaded with sizzling patties. A Little League team had taken over the three booths in the center of the restaurant and a young couple was sharing a hot fudge sundae in the corner. In the center of all of this ordered chaos, I spotted a tall, lanky man with a bushy mustache sweeping up around a booth. The busboy? Nope, this was none other than owner of thirty-five years George Nickol-opoulos. I asked him why he was sweeping, and he replied flatly, "I never stop." I soon realized that after over three decades of ownership he still does everyone's job, making rounds at tables, the grill, the register, constantly checking and making sure the dinner rush is going smoothly.

Before the arched, wood-ceiling diner with its large windows was built in 1958, Val's was a small barbershop across the parking lot. The original Val's eventually morphed into a variety store and post office run by George's aunt and uncle, Carmen and Al Valenzuela (hence the name Val). At some point, Al decided to start selling "charcoal burgers," and they quickly became the core of his business. Building a larger building with the focus on burgers and shakes was a foregone conclusion.

The burgers at Val's come in three sizes—the one-third-pound Baby Burger, the half-pound Mama Burger, and the one-pound Papa Burger. On my first visit, I was drawn to the Papa Burger mostly because of its absurd size sporting two half-pound patties on a toasted bun. I tried to compress the burger to fit into my face but still could not ram it in. I actually finished the mountain of meat-and-cheese and was amazed to find that even though the burger was cartoonish in size, it was still exploding with flavor and juiciness. It seemed from looking around that the Mama Burger was the way to go.

I asked George how many burgers he could sell on a busy day, and he quickly replied, "If you have time to count, you are not doing enough." Other questions about how he runs the business were met with similar responses. I had nothing but respect for this icon of the burger world and was enjoying his caginess. He did however offer one nugget of advice: "I'll tell you this. Our meat is far superior than anyone else's. It's also in the way you prepare the burgers that separates the men from the boys. No one would ever consider putting as much time as we put into these."

Don't miss out on the shakes at Val's. Long-time counterperson Valerie told me, "The best milkshake I've ever had is the Root Beer Banana shake. It's like milkshake crack." She wasn't kidding. The signature shake, also known to regulars as the Rootanana, has only three ingredients—vanilla ice cream, root beer syrup, and an entire banana. A friend of mine along for the trip took a sip of his and shouted, "That's insane!" I agree.

Val's is a Bay Area must on a hamburger tour of America and not just for its great burgers, shakes, and easy-going atmosphere. Go to Val's knowing that it is a family place. Not only are generations of regulars still enjoying Val's, but George's entire family works there in some capacity. It takes a family to run a true family restaurant.

COLORADO

BUD'S CAFE & BAR

5453 Manhart St | Sedalia, CO 80135 | 303-688-9967
Mon–Sat 10 am–9 pm | Sun 11 am–6:30 pm

Bud's Bar is not in Denver. On a map, the town of Sedalia, Colorado, looks like it could be a suburb of the Mile High City, but in person the tiny town, surrounded by cattle farms, feels as remote as any town on the Kansas Plain.

Bud's is one of only a few businesses in the small downtown of Sedalia. The seventy-year-old bar sits between two busy railroad rights-of-way that are only a few hundred feet apart. It's not uncommon to be stuck at either crossing for longer than twenty minutes waiting for a long coal train to pass. "Some guys walk out, see the train, and say 'Oh well!' and head back inside for another beer," Mike Steerman told me. Mike should know. He owns the place.

Mike is only the third owner of Bud's since Calixte "Bud" Hebert converted an auto shop into a bar in 1948. In the 1960s, Bud became a local judge and decided that judges shouldn't own bars. He sold his tavern to an employee, Thurman Thompson. In the 1980s, current owner Mike started tending the bar part-time to relieve stress from his job as a salesman. When Thurman decided to sell the bar, he set his sights on Mike, knowing that he would change little about the place.

The one thing I'll bet most people were afraid he would change was the burger. Rest assured that Mike has kept it the same. With a name like Steerman, it would be stupid to question his Colorado heritage or his affinity for fresh beef. The burger at Bud's is a classic griddled quarter pounder with american cheese on a white squishy bun. It's absolutely amazing and transcends the standard notion of bar food. The burger bursts with flavor and is one of the juiciest griddled burgers I have ever eaten.

People go to Bud's for two reasons—because they know everyone in the bar and for the burgers. Outside of drinks at the bar, Bud's has served only burgers since the beginning. "It's simple," Mike explained, "we don't offer lettuce, we don't offer tomato, and we only use one kind of cheese." Fries? Nope. Chips will have to do. But trust me, you'll be focusing on this burger and nothing else.

The burgers start as 80/20 chuck hand-pressed in a single patty maker. They are cooked on a smallish flattop griddle in a bright, clean kitchen next to the bar. As a burger nears doneness, both halves of a bun are placed on the burger and covered with a lid to steam the bun to softness. Your order is served with a bag of chips and a slice of onion in a plastic mesh basket lined with waxed paper. "That's it," Mike told me, proud of the simplicity of his product. Locals in the know request jalapeño slices that Mike has stashed in a small jar in the kitchen.

Sunday is the busiest at Bud's, a day where the griddle can see up to five hundred burgers. "That griddle stays full for six hours on Sunday," Mike told me.

Mike seems to be one of the newer members of the Bud's family, and one of the only males in a female-strong staff. Amiable bartender Nancy has been serving drinks for three decades now and most staff has been there forever.

Bud's interior is cozy and simple. One side is lined with vintage stools, there are booths on the other side, and a few tables in the middle. An original jukebox sits just inside the front door, and one wall displays a unique item—the branding board.

Of course being from New York, I was very intrigued by the branding board, something that probably seems mundane to a ranching community. The idea is simple—it's a long piece of wood attached to one wall of the bar that displays actual cattle brands of the local ranchers. To me, it was a viable piece of "bar art." One glance at the board and you are reminded of just how close you are to fresh beef.

Despite its roadhouse appearance, Bud's has become a place for family and friends. Since smoking in bars was banned in 2006, Mike has seen an increase in business. "A little while ago we had an entire Little League team in here."

CLAMP'S HAMBURGER STAND

Route 202 (Near Marbledale, CT) | New Milford, CT 06776
No Phone | Open Daily 11 am–2 pm, 5 pm–8 pm | (Late April to Labor Day Only)

Way up in the northwest corner of Connecticut is a tiny burger stand that is definitely worth the drive. It has no real address and no phone but it doesn't need these things. If you show up on a summer day at lunchtime, you'll find a crowd that somehow found its way there regardless of its off-the-grid status.

I asked owner Tom Mendell why, after all these years, there still was no phone at Clamp's.

He told me, smiling, "It's always been that way and I don't see any reason to change it." Tom's great-uncle Edwin Clamp opened the little white-shingled stand in 1939 because he had tired of his job as a door-to-door hardware salesman. "I think he came up with this idea because he didn't like to work," Tom told me. The stand is still open only during the warmer months, which gave Edwin the winter off.

When World War II started, meat rationing caused Clamp's to shut down temporarily. During that time, Edwin used the tiny stand to manufacture a faucet washer that he had patented. After his death, Edwin's wife, Sylvia, ran Clamp's and worked there into her late eighties. "She was a worker," Tom told me.

Tom, who lives in Baltimore in the winter and assumed the business twenty years ago at the young age of thirty, has changed very little about Clamp's. He expanded ever so slightly the tiny kitchen, but the structure still remains under 450 square feet. Tom himself mans the griddle at the front of the stand and spends most of his day flipping patties to perfection. And like most great keepers of the lunchtime grill, Tom stays focused and politely refused to answer my questions as he managed the incoming orders.

Tom picks up fresh ground quarter-pound patties every morning from a local butcher. He is very serious about the quality of the ingredients that go into his roadside fare. Everything is fresh, and he makes his own coleslaw and the chili that goes onto the hot dogs and hamburgers.

Somewhat recently, the griddle was replaced. Tom wasn't exactly sure but he thinks it happened around twenty-seven years ago because the original finally gave up. Janine, a former employee once told me, "The old griddle had a big slope in the middle from being cleaned so much."

Clamp's is an outdoor place. The stand is basically a kitchen with walk-up order windows. You place an order at one of the windows, find a table in the grassy grove on either side of the stand, and wait for your name to be called. Don't expect a loudspeaker to summon you back for pickup. The girls that take your order literally shout your name, sort of like your sister calling you for dinner.

The cheeseburgers are served on white squishy buns with the traditional Yankee white american cheese. Locals know to order theirs topped with a Clamp's specialty—a pile of sweet, slow-cooked, caramelized onions.

The drive to Clamp's is half the fun. If you are coming up from the quaint, historic town

of New Milford, Clamp's is exactly 5.9 miles north on Route 202 from the gazebo on the town's square. Trust me, you'll need this info as you pass farm after farm, nearly hit a deer (as I almost did), and wonder if you've gone too far. Look for the small white building tucked into the trees with an American flag displayed on its side. The only identification the building offers is a postcard-sized sign just over a side door: a small plaque that reads "Clamp's Est. 1939." And don't show up at 2 p.m. looking for a burger. The stand is strict about their afternoon break, which reopens at 5 p.m. for dinner. "We slam it down," Tom said of the sign at 2 p.m.

"We've had the same hours for seventy-eight years, and if we help one person after 2 p.m., we would need to help the next. . . ." It the spirit of fairness, the policy makes sense, and Tom added sheepishly, "I may have shut out Michael Stern once (beloved national food writer who happens to live nearby)."

Tom told me, "Most of the time I'm as busy as I can possibly handle." The only break he gets is when it rains, but even then, some like to show up for his famous burgers. "I think we have a cult of people who like to show up during thunderstorms," Tom told me. "It's funny. They sit in their cars, eat burgers, and watch the rain."

HARRY'S PLACE

104 Broadway St | Colchester, CT 06415 | 860-537-2410 | Mon–Sun 11 am–8 pm
Open March to October | March Hours 11 am–7 pm | www.harrysplaceburgers.com

Harry's Place is a classic roadside burger stand painted bright white in western Connecticut. Unlike most stands of this vintage (almost 100 years old) Harry's is very large and does a tremendous amount of business. When you walk up choose one of two ordering windows, or the separate ice-cream window around the corner of the building. Once you have your order, find a spot at one of the many picnic tables surrounding the stand. It's a real family place and on weekends expect a vibrant scene filled with kids, strollers, moms, dads, and old-timers.

Harry's, which is now on the National Register of Historic Places, was opened by Harry Schmuckler in 1920. In the beginning, the stand only sold four things—doughnuts, coffee, hot dogs, and burgers, and the burgers cost a quarter. Harry ran the place for only about a decade before Ruby Cohen bought Harry's and ran it for almost fifty years. In 1978, Romilda Garet-Neville

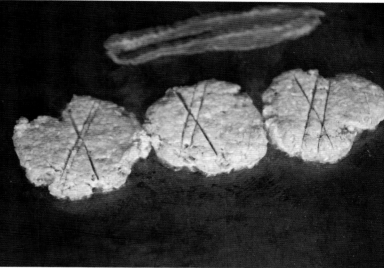

bought the stand from Ruby, and it has been in the family ever since. Today, Harry's is owned and operated by Suzanne Caruso and John Garet, both children of Romilda, who at 75, still run the office and payroll.

Although the menu has grown since 1920, expanded to include sandwiches, soups, fried clams, chili cheese fries, and much more, the burgers are still first and foremost the reason for Harry's continued success. Today, the burgers outsell the hot dogs by 2 to 1.

Place your order and find a seat, or do what I do and loiter at the large pickup window which has an up close and personal view of the large griddle. Watch as the grill cook deftly maneuvers large orders with ease by employing a method of organization that involves hieroglyphic-like slashes and marks on every patty that hits the griddle. Longtime grill cook

Nicole explained, matter-of-factly, "That's how I know which burger gets what." For example, one horizontal slash gets cheese and a vertical slash does not. 2 diagonal slashes gets bacon, and 2 diagonal and one horizontal slashes is a bacon cheeseburger, and so on. It's fascinating to watch and try your hand at decoding the slashes for fun. The foolproof system was put in place by Romilda's husband, Jim Neville, who is also credited with turning the stand around after marrying Romilda in 1985. "He took it from a mom 'n' pop run by kids who didn't know what the heck they were doing to what it is today," John told me.

The burger to order at Harry's is the bacon cheeseburger with fried onions (3 diagonal slashes and a horizontal). Beef for the burgers at Harry's comes from the butcher at Noel's directly across the street. They use an 80/20 butcher's blend and portion into 4-ounce balls. The ball hits the flattop and gets a gentle smash to the size of the patty. The smash creates the most incredible griddle crust. The cooked patty is then married to a pillowy soft, untoasted local bakery bun (from Nardi's, open 1908). You can request to have yours toasted but it's unnecessary. John told me, "95% go out not toasted." On a busy Saturday, Harry's can pump out over 850 burgers.

Because Harry's is a walk-up burger stand with outdoor seating only, the business is seasonal. Don't show up in the cold months looking for a burger. Harry's closes at the end of October mostly because the stand is not winterized and has no heating. By March 1st when the stand reopens, all of Colechester and the surrounding area are very ready for a burger. "We crush March," John told me with pride, "and I think because we close, people are pent up and can't wait for it."

LOUIS' LUNCH

261 Crown St | New Haven, CT 06511-6611 | 203-562-5507
Tues & Wed 11 am–3:45 pm | Thurs–Sat 12 pm–2 am | Closed Sun & Mon
Closed During August | www.louislunch.com

There are many claims to the origin of the first hamburgers in America. One of them is Louis' Lunch (pronounced LEW-EEZ). Even if the claim here can be disputed, it is without a doubt the oldest continuously operating hamburger restaurant in the country. What's more, one family, the Lassens, has owned and operated the tiny burger haven since 1895—four generations of passionate hamburger making. Operating Louis' today is the fourth generation: Jeff and Ken Lassen Jr. In 2010, the burger world lost an icon when their father, third-generation owner Ken Lassen, passed away at ninety-three. His life was the restaurant, and it was Ken who fought tirelessly to get Louis' Lunch on the National Register.

A friend of mine likens the quiet atmosphere at Louis' to church—there is rarely music heard, no excessive banter, or typical diner orders being barked. Just the clanking sound of the upright flame broilers opening and closing and the crinkling of wrapped burgers going into paper bags. People stand at the counter waiting patiently in silence for their order to be handed to them.

The structure that houses Louis' Lunch is a tiny box with one-hundred-year-old Victorian flair. Small as it seems, it's the largest it's ever been. The original Louis' was a tiny-wheeled lunch cart that eventually went terrestrial as a three-sided brick cube attached to the side of a large downtown New Haven tannery. When the tannery was torn down in the early 1970s, the three remaining sides were salvaged, dragged four blocks, and an expanded fourth wall was constructed, along with a basement.

A burger at Louis' starts with fresh ground lean beef, ground daily in the spotless basement. Every morning, Ken Jr. rolls the meat into small balls. Two balls are pressed together to make a patty, which is placed vertically in a metal grate and then slid into an ancient upright broiler. The grill cooks from both sides and juices drip into a pan below. The burgers are then placed on Pepperidge Farm white toast, simply because when Louis Lassen invented the "hamburger sandwich" in 1900 there were no buns (in fact, buns didn't come around for almost another twenty years).

In the 1970s, Ken felt the pressure to add cheese to his famous sandwich, but if you ask for cheese, you'll get a Velveeta-esque cheese spread. Due to the unique method for cooking the burgers, cheese slices take a back seat to the spread. Fresh-cut tomatoes and onions are standard, but don't ask for ketchup or you may be shown the door. As Jeff Lassen explains, "We honestly believe you don't need ketchup because it's the best burger there is." And Ken once told me, "Ketchup is a strong flavor. If we gave you that, it would destroy everything we are trying to give you." Jeff also pointed out that students from nearby Yale frequently try to sneak in small packets of ketchup only to be told that the burger they wanted to sit down and eat is now a to-go order.

Ken's wife, Leona or "Lee" as she is affectionately known, has finally retired. For over half a

Louis Lassen in his lunch wagon, 1907

century she could be found working at fever pitch at the upright broilers. A heart condition and a hospital visit did little to slow her down, and she surprised us all when she returned to work a few months later. But in 2010, she called it quits.

The Lassens are salt-of-the-earth burger royalty, and they are quite aware of their status in American food history. Regardless of the provenance that surrounds Louis', the prices are fair and the burgers are always fresh and tasty. And now that Jeff has started a family, he has potentially begun the next chapter in this restaurant's long history. Will a fifth-generation Lassen run Louis' someday? "Ahhhh, we'll see," Jeff told me. "You know how kids are."

SHADY GLEN

840 Middle Turnpike East | Manchester, CT 06040
860-649-4245 | Sun–Thurs 7 am–10 pm | Fri & Sat 7 am–10:30 pm

The inside of the Shady Glen looks like a cheeseburger. The yellow-striped wallpaper, warm lighting, and low brown Formica countertops mimic the colors of their famous cheeseburger concoction. Ice cream may be the number-one seller at this Manchester, Connecticut, institution, but the cheeseburger is what has made them famous. In 1949, Bernice Rieg invented the "Bernice Original," which became an immediate success and still accounts for 80 percent of their sandwich sales today. The four-ounce cheeseburger comes with four slices of cheese. The cheese is not just stacked atop the burger; it is symmetrically placed, centered on the burger as it cooks on the hot griddle. An understandably large portion of this cheese makes direct contact with the griddle. When the cheese cooks through, it is curled skyward by the deft grillman until it resembles a cheese crown. Amazingly, I watched burger after burger leave the grill with the same dramatic cheese. The same burger, over and over, since 1949.

"It's a special cheese, but that's all I can tell you," Michael the manager said with a smile. Michael started working at the Shady Glen almost three decades ago as a dishwasher. "At thirty years, I'm still the new kid on the block." Shady Glen is a very busy place. There are more than fifteen employees in constant motion, waitresses in little ruffled aprons, and grillmen in paper caps and black bow ties. This is the real deal, not a mock-up like Johnny Rockets.

There are no menus at the Shady Glen, just wall menus, and they are basic. You can order a "cheeseburger" or a "big cheeseburger"; the latter comes with the four slices of cheese. The smaller "cheeseburger" comes with only three slices. It's served on a white squishy bun and delivered to your spot at the counter with your own personal condiment tray of relish, raw onion, mustard, and ketchup. The Shady Glen can sell up to four thousand Bernice Originals on a busy week. That's a lot of cheese sculpture.

I stood by the grill and watched closely—the cheese, which looked like a house-sliced mild cheddar, really does not stick. One of the grillmen offered some shaky science. "The carbon, uh, buildup on the griddle over the years acts sort of like Teflon." I think he's right. I had a hard time trying to figure out what do with my cheese wings once I had my burger in front of me. Two guys sitting near me at the counter had opposing views. One told me, "Fold the crisps onto the burger and eat it that way." "Not me," said the other, "I like to break them off and eat them separately." A girl sitting on the other side of me was chewing on some cheese crown crisps with no burger in sight. "This is an order of Crispy Cheese," she told me. This guilty pleasure is served on a bed of lettuce and is not on the menu.

In 2008, Bernice passed away and a long-time employee Bill Hoch and his wife, Annette, became owners of the sixty-nine-year-old restaurant. They did not change a single thing about the place, probably because Bill started working at Shady Glen in 1954. He told me with a chuckle, "I've been a lifer here."

At first, I was concerned about the large mural that spans the entire west end of the restaurant. It depicts strange elves having a picnic of burgers, hot dogs, and ice cream. As I left the restaurant, I looked again at the mural and fully understood its significance—the Shady Glen is a necessary fantasy. I hope it never goes away.

TED'S RESTAURANT

1046 Broad St | Meriden, CT 06450 | 203-237-6660
Sun–Wed 11 am–9 pm | Thurs–Sat 11 am–10 pm | www.tedsrestaurant.com

If you are looking for a truly unique hamburger experience, go to Ted's. If you are looking for a potentially healthy burger, go to Ted's. If you are looking for a chargrilled cheeseburger, don't go to Ted's. Ted's Restaurant is at the epicenter of the steamed cheeseburger world—a burger that only exists in central Connecticut. Today, there are only two true steamed cheeseburger places left in the area, and as owner Bill Foreman pointed out, "If you are looking for a steamed cheeseburg around here you are probably coming to Ted's. Ninety-five percent of what we sell are cheeseburgs."

The steamed "cheeseburg," as it's referred to at Ted's mostly by old-timers, is just what you'd think it would be—a steamed patty of ground beef on a bun. What you wouldn't expect is that the cheese is steamed, too, steamed to a molten goo. The process starts with steaming cabinets that each hold twenty small stainless-steel rectangular trays. Specially ground fresh chuck is pressed into the trays, which are placed in the cabinet. The meat cooks through but stays amazingly moist and unfortunately, looks like gray matter. The result is a burger that loses a lot of its fat content (it gets poured off) but retains a truly beefy flavor. A "secret" mild Vermont cheddar cheese is also placed in the small trays in a separate steamer. Once gooey, the cheese is poured onto the burger,

served with tomato, lettuce, mayo, ketchup or mustard (or both), and a slice of raw onion, and placed on a soft kaiser roll. It's a very unique burger experience that is not to be missed.

The cheese is key to the success of a great Steamed Cheeseburg. Since this is a science project, the elements involved make all the difference. Former owner for over forty years (and Ted's son) Paul Duberek once told me, "I've heard some people that have used yellow american cheese on the burger—that's just an insult to the Steamed Cheeseburger."

With its narrow dull pink Formica countertop, nine stools, and a handful of booths, Ted's can fill up on the weekend. The orders come fast, though, so the wait can be from volume alone. Longtime employee Abby pointed out, "There's no one complaining about waiting." Grab my favorite stool if you can (third from the back) and be almost too close to the action. Only about three feet separate you from the opening and closing of the steaming cabinets with their huge plumes of steam escaping each time the drillmaster reaches in to grab some meat or cheese.

The origins of the steamed cheeseburger are a bit murky, but it's believed to have originated at Jack's Lunch in Middletown sometime in the '30s. Ted Duberek opened his restaurant in 1959 to feed the large local factory worker population. For

over one hundred years, that area of Connecticut was home to some of the largest silverware manufacturers and they had shifts around the clock. Ted's used to stay open until 4 a.m., but started closing earlier as the factories moved their business overseas.

In 2007, suffering from back trouble, Paul Duberek decided to leave the business and sold Ted's to his nephew Bill. He told me, "It was important for him to keep it in the family." Bill was no stranger to the steamed cheeseburg and has worked at Ted's since he was thirteen. Not surprisingly, Bill made a few needed changes to the menu and recently added fries. Since the beginning, Ted's only served home fries. "I wanted to do it for a while," Bill said of the fries, which sell well, "but our regular customers still want the home fries." For a real treat, get Ted's home fries with steamed, gooey cheese on top.

Bill plans to own Ted's for a very long time. He told me just after assuming Ted's full-time, "I count my lucky stars every day."

DELAWARE

CHARCOAL PIT

2600 Concord Pike | North Wilmington, DE 19803 | 302-478-2165
Mon–Sun 11 am–10 pm | (Two Locations around Wilmington) | www.charcoalpit.net

When Charcoal Pit opened in 1956, it was way out on the Concord Pike surrounded by fields and very few other businesses. "It was all farmland and nothing but a two-lane road," longtime general manager Frank Kucharski once told me, looking out the front window of this time-warp diner. "Hard to imagine now." Yes, it is. Concord Pike today is a densely packed commercial strip. It's a wonder this burger gem is still standing.

From the outside, Charcoal Pit looks virtually unchanged since the 1950s. The restaurant's boomerang-inspired marquee with its pudgy pink neon lettering is authentically retro. The interior has seen a few upgrades and design changes over the years and blends styles from the past six decades. If you're lucky, you'll be seated at a booth with a tabletop jukebox. These are not props. They actually work. The late Holly Moore, Philadelphia area food writer and a man who knew where to find the best greasy food anywhere, once told me, "Think Richie, Potsie, and Ralph Malph in a corner booth and Al flipping burgers behind the counter. There's something unmistakably genuine about eating at Charcoal Pit that needs to be experienced."

The burgers are cooked over an open flame, as the restaurant's name implies. The large gas grill, in full view of the dining room, is outfitted with a bed of lava rocks that help to evenly distribute the heat. Grillman of twenty-seven years, Lupe spends hours inches from the flames, flipping hundreds of burgers a day.

The half-pound burger is served on a kaiser roll and the quarter pounder comes on a seeded, toasted white bun. The larger burger is definitely the way to go and is exploding with juices. It seems as though someone was paying attention to burger physics when bun decisions were being made. The fresh Angus patties are delivered daily to Charcoal Pit from a local supplier. They go through over a thousand pounds of meat a week, and it's always fresh.

Not only are the burgers fresh, other items on the menu are housemade, like their crab cakes, soups, and coleslaw. The first time I visited

Charcoal Pit I found a few employees in the kitchen straining what looked to be about ten gallons of homemade vegetable beef soup.

Outside of burgers, Charcoal Pit is ice-cream nirvana. A sign out front proclaims simply, Ice Cream Creations and they are not kidding. The menu is heavy on ice cream and there is a sundae named after each of the nine local high schools. The thick, hand-dipped milkshakes are enormous and not to be missed.

Every year as the local high schools are letting out for the summer, Charcoal Pit can count on one thing—the prom. "It's total chaos in here," manager Joseph Grabowski told me, "They're really into the Kitchen Sink." For a second I thought he was referring to a burger and imagined a burger with enough embellishment to fill a sink, but Joe explained, "It's twenty scoops of ice cream, whipped cream, nuts, etc., and two bananas." Whoa.

DISTRICT OF COLUMBIA

BEN'S CHILI BOWL

1213 U St NW | Washington, DC 20009 | 202-667-0909 | Mon–Thurs 10:45 am–2 am
Fri 10:45 am–4 am | Sat 10:45 am–4 am | Sun 11 am–12 am
(Three Other Locations) | www.benschilibowl.com

Most people don't want to eat with a lot of loud music. "It's just part of our culture," a regular for four decades named Marshall Brown told me as we sat at the counter of this sixty-year-old Washington, DC, landmark chili restaurant. Marshall was referring to the sounds of Bob Marley and Luther Vandross that were oozing out of the jukebox, not necessarily loud, but definitely present. One time when I was enjoying a breakfast chili cheeseburger, the guy next to me at the counter was eating his eggs, so consumed by the music that he started dancing in his seat. I'm positive that moving to the music made the food taste that much better.

Ben's was opened in 1958 by Ben and Virginia Ali in a former silent movie theater known as the Minnehaha. Ben, who had emigrated from Trinidad, met his wife at the bank just down the street. "She was a bank teller," the couple's son Nizam told me. Ben passed away in 2009 and Virginia has retired, but two of their sons, Nizam and Kamal, run the restaurant today.

Ben's is known for its tasty chili that gloriously adorns hot dogs, half smokes, and hamburgers. The bright, airy, neighborhood restaurant, with its incredibly colorful facade, also serves a memorable breakfast, but many return from all corners of the country for their chili dogs and burgers. Over the years, it also became known for the role it has played in Black American history. Ben's fed many celebrities performing at the clubs along the U Street corridor in the '50s and '60s, including Ella Fitzgerald, Miles Davis, and Cab Calloway.

The 1968 riots sparked by the assassination of Martin Luther King Jr. started just a block away when someone threw a brick through a drugstore window. The riots devastated the neighborhood, a curfew was imposed, and the city shut down while attempting to restore order. But Ben's remained open by special police permission to feed firefighters, police, and members of the Student Nonviolent Coordinating Committee located just across the street. When they did close for the night, Ben stayed behind to protect the business from looters. "He kissed my mom goodnight, sent her home, and sat inside with a gun all night," Nizam told me. To identify the restaurant as a black business Ben painted the words *Soul Brother* across the front window.

Ben's survived the riots, the crack hell of the '70s and '80s, then the construction of a Metro extension that cut off traffic on U Street for almost five years. "We had two employees and were making only about two hundred dollars a day during that time," Nizam told me. "The construction was more devastating than the drugs." Massive publicity from Bill Cosby and other black luminaries kept the business alive during the bad times. Cosby and his wife had many dates there while he was stationed in the navy nearby.

Today, Ben's thrives. President Bill Clinton was a fan. Nizam told me, "We sent a lot of takeout over to the White House when he was in office." President Obama paid a visit in 2009 and indulged in their famous chili dog (and humorously complained when he noticed that the guy sitting next to him had cheese and he didn't). The U Street corridor is in the midst of a revival and the new Metro stop is directly across the street. There must be twelve people behind the counter, and the atmosphere is lively and fun, with all of the employees joking and flirting with each other. The large front room with its long counter and booths gives way to two more rooms that are somewhat hidden from view. The enormous dining room in the back has a projector and screen, and the walls are lined with adoring photos of a virtual who's-who in Black America.

The burgers are quarter-pound patties and arrive fresh daily from a supplier in Baltimore. The chili that goes onto the burger is a simple family

recipe that contains only finely ground meat in a dark red, tangy sauce. The burger comes on a toasted bun in a plastic basket with a side of potato chips. If you need more, go for a chili dog, or better yet, the sublime chili cheese fries.

Ben's is a successful family business that has endured incredibly hard times. "We've gotten the most ridiculous amount of press, more than we could ever dream of," Nizam pointed out. Much of their continued success may come from a promise they've made to their adoring clientele to not change a thing. Ben's is a big part of the collective histories of all of the diners who have passed through its doors, and the future stories that have yet to be written there.

TUNE INN

331½ Pennsylvania Ave SE | Washington, DC 20003
202-543-2725 | Sun–Thurs 8 am–2 am | Fri & Sat 8 am–3 am

Johnny Cash on the jukebox, cheap beer on tap, and copious amounts of taxidermy on the walls . . . sounds like a recipe for your favorite country crossroads bar. But the bar is the Tune Inn and it's only steps from the Library of Congress and the Capitol Building in our nation's capital. It'd be easy to assume the country bar trappings are an urban design choice, but all of the stuffed game was bagged by the three generations of the Nardellis, owners of the Capitol Hill watering hole since 1955. This place is the real deal—a comfortable neighborhood dive bar with an excellent burger on the menu.

"I shot that one. That's my first doe," Lisa Nardelli told me, pointing to a stuffed deer head directly over the bar. Lisa is young and pretty and doesn't strike you as the hunting type. Her grandfather, Joe Nardelli, hunted most of the stuffed game, ranging from deer to squirrels to pheasant. "They would get drunk and shoot at anything," Lisa said of her father, Tony, and grandfather hunting together. Mounted over the bathroom doors in the rear of the narrow tavern are the other ends of deer. "That's my grandfather's sense of humor— deer asses over the bathrooms." The collection is so vast that the local Shakespeare theatere once borrowed a bunch of the Nardellis' stuffed birds for a production of *King Lear*.

Lots of well-known politicos and other Capitol Hill heavies have been drinking and eating at the Tune Inn for the last five decades. One of the most famous couples in American politics, James Carville and Mary Matalin, had their first date here (they left abruptly because it was too crowded). Janet Reno was a regular (for the burgers) and JFK, the senator, had his favorite booth (second one on the left). The bar also hosts regulars who have been coming in for decades. "It's like a big family, which is unusual in a big city, so close to the Capitol," Lisa pointed out. It's also home to countless numbers of students looking for cheap beer and good burgers, yours truly being one of them a few decades back.

The menu is mostly modest comfort food but the burger takes center stage. It starts as a six-ounce ball of 80/20 ground chuck. Chef Mike Tate told me, "We use a measured scoop, then form a patty." The meat is delivered fresh every morning from a local butcher that also supplies the well-known upscale Old Ebbitt Grill, a Washington landmark near the White House. "It's the same exact meat," Lisa told me.

Most of the staff at Tune Inn has been there forever. Bartender Susan Mathers has been pouring drinks for twenty-seven years and others have been there over twenty. When Chef Tate did the math (going on twenty-one years in the kitchen) he asked, "Does that mean I'm getting a raise?"

The patty is cooked to perfection on a flattop griddle and served on a buttered, toasted bun. The result is a loose, moist burger that melts in your mouth. It really is the perfect bar burger—not so big that you can't finish your beer and not so small that you go hungry.

The Tune Inn was the fifth bar in the District to receive its liquor license after Prohibition was repealed, and today is the oldest drinking establishment on Capitol Hill. During Prohibition the bar served as a speakeasy and regulars have told stories about that time for decades. One day recently, Lisa was wondering about a certain out-of-place wall in the basement. She tapped on it, found it hollow, and proceeded to smash the wall with a sledgehammer. What she uncovered was an indelible piece of American history. "There was a trap door that led to right here," she said, pointing to a spot behind the bar. "Apparently they used to pass the booze through here to the bartender."

You can visit the Tune Inn for a burger, for a few drinks, or as longtime bartender Susan believes, for love. "You think I'm kidding. Many people find their own true love at the Tune Inn," Susan told me with a straight face. "I have observed many people meet and fall in love here." She looked over at the third-generation Nardelli. "Lisa met her husband here."

FLORIDA

EL MAGO DE LAS FRITAS

5828 SW 8th St | West Miami, FL 33144 | 305-266-8486 | Mon–Thurs 10 am–8 pm
Fri & Sat 10 am–9 pm | Closed Sun | www.elmagodelasfritas.com

Erase any preconceived notions you have about the traditional American hamburger. If you find yourself in Miami, get away from the glitz of South Beach, brush up on your Spanish, and prepare for the taste explosion that is the "frita." Also known as a "Cuban Hamburger," the frita is a genuine gastronomic expression of the Cuban American experience.

In the middle of the twentieth century, the frita was a ubiquitous street food of Havana. By 1959, when the smoke from the Cuban Revolution had cleared, many fled to set up shop in America. As entrepreneurism was squashed in the new Cuba, it flourished in Miami. Today, the best examples of the frita are found not in its birthplace but in its adopted home of South Florida.

At a bright and tidy lunch counter, tucked into a strip mall with only three parking spaces out front, you'll find, arguably, one of the best fritas in Miami. The man behind this tasty Cuban treat is the affable septuagenarian, Ortelio "El Mago" Cardenas. El Mago opened his lunch counter in 1984 after splitting from his brother-in-law's successful Miami chain, El Rey De Las Fritas (see page 62). Both restaurants are on 8th Street, aka Calle Ocho, which is the main artery through Little Havana in South Miami. Many lunch counters on Calle Ocho serve fritas but El Mago is in a league of its own.

El Mago's frita is made with fresh ground beef and what seems to be chorizo and several spices mixed into the patty. I sat at the counter one day with friend, guide, and translator, the Florida burger blogger Burger Beast, Sef Gonzalez, and asked El Mago what else was in the patty besides chorizo. He turned from the griddle and shouted with a smile, "No chorizo!" Burger Beast was confused and I was in disbelief. The presence of another red, spiced meat was undeniable, but what was it?

When you place your order, El Mago disappears into the back and returns clutching a wad of refrigerated ground meat. The multihued chunk is tossed onto a hot griddle and pressed flat. He reaches for an unmarked plastic bottle and gives the patty a generous squirt of a thin, deep red liquid. A handful of chopped onion is sprinkled on as the patty cooks in the red, bubbling sauce.

What makes a frita a frita is the generous heap of superthin, fried potatoes that virtually obscure the patty on the bun. It's presented on a soft, warmed Cuban roll with more chopped onion, a squirt of ketchup, and a bird's nest of the wiry potatoes. The extraordinary flavor profile made me nearly fall off my stool the first time I ate one. When I told El Mago how happy I was, he just looked at me and smiled. After inhaling that first frita, I did the only sensible thing I could think of. I ordered another.

Burger Beast told me, "There are frita places that use those canned potato sticks instead of fresh and that's just wrong." El Mago makes a batch of his ethereal fried potatoes every morning.

El Mago De Las Fritas has refreshing watermelon juice and the old Cuban standby soda, Materva, on the menu. But don't leave El Mago without trying one of his batidos, or Cuban milkshakes. You won't find American classics like the chocolate malt here. Instead, indulge in tropical fruit flavors like guanabana, papaya, or the amazing mamey fruit. Or get the incredible flan de leche. I swear I've never had a better flan.

Directly translated *El Mago* means "The Magician" and this one hails from a long line of Cuban frita purveyors. Like a good magician, El Mago harbors trade secrets that only his daughter, Martha, and her husband, Barry, seem to know. It's safe to say that in their hands the future of El Mago's frita is secure.

EL REY DE LAS FRITAS

1821 SW 8th St. | Miami, FL 33135
305-644-6054 | Open Daily 8 am–10 pm | www.elreydelasfritas.com

If I'm in Miami, I must get my hands on a frita (or three), otherwise my visit would not be complete. When most people think of fritas in Miami, they think of El Rey. That's because this popular frita minichain has been serving the Cuban hamburger for decades. Like El Mago just down 8th Street (see page 60), El Rey serves easily some of the very best fritas in Miami.

A man named Ramon Estevill is credited with bringing the first frita to South Florida. The Cuban Revolution in 1959 sent many fleeing to the United States and so went the Cuban hamburger. After settling in Miami, Ramon opened the first frita counter in 1962 and called it Fritas Domino.

Other shops popped up over the next decade, including El Palacio Des Las Fritas. Benito Gonzalez, who had sold fritas on the streets of Havana, worked at Palacio before opening his own frita shop in 1976 with wife Angelica, calling it El Rey (The King) de las Fritas.

In 1982, Fritas Domino closed and El Rey took over the iconic frita counter on 12th Avenue and 8th Street (their second location) preserving a legacy. But in 2005, El Rey was forced to relocate after a fire destroyed the iconic twenty-three-seat frita counter. The newer flagship Calle Ocho (8th Street) location is in a small strip mall near the heart of Little Havana where Spanish is the predominant language. Second-generation owner, Mercedes "Mercy" Gonzalez, runs the place with her mother who at seventy-seven years old still works in the kitchen. "She is very hard working," Mercy said of her mother who, every day, makes all of the desserts and helps to roll hundreds of balls of beef.

The bright, sparkling counter is packed at lunch but stools turn over fast. You'll likely be just outside your comfort zone here but it's a very good place to be, especially when the reward is one of the best burgers in America.

The frita is a taste explosion that must be experienced. At El Rey, fritas start as fresh ground 90/10 chuck and a very secret family spice-blend is added in. Traditionally, paprika and garlic are included. It's obviously an untraditional burger patty. The beef is rolled into roughly three-ounce balls and pressed flat on the griddle. The patty gets a big squirt of a tomato-based, secret sauce, then sprinkled with raw chopped onion. "The sauce is our version of Cuban ketchup," Mercy told me. The patties burble away in the sweet/hot sauce, are flipped, then transferred to a feather-weight Cuban burger roll. The patty is topped with a nest of traditional, thin, crispy, fried potatoes called "papas julianas." The taste is incredible, a combination of savory onion, garlic, and paprika, mixed with the delicate crunch of

the fried potatoes, and the sweetness of the caramelized secret sauce. I usually get two—not because I'm hungry, but because it's hard to walk away from that taste.

Get a mamey batido, a Cuban milkshake made from the Caribbean mamey fruit, to complete your El Rey counter experience. Or for the real deal get a small cup of guarapo, a drink made fresh in a machine behind the counter that squeezes the juice out of a stalk of sugarcane.

What is shocking to me is that apparently the frita no longer exists in the country where it

was born. Decades of dictatorship and corruption has made it impossible to collect the myriad ingredients necessary to make a proper frita. This makes the friteros of Miami the keepers of a significant piece of food history. Mercedes once told me that when things finally settle down in Cuba she'd like to go back and open the first frita drive-thru joint. I told her to make it wide enough to fit the cars from the fifties that were frozen in time before the frita left for Miami in the wake of a revolution, the most identifiable aspect of culture in Cuba today.

LE TUB

1100 North Ocean Dr | Hollywood, FL 33019 | 954-921-9425
Mon–Fri 11 am–1 am | Sat & Sun 12 pm–2 am | www.theletub.com

After Le Tub was chosen by *GQ* magazine in 2005 for having the number-one burger in America, *The Oprah Winfrey Show* did its own report backing up the claim. The only problem is, the most crowded no-frills burger shack in Florida just got more crowded.

Located on a stretch of A1A just a half hour north of Miami, Le Tub is a former Sunoco gas station converted into a strange pile of flotsam collected over three decades. Most of Le Tub's seating is outside on a meandering multilevel porch surrounded by lush foliage, worn wood, chirping birds, and hot breezes. Its proximity to the Intracoastal Waterway offers a constant boat show. I once sat at a table on the water and watched an

entire bachelorette party in bikinis float by, the bride opening gifts of lingerie and giggling.

The restaurant got its name from owner Russell Kohuth's collection of discarded commodes, tubs, and sinks, which basically hold the place together. In addition to the porcelain collection are parts of boats, buoys, and other planks that actually make up the basic structure of the restaurant. Russell started collecting stuff on early morning jogs along Hollywood beach and opened the restaurant in 1975. "This place wouldn't hold up in a hurricane," the guy at the next table told his wife.

Russell passed away in 2010 and willed the place to longtime employee Steve Sidle. Since

Steve basically ran the place for the twenty-five years leading up to Russell's death not a thing has changed at Le Tub. "We replaced a few pieces of wood here and there that have rotted," manager Brian told me, "but that's about it."

The Sirloinburger at Le Tub is a beast—thirteen ounces of fresh ground, hand-pattied, chargrilled 85/15 sirloin-chuck blend, served on a soft kaiser roll. When I prodded the waitress for the actual size of the burger, she told me, "They are big and messy!"

The grill cook works at a small three-foot-square grill on a level just below the bar in basically an enclosed, un-air-conditioned space. There is smoke everywhere and the smell of searing beef permeates your clothes if you spend any time at the bar. How the grillman does not pass out from the heat three times a day is beyond me.

The crowd at Le Tub is a mixed bag—confused tourists, beachgoers, and boaters fill the tables. A dock on the patio allows you to arrive by water if so inclined. If you are arriving in at peak times, it would be wise to order your burgers THE MINUTE YOU WALK IN THE DOOR. I'm not kidding when I say that mine took one hour and twenty minutes to arrive. When I asked our waitress upon ordering if their famous burgers really took that long, she warned, with a straight face, "Could take up to an hour and a half." I placed an order for myself and a friend who had just landed at Miami International Airport. By the time she got off the plane, got her luggage, rented her car, and drove to Le Tub, she still had to wait forty-five more minutes for her burger. "It's not always that bad," Brian confessed. If you don't like to wait, go at off-times.

The good news is that the burger is worth the wait. Also, don't forget, you are in a bar, on the water, in Florida—the beers will go down easy, especially because you'll be sitting there for a while.

IS THERE REALLY A "CHEESEBURGER IN PARADISE"?

Imagine that you are sitting in a beachside bar somewhere in the Caribbean or south Florida eating what you consider to be, at that moment, the best-tasting burger you have ever had. You tell the waitress or bartender, and they say, "Well, it should be the best. This is the burger Jimmy Buffett wrote the song about!"

This hypothetical conversation plays out every day somewhere in the warm climes of vacationland, in claims that stretch from the Bahamas to New Orleans and back to the Florida Keys. Places like the Cabbage Key Inn on the west coast of Florida, where many show up just for the burger "Jimmy sang about." Or Le Select, a comfortable beach dive on St. Barts where the claim has some merit because Buffett had been known to swoop in on his Cessna seaplane, go straight to the bar, and put on an impromptu concert.

One claim that seems to make the least sense but is worthy of inspection comes from Rotier's in Nashville, Tennessee. The burger at Rotier's has been on the top of every poll in Music City for decades. It's a worn-in, dark, friendly place that has served excellent burgers since 1945. Pointing at the bar, Margaret Crouse, the giggly owner and second-generation Rotier, told me, "He used to sit right here and write songs," referring, of course, to Buffett, who lived and tried to make a go of his music career in Nashville in the late '60s. It's easy to see how over the years a connection could be made between the best cheeseburger in town and a starving artist-cum-star's early low-income diet. Alas, there is no connection.

Where is the famed cheeseburger then? Turns out Buffett came clean a few years back and told the truth. The "cheeseburger in paradise" stemmed from a hallucination. As the story goes, he was sailing near Puerto Rico in the mid-'70s and ran into weather and equipment trouble. He and his crew floated at sea for over five days eating nothing but canned food and peanut butter, and naturally fantasized about juicy cheeseburgers. Eventually the ship limped into the Village Cay Marina on Tortola, BVI, and the hungry sailors headed for the dock bar. There they feasted on what he recalls as overcooked American-style burgers on burnt buns that tasted "like manna from heaven." The song that followed was not about that burger, but about the fantasy. Buffett made his dream burger a reality in 2002 when he opened the first of his eight Cheeseburger in Paradise restaurants.

ANN'S SNACK BAR

1615 Memorial Drive SE | Atlanta, GA 30317
404-687-9207 | Mon–Sat 11 am–7 pm | Closed Sun

"When I die, I want them to say, 'She was a mean bitch but she made a great hamburger!'" And she did. In 2015, Ann Price lost her battle to cancer and passed, and all that sass and bravado went with her. She also made a great hamburger.

The first time I stopped in she was working alone in the burger and hot dog shack she opened in 1972 in Kirkwood, a neighborhood on the southeast side of Atlanta. She kept the waiting patrons amused with a running comedy routine that covered everything from politics to real estate

★ **67** ★

and no one was spared. A guy sitting next to me explained once, "It's like a barbershop in here." The routine was real, though, and I found out the hard way on my first visit when she threw me out of the restaurant for wanting to interview her. "I threw *Southern Living* out just last week! I don't give a damn . . . Get *out*!" That day I refused to leave and was rewarded with the only thing that seems to get ordered from the short menu at Ann's—the "Ghetto Burger."

In 1994, a Checkers drive-in hamburger stand opened up just two doors down from Ann's. Realizing that she had to offer something different to maintain her business, Miss Ann (as she was affectionately called by regulars) ditched the frozen patties she was serving for fresh ground beef, and lots of it. The gimmick worked. "If I had known that's all it took to be world-famous I would have done this years ago," she told me once. Fresh beef was only the beginning. The Ghetto is an enormous burger; a glorious heap of sin; a pile of just about every ingredient in the restaurant. Two hand-formed patties that are unmeasured but look close to a half pound each are slow-cooked on a flattop griddle and sprinkled often with seasoned salt as they cook. The construction of the Ghetto Burger includes the two patties, toasted bun, onion, ketchup, mustard, chili, lettuce, tomato, cheese, and bacon. If that wasn't enough, the bacon is deep-fried. The finished product resembles a food accident and tastes as it should—amazing.

The Ghetto Burger looks absurd, but this type of beauty is in the eyes of the beholder. Some see this cartoonish burger and will write it off instantly with a silent whisper of "no way" (which I did), while others fall under a spell as the food pornography switch is flipped in their brain. Somehow I never fail to finish this burger.

In one of the most telling stories Ann shared years ago, she told me, "A lady came in here and watched everything I did and said 'Miss Ann, how come I can't make a burger at home like yours?' and I told her 'Because you ain't Ann, and you ain't BLACK!'" She always punctuated her delivery by repeatedly slapping the counter hard. The mostly black crowd would laugh at all of it as they waited patiently for their burgers, which could take up to forty-five minutes.

In 2012, Ann's sister, Josephine Culver, stepped in to help Miss Ann after she was diagnosed with cancer. Josephine's brothers and other Price family members also came in to help after Ann passed and they have managed to keep things the way they've always been. I've heard that the "fear" of entering the Snack Bar and being cut down for breaking a rule or two has dissipated and that the new staff is actually very friendly. It's a first for me—people complaining about *not* being abused by the staff at a burger counter.

IDAHO

HUDSON'S HAMBURGERS

207 East Sherman Ave | Coeur d'Alene, ID 83814
208-664-5444 | Mon–Fri 9:30 am–5:45 pm | Sat 9:30 am–5:15 pm
Sun 11 am–3 pm (June–August) | www.hudsonshamburgers.com

I f you found yourself in Coeur d'Alene at the turn of the century, chances are you would have paid a visit to Harley Hudson's tiny canvas burger tent for some greasy nourishment. The great news is that over a hundred years later you can still visit this landmark burger counter for the same greasy nourishment. The tent may have gone brick-and-mortar and has moved four times (only a few blocks each move), but the burgers are still made with pride by the fourth generation of the Hudson family.

This classic burger counter is just what you'd expect to find in picturesque downtown Coeur d'Alene, Idaho. From the front window of the restaurant, you can see a piece of the enormous Lake Coeur d'Alene and imagine the hydroplane speedboat races that took place there in the 1950s and 1960s. Find a spot at the long counter and order a burger, the only thing on the menu.

They also have drinks and pie, but that's it. No fries, no chips. By design, the menu focuses on

the hamburger, as it should, because this one was worth the drive.

The choices are single or double, cheese or no cheese. Condiment options are pickle and a slice of raw onion. If you request pickle, watch closely what happens. You'll witness something you'd be hard-pressed to find anywhere else in America. The grillman takes a whole dill pickle and hand-slices five or six pieces and neatly arrays them on a waiting steamed bun. The same happens for a slice of onion, sliced in a worn groove on the butcher block in front of the griddle. Nothing is presliced.

A pan of high-quality, fresh ground round sits to the left of the small flattop griddle. The grillman takes a guesstimated quarter-pound wad of the fresh beef and swiftly forms it into a patty, and it hits the griddle with an audible splat. The griddle only holds eighteen burgers at a time, so expect to wait for a stool during peak times. During the summer the line can go out the door and down the street.

Today, brothers Todd and Steve Hudson run the historic burger counter. They each take a two-day shift and do their share of burger flipping. Longtime employee Angela takes up the slack at the griddle. Hudson's serves what could be considered a nearly perfect burger. Relish the moment and plot your return because you'll be forever changed. The simplicity of the elements and the burger's ideal proportions will win your heart (and stomach).

One unique feature of the burger experience at Hudson's is a proprietary "spicy ketchup" that locals and regulars put on their burgers. Fair warning: this stuff is HOT and looks like regular ketchup in its traditional squirt bottle. The ketchup was invented not for culinary reasons but for economic ones. Todd explained, "During the Depression, some people would come in and load up their burgers with ketchup to stretch the meal." Todd's grandfather added fiery spice to discourage the practice. Almost eighty years later, Hudson's still does not offer the classic red stuff. Nothing much ever changes at Hudson's, except that an ATM was recently installed and Dr Pepper was added to the menu. Todd explained, "That's huge for us!"

Burgers have not been the sole passion of the Hudson family, though. Their proximity to the lake has led to a lifetime on the water. Great-grandfather Harley flipped burgers in the early part of the century, but also owned a steamboat that he rented for excursions on the lake. During the decade that speedboat racing was allowed on the lake, it was the Hudson family's unofficial job to set up the racecourse markers. When you have finished your burger at Hudson's, wander into the back of the restaurant, where you'll find one of the most impressive collections of hydroplane racing ephemera and memorabilia anywhere.

"The secret is our longevity," Todd explained as he smiled and shrugged. In 2007, that longevity was recognized when the state of Idaho issued a proclamation to honor the Hudson family for a hundred years of business. One hundred years of great burger making is definitely cause for celebration.

BILLY GOAT TAVERN & GRILL

430 N. Michigan (Lower Level) | Chicago, IL 60611 | 312-222-1525
Mon–Thurs 6 am–1 am | Fri 6 am–2 am | Sat 6 am–3 am | Sun 9 am–2 am
(Seven Other Locations) | www.billygoattavern.com

The Billy Goat is responsible for one of the most famous lines in hamburger history, delivered by John Belushi on *Saturday Night Live* on January 28, 1978. But the Goat is more than just "Cheezborger! Cheezborger! No Pepsi, Coke! No fries, cheeps." The Goat is steeped in history, so much that it makes you wish you were a Chicagoan, and definitely makes many Chicagoans proud. All this from a tavern opened in 1934 by Greek immigrant, William "Billy Goat" Sianis.

No one is really sure if the Billy Goat got its name from the far-fetched story of how a goat wandered into the bar one day and became a mascot/pet, or if the name came from the gray goatee Sianis sported, but the nature of its origins is part and parcel of all stories emanating from the Goat. The famous "Curse of the Billy Goat" was also dreamed up by Sianis, a curse that spiritually kept the beloved Chicago Cubs out of the World Series for seventy-one years despite Sianis's nephew Sam's attempts to "remove" it. It's all because the media-friendly tavern owner and his smelly goat were

denied entry to the 1945 World Series. In 2016, the Cubs finally managed to eek out a championship and the famed curse was lifted.

The history of the Goat, carried on today by Sam Sianis and his son, Bill (Billy Goat Jr.), along with the eight-by-ten glossies of past newspapermen who drank and debated there and the bizarre subterranean location, actually add a different

type of flavor to the burger. The Goat has what I like to call the "whole burger experience"—it's not just about the burger. It includes the place you are eating it, and who you are eating with.

The "cheezborgers" at the Billy Goat start as fresh beef that is machine-pattied into quarter-pound slivers. "Triple much better!!" is the call

you are likely to hear as the countermen take your order. Just try and order a single cheeseburger. A "Sosa" is four patties, named after the home run king of the Cubs. There really are no fries so don't even ask. You remember the call "No fries, cheeps, no Coke, Pepsi!"? Belushi accidentally flipped it in the skit—the Goat serves Coke, not Pepsi. You dress your own burger with onions and specially made pickle slices, then grab a seat at the bar (one of the longest I've ever seen) or at one of the many red-checked tables. There are so many things to look at that it would take days to read all of the clippings and photo captions. Not a problem here, since the Goat is open every day, twenty hours a day.

Probably every old hamburger joint has its share of stories and lore, but none wears it on its sleeve like the Billy Goat. There are so many stories to hear that you'll have to go there and ask Sam or Bill yourself. I'm sure they'd be glad to tell a few—ask about the butter on the ceiling, or the goat that ate the twenty-dollar bill.

CHARLIE BEINLICH'S FOOD & TAP

290 Skokie Blvd | Northbrook, IL 60062 | No Phone
Tues–Sat 11:30 am–10:45 pm | Closed Sun & Mon | www.charliebeinlichs.com

There's a sign behind the bar at Charlie Beinlich's that says, "Business hours subject to change during fishing season," and I believe them. This sixty-year-old bar in the suburbs north of Chicago is filled with an impressive collection of mounted fish, most of them caught

by Charlie himself. "Grandma caught that one," third-generation owner Linda Rainey told me, pointing to what looked like the largest in the collection. Her father, John Barnes, who retired after running Beinlich's for over thirty years, is also a fisherman and can claim two of the large fish on

the walls as well. John told me, "Charlie used to say, 'The time you spend fishing doesn't count against your lifespan.'" In his retirement, John spends a fair amount of time in Florida . . . fishing.

Linda recently assumed ownership of the bar with her husband, Tom. "He [Tom] got this place the same way I did," John joked loudly sitting at the bar, "the old-fashioned way: he married the boss's daughter!" The bigger-than-life former owner married Charlie's daughter, Karen, and helped run the business side by side with him. Over the decades virtually nothing has changed at Charlie Beinlich's. "We added an ATM and switched to a soda gun from canned soda," John told me. "That's about it."

The interior of Charlie Beinlich's looks more Northwoods tavern than suburban hangout. The long bar sports thirteen very comfortable stools and the dining area is a sea of no-nonsense black tables. The place is spotless and attracts a slightly

older crowd that come for Bleinlich's famous shrimp cocktail and, of course, the burgers. Families and kids are welcome but Beinlich's offers no booster seats. "We have phone books and duct tape for the kids," Tom pointed out. The servers all wear white oxford shirts and crisp maroon aprons that have their names embroidered on them. They can be seen rushing through the packed dining room with sometimes five burger plates up each arm.

Burgers were introduced to Beinlich's customers a few years after Charlie opened the place. "He used to give food away," John told me. "He'd have big platters of cold cuts out." Tom told me there used to be a sign near the bar that stated simply, "Food is served for the convenience of our customers drinking alcoholic beverages." Eventually, a kitchen was constructed off the back of the bar and a booming burger business was born.

There's only one burger to order and your choices are with or without cheese, swiss, american, or cheddar. Lettuce and onion are available but you'll have to forgo the tomato. In the half century that Beinlich's has been serving burgers, not one has ever seen a tomato and probably never will. If you ask for a "deluxe" burger, you'll get coleslaw and fries on the side, and longtime customer Jeff Goldman told me, "I put the coleslaw on the burger." Slow-cooked and very tasty sautéed onions are also available.

The beef for the burgers is, as John described it, "a sirloin and chuck combo, supposedly," and is amazing. In the early '70s, John switched from hand-pattying to pressing the patty and purchased a patty maker. "I wanted a third-pound burger but the guy cut the mold too big," John explained, leaving Beinlich's with a burger that still today is something closer to a half pound.

As you've probably guessed at this point, there are a lot of great signs to read at Beinlich's. One of my favorites hangs just inside the front vestibule and says, "No tank tops, muddy boots." The suburban setting and mall across the street are hardly the place to find hungry burger-seekers wearing muddy boots so there had to be a story. As construction began nearby on what was the first expressway out of Chicago in 1950, workers would naturally find their way to Beinlich's. "They were building the Edens when this place opened," Linda told me. "My grandmother wanted to have none of that." Although the Edens Expressway has been finished for over half a century, the rule is still enforced.

Charlie Beinlich's future looks strong even though John joked, "When I die, Linda's selling the place!" Linda and Tom have two girls and no intention to sell. Linda told me, "We hope they'll want to take over the business." Their future husbands may get to own Beinlich's, too, the old-fashioned way.

FAST EDDIE'S BON AIR

1530 East 4th St | Alton, IL 62002 | 618-462-5532
Mon-Thurs 1 pm–1 am | Fri-Sun 11 am–2 am | www.fasteddiesbonair.com

The first time I visited Fast Eddie's it was the end of July and it was hotter than hell. But inside the vast, low-ceilinged, dark roadhouse it was as cool as the produce section at the supermarket. The clean-but-broken-in bar is ready for serious crowds, and they get them. Fast Eddie's has an astonishing capacity of one thousand customers.

It's a biker bar, but at the same time caters to all. There's a special parking lot out back designed just for motorcycles, and it's larger than the car lot. When I say "designed" I mean literally—the entrance to the lot is curbed and only about three feet narrow so that cars cannot sneak in. It may look like a playground for bikers only, but longtime manager Christian told me, "We get people of all walks, college kids, judges, lawyers. . . . You name it." That is, except for kids. Fast Eddie's is a twenty-one-and-over bar. I once tried to get food to go since my eight-year-old son was with me but that wasn't happening either. All food must be consumed on the premises, no take-out orders or delivery.

In the beginning, before Budweiser flowed freely at the bar, Anheuser-Busch built the bar in 1921 just as Prohibition was taking root. They were probably only serving "near beer" back then, a non-alcoholic malt beverage called Bevo and waiting for Prohibition to be repealed. But as we know, when

the law was repealed a new law was also created preventing breweries from owning bars. Two generations of the Balaco family owned the Bon Air until "Fast Eddie" Sholar bought the place in 1981. Eddie has since passed away and Eddie Jr. now runs the enormously successful roadhouse.

I always have to flat out ask the question, "Is your beef fresh or frozen?" Eddie Jr. looked at me like I was insane. "Hell no!" He blurted loudly, "We grind our own here!" I ask this question for the reaction, not the content. Eddie's reaction was perfect.

The food operation is separate from the bar operation, and there's no table service unless you are ordering a drink. You can get a drink at the bar, or get a drink from a cocktail waitress, but if you want food, you'll have to get in the line, which is probably long, to order food. Look for the open kitchen just beyond the large bar. Behind a counter are eight electric indoor flame grills. "On

Saturday," Angie, in the kitchen, told me, "all these grills are full." That is a lot of food to grill. Each one holds sixteen burgers. The kitchen also serves hot dogs and a "Hot Chick on a Stick" (grilled chicken), and shrimp cocktail for thirty-nine cents a shrimp. The shrimp is on display, on ice at the kitchen counter and is actually really great. (I usually stay away from shellfish in landlocked restaurants.) "Eddie Sr. got the idea from Vegas casinos," Christian told me "and Eddie Jr. spends a lot of time on quality." All of the food coming out of the grill area tastes incredible, especially after a few drinks, which is what will happen if you get sucked into Fast Eddie's for the night.

The burgers start as quarter-pound fresh ground (in-house) beef that are machine-pattied. They are cooked over a flame and served with nothing but cheese or not. You'll be able to dress you burger with the minimal toppings offered (raw diced onion and pickles) and an array of sauces (hot sauce, mustard, ketchup, Worcestershire sauce among others. And the price of the burger is ridiculously low—only $1.99, or $2.39 with cheese. Don't ask for tomato or lettuce. Angie pointed out, "If we had that, we'd have to charge more!" The burgers are incredibly juicy since they are cooked over a flame grill. The grill gives the burger a pronounced flame-kissed char so the burger tastes like a steak. Maybe that's why the condiment of choice seems to be steak sauce.

The guys will probably take a spin in the men's room at some point, keep an eye out for the old-school rubber dispenser and the ashtray mounted between the urinals. It was a different time back then.

Fast Eddie's is a short drive from St. Louis in the southwestern tip of Illinois so if you find yourself in the area you have to visit. Just bring a designated driver—between the live music, great bar food, and drinking it's hard to not have a good time here.

HACKNEY'S ON HARMS

1241 Harms Rd | Glenview, IL 60025
847-724-5577 | Open Daily 11 am–9 pm | www.hackneys.net

Before there were suburbs, there was Hackney's. "There was nothing out here in the beginning," third-generation owner Mary Welch told me. Hackney's sits way back from Harms Road on a lush, tree-filled piece of property. Across the street is a large forest preserve. It still sort of feels like the middle of nowhere, but drive a few hundred feet in either direction and you'll find yourself in the center of Chicago's suburban sprawl.

The history of Hackney's is so complicated that Mary actually drew a chart for me on the back of a paper placemat. Here is the abridged version. In the '20s, Helen and Jack Hackney converted the back patio of their home into an illegal Prohibition-era bar that served burgers. "It was so deserted out here that they thought they'd make money on booze," Mary explained. Eventually, the Hackneys moved the business from their backyard to a barn-like structure opposite the house. "We're not really sure what it was," Mary told me. "Maybe a chicken coop or a barn." In 1939, Mary's father, Jim Masterson, who was Helen's nephew, and her mother, Kitz, purchased Hackney's for one dollar and endured the slow war years with business being fueled by soldiers from a World War II POW camp in the forest preserve across the street. When the war ended, the suburbs exploded and Hackney's was suddenly surrounded by hungry families. "There were mostly German bars here then," Mary explained, "and this was the first real family place." It was a mixed blessing, however. Thanks to new residential zoning after the war, Hackney's was not able to expand the restaurant on the property. In 1955, Jim and Kitz were turning away one hundred people a day. Their solution? They opened a second Hackney's just down the street.

When the Mastersons assumed ownership of Hackney's, they introduced a burger to the menu that remains today—the "Hackneyburger." This North Suburbs classic is unique to the burger world because, since day one, it has been served on dark rye. And not just any dark rye, homemade dark rye prepared daily in Hackney's own bakery. "Originally, my parents made the bread at home," Mary told me, in the house that sits just opposite the restaurant. The bread is soft and sweet, not what you'd expect from dark bread. In fact, it's so soft that it has a tendency to disintegrate quickly thanks to the juicy eight-ounce burger that it cradles.

The Hackneyburger comes unadorned, with lettuce and tomato on the side. Onions are available, and if you ask for them grilled, you'll get an entire onion's worth on the side. Cheese choices are american, swiss, and cheddar. The half-pound burger, kept thick, is cooked on a flattop griddle and can be prepared to the temperature of your choice. Hackney's used to buy ground beef from a local butcher and Mary's parents would hand-patty the burgers daily using a coffee cup as a mold. They eventually purchased a patty machine, and one day gave the patty machine to their butcher. That butcher, who has been supplying Hackney's since the beginning, is now the sole provider of hamburger patties to the six Hackney's locations in the

Chicago area. "That's all he does for a living, makes burgers for all the Hackney's," Mary told me.

No visit to Hackney's would be complete without trying one of their signature sides, the french fried onions. It arrives as a deep-fried brick of thinly sliced onions fused with fried batter standing tall at about seven inches. It's an impressive presentation and was invented by a cook at Hackney's in 1962. In an effort to placate a customer who had missed out on the perch-one-fish-fry Friday, a cook named Carmen tossed a handful of battered onions into the deep fryer and invented a new side dish. The concoction emerged whole, in the shape of the fryer basket, and to this day is still served as a block of deep-fried goodness on a plate.

Not surprisingly, Hackney's has a great selection of German beers on tap and a solid bar lined with substantial leather-topped stools. The bar is carpeted, quiet, and dark, even on bright, sunny days. I could see myself passing many hours there. The small dining room is also clean and dark, and a young, cute server told me, "It kind of reminds me of a cozy Wisconsin bar." Me too, but Hackney's is even cozier than what I've seen in Wisconsin. Across the parking lot, behind the original house, Hackney's also operates a patio that seats two hundred in the warm months.

"It hasn't really changed since my parents were here," Mary told me, which is a good thing because everything seems to work just fine. Mary is one of seven children, all of whom are partners in the business and separately manage the six Hackney's in the area. Mary has the shortest commute, though, a short walk across the parking lot from the family home she grew up in. "I'm not complaining," she told me with a smile.

MOONSHINE STORE

6017 East 300th Rd | Moonshine (Martinsville), IL 62442 | 618-569-9200
Mon–Sat 6 am–1 pm, Grill Closes at 12:30 | Closed Sun & Major Holidays

The Moonshine Store is one of those places you hope no one finds out about. I never would have known about the Moonburger if I had not seen a clip on *CBS Sunday Morning* calling it the "Best Burger in America." A claim like that makes me a skeptic from the start but naturally my interest was piqued. I had all but written the place off when I just happened to be in the neighborhood. Believe me, this is not an easy thing to do.

The Moonshine Store is at a crossroads in east central Illinois surrounded by cornfields. The drive to Moonshine (population two) is a blur of cornstalks and soybean fields for hours on two-lane roads and the nearest city is Terre Haute, Indiana. There's a reason the lines are not out the door with city people—it's too damn far away. But it's true; the Moonshine does make one of the best burgers in America.

The large country store turned burger spot does a brisk business regardless of its remote locale. There are no tables inside, just recycled church pews and chairs that line the counters and cases. You place an order at the back of the store and when your burger is ready, you take it to the bountiful condiment table in the center of the room. If you can't find a spot on a pew, there is ample seating out back at the picnic tables.

The staff is a sight to behold—a bevy of chatty country women all taking turns at the grill

and register. "I don't work here, I'm just helping today," laughed one behind the counter. Owner Helen Tuttle once explained, "Friends and family all come down for the lunch hour to help out. When we're busy we'll even ask someone in the store to do dishes—we're not bashful." Today, Helen has retired from day-to-day and has left her two daughters-in-law in charge, Lisa and Jackie, and they've changed absolutely nothing.

The Moonburger is a beauty: pure and simple, 80/20 ground chuck cooked on a hot gas griddle until moist inside with a delicately crunchy exterior. I asked what the size of the burger was and Helen told me, "All sizes. Depends on what my hand grabs." They look to be around a third of a pound and served on an untoasted white squishy bun. Cheese is treated like a condiment and tossed on cold. Trust me—this burger needs no cheese.

The three new gas griddles can hold up to 150 burgers, which is an improvement over the previous electric griddle that only held fifteen. "We can sell fifty to six hundred burgers a day depending, and at least four hundred on a Saturday," Helen once told me. Many motorcycle tours make the Moonshine a destination for burgers, and every year a group called the Moonshine Lunch Run tries to break the previous year's record. On April 8, 2017, almost three thousand motorcycles descended upon the country burger joint and set an astonishing new record of 3,362 burgers, all made and consumed on the same day.

In a moment of introspection standing on the front porch of the Moonshine, Helen once told me, "We do no advertising. I believe the Lord has a hand in this business." Believe it. These burgers are touched by something.

PARADISE PUP

1724 South River Rd | Des Plaines, IL 60018
847-699-8590 | Mon–Sat 11 am–5 pm | Closed Sun

There are plenty of places in Chicago proper to find a good old greasy sustenance thanks to the thriving hot dog stand culture that the city is known for. I love a good Chicago dog, "dragged through the garden" as I've heard the classic fully loaded char dog described. But what took me years to discover was that many of these stands also serve excellent char burgers. And one of the best Chicago char burgers is not even in the city.

We are specifically talking about the Char Cheddar Burger, one of the greatest confluences of flavors and textures anywhere. There is nothing to a great Char Cheddar but flame-grilled beef, sautéed onions, and a heaping helping of soft Wisconsin cold-pack cheddar spread. These simple elements together easily create a sum greater than its parts.

Paradise Pup is way out in Des Plaines but very close to O'Hare and I've been known to book flights that correspond to their opening hours. Once in a car, you are only minutes from this fully satisfying burger experience.

True to its roots, Paradise Pup is a no-frills place. Jump in line and be ready with your order. Thankfully for you there's not much to choose from so try not to hold up the regulars behind you who are hungry. There are a few stools inside and narrow counters but you'll probably just be in the way if you sit down when they are busy. If it's warm, sit outside at one of the picnic tables, or in your car, assuming your Char Cheddar will make it that far.

Brothers George and Tony Manos opened the stand in 1983 after friends told them they should go into business. "We used to make burgers at home for the neighborhood," Tony told me from his spot at the grill. They converted a small sandwich shop into the Pup and thirty-five years later they are still there. Chances are you'll always find Tony at the grill at the Pup and George taking orders because that's the way it has always been. Tony has never missed a day of work, EVER. "His wife gave birth and he was back by noon," George told me with a straight face. Tony is also mildly obsessed with the quality of his grills. "We have a grill graveyard," he told me, "and I've gone through at least forty in the last thirty-five years."

The burger at Paradise Pup starts as a six-ounce fresh patty of 80/20 ground chuck steak

that comes from a supplier the brothers keep very secret. "I see people dumpster diving," George told me, but that will do no good since the packaging is not disposed of there. Tony flame-grills the thick patty, which develops a serious char and deeply smoky flavor. The bun is pillowy and fresh and comes from a local Jewish bakery. "They used to deliver to my house at 4 a.m.," George told me. "They had the keys to my car and would leave them there." The flattop at the Pup is for nothing but cooking large quantities of chopped spanish onion until they are caramelized and perfect. The onions luxuriate in their own juices on the flattop until married to a burger.

And then there's the cheese. The brothers were arguably one of the first to use the beloved

Wisconsin cold-pack cheddar spread from Merkts on a burger. The result is downright orgasmic, especially when combined with a smoky, beefy patty and sweet, caramelized onions.

The shakes are something else at Paradise Pup and you'll definitely want to get one. "We always use fresh fruit," George told me. If raspberries are in season, indulge in a raspberry shake for sure.

The name, according to George, just popped into his head, *paradise* meaning a happy place and *pup* for the char dogs they sell. But the Pup is only open six hours a day so plan your visit to paradise accordingly.

Tony's son, Anthony, now twenty, works in the stand regularly and will hopefully run the place one day. "I love food and cooking," he told me, "and I grew up with it." Even if young Anthony possesses one-tenth of his father's passion he'll be fine and the restaurant will have a great future.

TOP NOTCH BEEFBURGER SHOP

2116 West 95th Street | Chicago, IL 60643 | 773-445-7218
Mon–Thurs 8 am–8 pm | Fri & Sat 7:30 am–8:30 pm | Closed Sun

Not everyone wants to go to Top Notch and that's a shame. That may be because although the address says Chicago it is very far from Chicago proper. In fact, it's about twenty-five minutes by car south of the Loop in a neighborhood called Beverly. When I tell people where Top Notch is, the response is usually, "All the way down there?!" C'mon, Chicago, the journey to Top Notch is worth it because they make, without a doubt, one of the best burgers in town.

In 1942, the Soulian Family opened the first Top Notch on 79th Street across from Leo High School. In the early 1980s, they moved to a new location on 95th Street, and moved again to the current location further west on 95th in 1983.

Top Notch has standard-issue brown Naugahyde booths, fluorescent lighting, and wood paneling from the 1980s but takes it a step further to include Bob Ross–inspired oil paintings of soothing waterfalls and mountain scenes. It's a big, bright place that looks as if nothing has changed in decades. The staff is extremely friendly and the menu lists true diner fare. The shakes, fries, and tuna sandwiches are all good, but the reason to visit Top Notch is for the "beefburgers." They come in three sizes—the quarter pounder, the half-pound "King Size," and the three-quarter-pound "Super King Size." A deal breaker for me is the absence of fresh ground beef in a burger restaurant, so I always ask the question "fresh or frozen?" I was directed to the manager of thirty years, Sam Gomez, who, without asking for credentials, dragged me into the kitchen and into their small meat locker. There I was surrounded by the real thing—about five sides of beef and various cuts waiting for their turn in the grinder. Sam told me "our burgers are very fresh." I had a hard time doubting him and I've been back countless times since then.

The burgers are cooked on a large vintage cast-iron griddle in view of a few lucky counter seats. They are griddled wide and flat, allowing more of the beef to have contact with the griddle surface. A favorite condiment at Top Notch are grilled onions, so much so that burgers requested without onions still gather an onion essence. The bun is my favorite kind—white and squishy with sesame seeds, probably six inches across, toasted in the same upright conveyor toaster that Louis' Lunch in New Haven uses. Sam describes the fries as "pre–World War II," which I took to mean from a time before fries were frozen. Sure enough, there in the kitchen one employee had the task of gathering up fresh-cut fries that soak in cold water and bringing them to the fryer. The fries are excellent.

Darrin Soulian, the son of the founders, owned and ran Top Notch until he passed recently, leaving the restaurant to his widow, Louis. She does not handle day-to-day, that was left to Sam and an old friend of Darrin's, Jim Quigley. Jim is at the restaurant daily, handles the books for the family, and dispenses hamburger lore to whoever will listen. He has become a fixture at Top Notch and the only link to the burger joint's glorious past. Nine years ago, Jim saw his friend Darrin struggling with restaurant paperwork and offered to help. "I came in for two weeks to help," Jim told me, "and I'm still here!"

KNOW YOUR BUTCHER

Okay, I've given you two hundred reasons to eat out and you still want to make a burger at home? No problem. All you'll need to do is drop in to your local big-box supermarket and grab a plastic-wrapped wad of ground meat on the Styrofoam tray, right? Wrong. The first step is getting the right meat from the right people. It's time to make friends with your local butcher.

Fresh ground beef is the prime ingredient of an excellent burger. Supermarket ground beef can be fresh, but unless a butcher is handing it to you, it has probably been on the shelf for a while. Also, the origin of the cow (or cows) that is in supermarket beef is usually unknown. If you go to a butcher, chances are the beef comes from one cow and will be ground right in front of you.

Depending on your preference, choose a fat-to-lean ratio. The best hamburgers have more fat (surprised?). Most butchers will choose an 80/20 percent ratio of muscle to fat if you don't ask. This is because beyond 25 percent fat will cause the burger to shrink substantially as it cooks. Less than 5 percent fat may cause the burger to stick to the cooking surface.

Ask for chuck shoulder. This is the most common part of the cow used for hamburger meat because of its high fat content and excellent marbling. Some butchers will blend fatty chuck with sirloin in the grinder to increase the leanness of the mix.

Ask your butcher to send the beef through the grinder twice. This means the butcher will put it through the grinder twice to ensure that the fat and muscle fibers are well blended.

It's wise to use the ground beef the day you purchase it. After a few hours, refrigeration causes the juices to separate from the meat. These are the juices you'll need to create the perfect burger.

You may also want to invest in an inexpensive countertop meat grinder and experiment with whole cuts of beef. This is an excellent exploration, but I can guarantee you'll be back to your butcher for ground beef sooner than you think.

INDIANA

HEINNIES

1743 West Lusher Ave | Elkhart, IN 46517 | 574-522-9101
Mon–Thurs 11 am–10 pm | Fri 11 am–11 pm | Sat 4:30 pm–11 pm | Closed Sun

Friend and food columnist Marshall King led me to this hamburger. He told me about a decades-old bar down by the train tracks in an industrial part of town that had been serving burgers forever—I was sold.

When I first visited Heinnies, Bill DeShone, third-generation owner, was doing what his grandfather and father did for decades before him—he was walking around the dining room, greeting people, and checking on their food. "There's always a family member here," Bill told me, "whether it's me or my brother." It's that kind of pride of place that keeps people loyal. That and, of course, a world-class hamburger.

In the early 1950s, Henry "Heinnie" DeShone chose a spot for his tavern that was a bit remote for the residents of Elkhart. His new venture would be located across the street from one of the busiest railroad hubs in North America. "There was nothing else out here," Bill explained, and told me that most of the clientele were railroad men. "It has always been a place where the working man could come get a burger, though back then it was a beer and a burger."

When Heinnies opened in 1951, the low-ceiled bar had a sign on the door prohibiting women (but by 1956 the sign was removed). A small dining room was added to the bar in 1983, and in 1996 a full renovation was completed. Bill's younger brother, Troy, did the decorating and his obsession with NASCAR and open wheel racing is apparent—the walls are lined with an impressive collection of American racing memorabilia.

The menu is loaded with burgers, but the ones to focus on are the classic "Heinniecheeseburger" and the "Claybaugh." The latter is a larger version of the classic that includes two one-third-pound patties and a wild pile of ingredients including, but not limited to, bacon, mushrooms, and four types of cheese. This one should be reserved for the truly starved. The burger is named after a local policeman and regular named Scott Claybaugh who, Bill explained, just like the burger, "is big and full of shit." But it's the Heinniecheeseburger that they come back for, a moderately priced, well-seasoned, great-tasting burger.

Made from fresh ground prime beef, the Heinniecheeseburger in its simplest form (no condiments, on a bun) is a taste explosion. That's because of a not-so-secret ingredient included in the DeShone family burger recipe—chopped onions mixed into the beef. "We used to mix in bread crumbs and egg, too," Bill told me. "It was sort of like a meat loaf." But because the meat turned bad quickly, the DeShone family decided to stick with the basics—chopped onion, salt, and pepper.

The meat for the Heinniecheeseburger comes from a local butcher, the same butcher Heinnies has been using forever. The butcher uses scraps from sirloin, filet, and strip steaks and grinds them for the restaurant. After the ground prime arrives, it is blended with chopped onion and pattied on an ancient family heirloom. The tool is a unique patty maker that presses the burgers one at a time to the proper thickness without forming the traditional cylindrically "squared" sides. The result is a patty with craggy edges that looks hand-formed.

Bill is slightly befuddled by a group of fans who have discovered the decades-old tavern—the Amish. On Friday nights, the back room is full of people from the nearby Amish communities of Nappanee and Shipshewana. Bill assumes that they are drawn to the restaurant by the huge, horse stable–themed dining room that was added in 1985 to the back of the restaurant called "Heinnies Back Barn." Knotty pine frames each booth like a horse stall and vintage farm equipment lines the walls. "They come in by the vanload," Bill told me. "Strawberry daiquiris and steak for two!"

HINKLE'S SANDWICH SHOP

204 West Main St | Madison, IN 47250 | 812-265-3919 | Mon–Thurs 6 am–10 pm
Fri & Sat Open 24 Hours | Closed Sun | www.hinkleburger.com

Hinkle's is a tiny diner with a big, eighty-five-year history. The trolley no longer rumbles by out on Main Street, and the place underwent a face-lift after a fire, but the soul of the diner remains, and so do their very addictive sliders.

In 1933, Winfred Hinkle decided to expand his growing empire of burger joints and opened in Madison. The Hinkle brothers had opened other units in Bloomington, Columbus, and North Vernon as well, all during the 1930s (in fact, the Bloomington location, which is still open, was owned by Winfred's brother, Leon, up until he retired in 1989). The Madison location changed hands two more times before local business-man Jack LeGrand bought the diner in 1998. His daughter, Amber, became part owner in 2003 because, as Jack put it, "I'm getting up there."

It's counter service at Hinkle's and that means fast turnover. So fast that the waitstaff serve most drinks in to-go cups—it's assumed you are eating quick and taking your drink with you. There are only 11 stools at Hinkle's so if you plan to linger, go next door and sit in the newish dining room. But to enter the other half of Hinkle's, you'll need to

The burgers are cooked on a large flattop just inside the front door, a griddle placement that goes back almost a century for most burger joints with any history. Hinkle's uses tiny 1.5 ounce patties that cook fast. Bubby tosses a handful of minced onion onto each patty, then flips, adds cheese and the bun top. They are served on tiny, tasty buns that are pillowy soft, partly from being steamed on the burger. For years Hinkle's used buns from a local Hostess Bakery, but they shut down suddenly overnight a few years ago and Jack was in search of a new bun vendor. The new bun, a change which regulars are still reticent to accept, are tasty sliced dinner rolls from another local baker.

Hinkle's uses high quality beef, specifically expensive, pasture-raised Certified Angus Beef. "It makes a difference," Jack told me. He is mildly obsessed with quality and cleanliness, two things anyone can appreciate.

exit the diner, make a right turn and go in the first door you see. I accidentally tried to cut through the kitchen to get there once and was told jokingly by waitress Debbie, "We'll put you to work if you go that way!" Debbie has been at Hinkle's, on and off, for over 23 years. "We always leave and come back," waitress Alica told me, "they recycle us!" Alica started at Hinkle's when she was 15 and has been there now for 20 years.

Grill cook of 26 years Bubby is focused and cranks out burgers, breakfast and beyond nonstop with ease. The burgers are small so you'll need to order a bunch or leave hungry. It's one of the only places in America where an order of two triples with cheese is not absurd, in fact it's the perfect order.

When a restaurant suffers a catastrophic fire the blame is usually faulty, ancient wiring or a buildup of grease in the exhaust fan. But the day Hinkle's caught fire in 2000 a tenant smoking in bed upstairs was to blame. "Flames were shooting out of the window when I got here," Jack told me. The building inspector almost declared the building unfit, but at the last second it was spared and renovation began. The iconic diner was shuttered for 3 months for extensive repairs, though Debbie joked, "We were closed for a minute!" And she's absolutely correct—when a diner has a history as long as Hinkle's, 3 months is a minute.

POWERS HAMBURGER SHOP

1402 Harrison St | Fort Wayne, IN 46802 | 260-422-6620
Mon–Sat 5 am–12 am | Closed Sun

Powers is the real deal. Not unlike White Manna in New Jersey or The Cozy Inn of Kansas, Powers is a complete time-warp hamburger joint. You'll be sent straight back to 1940 and a simpler time when the all-American slider was made with fresh ground beef and your only option was with or without onions.

You will smell Powers a block away as you approach old downtown Fort Wayne. Across the street from the beautiful, well-preserved art deco burger joint are two stately federal buildings. If you snapped a photo of the corner in black and white it may look identical to one that could have been taken in the '40s—virtually nothing on this corner has changed.

Onions are the name of the game at Powers. There'll be no hiding the fact that you grabbed a few sliders here because the deep essence of steam-grilled onions will stick with your clothes for hours after. The bouquet of sweet onion wafts throughout the parking lot the minute you step out of your car.

I was clearly the only nonlocal regular in the place the first time I visited. Two women ran the place—one named Sarah took orders and served pop and made change while the other managed the tiny, crowded flattop griddle. Country music played and both women sang along and knew every word. Sarah greeted each person that walked in the door by their first name and said, "Bye, honey," as they left.

★ 89 ★

The classic sliders at Powers are the primary source for the American hamburger. Tiny two-ounce balls of fresh ground beef are grabbed from a pile in a fridge adjacent to the griddle. The balls are tossed on the griddle and covered with a thick wad of thinly sliced sweet onion. The griddleperson gives the onions a gentle press until the balls of beef are flattened. When the patties are flipped, a locally made, sliced "dinner" roll is placed on the burger to steam until soft. A burger with everything comes with cheese and onions. Pickles are available, but as Sarah curtly pointed out, "Only if you ask." If you require a double, two balls are pressed together to make a larger patty. Several doubles with everything is the way to go.

The soft, limp onions easily make up 50 percent of each burger and rule the flavor profile. The cheese acts as a sort of glue for the whole glorious mess and the soft dinner roll completes the package. As I was thinking about this, a customer walked in and ordered a bunch with extra onion, which was hard to imagine. As I popped the last bite in my mouth, I placed an order for two more. The fear of walking out of a place like Powers unsated was too much to bear.

All types of folks dine at Powers. Next to me was a tattooed dude with a Mohawk and next to him a clean-cut man and his daughter. Harley types and old-timers also occupied stools and nary a word was spoken, just quiet consumption and the dull thwack of onions being pressed into beef.

In the beginning, Powers, like many other burger stands of the day, was open around the clock. Today, they have fairly normal hours, opening at 5 a.m. Six days a week. In 1999, the mild-mannered Michael Hall bought the vintage burger joint and changed nothing. Michael still works the griddle daily during the morning shift. I asked him recently what compelled him to buy the place and he responded (with a wry smile), "Somedays I ask myself that same question."

TRIPLE XXX FAMILY RESTAURANT

2 North Salisbury St | West Lafayette, IN 47906 | 765-743-5373
Mon–Sat 5:30 am–11 pm | Sun 5:30 am–10 pm | www.triplexxxfamilyrestaurant.com

"This place was on the brink of folding," owner Greg Ehresman told me as I sat at the twisting short-order counter for the first time. Greg would know, because he flipped burgers at the Triple XXX decades before he was an owner. He obviously saw the value in this burger counter at an early age and told me, "I wanted to buy this place when I was seventeen."

The Triple XXX opened in 1929 as a seasonal root beer stand, or "Thirst Station," only a few blocks from Purdue University. At one point, there were one hundred Triple XXX Thirst Stations

caught my eye, something I had never seen before in my endless hamburger research: the patty was nonchalantly tossed into a bin of flour before it hit the griddle. Perplexed, I asked him why. Like all great stewards of tradition his only response was, "Because that's the way we've always done it." The result was predictable and amazing. The flour mixes with the sizzling fat to create an even more pronounced griddle char and flavor.

If you are looking for a hamburger on the extensive menu, you'll need to search for the "Chop Steak." A cheeseburger is a Chop Steak with cheese. Skip those, however, and head straight for their signature burgers, all named after All-American football stars from Purdue. One of the most popular is the "Boilermaker Pete," a triple with cheese and grilled onions served on a toasted white squishy bun. A triple sounds unmanageable but the proportions are perfect on this beauty, a pure expression of the classic American burger. Wash your burger down with the restaurant's namesake root beer, still made on premises as it has been for almost ninety years.

The Triple XXX is a twenty-four-hour restaurant. That's right, you can show up at any hour of the day to eat amazing burgers. Students make great use of this feature by filling the place well past 4 a.m. on weekends. "On a football weekend," Greg told me, "we'll go through seven hundred pounds of beef easily."

Today, Greg and his wife, Carrie, run The Triple XXX and stay very busy thanks to a visit by Guy Fieri in 2007. "We saw a 40 percent uptick in business since that show aired," Greg told me. For

around the country selling root beer by the mug to a population in the midst of Prohibition. Over the decades, the stand morphed into a full-scale diner with carhop service but slipped into decline in the 1970s. Greg's father, Jack Ehresman, who grew up only a block from the restaurant, swept in and saved the iconic hamburger stand in 1980, even though, as Greg put it, "He was not a restaurant guy." Jack, his wife, Ruth, and son, Greg, decided that the key to their success would be to go back to the old way of making everything by hand—a failsafe measure that has proved to be an enormous success.

The burgers at Triple XXX start as sirloin steaks from a local butcher that are ground daily upstairs in the restaurant and formed into tall "pucks," not thin patties. The puck is smashed thin with great force by the hand of the grillperson just before it hits the hot griddle. As I watched Greg make a burger for me, he did something that a college-town watering hole surrounded by soulless chains that is music to my ears. Even though the McDonald's only one hundred feet away from the Triple XXX is open twenty-four hours, Greg confidently told me, "It does not affect business here at all."

WORKINGMAN'S FRIEND

234 North Belmont | Indianapolis, IN 46222 | 317-636-2067 | Mon 11 am–3 pm
Tues–Thurs 11 am–5 pm | Fri 11 am–8 pm | Sat 11 am–3 pm | Closed Sun

The gloriously unpretentious Workingman's Friend sits on the edge of a working-class neighborhood only a few miles from the famous Indianapolis Motor Speedway. Look for the bar with the large vintage Pepsi sign and a facade made almost entirely of glass block.

Opened in 1918 by Macedonian immigrant Louie Stamatkin as Belmont Lunch, the place mostly served sandwiches and burgers to workers at the nearby B&O Railroad maintenance facility. In 1922, there was a railroad strike and times were tough, so Louie would run tabs for the workers knowing that they had little money to spend. The workers dubbed Louie the "workingman's friend." In the late '40s, Louie passed away and his two sons, Carl and Earl, assumed ownership of the bar. They changed the name out of respect for their father. They began construction on a new, larger building to replace the converted house that Louie called Belmont Lunch. To avoid shutting down for months, the brothers instead built around the existing structure. During construction, pieces of the old structure were carted out the side door and they were never once closed for business. "They did

it to stay open," Becky Stamatkin told me. Becky is Louie's granddaughter, daughter of Carl and the third generation of the Stamatkin family at Workingman's Friend. She has run the bar and smashed burgers to perfection for almost forty years.

★ 92 ★

Today, the large, open tavern is a sea of utilitarian red chairs and tables. Sixty feet in length, it boasts one of the longest bars in Indy. The bar sits atop a wall of glass block that is backlit by two tubes of pink neon. Decoration is minimal, and sections of the linoleum flooring have worn through to the concrete. Two nonfunctioning vintage cigarette machines sit by both doors to the bar as a vestige of the Workingman's past, not some purchased history for the sake of kitchy decor.

"99.9 percent order the double cheeseburger," Becky told me. And there's a good reason for that—it's amazing. Becky takes two balls of fresh ground 80/20 chuck and smashes them super thin on the nearly half-century-old flattop griddle. The burger cooks through but stays moist and the edges become lacy and crisp. The double is served on a toasted white squishy bun with a third bun inserted to separate the two patties. If you ask for everything, your double will come with shredded lettuce, sliced tomato, raw onion, and mayonnaise with pickle slices on the side. The grease, cheese, and mayo worked well with the beef, and I asked Becky if there was more than just mayo between the buns. She told me with a wink, "It's only mayo, but I tell people it's a special sauce."

The double cheeseburger is a sight to behold. The floppy edges of the smashed-thin burger hang far outside the bun, making this beast seem unmanageable. Fortunately, the entire package is quite manageable. The patties each weigh in at around a quarter pound but Becky could not confirm this. "Ah, I don't know how big they are," she confessed. "I've been doing this for so long that I don't know anymore. I make balls of beef, then I smash them." Whatever the size, it's perfect.

One thing at the bar that is almost unmanageable is the beer. If you like your tap beer large, then don't miss the thirty-two-ounce "Frosty Fish Bowl." Bartender Terry, Becky's half brother, pulls a heavy goblet out of a freezer behind the bar and fills it with ice-cold Budweiser or Bud Light. That's a lot of beer and it's almost hard to heft when the glass is full. If you don't want to look like a medieval king at a banquet with this ridiculously large goblet, go for the smaller sixteen- or ten-ounce sizes.

On a diet? Workingman's Friend offers a burger called the "Diet Special" that sounds crazy but good. Becky takes the same smashed-thin patty and serves it on a plate with lettuce, grilled onions, pickles, cottage cheese, and no bun. "We sell maybe five a week," Becky told me. But hey, you didn't come in here because you are on a diet.

I was across the street once snapping a few photos after leaving Workingman's Friend when an old-timer on mobility scooter rolled by and offered his own review. "It's the best burger in Indy!" he shouted and kept rolling. And he's absolutely right.

ZAHARAKOS ICE CREAM PARLOR AND MUSEUM

329 Washington St | Columbus, IN 47201 | 812–378–1900
Open Daily 11 am–8 pm | www.zaharakos.com

When I first stepped into Zaharakos, my jaw dropped. What you'll find at this 118-year-old ice cream parlor will astound you. In 2009, after being purchased (and saved) by local businessman Tony Moravec, Zaharakos reopened completely renovated to its original decor from opening day in 1900. During the century that the Greek-owned restaurant was in business, the place saw many renovations (and a car through the front window) but when Tony purchased the parlor his goal was clear—to restore Zaharakos to its original grandeur, complete with period marble soda dispensers, stamped tin ceilings, wire-back café chairs, and an enormous vintage Welte player organ. I have never seen anything like this in my life.

Tony Moravec is extraordinarily passionate about ice cream parlor memorabilia, ephemera, and history. His passion is fueled in part by his very successful pharmaceutical company located nearby in Columbus. The renovation cost Tony $3.5 million and took two years to complete, but as he explained to me, it was his pleasure. "It was a fascinating trip," he told me. The last Zaharakos family member running the parlor passed away in 2006 as the restaurant was in decline. Tony saw his purchase of the aging relic as a chance to give back to the community.

"In the renovation, we kept the original bones of the place and renovated around that," Tony explained. But this wasn't just any renovation. Tony had specialists come in from all over the country to manage things like restoring and cleaning the original marble, repairing the vintage soda dispensers, and most notably to bring the Welte organ back to its former glory. "I wanted to make it first-class and make Zaharakos a destination." He most certainly has, with stunning detail and unfaltering commitment.

The menu was also restored and updated but still reflects some of the early offerings from the Zaharakos family, like the dizzying selection of fountain soda favorites and the famous "Gom Cheese-Brr-Grr." The Gom is not really a burger but, like the Maid-Rite "loosemeats" sandwich of Iowa, it is an intriguing take on the marriage of beef and bread. There is a regular burger on the menu at Zaharakos but trust me, go for the tasty Gom.

The Gom Cheese Brr-Grr is basically a Sloppy Joe fused with a grilled cheese sandwich, although this one has far less tomato sauce than a typical Joe. Its history is mostly unknown but it is believed that over seventy-five years ago the Zaharakos brothers may have actually invented the original Sloppy Joe. The general profile of the slop is kind of sticky, or "gommy" (from the German slang for "sloppy") and is loaded with tasty spices and a little bit of brown sugar. The buttered, toasted white bread and gooey cheese make this one savory sandwich.

I glanced around the restaurant and noticed that most people were enjoying Gom sandwiches, with and without cheese. The cheese is great on this concoction because it acts like glue to keep the loose contents together. Tony told me, "It still outsells everything we do."

You'll need a drink with your Gom and good luck trying to choose just one. The original soda dispensers behind the long marble counter are still functional for the most part and operated by an actual soda jerk with experience, the sassy Wilma. She suggested the "Jerk's Special," a cinnamon Coke, "Because that's what the jerk likes!" The cinnamon Coke, hand-mixed from Coke syrup, cinnamon syrup, and soda water, is intoxicating. "The cinnamon enhances the flavor of the Coke, right?" Wilma asked. You can also get a number of other fountain sodas, like chocolate Coke, red Raspberry Coke, and the old Prohibition-era favorite, the neon green "Green River" (lemon-lime-flavored).

At some point during your meal, you may hear the towering Welte player organ come to life. This perfectly restored centerpiece of the dining room was originally installed in 1908 and remained in place until the Zaharakos family, in need of cash, sold it to a California collector. Tony, hell-bent on a perfect restoration, tracked down the original

and spared no expense to bring it back. He found an automatic musical instrument restorer in Baltimore who admitted that his love of player organs came from a visit to Zaharakos in his teens. The restored organ sounds like an entire orchestra in a box and is probably just as loud. If you want to be transported back to the glory days of ice cream parlors, just ask a manager to crank it up for you. You'll probably hear the Zaharakos theme song, Scott Joplin's "The Entertainer," though Tony personally changes the reels every few days from his collection of over two hundred.

The Smithsonian Institution should honor Tony Moravec for his role in preserving this piece of long-gone history. His commitment to the culture of ice cream parlors makes him a true American hero. "I don't think he'll get rich from it," former manager Gary mused once and he's probably right. But we are all richer for Tony's service to America.

B&B GROCERY, MEAT & DELI

2001 SE 6th St | Des Moines, IA 50315 | 515-243-7607 | Tues–Fri 8:30 am–6 pm
Sat 8:30 am–3 pm | Closed Mon & Sun | www.bbgrocerymeatdeli.com

'

've never been in a butcher shop quite like this before. Other than cases filled with every type of meat known to man, you'll likely come across co-owner and butcher John Brooks. Trust me, you'll be able to pick out which one is John. Just look for the outgoing guy behind the counter with a vintage *Coke Is It!* paper cap. His dry sense of humor is infectious and his runner banter priceless.

"I used to hate this place," were the first words out of John's mouth when I met him. "It's because I grew up here. Now I love what I do." John is a beef savant and seems genuinely passionate and endlessly fascinated by it all. Each time he tried to describe to me where a certain cut was on the animal, he'd start drawing detailed diagrams on butcher paper.

John did grow up at the shop. His grandfather, John, and great-uncle, Joe, opened the place in 1922, then his dad, John, and uncle, Joe, took over. When John (2) had his own John and Joe the third generation was set. Today, John co-owns B&B with his brother—you guessed it—Joe. The B&B stands for Brooks & Brooks. I probably didn't need to spell that out for you.

Throughout American history, butcher shops have sold burgers. Most took the path of least resistance, shut down the butcher side of the business and today only sell burgers (Stanton's in Houston and Kincaid's of Fort Worth, for example). It's rare

Place your order with any one of several family members at the same counter where orders are being placed for holiday standing rib roasts and T-bone steaks. The burger is cooked on a very small flame grill behind the counter and the patties get a sprinkle of B&B's secret seasoning, a combo of three types of pepper, garlic powder, and "other stuff," John told me. Your choices are single, double, or triple and they come with mustard, ketchup, pickle, and diced onion. The standard white bun is also toasted on the flame grill. My favorite is the bacon double cheeseburger with everything. The fast cook time on the flame grill leaves the burger nicely charred and smoky on the outside, juicy as hell on the inside.

to find a fully-functioning butcher shop that also sells sandwiches and burgers. "We are unique," John told me standing in the shop's enormous walk-in cooler. "The beef for our burger comes from one cow. Not many can say that." John grinds 83/17 beef for the burgers from a hanging cow in his walk-in. Not only are the Brooks brothers involved with whole animal butchery, all of the cows for B&B come from within thirty-five miles of Des Moines. "We sell everything from the snooter to the tooter!" John told me, eloquently describing the family's full-serve butcher business.

There's something about eating a burger in a butcher shop that is like eating sushi on a dock. B&B has converted a bunch of the original grocery shelves into counters for eating.

The sandwiches and burgers started out years ago as a staff meal. Customers took note and demanded they sell them. Today, the lunch crowd is all about prepared food, not lamb chops. "Sometimes were are five deep in here at lunch," John told me. They get all types, "teamsters, high school teachers," John told me. "We get strippers, too. I'm not kidding."

CANTEEN LUNCH IN THE ALLEY

112 East 2nd St | Ottumwa, IA 52501 | 641–682–5320
Mon–Sat 10 am–7 pm | Closed Sun | www.canteenottumwa.com

"It was time," Lindsey Newland told me. She was referring to the previous owners' retirement at Canteen Lunch. "They didn't want to sell it. They were in their eighties." When Lindsey's parents, Jan and Scott Pierce, sent longtime owners Ernie and Shirlee MacBeth a letter in 2015 stating their interest in purchasing the business, they already knew all about the restaurant. Scott grew up in Ottumwa eating the tasty loosemeat sandwiches at Canteen Lunch. The MacBeths owned the tiny lunch counter for almost forty years and were not going to sell to just anyone. "They wanted it to go to someone committed to keeping it the same," Lindsey told me. Looks to me like the new owners have clearly kept that promise. "There's a crack in the window of the pie case," Lindsey pointed out, "and if we fixed it people would complain."

A must-visit spot on the loosemeat sandwich trail, Canteen is the real deal and was opened in 1927 just as the popular Maid-Rite sandwich was sweeping the state. Dusty Rhoades opened a five-stool counter in an alley in downtown Ottumwa, but sold only two years later to the Carter family who would run the icon for almost fifty years. In 1936, they moved the business to its current location, a whopping thirty feet to the west.

Canteen serves loosemeat sandwiches under the proprietary name "Canteen." They are not Maid-Rites. "We don't like when people call them Maid-Rites," Lindsey told me. "We like to say, 'yeah we make 'em right!'"

Those who have been to Taylor's, Tendermaid, or NuWay know exactly what a loosemeat sandwich is. It's not a hamburger but shares a very similar profile. Crumbled beef is cooked in a contraption that steams the meat. The crumbled beef is spooned onto soft white squishy buns with a bricklayer's trowel and served with ketchup, mustard, pickles, and chopped raw onion. If you want yours "dry," you'll get a scoop off the top of the beef in the cooker. If you ask for "wet," a scoop comes from the bottom and contains more rendered beef fat. My advice: go wet.

The cooker has a divider to keep the ten pounds of fresh cooking beef separate from the ten pounds of cooked beef being served. Canteen uses fresh 80/20 chuck for their sandwiches.

When Lindsey first started at Canteen as general manager, there was some confusion as to why she was behind the counter. Traditionally the Carter and MacBeth families only hired older women to work at Canteen Lunch. Lindsey, a youthful doe-eyed beauty told me, "When I started, it was rough. Customers were like, 'Who are you?'" Things have mellowed since.

Actor Tom Arnold is from Ottumwa and on the TV sitcom *Roseanne* the fictional loosemeats

restaurant Lanford Lunch Box is based on Canteen Lunch. Also, Ottumwa has a special place in my heart as the home of Radar O'Reilly in *M.A.S.H.* When I mentioned this to Lindsey she said, "You know that's a fictional character, right?"

To a first-time visitor, Canteen Lunch looks odd, wedged underneath a slab of concrete. As the story goes, about a decade ago the city wanted to build a new parking structure and offered to move Canteen to a new location about a half mile away. The people of Ottumwa petitioned the city and Canteen stayed right where it has always been . . . and the lot was built around the tiny brick building.

Regulars populate the seventeen stools at the tiny horseshoe counter for most of the day, especially on Tuesdays when a group of old-timers in their nineties take over the Canteen. Cook Debra, calls it "Comedy Night" because, "you never know what's going to come out of their mouths!" The nonagenarians hold court and Debra told me, "people don't want to leave because it's so entertaining." On any given day, there are people stopping in to the restaurant for nostalgic reasons, and many will pop in for a Canteen as a first stop home in Ottumwa, "before they get to where they are going," Lindsey told me. In fact, as she was telling me this, the girl next to me admitted she stopped in on her way to see her mother. Just then another guy walked in and announced to me that he knew who made the ancient cooker in the center of the restaurant. It's that kind of a place—warm, friendly, and full of great stories.

HAMBURG INN NO. 2

214 North Linn St | Iowa City, IA 52245
319-337-5512 | Open Daily 6:30 am–11 pm | www.hamburginn2.com

Chances are that if you've been to Iowa City you've been to the Hamburg Inn. Since 1948 this hamburger destination has been serving fresh ground burgers to University of Iowa students, professors, and faithful regulars, and more recently has become a sort of base camp for politicos rambling through town on the campaign trail.

Everyone from local politicians to presidential hopefuls has made press stops at the Hamburg Inn. They are there to talk to the people and, naturally, be photographed enjoying America's favorite food. But the burger at Hamburg Inn is not just a photo-op prop, it's the real deal.

Dave Panther inherited the Hamburg Inn No. 2 from his father, Fritz Panther. Fritz's older brother, Joe, opened Hamburg Inn No. 1 in the mid-1930s, a small, classic ten-stool hamburger stand featuring burgers for a nickel. In 1948, Fritz and another brother, Adrian, bought a defunct restaurant (the current location) and called it Hamburg Inn No. 2. At one point there was a No. 3 in Cedar Rapids but today, both No.1 and No. 3 are long gone. Only No. 2 remains.

Dave started working for his parents at the restaurant at age thirteen, peeling potatoes. After a stint in the U.S. Air Force, Dave started working full-time at the Hamburg Inn and in 1979 assumed ownership. After thirty-eight years, Dave decided it was time to retire and sold the historic burger joint to Michael Lee in 2016. "He's still here at least once a week," longtime manager Seth Dudley told me. Dave's title in retirement is "consultant."

Since the beginning, chuck steaks have been ground daily on the premises. A six-ounce ice-cream scoop is used to measure the balls of ground beef. The balls of meat are pressed on the griddle and assume a somewhat uneven beauty. Fritz bought a patty maker back in the 1950s but returned it after three days, fully dissatisfied with the results. "He said the patty maker changed the complexion and nature of the whole product," Dave remembered. Over six decades later, not a single pre-formed patty has ever graced the griddle at the Hamburg Inn.

The burgers are served on large, toasted, cornmeal-dusted kaiser rolls. Five different types of cheese are available, as are an abundance of toppings ranging from the standard tomato and lettuce to the slightly bizarre pineapple. Honestly, don't be blinded by the options—this burger, made from choice beef, is so fresh it'd be a shame to cover it with anything other than a bun.

The menu at the Hamburg Inn is enormous, offering every type of comfort food imaginable. Dave gradually expanded the menu over the decades and was responsible for adding a favorite breakfast item, the omelet. The burger takes center stage for lunch and dinner but it's the omelet, served in unlimited combinations, that captivates the morning crowd. "We have a guy that comes in and orders a cream cheese, black olive, and raisin omelet," Dave told me once, "That's about the weirdest combination we've made." One of the restaurant's most popular omelets contains, not surprisingly, a healthy dose of the Hamburg Inn's ground beef. With ground beef and american cheese, it's basically a hamburger omelet. A great idea and probably the only one of its kind in America.

While campaigning for the presidency, Obama stopped in but got an omelet to go (apparently it was early in the morning). The walls of the Hamburg Inn are covered with vintage photos and one wall is dedicated to American politics. There's even a plaque over table number six that trumpets a visit by former president Ronald Reagan. President Clinton visited as well and chose the seat just "to the left" of Reagan's. On the most recent election cycle all of the candidates made it through the Hamburg Inn with the exception of one. "I'm not sure why Trump didn't come here," Seth mused. "The crowds probably would have been too much for the place anyhow."

THE IRISH SHANTI

17455 Gunder Rd | Elgin, IA 52141 | 563-864-9289
Tues–Sat 10 am–10 pm | Sun 11 am–5 pm | Closed Mon | www.thegunderburger.com

If you find yourself eating a burger at the Irish Shanti, deep in the rolling farmland of northeast Iowa, it's because you've made a point of being there, or you are lost. The town of Gunder, Iowa, is barely on the map and the Irish Shanti, across from a defunct gas station, is the only business in town. Though remote, this destination restaurant manages to fill the dining room on most nights and suggests reservations on weekends. Some will drive for hours to eat at the Shanti, and many of them are in search of a menu item that has made this corner of Iowa famous—the "Gunderburger."

The Irish Shanti has only been around in name since the midseventies but the building itself dates to 1929 when it opened as a grocery store. The restaurant has changed hands many times over the years, and today, it's owned by the Boston transplant, Kevin Walsh. At one point, the tiny town of Gunder was in danger of being literally wiped off the map. The unincorporated town with a population barely in the double digits was rescued by a grill cook at the Irish Shanti named LaVonne Christianson. In 1985, she had an idea to concoct a colossal burger for all to see and name it after the town. The plan worked and today, Gunder remains on the map, and the enormous Gunderburger remains on the menu.

The Gunderburger must be seen to be believed. It starts with a twenty-ounce ball of fresh ground beef that is slapped on the flattop and pressed into

a patty by hand. The chef sprinkles a bit of a "secret fairy dust" on the patty, then drops a bacon weight on it. The burger cooks slowly over low heat on a griddle that has an excellent, dark patina.

If you order a Loaded Gunderburger, get ready to flex those jaw muscles. To the one-pound cheeseburger, the Shanti adds lettuce, tomato, bacon, sautéed onions, and grilled mushrooms and they are not stingy. After construction, this burger weighs in at around one-and-a-half pounds.

The appearance of the Loaded Gunderburger is part of its shock value. To say that the bun is disproportionate to the patty is an understatement. The Shanti purposely uses a standard-sized bun that does

not stand a chance in holding back the burger's contents. The patty and piles of condiments protrude cartoonishly from under the bun leaving the uninitiated with a challenge. I actually tried to heft the beast to my face only to find that the bottom half of the bun had virtually vanished into the copious juices. I ate the burger gripping the patty but eventually had to use a fork because stuff was falling everywhere. "The strategy I tell people is to go around the outside of the bun with a fork first," Kevin's son, Hans, told me years ago (he used to be their chef). The Gunderburger was a mess but well worth it. You'll need a hose-down after this one.

Kevin moved from his native Boston leaving behind a job as a registered nurse and bought the restaurant in 2005 with his wife, Elsie. One of the first major changes he made was to add a sizeable kitchen. "It used to be here," Kevin explained with his arms outstretched at the end of the bar. Kevin is Irish and this probably explains the proudly displayed Irish flag in the center of the dining room and the Guinness on tap. "We have a lot of Irish whisky, too," Kevin told me. The Irish Shanti also serves fried cheese curds, one of my absolute favorite guilty pleasures available in this part of the country. Everything at the Shanti is made fresh in-house and most of the produce during the warmer months comes from their garden.

Car and motorcycle clubs find their way to the remote burger outpost, as would be expected, during warmer months, but the Shanti also gets its share of snowmobile clubs in winter as well (that's a new one for me). Kevin told me recently, "We have guys that ride their tractors here like they are motorcycles. Sometimes there are twenty of them out there!" There's no denying that the Irish Shanti is in the heart of a farming community.

So if you are rambling around northeast Iowa in search of nourishment, seek out the Irish Shanti. Indulge in a few pints of Guinness or two fingers of Jameson, and eat the burger that saved a town.

PAUL'S TAVERN

176 Locust St | Dubuque, IA 52001
563-556-9944 | Mon–Sat 10 am–2 am | Sun 10 am–12 am

There was a time in American tavern culture when the drink reigned supreme. Certain bartenders probably noticed the need to serve a modicum of edible nourishment to keep their customers from leaving for meals and the bartop grill was born. The foodservice at Paul's is a vestige of this tavern's past that holds a tiny footprint behind the bar. Although small, the bar kitchen at Paul's still cranks out amazing burgers to comfortably buzzed patrons.

I've heard people refer to Paul's as a "dive," and after my first visit I have to say that Paul's is the cleanest dive I've ever set foot in. Somehow, this broken-in bar shows its age but maintains its gritty character without coming off as a dump. The place is filled with perfectly preserved vintage beer signs and the most amazing collection of taxidermy you'll ever see while sipping a Miller High Life. The bears, bighorn sheep, deer, and alligators that line the walls were all hunted by former owner Paul Schollmeyer. The displays go beyond the traditional random, dusty, deer head over the bar. The work that went into these displays is astounding and the taxidermist was clearly a master at the craft. Think Museum of Natural History in a bar setting. There are large, well-lit glass cases on either side of the bar and

one that is actually mounted on the ceiling for effect. That case contains a massive polar bear, shot in 1966. Paul, who is now ninety and still visits the bar frequently, told me he bagged the polar bear years before restrictions were placed on hunting them. As I surveyed the impressive collection of mounted big game overhead, Paul leaned and whispered to me, "I don't mean to brag, but I can shoot."

The centerpiece of the tiny kitchen area at the end of the long bar is an ancient Norge Broilator. The thick black stove is one of the more unique cooking apparatuses I've seen for burger making and clearly the precursor to the salamander broiler found in many professional kitchens. The most obvious difference in the Broilator is that the burgers cook on a small, well-seasoned flattop that can't be more than

two feet wide and only one foot deep. Burgers are slapped onto the tiny flattop and the operator pulls on a bar that simultaneously closes the door and sends the burgers up and into the center of the stove. The burgers then cook from above by indirect flame as they sizzle on the griddle. Totally unique.

Though the cooking area inside the Broilator is limited, bar manager Dave explained, "It can cook eight at a time." The burgers start as quarter-pound scooped balls of 90/10 fresh ground beef that are placed in a single-patty press. "We use lean beef because anything too fatty and it'll flare up and burn," Dave told me. Soft white buns are warmed in a nearby toaster oven and the burgers are served on tiny paper plates with pickles and a slice of raw onion. When I inquired about additional condiments, Dave responded gruffly, "No lettuce, tomato, or any of that stuff." The burger at Paul's is simplicity personified.

Today, the tavern is owned by a former manager from McDonald's, Tom Koch, a friend of Paul's who purchased the place in 1991. Paul actually approached Tom and asked him to take the reins, probably so that his big game collection would remain intact. "Everybody loves this place," Tom told me. "I told Paul I'd try it for a year and [twenty years later] I'm still here." Tom's brother, Dave, helps manage the tavern and his daughter, Amber, bartends and makes burgers. I believe the future of Paul's is secure.

As we polished off our fourth or fifth beers and finished our burgers a friend of mine, surrounded by the taxidermy said, "Every bar in New York City wishes they were this cool." It's true. Paul's Tavern is the real deal. Everything else is just trying to be Paul's.

TAYLOR'S MAID-RITE

106 South 3rd Ave | Marshalltown, IA 50158 | 641-753-9684 | Mon–Sat 8 am–9 pm
Sun 11 am–7 pm | (Winter Hours: Mon–Sat 8 am–8 pm) | www.maidrite.com

Taylor's does not serve hamburgers. Taylor's serves a "loosemeats sandwich." For those not familiar with the popular Iowa hamburger-influenced sandwich, a loosemeats, or Maid-Rite (and sometimes referred to as a "tavern"), is basically a deconstructed hamburger, or a Sloppy Joe without the slop. The recipe is simple: fresh, ground-on-premises beef is steamed and crumbled in a cast-iron cooker. Nothing is added but salt. Upon getting an order, a member of the extended Taylor family or a longtime employee grabs a bun that has been "doped" with pickle and mustard, and with the other hand, scoops up an impossible amount of the pebbly, moist meat. That's it, and there's nothing else on the menu but shakes, ice cream, pie, and soft drinks. They have been doing it this way since 1928. The order is wrapped up, even if you are eating at the counter. "Wrapping makes the bun soft," Zac told me. Zac, visiting for a short stint to help out, is a fifth-generation Taylor proving that Taylor's is clearly a family-run business.

Cliff Taylor purchased the franchise for the third Maid-Rite in Iowa for three hundred dollars and called it Taylor's. His son, Don Taylor, took over the business in 1944. In 1958, Taylor's moved across the street into a new, modern building, its current location. Cliff Taylor's granddaughter, Sandy, remembers the move well. "We moved the entire contents of the restaurant overnight making trips back and forth across the street. I remember helping and carried the plates." One element of the

move that didn't work out so well was the new steam cooker. "My dad thought the meat just didn't taste right so he brought the cooker over from the old place," Sandy told me. "This could be the same cooker from 1928," Sandy said, pointing to the strange stainless cabinet with the deep, cast-iron trough.

Taylor's is a bright, clean, friendly place with floor-to-ceiling windows in the front of the restaurant. A large horseshoe counter surrounds a short-order kitchen that offers amazing views of your food being prepared. One wall of the restaurant is covered with enormous world and U.S. maps with the phrase above, "Go 'round the world, but come back again."

Unlike other Maid-Rites in the well-known, midwestern franchise, Taylor's has kept things simple. The other Maid-Rites offer everything from roasted chicken and corn dogs to tacos. At Taylor's, a loosemeats sandwich has always been the solitary sandwich on the short menu.

The loosemeats sandwich may be some of the fastest food you'll ever come across because the meat is already cooked and warm. An order can arrive at your spot at the counter in under a

minute. Unwrap and sink your teeth into one of the softest, tastiest sandwiches around and you'll start wondering why the rest of the country has not caught on yet.

The first time I visited this Central-Iowa eatery there was a debate going on about the proposed introduction of ketchup, not to the sandwich, but to the *counter*. A sign out front announced "Stop In Vote Yes Or No For Ketchup." The votes were tallied, and in August 2006, ketchup was introduced to the counter, seventy-seven years after opening day.

Sandy retired from a job as a schoolteacher in North Dakota only to return home and find herself drawn to Taylor's. Her son, Don Taylor Short, was looking to move on after twenty years managing the popular loosemeats institution and Sandy agreed to jump in. "This is my retirement!" she told me laughing. She's there every day and makes a point to warn customers about the pitfalls of the metal cup that holds your "extra" milkshake. "You need to stir it before you pour it," she reminds me. "Someone dumps their shake on the counter every day."

THE LOOSEMEATS SANDWICH

This is an interpretation of the Iowa classic loosemeats sandwich. At Taylor's Maid-Rite in Marshalltown, there are no secrets and their recipe is simple. They grind meat at the restaurant, add salt, and use a cast-iron steam cooker that has been in use for almost eighty years.

Makes 6 sandwiches

Equipment

A seasoned cast-iron skillet

A wooden spoon

A perforated serving spoon

The Burger

1 pound (500 g) fresh ground 80/20 chuck

1 cup (250 mL) beer (use a Pilsner or other light beer; save the remainder to wash down the burger)

3 squirts of yellow mustard

Salt, for seasoning

The Toppings

6 classic soft white hamburger buns

Dill pickle chips

Yellow mustard

1. Preheat the seasoned cast-iron skillet over medium heat. Add the beef and, using the wooden spoon, crumble the beef as it cooks, as if you were making ground beef for tacos.

2. Once the meat is pebbly, kick the heat up to medium-high and cook for about 4½ minutes, until lightly browned.

3. Pour in the beer and continue to stir and crumble the meat frequently as the beer cooks off, another 9 to 10 minutes.

4. While the meat is steaming, prepare the hamburger buns with a slather of mustard and 2 or 3 pickle chips on the bottom half of each bun. Set aside.

5. Just before all the beer has evaporated from the skillet, mix in the mustard and salt to taste. Continue to cook until all of the liquid has evaporated. Remove from the heat.

6. Use a perforated spoon to scoop up a pile of meat, draining any remaining fat, and press onto a prepared bun. Repeat with the remaining meat and buns.

7. Enjoy with remaining beer, and maybe one or two more.

KANSAS

BOBO'S DRIVE IN

2300 SW 10th Ave | Topeka, KS 66604
785-234-4511 | Mon–Sat 11 am–8 pm | Closed Sun

Bobo's is one of only a handful of original drive-ins in America still using carhops. That's right, the ones who come to your car, take your order, then come back with food and clip a tray onto your car door. Sonic may have capitalized on the modern version of the drive-in, but there's still nothing like an original one-of-a-kind like Bobo's.

At one point there were two Bobo's Drive Ins in Topeka. The one remaining opened in 1953. The first location was opened just a few blocks away in 1948 by Orville and Louise Bobo. In fact, Mrs. Bobo still comes in and buys pies two to three times a week with her nephew. "It's so adorable," cashier Sharon Rodriguez told me. Bobo's is now owned by Richard Marsh who purchased the drive-in from Bob Hume in 2007. He is only the third owner in the restaurant's more than six decades of operation. Richard bought Bobo's and all of the secret recipes and for a decade has kept everything pretty much the same. "That's the thing about this place," Sharon offered, "it's always been run by families." Sharon herself is related to Richard.

Bobo's plays the part of the midcentury American road icon with a neon tower shooting out of its roof and a large arrow pointing the way. There are twelve stalls for cars and two carhops during the day running orders and food back and forth from the kitchen to waiting drivers. You can see why so many fast-food restaurants moved to the economical drive-thru; the drive-in

is without question a lot more work. There's also a beautifully dated dining room if you prefer to not eat in your car. It has a tiny horseshoe counter with eleven sturdy stools and a handful of booths, all of it covered in dusty rose-colored leather. The walls are partly sheathed in a burled-wood Formica.

The burgers at Bobo's are excellent. They start as fresh ground 90/10 lean one-sixth-pound patties and are cooked on a superhot flattop griddle, pressed flat. "You don't always get a perfect circle," the grill cook admitted to me once. The thin patty is sprinkled with salt and pepper, then griddled until crunchy on the outside but perfectly moist inside.

Not to be missed are the onion rings. I mean it when I say that these were probably the best I've ever eaten. I still think about that inviting pile of not-too-greasy gnarled, deep-fried onions. I couldn't stop eating them. The homemade root beer is also a draw.

A strange burger creation proprietary to Bobo's competes equally with their flavorful double cheeseburger—the "Spanish Burger." On my first visit I inquired, "What's on the Spanish Burger?" "Spanish sauce," a waitress told me bluntly. Settles that. Turns out the spanish sauce is a tangy, sweet tomato sauce. Just then, someone sat down and ordered one. "You see?" the waitress said, "We sell as many of them as cheeseburgers."

COZY INN HAMBURGERS

108 North 7th St | Salina, KS 67401 | 785-825-2699
Mon–Sat 10 am–9 pm | Sun 11 am–8 pm | www.cozyburger.com

The Cozy Inn is a classic, well-preserved hamburger stand built in 1922 in Salina, Kansas. Not surprisingly, the Cozy, with its six white-painted steel stools and short counter, was modeled after the successful White Castle hamburger chain. In 1921, only one year earlier in nearby Wichita, a man named Walt Anderson had opened the first White Castle: it was to become the first hamburger chain in America. In the next few years, the White Castle model, a clean, small stand serving wholesome burgers, would be copied by entrepreneurs all over the country. The secret ingredient to White Castle's success was chopped onions that, when cooked with the burger, created an intoxicating smell that drew customers from near and far. Bob Kinkel, an amateur baseball player from Salina, liked what he saw (and smelled) and immediately opened the Cozy Inn.

On one of my visits to Cozy, a woman sitting at the counter named Phyllis told me, "My father built this place for Bob—five-hundred-dollar turnkey." This would have been a bargain even by 1922 standards, with the possible exception that the place is incredibly small. It takes only a few people to fill up the low-ceilinged burger joint, so understandably, a line builds quickly outside at lunchtime.

To sit and watch the grillman at work is a treat. He stands in front of a smallish recessed griddle that has room for sixty of the aromatic sliders for which the Cozy has become famous. A steam cloud envelops his head as he flips row after row of the small onion-covered burgers. The cloud fills the tiny restaurant with an aroma so thick your eyes will tear and make your clothing smell for days. It's an oniony goodness that once saturated thousands of burger stands just like the Cozy Inn from the 1920s to the 1950s. Today, Cozy is one of only a handful of its kind still in operation.

So now you're thinking, can I get a slider without onions? No. For over eighty years the same sliders have been sold at Cozy. If you don't like onions, you won't like their burgers. But if you do, you'll be in heaven. A burger "all the way" comes with ketchup, mustard, pickle, and a pile of steam-cooked onions. Today, you can choose any combination of these condiments, but in the old days you had no choice—a burger

at the Cozy came "all the way" and that was that. And for all of these decades, cheese has never graced a burger at Cozy, so don't even ask. "It's amazing how many people come in here and ask for a cheeseburger," former manager Nancy Durant once told me, "even though we have 'no cheese' signs everywhere." No fries either. Grab a bag of chips at the counter.

The burgers are small, so order a bunch. A familiar call from a customer might be, "A sack and a pop, please!" Which is local vernacular for "six sliders and a soda to go."

"We roll our own meat here," Nancy said, referring to the one-ounce wads of fresh bull beef that make up a Cozy slider. The tiny stand will go through five hundred pounds of onions and an incredible one thousand pounds of meat a week. "On our eightieth anniversary we sold 8,800 burgers in three days," Nancy boasted. The buns, soft and pillowy, are made especially for the Cozy Inn and come all the way from Missouri.

For the first time in almost ninety years, a second Cozy Inn location opened. The lucky college town of Manhattan, Kansas, is now able to indulge in a sack and a pop.

On my first visit to the Cozy Inn, I was walking out, reeking of onions, and an older woman on her way in stopped me and excitedly asked, "Was it as good as you remembered?" Now that's the kind of sentiment the Cozy deserves.

NUWAY CAFE

1416 West Douglas Ave | Wichita, KS 67203 | 316-267-1131
Open Daily 10:30 am–9 pm | (Four Other Locations in Wichita) | www.nuwayburgers.com

When we rolled into Wichita looking for burgers, I was shocked when we came across the NuWay Cafe. I know a lot about regional burgers in America and where these microcosms exist. I'm also pretty familiar at this point with how far certain burger trends have traveled, but most crazy ideas usually remain within the city limits. The Jucy Lucy has not gone much farther than a handful of burger joints in Minneapolis, the steamed cheeseburg only exists in the geographic center of Connecticut, and, as far as I know, you can only find an authentic Cuban Frita on Calle Ocho in Miami. So when expert burger taster Kris Brearton and I plopped down at the counter at NuWay, we found that the loosemeat phenomenon of Iowa may have found its way to Kansas.

Of course the loosemeat sandwich is not entirely a hamburger. I put Taylor's Maid-Rite in this book as a fine example of where to find the sandwich; a deconstructed burger of sorts. All of the elements for a great burger are there—the soft, white bun, fresh ground beef, pickles, mustard, and onion. But the beef, instead of being a patty, is crumbly and moist. It's a Sloppy Joe without the slop and it's heavenly.

At NuWay they call them "Crumblies," or the "Crumbly Sandwich." The menu lists them as the "Original" and I've also heard them referred to as simply "NuWays." Whatever you

decide to call them, they come in various sizes and configurations. The traditional size is the large, which is about a third of a pound of super-moist, crumbled meat that has been scooped by a spatula into a soft white bun and served with pickle, onion, and mustard. The amount of meat you'll find in a NuWay varies but usually in your favor. "It's a very unscientific method," owner Neal Stong said of the amount that gets scooped into a NuWay. "We try to overserve rather than underserve."

Neal did not open NuWay but he is certainly the protector of this Wichita tradition. In 1930, Tom McEvoy opened the first NuWay on Douglas Avenue after leaving a partnership behind in Iowa of (you guessed it) a new concept called the Maid-Rite sandwich. In search of warmer weather he headed south and settled on Wichita. He found a potato patch to lease just east of downtown for twenty-five dollars a month and built the location that still exists today. McEvoy brought with him his patented cooker for making the crumbly beef sandwich and guarded the process. People would try to get a glimpse of the cooker in action and according to local legend McEvoy would chase them out of the restaurant.

The cooker is still out of view and the process of making the NuWay sandwich kept a secret. "We only use high-quality USDA ground beef but we have a secret grind," Neal told me. And unlike the chain of Maid-Rites in Iowa and beyond (with the exception of Taylor's in Marshalltown) the meat is not spiced. As Neal put it, "Tender love and care is the only thing we add. People think we put something in there but we don't."

The NuWay is similar to the Maid-Rite sandwich but actually beefier and definitely moister. "The fat is where the flavor is," Neal told me. Some call it sauce, some call it grease, but in reality, the NuWay is so good because some of the fat is not drained off when you get your sandwich. "You can ask for it 'light,'" said Neal, but the sauce, soaked into the soft bun, is where the flavor is.

In the beginning, NuWay only served NuWays, malts, and root beer. Today, the menu has expanded greatly, but the core menu is still available. A regular at the counter named Vicki told me, "I've been coming here for forty years

and back then there was only NuWays on the menu." Everything is made fresh in the restaurant, including the popular garlic salad (which is basically coleslaw spiked with garlic) and the homemade root beer.

Neal became a partner in the business in 1981 with Gene Friedman after buying out McEvoy's widow, and Neal has owned NuWay on his own since the late 1990s. Under their leadership four new locations have been opened around Wichita and the original location has been kept intact. "It's an icon," Neal told me. "I see it as a museum. Other than a coat of paint we're not going to change a thing."

KENTUCKY

DOVIE'S CAFE

107 W 4th St. | Tompkinsville, KY 42167
Mon–Fri 8:30 am–4 pm (Winter Hours: 8:30 am–3 pm) | Sat 8:30 am–2 pm | Sun Closed

It's very rare to find a burger joint in America these days that has the distinct honor of being open for eighty years. Dovie's, which opened in 1938, has been owned by different members of the Moore family but has hardly changed since opening day.

Rolling hills and red barns give way to rural Kentucky and the town of Tompkinsville. Dovie's has been a staple in the town forever and is beloved by generations of happy customers. When I first visited Dovie's, the clientele was 100 percent local—not an interloper in sight. The remote location (it's about two hours from Nashville) has kept Dovie's a secret and the lack of a phone probably doesn't help. Regardless, I've never met a friendlier bunch of burger lovers. Whenever the door opens and a customer walks in, they are greeted by a chorus of "*HELLO!*" by the entire staff of seven women behind the counter.

Stanford Jefferson Moore opened a burger joint and named it after his sister, Dovie (who eventually owned and ran her namesake restaurant after Stanford). Today, Stanford's grandson,

Butch Reed Moore, is a co-owner with his two cousins, Ronnie and Karen. Regardless, it's really Tina McIntyre that keeps Dovie's humming these days. She's been the manager since 2012 and is at the restaurant six days a week, which is every day that Dovie's is open.

At Dovie's the burgers are cooked in a way that dates all the way back to the beginning of hamburger history: deep-fried in a skillet.

In the old days before flattops, short-order cooks would use large skillets to make burgers. Today's commercial flattops have a drain for grease to run off, a convenience not available to the skillet cook of yesteryear. If the burger joint had a crowd for lunch, you can guarantee the skillet would be filled with rendered beef fat, which in effect would deep-fry the beef. It's likely that the burgers are fried at Dovie's because local tastes going back to the 1930s dictated and prevailed.

Three large rectangular "tanks," fabricated by a local welder, filled with soybean oil sit in the center of the restaurant surrounded by three long counters. "Years ago it was pure lard," Tina told

me, but health trends prevailed and Dovie's made the switch to soybean oil years ago.

The burgers at Dovie's are addictive. They start as quarter-pound patties that are made every morning and have fine bread crumbs and water mixed in. This, of course, is likely a nod to the historically significant Slug Burger, found throughout northern Mississippi today. The patties bob in the oil and are transferred from tank to tank depending on doneness and apparently each tank is at different temperatures. At the end of the process, depending on preference, your burger will be "squoze," or not. This is where any excess oil is squeezed out of the patty (which is really beef juices). I would highly recommend NOT

getting your burgers squoze. Tina pointed out correctly, "If you do that you're squeezing a lot of the flavor out, too." And if you want cheese, your patty makes a return to the oil to melt. "But not if you want yours squoze," Tina warned. Patties that are squoze get a piece of cold cheese.

The burgers are served on regular-sized, soft, white buns that have been prepped with a "special" sauce made from a proprietary blend of mustard, ketchup, pickle juice, and finely chopped onion. A few pickles and a slice of raw onion are placed atop your burger and delivered to your spot at the counter on waxed paper. A common order is for two burgers. If you just order one, I'll bet you'll order another soon after.

The regulars are openly addicted to their burgers and share stories about why and what they order. The bread crumbs when deep-fried make the exterior of the patty crunchy and the water helps to keep the center very moist. It's a truly tasty hamburger science experiment.

One curiosity about Dovie's is that all the women wear skirts behind the counter. "It's just always been that way," Tina pointed out. But it was actually the subject of a precedent-setting case for the state of Kentucky. When an employee arrived one day for work in pants, Butch told me, "She was asked to go home and change into a skirt or stay home." The case was decided in favor of Dovie's because in Kentucky restaurateurs make their own rules.

The exhaust fan does minimal work to remove the thick scent of frying burgers. On most days, the windows are fogged and I can guarantee you'll smell like Dovie's all day, which is a good thing.

LAHA'S RED CASTLE HAMBURGERS

21 Lincoln Square | Hodgenville, KY 42748 | 270-358-9201
Mon–Tues & Thurs–Sat 9 am–4 pm | Wed 9 am–1:30 pm | Closed Sun

The first time I walked into this tiny sliver of a burger counter on the circle in the center of Hodgenville (the birthplace of Abraham Lincoln) I spied a custom spatula in the hands of the grillperson. It was a mason's trowel with the long tip cut off, an item I've seen around America at some of the greatest burger joints. "My husband used to be a bricklayer," Anita Laha told me. Anita is married to Kelly Laha whose grandparents, William and Sally, opened the burger restaurant a few doors down in 1934. Anita joked that the place was called Red Castle, "because White Castle was already taken." She added that Sally loved the color red and wore bright red lipstick every day.

A meal at Laha's (pronounced "LAY-HAY") is fast with most customers spending only about ten minutes at one of a handful of stools at the counter-only restaurant. When the stools fill up, customers wait against the wall, patiently, for a stool. A large portion of the lunch hour is spent putting together to-go orders. I asked when the lunch rush started at Laha's and Anita joked, "Sometimes at 9 a.m."

Consider yourself lucky if Edna Mae Owens is on the griddle when you walk in. Mae has been at Laha's for over thirty years now and makes one tasty burger. "Many come back for the burgers, but also to see Mae," Anita told me. Mae is

a machine and keeps all of the orders perfectly straight. To-go, to stay . . . cheese, no cheese . . . she's on it.

The menu is short and sweet with the burger, of course, being the biggest seller. Your options are hamburger, cheeseburger, double hamburger, double cheeseburger. Don't be confused when you order a double and it's a single patty on the bun. "Some people, when they don't see two patties, come and cuss at me," Mae told me with a dismissive wave of her hand. The double means double *meat*, where two portions are pressed together to make a larger patty. Traditionally, this burger method predates the classic double patty burger by almost fifty years.

All burgers at Laha's get a sprinkling of salt and pepper and a pinch of minced spanish onion as the fresh beef is pressed onto the griddle. The elements create an aroma that can't be beat, one that will stay with you all day. Anita told me, "It's our secret weapon." If someone in town smells like onions and beef grease, it prompts others to say, "Oh my God, you've been to Laha's, you are making me hungry!"

The burgers are small so order at least two doubles. They are served on waxed paper at your spot at the counter, or wrapped up in the same paper to go. The vintage flattop griddle, a thing of beauty, which dates back to 1951, is usually full of burgers all day long. The simple combination of beef, cheese, and onions is all you'll need. Resist the temptation to load this burger up with condiments—they are unnecessary.

As if the regular burger wasn't flavorful enough, Laha's also offers an odd, off-menu item call the Nasty Burger. This baby is loaded up with some of the griddle scrapings, which is basically deeply cooked, chopped onion basting in rendered beef fat. Professionals only, please.

Anita told me one of the funniest burger stories to date, which happened one day at Laha's. Kelly works the griddle on Saturdays to give Mae a break. On this particularly busy Saturday, Kelly noticed a man out front arguing with a police officer about parking. Anita watched Kelly go outside, and within minutes noticed that, for whatever reason, he was suddenly in handcuffs! Sitting at the counter was the sheriff and his wife trying to stay out of the way when Anita said, "Get out there and do something! I need my cook back!" I love small town America.

CAMELLIA GRILL

626 South Carrollton Ave | New Orleans, LA 70118
504-309-2679 | Sun–Thurs 8 am–12 am | Fri & Sat 8 am–2 am

I've been eating at the Camellia Grill for almost thirty years, but only for breakfast. Every visit to New Orleans has always included a blurry hungover pilgrimage to get pancakes, bacon, and french toast at this uptown favorite. There was generally a line out the door but it dissipated quickly because the countermen knew how to move people along. Then a few years ago, good friend and New Orleans local T. G. Herrington asked me if I'd ever had the cheeseburger there because it was one of his favorites in town. I had never even given the burger at Camellia Grill a thought. I felt pretty stupid.

Turns out it's true, they do serve a world-class bacon cheeseburger and it took me decades to figure it out. The regal exterior is painted bright white and features tall, two-story columns. The friendly, high-ceilinged interior has pale pink walls, marble countertops, and green leather stools giving the Camellia Grill a timeless, classy look.

The next and most obvious feature at Camellia is the upbeat, all-African American waitstaff in crisp white linen coats and black bowties behind the counter. It has been like this at the diner since opening day in 1946, making Camellia one of the first in New Orleans to employ African Americans for the front of house. Most of them will work at the diner for more than forty years. The banter between the staff is worth a counter seat at Camellia alone. There's lots of razzing by waiters directed at the cooks, all of it boisterous, all of it fun.

The Camellia Grill makes a helluva lot of breakfast. Because of this they've installed two separate flattop griddles, one to service each of the two horseshoe counters. Upward of ten pounds of bacon is cooked on each of the griddles daily, which naturally flavors the burgers at lunch.

The burgers are hand-formed from fresh ground 80/20 chuck. "We've tried other ground beef and pre-formed patties," longtime general manager Ron Jaeger told me, "but it's just not the same." The cheeseburger has always been on the menu but under the radar. For many a visit to Camellia will be about the signature oversized omelet, which starts in a milkshake blender whipped to a frothy foam (poplular in New Orleans and of which Camellia is arguably

★ 121 ★

the progenitor). But today, sales are shifting. Ron told me, "We'll sell more burgers than omelets these days."

In the beginning, it was the legendary Harry and Bat who led the waitstaff at Camellia, Harry being the very first hire at the restaurant in 1946. For over fifty (!) years, Harry and Bat played off each other and dispensed untold amounts of omelets, burgers, and advice over half a century. The two were also annually recognized as the best waiters in the city.

Hurricane Katrina affected the business and lifestyles of every resident of New Orleans in 2005. The Camellia Grill was spared major damage but the city was in shambles. "It was bad," Ron told me, "You didn't know if [the city] would come back or not." A local restaurateur bought the business from the original family and began the eighteen-month process of upgrading and reopening. He brought back the original black marble countertop from the 1960s (it was Formica up until Katrina) as well as switching out paper napkins for linens. "That's what set this place apart back then," Ron explained, pointing out that the upscale feel of the place kept the "riffraff" out.

During its closure, the front door of Camellia became covered with thousands of notes begging for someone to reopen the iconic diner. And on opening day, the line went down the street, all day long. "It was like that for five months," Ron told me.

When we filmed our Camellia episode of Travel Channel's *Burger Land* we were fortunate enough to plop down in Marvin's section and he took care of us. Marvin, an employee of almost thirty years, greeted everyone with a fist bump, his signature. When I returned recently, I saw something I didn't want to see—the west wall of Camellia has a few painted portraits of waiters that have passed. I was shocked to see Marvin up there, who had suffered a heart attack at age fifty that year. "He was family," Ron explained, tearing up. Today, when you walk into Camellia you'll be greeted by a fist bump by one of the waitstaff, in memory of their friend Marvin.

JUDICE INN

3134 Johnston St | Lafayette, LA 70503 | 337-984-5614 | Mon–Thurs 10 am–10 pm
Fri & Sat 10 am–10:30 pm | Sun Closed | www.judiceinn.com

I n a part of America dominated by gumbos, crawfish, and other Acadian/Cajun goodies, there is an old-time burger joint that is about as authentic as it gets. The low, white structure proudly displays a new red awning (it was green for years) and stands out on this busy strip of Route 167 southwest of downtown Lafayette. It's a local destination for burgers and has a robust regular clientele that ranges from high schoolers to UL Lafayette students to old-timers.

The Judice Inn was hand-built and opened by brothers Alcide and Marc Judice in 1947 after they both served in different branches of the U.S. military. Today, it is still owned and operated by numerous members of the Judice family and over the past seventy years just about every Judice family member has worked at the burger joint. Some have started part-time as early as seven years old and continue to return to help out when needed.

There's not much to the simple menu, and very little has changed at the Judice since the day it opened. Cheeseburgers are king here, and the

double cheeseburger is the call. The Judice grinds beef every morning and uses a proprietary seasoning on the burger that is adjusted to the tastes of locals. It's peppery without being spicy hot and is similar in flavor to what you might find at a crawfish boil.

The burgers are cooked on a flattop griddle in a tiny kitchen in the rear of the restaurant. The Judice family has a tomato-based "special sauce" that goes on every burger as well as shredded lettuce and a mustard/mayo mixture. Ask for grilled onions to take this already flavor-packed burger to the next level. All burgers are served on soft white squishy buns and wrapped in waxed paper (no plates). Unwrap your burger to reveal a most beautifully sloppy, cheesy burger.

Unlike many tiny burgers-only joints in America, beer is available as well as a bar to sit at. Or sit at one of the fancy new wood slat booths inside (which replace a sea of retro, curved wood yellow Formica seating). There have never been fries at the Judice Inn and most likely never will be so grab a bag of the locally favorite potato chip brand Zapp's hanging over the bar.

Ham-and-egg sandwiches are also popular at Judice, but don't try to order one on Saturday. Gerald Judice, the son of founder Marc, explained to me once, "We are so busy on Saturday at lunch, there's no room for eggs." Ahh, tradition. It's why we love these places and pray they never change.

PORT OF CALL

838 Esplanade Ave | New Orleans, LA 70116 | 504-523-0120
Sun–Thurs 11 am–12 am | Fri & Sat 11 am–1 am | www.portofcallnola.com

Port of Call is a bar and restaurant that sits on the far northeast end of the French Quarter in New Orleans. I say this because when people tell you this place is in the quarter your thoughts first go to drunken tourists with their souvenir hurricane glasses, lame strip clubs, and big-ass beers. Not so here. Port of Call is on the other end of the quarter, in a quiet, beautiful neighborhood.

The building Port of Call calls home dates back to the turn of the century, where it started as a sailor bar. Over the years, it went from grocery store to tavern and then opened as a steakhouse in 1962. Burger sales one day eclipsed the steak, and today, Port of Call is the most popular (and best) burger destination in New Orleans.

The decor is comfortably nautical and has dark wood floors, wood walls, wood tables, and a wood bar. The entire ceiling is a web of sisal rope and the whole place feels like it might start creaking and rocking with the tide.

There are four burger choices—Hamburger, Cheeseburger, Mushroom Burger, and Mushroom Cheeseburger. Don't mess around, get the Mushroom Cheeseburger. It's the one that keeps them coming back.

Port of Call grinds its own chuck and forms burgers into eight-ounce patties. The burgers are chargrilled and served on a bun that seems too small for the amount of meat provided. In order to make the patty fit, the burger is a tall, inch-and-a-half-thick, perfectly cooked fist of meat. The

cheese is soft, shredded cheddar and the mushrooms are sautéed in wine, butter, and garlic (and melt in your mouth). It looks like a mess when it arrives at your spot at the bar (or at one of the many tables in two dining rooms) but is actually easy to handle once you get going.

As if the burger were not enough, make sure to also wave in Port of Call's famous baked potato. Fully loaded and photo-worthy, with mounds of sour cream, bacon bits, more mushrooms and shredded cheddar, and a sprinkling of chopped chives, it's a meal unto itself. Get ready for the food coma.

Port of Call was spared major damage during the devastating Hurricane Katrina in 2005. "The flooding stopped two blocks that way," general manager of forty-two years Mike Mollere told me, pointing north. "We were extremely fortunate and had little damage. After the neighborhood opened

back up, I just turned the key and we were open for business." Mike followed his post-hurricane opening by serving first responders and the press.

In high season (January to "hurricane season"), the place fills up fast so get there early (a line may start to form thirty minutes before doors open). When the ancient, windowless wood doors are unlatched, the entire line pours into Port of Call to find a seat. "It's like that every morning," Mike said, shaking his head. I took a spot at the bar and watched as the restaurant filled almost to capacity with hungry tourists, locals, and construction workers. Inside of ten minutes the Port of Call was transformed from an empty, dark bar into a bustling, lively hot spot. They also have one of the best jukeboxes in town. Mike pointed out once, "Hey, where else can you hear Zappa on a jukebox?"

TED'S FROSTOP DINER

3100 Calhoun St | New Orleans, LA 70125 | 504-861-3615
Mon–Fri 7 am–5 pm | Sat & Sun 8 am–3 pm | www.tedsfrostop.com

was nineteen when I first stumbled into Ted's with a mean hangover after an all-night bender. At the time, my brother, Tim, was a freshman at Tulane and we had painted the town (easy to do in New Orleans). He assured me that the only cure was a cheeseburger, or two at Ted's, and more sleep. He was absolutely right and my appreciation of Ted's continues to this day (and has come to the rescue on numerous occasions).

Pronounced "FROS-TOP," the Ted's of my teens is a slightly different place today. Back then it definitely was a fading greasy spoon (which has appeal, too), but today, the kitchen (which is completely visible from the cash register) is a gleaming version of its former self.

L.S. Harvey opened the first Frostop Root Beer stand in Ohio in 1926. By the mid-1960s there were over 350 locations across America, all owned by independent franchisees. One of those owners was Ted Sternberg, a New Orleans native who, after returning from the Korean War, started to buy up Frostop franchises and opened fifteen drive-in stands. The South Claiborne location remained, survived Hurricane Katrina, then finally sold in 2011.

The buyer couldn't have been a better fit. Downtown antique dealer Peter Moss and his brother purchased Ted's and returned the iconic drive-in to its former glory. At some point the root beer changed, but Moss brought back Frostop-brand root beer (still being produced) and switched from frozen burger pucks to fresh ground 80/20 chuck. Moss also repaired the original fourteen-foot-tall root beer mug that was knocked off its signpost by Katrina.

"In the old days, they used to put butter chips in the ground beef," general manager Derrick Todd told me, probably before the place began a decline into frozen patties. Today, you can still order the very popular Lot-O Burger and it's made with fresh beef cooked in full view on a large flattop griddle.

The Lot-O Burger is a loaded, tasty beast. To the quarter-pound griddled and seasoned patty Ted's adds tomato, shredded lettuce, red onion, pickles, and the special "Loto Sauce," which is just mayo and mustard. It's served on a large, floppy toasted, seeded bun and the special sauce gives the burger a very unique, mustardy zing. No longer on the menu (but available) is my favorite, the Lot-O PoBoy, where two patties are placed side by side on classic New Orleans po'boy bread and dressed the same. A definitive hangover helper. And the root beer is next-level stuff, ultra creamy and deep. Grab a frozen mug right next to the self-serve soda dispenser.

Derrick is obsessed with efficiency and makes constant adjustments to how the food at Ted's is made and served. He told me (in all seriousness), "Every five seconds you save in a day is going to add up to minutes." And he added, "Waiting is horrible." Derrick also created the current method for patty making at Ted's where portioned balls of beef are pressed into shape using a custom template made from a polyethylene cutting board.

Derrick also trains his staff to keep a chin up when dealing with customers. "You never know what happened to them before they walked in," Derrick explained. Could have had a fight, an accident, you don't know, "Our job is to make them happy, and not make them wait."

MAINE

HARMON'S HAMBURGERS

144 Gray Rd | Falmouth, ME 04105 | 207-797-9857
Mon–Wed 10:30 am–3 pm | Thurs–Fri 10:30 am–7 pm | Sat 11 am–7 pm | Closed Sun

When I first visited this tiny burger outpost just north of Portland back in 2006, it was called Harmon's Lunch. I made the mistake of asking why. Through his thick Maine accent Pete Wormell told me, "We're only open for lunch." Things have changed (slightly) since then and Harmon's is now open until 7 p.m. two days a week.

Pete and his friend Cliff, bought Harmon's in 1995 from Marvin Harmon, who opened the burger joint in 1960 and was looking for the right people to buy the place. Cliff had seen an ad in the paper that the restaurant was for sale. Within a few years of co-ownership, Cliff sold his portion to Pete, who joked, "We're still friends part-time." Cliff continued to work the grill with Pete until retiring in 2014. Pete's son, Jeff, picked up the slack while working a full-time job as a residential painter. Soon after, Jeff became a part owner with the understanding that he would eventually become full owner of Harmon's. "That's the plan," Jeff told me, and he had no problem leaving his painting career behind. "House painting is seasonal—this is much steadier."

Both Pete and Jeff share time at the busy seasoned griddle cranking out excellent burgers. The menu is limited to burgers, hot dogs, and grilled cheese, but fresh-cut fries and now onion rings are also available. If you ask for milk, specify either "white" or "chocolate" or be pegged a tourist. Jeff and Pete also added ice cream and shakes recently because they wanted to expand the menu.

The burger at Harmon's is small but tasty. Pete buys fresh ground beef and uses a patty former at the restaurant to make two-ounce patties. A fully loaded burger comes with mustard, fried onions, and a signature sweet red relish. "Most people think it's going to be hot because of its color," Pete told me. A local bakery provides preservative-free buns that are steamed to limp. The bun creates an impossibly soft, warm pillow that cradles the perfectly cooked thin patty.

The wait at Harmon's, especially on a Saturday, can be up to forty-five minutes. "We get backed up," Pete said, "but to have the quality you can't do more." Jeff told me recently, "Well,

I don't have a forty-five minute wait! [Pete] does sometimes."

When Pete and Cliff first took the helm at Harmon's, they decided to slightly alter the menu and offer a traditional Maine favorite—the lobster roll. The attempt backfired and the roll was pulled from the menu after only a few weeks. "This is a hamburger place," Pete once explained, and attributed the failure to the old adage "If it ain't broke, don't fix it."

MR. BARTLEY'S

1246 Massachusetts Ave | Cambridge, MA 02138 | 617-354-6559
Tues–Sat 11 am–9 pm | Closed Sun & Mon | www.mrbartley.com

Bill Bartley is an original. He stands at the griddle at his family's Harvard Square eatery shouting things at me like "We're the BEST!" and "This is the greatest burger ANYWHERE!" He's smiling and extremely energetic and has the kind of cocksure confidence and running dialogue usually reserved for someone like Muhammad Ali in his prime. Fortunately, all of it is true—the burgers at Mr. Bartley's are unbelievable.

"I've probably made over five million burgers in the last thirty years," Bill told me as he shifted some thick patties on the six-hundred-degree griddle, "All good ones, too, all cooked to temp." If you ask for medium-rare, that's what you'll get. Every burger goes out exactly the way Bill wants them to, which means perfect. If you ask for cheese, it's cooked separately from the burger. Where most chefs melt the cheese atop the burger as it nears completion, Bill cooks the perfect burger, tosses a thick slice of cheese directly on the griddle for a minute, then gently transfers it to the burger

as it is dispatched to a table. As Bill eloquently explained, "The cheese is ambivalent to the temperature of the burger."

Mr. Bartley's is a busy place. Just across the street is Harvard University, so you can imagine the crowd. The restaurant feels like a big broken-in bar, yet no booze is served and the walls are covered with Red Sox stuff, political ephemera, and the types of posters a student might have in their dorm room. Many tables, including a long communal one, and green plastic chairs complete the scene.

The first time I visited, there was a line out the door at 2:30 p.m. on a Thursday. The man who started it all, Joe Bartley, was taking names outside, his wife, Joan, was managing the tables inside, and their son, Bill, was at the grill cranking out perfect burgers. "You don't have a line outside because you're slow," Bill explained, "you have a line because you're GOOD." The turnover is quick and the service lightning fast.

The burger selection is enormous and specials are added and named after hypercurrent news events. With the same seven-ounce patty, Bill and his team can add any one of the over thirty printed burgers on the menu. Everything you can imagine on a burger is available here, from feta cheese to baked beans, but the big seller is the Viagra Burger. The Viagra is topped with creamy blue cheese and bacon, and the menu asks you to "rise to the occasion." The reality is that these burgers need no condiments. They are that good and don't even need a bun. Of course Bill put it best when he explained, "The bun is just the envelope for the good news that's coming."

Mr. Bartley's burger starts as fresh ground chuck that comes from a local butcher daily. A special patty former in the restaurant is designed not to compress the meat too much as it creates the fist-sized burgers. "We use an Acu-Pat," Bill told me. "It's made of stainless steel so it doesn't use heat during patty forming like most. Heat is the worst thing for an uncooked burger." On the intensely hot griddle, the burgers are seared to almost a burn to seal in the juices.

Even though the burger selection is daunting, your toughest choice will be deciding what to drink. Mr. Bartley's serves up some of the city's greatest frappes (milkshakes) and an amazing raspberry lime rickey. My advice? Get both.

Joe Bartley ran a lunch counter seven days a week in the back of a pharmacy in Garden City, New York, in the 1950s. "I was going to be a cop on Long Island, can you believe that?" He decided to move back to his native Boston one day and opened a grocery store in 1960 in Harvard Square. By 1962, he was making burgers because, as he told me, "When I started there wasn't a good burger around."

As I stood and watched Bill's genius at work, I tried to figure out what made these burgers so special. Without missing a beat, Bill offered this insight: "The person who has this skill level thinks they should be doing something better. Not me. I make the best burgers anywhere."

WHITE HUT

280 Memorial Ave | West Springfield, MA 01089 | 413-736-9390
Mon–Thurs 6:30 am–7 pm | Fri 6:30 am–8:30 pm | Sat 8 am–8:30 pm | Sun 8 am–6 pm
www.whitehut.com

White Hut is one of the few remaining "White" restaurants in America. During the 1920s and 1930s, America was blanketed with ten-stool hamburger joints with names like: White Tower, White Diamond, White Clock, and the one that started it all—White Castle. Placing the word *white* in your name conveyed a sense of cleanliness, an important tenet in a time when hamburgers were considered dirty food for wage earners. By the 1930s in America, thanks to the tremendous success of White Castle, the word *white* also became synonymous with quality fast food.

Then, along came White Hut. In the late 1930s, Hy Roberts opened a small three-stool hot dog shack on a busy corner in West Springfield, Massachusetts. A year after opening, Edward Barkett was asked by Roberts to run the stand for a few weeks. Barkett liked what he saw and negotiated the purchase of the business for three hundred dollars. He bought a plot of land across the street soon after and built a tiny six-hundred-square-foot burger counter. That same burger counter, almost eighty years later, serves a thousand burgers a day and is still run by the third generation of the Barkett family.

The interior of White Hut is a classic burger counter with twelve vintage stools facing a large flattop griddle, bare white walls, and a long counter supported by a wall of glass block. The place was built during the Depression, at a time when most building materials were scarce. "The White Hut was built with black-market lumber," current owner and grandson E. J. Barkett pointed out. "Nothing else was available during the war." His grandfather was also forced to use the only flooring available, a beige terrazzo. Booths lined the back wall of the restaurant for the first few months, but were removed when Barkett noticed that people tended to hang around in them too long. "My grandfather needed the turnover and replaced the booths with a large table to stand around."

White Hut offers only three things: hamburgers, cheeseburgers, and hot dogs. And, as of only a few years ago, fries. If you love onions, you'll love the burgers at White Hut. Every morning a large pile of chopped spanish onions is placed on the griddle. The onions cook slowly until they are translucent and limp, then hearty amounts are spooned onto the burgers. "We go through about 250 pounds of onions a day," counterperson Roberta told me. Roberta (now retired) is actually the owner, E. J. Barkett's, mother and is a fount of White Hut lore. White Hut receives an order of fresh, thin, two-ounce patties every morning made of a special blend they have been using for years. "There's less fat so there is less shrinkage," Roberta pointed out.

The daily lunch crowd is large and the method for ordering a burger at peak times requires well-tuned survival instincts. Order your burgers when a counterperson makes eye contact with you. Roberta told me, "People will stand four and five deep at the counter at lunchtime." Nothing is written down and somehow everyone's order is produced perfectly. Regardless of the hungry mob and apparent lack of order, the average dining experience at White Hut lasts only fifteen minutes. A unique rule, imposed at the counter, may help. "No newspapers between twelve and two," someone told me once, "because they are

not paying attention." But things have eased recently at White Hut, and newspapers have been replaced by cell phones. "My dad used to be serious about that," E. J. told me. "We are not so strict anymore because the lunch crowd is now spread out over four hours."

White Hut is a family place, run by family, and visited by families. A regular named Michael, in a suit, standing and eating a quick lunch told me, "I bring my kids here just like my dad brought me here years ago." "We've had four generations sitting at the counter at the same time," E.J. told me. "I love to see that." For many in this part of western Massachusetts, White Hut is an enduring tradition that shows no sign of fading any time soon.

MICHIGAN

GREENE'S HAMBURGERS

24155 Orchard Lake Rd | Farmington, MI 48336
248-474-7980 | Open Daily 24 Hours

Plain and simple. Greene's Hamburgers is living history. What you see is exactly what you would have seen if you popped in for a burger in 1957. Very little has changed at this authentic slider emporium despite being open around the clock for over sixty years. You'd think the wear and tear would have taken its toll, but the gleaming structure, sheathed in sheets of sturdy enamel steel panels inside and out, have worked to protect the joint. And the original, thick stainless-steel countertop, one of the most incredible I've ever come across, is smooth and mirror-like from decades of use, almost to the point of chrome.

And the menu remains somewhat unaltered as well, brief and to the point. There are breakfast options, and chicken fingers have been added, but the core menu of hamburger/cheeseburger/pop/coffee makes up the bulk of sales. "My dad always said he had no waste, which goes back to the war," co-owner Debbie Sutton told me. "The only waste was coffee grounds and onion skins." Debbie owns Greene's with her mother, Mary Jenkins. Mary's husband, Jake Jenkins, helped Jim Greene open

his third location in 1957 and in 1977 became the owner. Both Jim and Jake, not surprisingly, worked at White Castle before World War II.

Greene's is a true slider emporium. DNA of the original American hamburger are unquestionably at play here. Behold the simplicity of a tiny wad of fresh ground beef pressed thin and cooked with sliced Spanish or Vidalia onion (depending on season). Classic american cheese joins the party on the flip and white squishy buns are placed on top to soften. That is about as authentic as the burger can get. The result is a burger experience that is sweet and savory, evocative and historically accurate.

At one point, there were three Greene's. The first was built in 1947, the second in 1952, and the Farmington location in 1959. This location is the lone survivor in the minichain. You might notice that Hunter House Hamburgers up in Birmingham looks identical, that's because they used the plans from the original Greene's.

Did you know that you can find a nearly pitch-perfect facsimile of the Greene's slider at Cheesecake Factory? That's

because their CEO David Overton was raised eating the real thing. "I grew up three blocks from Greene's," he told me. "I would take my paper route money and spend it on burgers." When Overton opened his first Cheesecake in Los Angeles in 1978, he was determined to relive his youth and serve the burger that he remembered. "I was going to make the best darn burger I could," he said. "And I knew that if I liked something, others would, too." He was right. Today, you can find an appetizer called Roadside Sliders on any Cheesecake Factory menu, anywhere in the world.

Grab one of the eleven stools at the counter (the far left stool is closest to the griddle), or one of the eight stools with views out onto busy Orchard Lake Road. The building is so well constructed that you can barely hear the traffic, only the sound of orders being taken, the sizzle of burgers, and the exhaust fan. Or grab an order to go by using the old-school "curb house," a tiny room just off the griddle for walk-ups. Years ago this little structure was damaged when a drunk driver slammed into it. Debbie joked, "She tried to turn our curb house into a drive-thru!"

HUNTER HOUSE HAMBURGERS

35075 Woodward Ave | Birmingham, MI, 48009 | 248-646-7121
Mon–Thurs 9 am–10 pm | Fri & Sat 8 am–12 am | Sun 11 am–9 pm
www.hunterhousehamburgers.com

Hunter House is not a roadside burger joint or a fading relic of the past. It is a thriving sixty-six-year-old diner in a Detroit suburb that probably looks the same as it did on opening day in 1952. What's more, not only is the restaurant a historically accurate midcentury burger joint, Hunter House is located on Woodward Avenue, the first paved road in America. In 1904, when Detroit became the center of automobile production in America (thanks to the Ford Motor Company), it was inevitable that paved roads would follow.

The interior of Hunter House looks impossibly clean for a diner this old. It's clear from first glance that the stools, the long counter, the basket-weave tile floor, and the enamel-steel walls that this diner is no imitation. "Everything in here is original," charming owner Susan Cobb told me with a smile. The line of refrigerators and vintage appliances behind the counter are eye candy for the lucky ones that grab a stool, though apparently repairs to these beauties is not easy. Susan told me, "Servicemen come in here [for repairs] and always start by saying 'I'm not going to have parts for these.'" It's not uncommon for Susan to have parts fabricated for ailing appliances in order to keep Hunter House original.

The hamburger is the main attraction on the limited menu at Hunter House. "When you come here you need to order the burger the way we've always made it," Susan told me with a smile. The way they've always made the burgers is with paper-thin sliced spanish onion cooked with the burger. If you don't want onion, you have to ask for no onion, but the flavor profile of this burger is equally about the onions as it is the beef. Just about everyone orders theirs with onions and as the server's T-shirts aptly explain, *Onion breath is better than no breath.*

A flattop griddle sits at one end of the counter adjacent to a functioning carry-out walk-up window. The burgers start as 80/20 chuck that comes to the restaurant as fresh ground beef formed into "pucks," or tall patties. The puck is pressed thin into a patty on the griddle and covered with sliced onions. When the burger is flipped, the grillperson places both halves of the bun atop the patty (or patties if you are getting more than one) and with a squeeze bottle full of water sends a thin stream that encircles the patty. Not surprisingly this sends up an explosive vapor cloud. As grillman Bret once explained to me, "We do that to steam the buns." It looks like they also do it for fun. Who wouldn't want to spray cold water on a hot griddle and see what happens? "It's amazing," Susan told me. "The buns poof right up." The result is a bun-and-burger combo that arrives impossibly soft and tasty. A double is the way to go because the single patty, weighing only three ounces, is just a snack.

Red Hot Chili Peppers drummer Chad Smith is a huge fan of Hunter House and grew up on the famous sliders. "Whenever he comes home, his mom has a little white bag of burgers waiting for him," Susan told me. And when the Peppers were inducted into the Rock and Roll Hall of Fame recently a friend of Chad's mom drove a bunch of burgers to Cleveland for him. Susan recalled, "He sent me a picture of himself and two of the burgers!" It's official; Chad Smith is obsessed with the burgers at Hunter House.

On the third Saturday in August every year, Woodward Avenue is transformed into the world's longest, largest classic auto show in the form of the Woodward Dream Cruise. Over 35,000 vintage cars and one million visitors descend to "cruise" a section of Woodward that extends from Detroit out to the suburbs. The event is crushing to the tiny hamburger icon so Susan shuts down the restaurant and sets up flattops outside in the parking lot to feed the masses. "We use the restaurant for the crew to take breaks," Susan explained. During the Cruise, Hunter House has served up to forty thousand burgers to hungry car enthusiasts.

Susan's parents, Al and Martha Cobb, bought the vintage burger joint when it came up for sale in 1982. They were the third owners and ran the place until 2005 when Al sold Hunter House to his daughter. Fortunately, she hasn't really changed a thing, with the exception of adding two catering trailers for parties.

The future of Hunter House is secure and Susan's family is committed to hamburger excellence. "We just had a family meeting and discussed the future," Susan told me. "The kids never want to sell."

KRAZY JIM'S BLIMPY BURGER

304 South Ashley St | Ann Arbor, MI 48104 | 734-663-4590
Mon–Sat 11 am–10 pm | Sun 12 pm–8 pm | www.blimpyburger.com

A visit to Blimpy Burger can be a daunting but rewarding experience. Theatrically, the cooks behind the counter engage in a sort of Soup Nazi berating of customers who do not follow the cafeteria-style rules of ordering. "Just answer the questions I'm asking you," a grill cook told a group of newcomers the first time I visited. In reality, the rules are there to help you, not scare you. They are there to allow the cooks to get your food to you fast, which is a good thing because you'll need this burger in your mouth as soon as possible.

The interior of Blimpy Burger is wholly utilitarian and the opposite of a comfy dive. A collection of vintage cast-iron swivel stools bolted to the floor serve most tables. The original owner, Krazy Jim Shafer, purchased the stools from a department store that had gone out of business in the 1950s for $1.75 apiece.

For sixty years, Blimpy Burger was on the edge of the University of Michigan campus, surrounded by student rental houses with mud lawns. But in 2012, Blimpy owner Richard Manger was given the boot off the property under his business. He was told to match an offer of $1.075 million (which the university was willing to pay) in thirty days or be gone. "I was blown away," Richard told me. The story became very public and a number of "Save Blimpy" campaigns began. In 2013,

Richard closed Blimpy and reopened fourteen months later in busy downtown Ann Arbor, only a few blocks from the original location. Richard moved everything, even the vintage stools, to the new location, which looks a lot like the original, just larger and with more foot traffic.

In 1953, Jim Shafer turned a corner grocery into a burger stand to sell cheap burgers to University of Michigan students. At his previous burger venture, shoehorned into an alley in downtown Ann Arbor, a friend at a neighboring business called Jim "crazy" for selling food for so cheap. The moniker stuck, as did the famous phrase that greets customers at Blimpy Burger: "Cheaper Than Food." Richard told me, "Back then it was cheaper to buy a twenty-cent burger than to eat at home."

Richard bought the restaurant in 1992 from Krazy Jim, who was already in retirement. Jim and Rich had a past together at that point—Rich had worked as a cook flipping burgers in the late '60s for Jim at Blimpy, had met his wife, Chris, there (also a student), and had designed the Blimpy logo that is still used today. It's a drawing of a seated, chubby bear smiling and hoisting a burger. "Jim wanted me to draw a cow. I told him 'I don't draw cows. I draw bears.'"

Richard's menu design is an elaborate piece of R. Crumb–inspired line art that is suitable for framing. It lists a dizzying assortment of comfort foods and toppings for the burgers. Rich told me, "When Jim opened he only had burgers, american cheese, pie, and coffee." Not so today. The selection of toppings and burger sizing is so vast it prompted a math student to deduce that there are more than 2,147,483,648 possible burger combinations.

The fresh chuck that is used for Blimpy burgers is ground daily in the back. When you ask for a burger, you tell the grill cook how many you'd like (up to five, a "quint") and he'll grab that number of one-and-a-half-ounce balls of beef. The balls are tossed onto the hot griddle and smashed into smallish, beautifully sloppy flat patties. The burgers are pressed thin, flipped, cheesed, then tossed on a bun. The result is a glorious grease bomb—a pile of loose, griddled meat that is crunchy in parts and soft in others. The meat is so loose it's practically pebbly. A grill cook once told me, "These things are held together by hope."

The choice of bun for your burger, toasted on the griddle, includes pumpernickel, onion, or kaiser, the latter offered with or without sesame seeds because, as Rich explained with a shrug, "Some people have diverticulitis." The onion roll is hands down one of the best I have ever eaten, soft and tasty and able to soak up the copious amounts of grease a Blimpy burger produces. "Onion rolls most places suck," Rich told me bluntly. "These really are great rolls."

Following the rules for ordering is important. Start by grabbing a tray and getting in line. Everyone gets a tray because, as Rich pointed out, "It keeps the tables clean when we're busy." First, your

fry order; french fries and onion rings are offered, but skip the usual for excellent deep-fried vegetables like mushrooms and cauliflower. Next, order your burger, the number of patties you want, but hold your cheese selection until the end of the process. Then give your toppings selection. At the end of the process grab a drink. (NOTE: this is different from the old setup where you grabbed a drink *first*.) Follow the rules and no one gets hurt.

A group of healthy-looking sixtysomethings were enjoying their burgers the first time I visited and told me, "This is where we celebrate our birthdays. We've been coming here for over fifty years." When one of the grill guys, heard that, he blurted out, "And they STILL don't know how to order their burgers."

MILLER'S BAR

23700 Michigan Ave | Dearborn, MI 48124 | 313-565-2577
Mon–Sat 10 am–1 am | Closed Sun | www.millersbar.com

The first time I visited Miller's it was in the middle of a torrential springtime downpour. It was 11:15 a.m. on a Wednesday, the bar was packed and everyone was eating hamburgers. Doesn't that pretty much say it all?

Miller's is on a commercial stretch, six lanes wide, in Dearborn, Michigan. Across the street from a large Ford dealership, the windowless bar is painted with a fresh coat of red paint and emblazoned with enormous white letters spelling out the name of this seventy-seven-year-old institution. Despite the cool functionality of the exterior, the interior, with its original 1940s Brunswick bar of undulating high-gloss wood and booths made of supple deep red leather, feels more like a long-lost private men's club than the

bunker that the outside evokes. The immaculate well-preserved dining room is dark and cozy and, according to part-owner Mark Miller, has not needed renovation since 1964.

There is no menu at Miller's but the options are simple—burgers, fries, and onion rings are available, as are tuna, ham, and corned beef sandwiches and, of course, drinks from the bar. The clientele is mostly local devotees and regulars from the nearby world headquarters of the Ford Motor Company. They come for the burgers and have been since 1941, when Mark's uncle, George Miller, opened the bar. Today, thanks to topping many "Best-of" lists in America, Miller's Bar sells over 1,200 burgers a day. Every one of those burgers is cooked on a griddle next to the bar that is no more than three feet square.

"Our butcher starts grinding beef for us at 4 a.m. every day," Mark told me. Mark owns the bar with his brother, Dennis, and the two are second-generation owners. The Miller's father, Russell, bought the bar from his brother, George, in 1947.

The sprightly grill cook, Kim, who has been flipping burgers at Miller's for almost thirty years, is responsible for griddling the hundreds of perfect, award-winning burgers during the lunch rush. I once overheard her take an order for a few burgers "well-done." Well-done? "Oh gosh, yes," she said with a sigh. "People don't know how to order their burgers here." Mark told me he won't eat anything over a medium, and rightly so, because Miller's meat is ultra-fresh.

The Millers have been using the same butcher for almost fifty years. The bar used to get a four hundred–pound delivery daily of fresh ground beef that would have to be hand-pattied by the kitchen staff. "It got to be too much," Kim told me, so the butcher offered to start delivering pre-formed patties. Knowing that the Millers wouldn't accept just any patty, he employs a special patty maker that injects a blast of air back into the beef. "It makes the patty looser," Mark explained, "and it has an almost hand-pattied feel."

The seven-ounce burger is served on a steamed white bun and delivered to you on a square of wax paper. Lettuce and tomato are not offered. Swiss or Velveeta are available, as are the standard condiments like ketchup, mustard, pickle, and sliced onion. But this burger needs no embellishment—so forgo any condiments. The meat is so good you could eat it plain. I asked what it was that made the burger taste so great and Mark told me, "It's the meat. The meat is great. There are no seasonings and we have no secrets."

The secret may be in longevity. The staff is great and many have been with Miller's forever. The day-shift bartender, Jeff, has been pouring drinks for thirty-five years and a waitress named Linda has been delivering burgers at Miller's since Nixon was in office. The secret may also be in the Miller brothers' commitment to the family business. Every Sunday, when the bar is closed, Mark and Dennis take apart the entire kitchen and grill area for a thorough cleansing. Mark told me, "We completely disassemble the griddle, dishwasher . . . everything." What did you do last Sunday?

MOTZ'S HAMBURGERS

7208 West Fort St | Detroit, MI 48209 | 313-843-9186
Mon–Sat 10 am–4 pm | Closed Sun | www.motzsburgers.com

If I told you that when I first arrived at Motz's Burgers I ran into the place with unbridled enthusiasm, I'd be lying. On my first visit to the vintage burger joint that shared my name, needless to say, I was very nervous. What if the burgers were crap? What if this tiny ex-White Castle, nestled in an industrial neighborhood on the outskirts of downtown Detroit, was a washed-up version of its former self? How would I explain that this perfect little burger joint was a bust?

The first five minutes inside Motz's Burgers was a complete blur. I quickly spotted the griddle and a cook smashing balls of fresh meat, and noted the glorious smell of onions that filled the little diner. There were a few stools and a counter and people walking off with paper bags full of steaming sliders. The scene was right out of a Depression-era FSA black-and-white photo. I had stumbled into hamburger nirvana and I was beyond relieved.

Even though we share a name, the pronunciation differs. Originally, the restaurant was called "Motts Burgers," named after the man that scooped up a handful of Detroit-area White Castles that were being sold to offset the financial strain of the Great Depression. Motts purchased a few in the '30s and put family members in charge of each one. Robert Motts, the son of the original owner, decided to sell the West Fort Street location in 1996 to current owners Bob and Mary Milosavljeveski. Bob had just left his father's thirty-six-year-old local bakery and was searching for something new. Motts asked Bob to change the name since there was another Motts Burger still in operation down the street. Bob chose to replace the "t's" with a "z," thus making my visit to the place destiny.

Bob's wife, Mary, makes change and takes orders at the counter while grill cook of twenty-eight years Tammy (from the Motts days) flips burgers. At one point during my conversation with Bob, Tammy leaned over and audibly whispered to him, "Did you tell him the secret ingredient?" A pregnant pause followed and I was compelled to blurt out, "What is it?" "Love," Tammy told me with a straight face. "Love is the secret ingredient. If you don't love what you are doing, it ain't gonna taste good."

Mary and Bob's eldest son, Tony, has recently lent a hand at Motz's and does his part to recreate burger history at the griddle. "He's the next one in line" Mary told me with a smile, which means the future of Motz's is secure.

The burgers basically come in three sizes—a single, a double, and a "King Motz," which is a triple. "Motts said 'keep the burgers the same' and he was right," Bob told me at the counter during the busy lunch rush. The burgers at Motz's are really oversized sliders but cooked the exact same way a place like White Castle would have done it over eighty years earlier. Bob picks up fresh ground beef for the restaurant every morning. A rolled ball of 88/12 chuck and rump round mixture is tossed on the flattop behind the counter and pressed flat with a spatula. A handful of thinly sliced spanish onion is sprinkled on top that softens and intermingles with the patty once it's flipped. The result is, well, the burger that I make at home—the purest form of the American hamburger that I know of. An original Motz Slider is served on a white squishy bun with mustard,

ketchup, and pickles and is very tasty. Although I prefer my burgers without ketchup, I gave in to tradition and was pleasantly surprised.

When Bob and Mary bought the place in 1996, it was a dilapidated relic. "The place was a dump," Bob said with conviction and explained how he gave the interior a major facelift without destroying the integrity of the place. "We moved the griddle but kept it in sight." Bob explained, "Places like this will never die out because you can see the cook, see the meat."

The neighborhood surrounding Motz's Burgers ain't pretty, but it's getting better. When I first found the place ten years ago, the only other visible sign of life was the enormous Detroit Produce Terminal directly across the street. Truckers and employees from the Terminal make up the bulk of business back then, but that has changed. "Detroit is just . . . ," Bob said with wide eyes as he animated an explosion with his hands. "It's totally different now. . . . It's safer!" At one time in this neighborhood's history, West Fort Street was lined with factories and bars and this burger joint probably fit in perfectly. The fact that this national treasure is still standing and serving great burgers is an absolute miracle. I wondered why Bob and Mary would take a chance in a neighborhood like this but I got my answer. "If it has survived almost ninety years, it'll be around for a while."

REDAMAK'S

616 East Buffalo St | New Buffalo, MI 49117 | 269-469-4522 | Mon–Thurs 12 pm–9:30 pm
Fri & Sat 12 pm–10:30 pm | Sun 12 pm–10 pm (Spring & Fall) | Mon–Sat 12 pm–10:30 pm
Sun 12 pm–10 pm (Summer) | Closed In Winter | www.redamaks.com

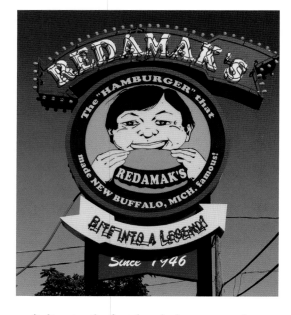

Redamak's is a burger destination. Vacationers come from miles around for a weekend at Lake Michigan and most visit Redamak's for nourishment. George and Gladys Redamak opened a tiny mom-and-pop burger restaurant in the late 1940s. In 1975, Jim and Angie Maroney bought the restaurant from Gladys, with the stipulation that they keep it the same. It didn't really turn out that way, though—they actually made it better.

Redamak's is enormous. Years of expansion and updating to the structure have created a profoundly successful restaurant that can comfortably seat four hundred. Crowd control is aided by two sets of double doors at the front—one marked *Enter*, the other *Exit*. If you have kids, you won't be alone here—kids and families populate the place. There are two separate video arcades and a sizable kids' menu. If you need a drink, there's a bar right in the center of it all. And, of course, if you need a burger, Redamak's makes one of the best in the country.

The menu is round, the size of a large pizza, and has more text on it than the front page of the *Chicago Tribune*. You won't believe the options you'll have. Everything from corn dogs to clam strips is offered, along with seven different types of french fries. There's even lake perch on Fridays. The endless selection of lakefront comfort food

can't disguise the fact that the burgers are the star attraction here. The menu proudly proclaims the Redamak's burger is "The Burger That Made New Buffalo Famous."

Fresh Iowa beef chuck steaks are ground in the kitchen for the six-ounce burgers at Redamak's. The kitchen can crank out over 2,500 fresh patties a day and Redamak's grinds over 135,000 pounds of beef every year, which is amazing for a restaurant with an eight-month season.

Since the beginning, the method for cooking the burgers at Redamak's was a curious

one. Up until 2016, the burgers were cooked in skillets on stovetops, five to a pan. As the business grew, the Maroney family scaled up the number of skillets and stovetops until they reached thirty pans. "It was a dishwasher's nightmare," second-generation owner Charles B. Maroney pointed out. Taking into consideration the labor it took to cook with and clean all of those skillets, they finally switched to a high-tech cooking contraption called the Steam Shell. "We were able to cook the burgers faster and with more consistency," Charles told me. Although the Redamaks said change nothing, this was a good change.

And that wasn't the only change the Maroneys have made in the past few years. "There were three things my dad said we'd never do," Charles told me recently, "pave the parking lot, offer lettuce and tomato, and serve coffee. Well, we still don't serve coffee." You read that correctly—Redamak's now offers, free of charge, fresh local tomatoes and lettuce for your burger. "We had some upset customers," Charles told me. Some people just don't transition well.

A burger with everything comes with ketchup, mustard, pickles, a slice of raw onion. Cheese choices are swiss, mild cheddar, pepper jack, colby, and Velveeta. Bring the family, bring your friends, bring everyone you know—Redamak's can handle the crowds with ease. You'll probably have to wait, so go to the video arcade or browse the merchandise at the front. It might be the only place in America where you can buy a souvenir yo-yo in the shape of a hamburger.

SCHLENKER'S SANDWICH SHOP

1104 E Ganson St | Jackson, MI 49201
517-783-1667 | Tues–Fri 11 am–7 pm | Sat 10 am–3 pm | Closed Sun

It doesn't look like much from the outside but if I've learned anything over the years about great burgers it's not to judge a burger joint by its cover. This is not to say that Schlenker's is a dump, not by a long shot. It is, in fact, a sparkling, unadorned restaurant that exists to do one thing—make consistently great burgers for adoring locals . . . for over ninety years.

Sixteen loose high stools surround a horseshoe counter in a tiny narrow space painted two-tone drab green and lit by a strip of fluorescent tubes that run the entire length of the restaurant. It has the look and feel of a place that means business.

In 1927, George and Bertha Schlenker opened the sandwich shop and it remained in their family until 1979. The Shaughnessy family owned until 1996 when current owners Bob and Sue Fitzpatrick became only the third family to operate Schlenker's in its long history. "I used to come in here to eat all the time," Bob told me. His wife is a real estate agent and had the listing for the restaurant, and Bob was looking to "retire." Twenty-plus years running a burger joint is one helluva retirement.

Regular cheeseburgers are available at Schlenker's, but for a real treat get your hands on the regional Michigan staple—the Olive Burger. To a regular cheeseburger loose, briny green

olives are added and the flavor is simple but incredible. In parts of the state the Olive Burger can be found with a topping mix of chopped green olives and mayo, but here the Olive Burger is served instead with sliced green olives and a special sauce created by Bob Schlenker many decades ago that contains mustard, relish, and chopped onion.

The burgers are cooked in plain sight behind the counter on a flattop, and a local butcher brings fresh beef daily. Printed on the glass right in the front door, "Schlenker's may close earlier than the posted hours if we run out of hamburger." The consistency in quality is implied.

Schlenker's is not just a burger counter, though, it also plays the part of a community center and Bob loves it. "Sometimes it's like a bar without the booze," Bob joked. "If I served booze I'd be a millionaire."

One of the best stories I've heard about Schlenker's involves the LeFere Family reunion. As sure as death and taxes, every Christmas the LeFere family takes over the tiny counter for their annual olive burger fix. But the family has grown over the decades and no longer fit in Schlenker's at one time. "They come in shifts, I shit you not," Bob explained, and their order exceeds three hundred burgers. And then he told me while laughing, "New family members have to order a double, initiation."

Schlenker's also had to move once, but not very far. The restaurant was deemed too close to the street in 1939 and the city asked Schlenker's to rebuild farther back on their lot. Instead, the entire high school football team paid a visit, picked up the structure, and moved it back from the street. True story.

Currently, Bob is getting ready to hand off the ownership of Schlenker's to the next family and actually retire. Future owner Kyle Alger was at the griddle last time I was there and he is ready. "I'm not changing anything about it."

BAND BOX DINER

729 S 10th St | Minneapolis, MN 55404 | 612-332-0850
Mon–Sat 9 am–9 pm | Sun 9 am–3 pm

When a top chef sees value in the classic American diner, I know there's hope for the future of comfort food and burgers. This point was made clear in 1998 when a chef from the now shuttered fine dining spot Cafe Solo put down his chef coat and squirt bottles and revived a run-down, iconic downtown Minneapolis diner.

"I burned out, it became ridiculous," Brad Ptacek told me, "It wasn't me anymore." Brad was there at the beginning of the star chef movement. "We were the first to start drawing on plates with squirt bottles and using fresh herbs," he remembered. Brad reviewed his life and asked himself how he wanted to live. I asked his longtime partner/love-of-his-life Heather, who works at the diner, why did he do it? She told me, "He wanted to make simpler food." Brad came to the realization that the KISS approach (Keep It Simple Stupid) was the best course and admitted, "All I really wanted to do was drink coffee and bullshit."

At one point there were fourteen Band Box diners in the Twin Cities. The name goes back

200-plus years and comes from the small box that stored men's detachable collars and cuffs while the shirt was being cleaned. If something was referred to as a band box, it was small, clean and special. The unit that Brad purchased, opened in 1939 by

Harry Wyman and his wife Bert, was the first Band Box to be built and oddly it's the last one standing. They were the result of a project by Butler Manufacturing, a well-known manufacturer of grain silos all over Minnesota and beyond. They built a handful of these prefab structures (called "boulevard buildings") in the 1930s then ceased production during WWII and never resumed.

The last time I was in the Band Box it was mid-morning and breakfast was on and the place was humming. There was a mix of eggs, pancakes and burg-

ers, coffees and Cokes in front of customers at the counter and at tables. I asked grill cook Aaron how often he sees orders for burgers for breakfast and he told me, "Sometimes it's my first ticket." Aaron works the griddle and seems half asleep but was actually cool under pressure, easily managing the array of confusing orders that kept coming in. "It's hard to find guys that can cook like that," Brad told me. It's definitely a dying art. To be able to cook the entire menu on one cooking surface takes a special brain and skill set. I made the mistake of calling him a chef and he corrected me, "Technically I'm a line cook. I don't think diners have chefs."

In the beginning, Brad opened the diner and served the basics. Once he got to know the neighborhood, the menu began to shift and he now has specialty burgers on the menu but still keeps it simple, "No truffle oil or any of that," he joked. The classic cheeseburger at Band Box is great, but one of the best and most visually stunning creations is the Lunch Box Burger. It starts with a fresh one-third pound Angus patty, cooked on the flattop with a nice griddle sear. The patty is transferred to a toasted, locally-made bun that has a wad of creamy coleslaw on it. A large haystack of ultra-thin, fried potatoes is placed on top and the bun is speared to the side as if the contents of the burger are exploding up and out. It's a very dramatic presentation and proof that Brad still has his haute cuisine gene intact. "I used to be known for my height and presentation," Brad reminded me. It may look insane but I'll bet you'll find a way to get this thing in your mouth.

The tiny Band Box is a beautiful piece of American road architecture with a red and white paint scheme. Since my first visit 10 years ago Brad expanded the footprint of Band Box. "When I bought the place there were only 5 stools and 2 tables," Brad told me, "We were busy all the time, but it's easy to be busy when you only have 10 seats." He need to expand and added a dining room wing, keeping the integrity of the building as intact as possible. Brad told me it had to be done. "It's hard to make a living selling 10 eggs at a time."

CONVENTION GRILL

3912 Sunnyside Rd | Edina, MN 55424 | 952-920-6881
Mon–Thurs & Sun 11 am–10 pm | Fri & Sat 11 am–11 pm | www.conventiongrillmn.com

There are times when a diner looks vintage inside and out but the menu and ownership fail to live up to its historical roots. The Convention Grill, a Twin Cities institution, looks the part as you first step in off the street, almost too much so. The original tiled floor, the red leather swivel stools, the off-white patina to the walls, and the griddle behind the counter all look too good to be true. The waitstaff, scurrying around in pressed white uniforms with white shoes, makes you feel like you've just stepped into a period film from the '30s. The good news is it's not all show. The Convention Grill is a perfectly preserved time capsule from diner culture of the early twentieth century. The burgers at Convention Grill stand up to the image, and the whole package makes for a genuine, throwback hamburger experience.

The Convention Grill opened in 1934, built by a diner fabrication company that had planned to start a chain. When the company struggled, a Greek immigrant named Peter Santrizos took the Edina location off the company's hands for paltry seventy-five dollars. Peter ran Convention Grill until Twin Cities restaurateur John Rimarcik came along in 1974 and bought the iconic burger counter from Peter. John, at the age of thirty-four, already the owner of several area restaurants, saw amazing potential in the Convention. He also knew that by changing anything he would destroy the ethos of the place. John has worked in the restaurant business since he was twelve years old, loves hamburgers, and clearly also has a soft spot for the classic American diner.

The only major change visible at the eighty-four-year-old diner is the expansion to the dining room. In the late '80s, and again in the early '90s, John purchased the neighboring beauty salon and barbershop, greatly increasing his seating capacity. The additions lack the genuine feel of the original section of the diner but most regulars don't seem to care.

The burgers are cooked on a flattop in plain view of anyone seated at the curved counter. The Convention Grill uses fresh ground 80/20 Angus beef that is hand-pattied daily to around a quarter pound. The burgers are basic because John believes that when you stray from the simplicity of an all-American burger you end up with, as he put it, "Something else." Stick with the cheeseburger and you can't go wrong. The Convention offers swiss, american, muenster, and an amazing smoky cheddar cheese and standard condiments like tomato, lettuce, and bacon.

There's a very curious burger on the menu at the Convention that I had been warned about—the "Plazaburger," served on a dark bun with a dollop of sour cream, chives, and chopped onions. In all my travels, I had indeed come across the actual Plazaburger at the Plaza Tavern in Madison, Wisconsin, and right there on the menu, the Convention was giving credit

to this University of Wisconsin staple. "It was suggested to me years ago by a regular named Dudley Riggs," John explained. Dudley told John that he ought to have the burger on the menu. "It sounded despicable," John told me, "but I put it on there out of respect for him and it became our biggest seller." Years later, John went to the actual Plaza Tavern to try the burger that made it to his menu. "Theirs was the furthest thing from what had been described to me, and ours was better." Thanks to a healthy dose of the telephone game the two burgers have very little in common. I know how tight-lipped Plaza Tavern owner Dean Hetue is about the recipe for his secret sauce and was actually happy to find that the code had not been cracked.

A large chunk of the menu at the Convention Grill is dedicated to ice cream and drinks. Indulge in a malted milk, the Convention's vernacular for a milkshake. They come ridiculously thick and with the steel cup it was mixed in. Or get a phosphate, the old-time terminology for soda water with flavors mixed in. The Convention offers cherry and lime phosphates, and they are pleasantly refreshing.

We should all be glad a guy like John Rimarcik owns the Convention Grill. He told me, in complete seriousness, "I love hamburgers and we take pride in serving them here." John explained that the name of the restaurant came from a "meeting place" or "a place for people to get together and have fun." Considering the Convention Grill's legacy its meaning is probably even deeper today.

GORDY'S HI-HAT

411 Sunnyside Dr | Cloquet, MN 55720 | 218-879-6125
Open Daily 10 am–8:30 pm | (Mid-March to Mid-September) | www.gordys-hihat.com

"We are the real deal drive-in," Gordy's owner Dan Lundquist said with confidence. "You won't find burgers with fancy stuff on them here." And you won't, because nothing has changed since what Dan's father, Gordy, refers to as the "good old days"—fiftysome years ago when the drive-in first opened. "Consistency is the key," Dan told me, and he was serious. Pretty much, the burger you ate there years ago will be no different than the one you'll get today.

Gordy's is a destination burger stand. "Forty percent of our business comes from people from Minneapolis stopping on the way to their lake cabins," Dan explained. Gordy's is just off I-35, the main artery connecting the Twin Cities to Duluth. "They get in a pattern of stopping here." And they do. During the six warm months that Gordy's is open, the restaurant will serve up to two thousand burgers a day. That's pretty impressive for a place that's not in or near a major metropolis.

The most popular burger at Gordy's is the double cheeseburger. Ask for everything, and you'll get a burger with pickles, ketchup, mustard, and raw or grilled onion. Other condiments are available like tomato, bacon, and lettuce but you really need to follow history and appreciate the simplicity of this amazing burger. Somehow this burger, even though it was soft, tasty, and loaded with cheese, managed to not drip or fall

apart before you finished. A perfect package of beefy goodness.

The fresh ground beef comes from a supplier in Minneapolis and is hand-pattied daily using an ice-cream scoop for sizing. Dan told me that they wear out the flattop griddle every seven years.

Today, Gordy's is owned by Dan but his parents, both in their eighties, still come up from Florida to spend the summer working at the drive-in. The first time I was there (during a busy early dinner rush), Gordy was sweeping up with a broom and dustpan and Marilyn was at her post in the kitchen warming and prepping buns at a griddle. "I've been doing this fifty-eight years," Marilyn said with a smile as she gave multiple buns a squirt of ketchup without looking. "Fifty-eight years!"

★ 153 ★

The kitchen is alive with energy and dozens of employees (a lot of them Lundquists). During a rush, the kitchen kicks into high gear, working like a well-oiled machine. Everyone has a task and repeats that task over and over again as the orders come pouring in. Marilyn is the point person, calling out orders from tickets as they are handed to her, all the while toasting and prepping buns. It's truly mesmerizing.

Before there was the Hi-Hat, Gordy and Marilyn Lundquist opened the first A&W Root Beer stand in Minnesota in 1950, and after that the wildly popular London Inn of Duluth in 1955. In the '40s, Gordy did some research out in California and came across a little-known burger stand called McDonald's Famous Hamburgers. He liked what he saw and immediately hatched a plan to replicate the stand in his home state of Minnesota. The London Inn became the spot to go in Duluth in the midfifties and Gordy told me, "It was a riot. I think we had every student from University of Minnesota–Duluth, every day!" Dan added, "My father used to always say, 'If I had a nickel for every time someone burned rubber in the parking lot, I'd be a rich man.'" Gordy and Marilyn sold the London Inn in 1960 because, as Gordy put it, "Someone offered us too much money to stay." They decided to move twenty miles west to the village of Cloquet to raise a family and set down permanent roots. Soon thereafter, Gordy's was born.

Gordy's has expanded many times over the years and started as a tiny box with a walk-up window to order from. Today, the kitchen area is still where it was half a century ago, but many rooms have been added, bringing the seating capacity to over one hundred inside and out. The efficient ordering system and enormous staff is all geared toward getting you a hot hamburger as fast as possible. This is the unwavering mission at Gordy's. Dan left me with these words: "We don't do anything magical. We just keep it simple and don't screw it up."

HI-HO TAVERN

10 Center Ave E | Dilworth, MN 56529 | 218-287-2975
Mon–Sat 11 am–9 pm | Sun 12 pm–8 pm | www.hihoburgers.com

"The original menu was burgers and fries," owner Rick Cariveau told me. "And that's what you got." This broken-in seventy-year-old neighborhood watering hole in the Fargo metro area has had a burger on the menu since opening day in 1947. "We added lettuce and tomato in 1977," Rick told me bluntly. Change comes slowly to the classic burgers of America.

Hi-Ho Tavern, named after the cracker brand, is part of a small cluster of businesses on Route 10 in the center of tiny Dilworth. Within one block there are four bars and a tattoo parlor, with a Dairy Queen across the street for dessert. Two of these bars are owned by Rick—he bought Mills Lounge in 2010, two doors down from Hi-Ho.

Rick's parents, Earl and Edith Cariveau, bought the Hi-Ho in 1960 and sold it to Rick and his wife, Cathy, in 1977. Not much has changed at the large, carpeted bar with standard issue chairs, tables, and booths. As old bars go, this place is neat and clean, and there's a game room on the way to the bathroom. "There was talk of remodeling in here," bartender Rachelle told me, "but the regulars were like 'NOOOOO.'"

The Hi-Ho Special is one way to go when ordering. You get a cheeseburger, all-you-can-eat fries (yep), and a bottomless beverage. The deal seemed too good to be true until I discovered that it did not include all-you-can-drink beer. Add a beer for $2.00 and pay only $11.50 for everything. Amazing.

I like the basic double cheeseburger with chopped, fried onions. The burgers are cooked on a large flattop behind the bar and served on a toasted white squishy bun in a plastic basket. A double is a half pound of beef so come hungry.

A local butcher has supplied quarter-pound fresh patties for the burgers for decades and Rick will still go and pick up the order daily. "Some see me at the butcher and say 'oh that's where you get it!'" Starting in 1960, Rick joined his dad on trips to the butcher, and when he turned sixteen, he was making the daily trip by himself.

The menu at Hi-Ho today has gone far beyond the days of burgers only and they now offer popular fried foods like popcorn chicken and cheese curds as well as hot dogs, grilled cheese, and a fish sandwich. But you didn't come all this way for a fish sandwich. The menu repeats itself at its second location in Fargo.

In 1996, Rick and his son, Rick Jr., decided it was time to open a location closer to the action when Rick Sr. noticed there were people traveling out to Dilworth for his burgers. "We take checks and noticed a lot were from Fargo," he told me. The plan worked and now the Fargo location, with an impressive selection of tap beer, does more business than the original. "My son ran with it, and he worked his butt off to make it happen."

Rick Sr. prefers to stay in Dilworth and let his son manage the business in Fargo. He holds court at Mills Lounge where I noticed there was a limited menu. Fortunately, if you are drinking at Mills an excellent burger is just steps away. Or if you ask nicely, the bartender will call in your order and have it delivered.

LIONS TAP

16180 Flying Cloud Dr | Eden Prairie, MN 55347 | 952-934-5299
Mon–Sun 11 am–10 pm | www.lionstap.com

Although it's basically in the Minneapolis metro area, Lions Tap is out there on its own, surrounded by no other businesses on Flying Cloud Drive. However, the semi-remote location for this enormous hamburger hotspot does not seem to affect business in the slightest. "It's definitely not a drive-by business because we are in the middle of nowhere," second-generation part-owner, Matt Notermann, told me. "This is a destination spot." The first time I visited it was between lunch and dinner on a Saturday and the two-hundred-seat family burger restaurant was almost full. By dinnertime there was a wait.

In 1933, before it was Lions Tap, it was a farm stand operated by the Peterson and Larson families. Soon after, the stand started selling beer, then gas, and eventually it morphed into a convenience store. A string of owners made changes to the store over the decades and in 1958 burgers made their debut at the location. In 1977, current owners Bert and Bonnie Notermann bought the place, which was then a small roadside bar and burger joint called Lyon's Tap, named after the previous owner, and slightly altered the name. Over the years the Notermanns made significant additions to the building with the largest doubling its capacity in the 1980s.

The Lions Tap method for making patties is fairly unique. Fresh ground beef is delivered in bulk daily and portioned into quarter-pound balls. The balls are pressed into patties with a cutting board between two squares of waxed paper. Three large flattop grills in the kitchen see some serious action during the lunch and dinner rush. "When we are busy," Matt told me, "these [griddles] are screamin.'" On a good day, the Lions Tap can crank out an astonishing two thousand patties a day. Many of those patties go into double cheeseburgers.

Make no mistake, Lions Tap is a burger restaurant. If you wanted something else to eat you'll be limited to french fries. Many other burger-only joints have succumbed to the pressure to diversify, but not the Tap. The burger choices are limited as well. Order a standard cheeseburger and you'll get a quarter-pound burger on a classic soft white bun with pickles on the side. You can add fried or raw onion, that's it. Ask for a California Burger and the kitchen will add lettuce and tomato. Bacon is available, too, as is a mushroom swiss burger. The most

popular burger, though, is the classic double cheeseburger with fried onions. It's a pretty perfect burger and at half a pound of beef it's almost too much for the bun. All Lions Tap burgers get a sprinkle of their secret seasoning (which can now be purchased in the gift shop), and if you want yours cooked to temperature, no problem. "People appreciate that," Matt told me.

The atmosphere in Lions Tap is very familiar and comfortable. It's a family place reminiscent of a north woods supper club. One of the dining rooms has a large mural depicting an outdoor scene, painted by well-known, local artist Leo Stans. The staff is huge and knows just about every customer in the place. "I think people come here for the staff, as well as the food," Matt told me. Half of them have been working at Lions Tap for over ten years and a few have actually been there for over thirty-five years. Matt added, "In this business that's just not normal."

MATT'S BAR

3500 Cedar Ave South | Minneapolis, MN 55407 | 612-722-7072
Sun-Thurs 11 am-10:45 pm | Fri & Sat 11 am-11:45 pm | www.mattsbar.com

If you have no connection to or have never visited the Twin Cities, then there's a good chance you have never met the beloved Jucy Lucy (correct spelling, read on). The famed burger concoction can be found all over Minneapolis, but the epicenter of the Jucy Lucy legacy is a small, friendly, lost-in-time bar on the south side of town. In 1954, then owner Matt cooked up the first Jucy Lucy for a customer sitting at the bar who asked for "something special." The result was two fresh quarter-pound patties crimped together with a folded slice of american cheese hiding inside. When the customer bit into Matt's burger science project and the cheese came oozing out, he exclaimed, "Now *that's* a Juicy Lucy!" Other customers needled Matt and within six months the "Jucy Lucy" was on the menu, misspelled, and never corrected.

Over sixty years have passed and the burger recipe remains unchanged. The burger is griddled and closely monitored (much like a science project), delicately flipped, then pinpricked to release pressure and prevent it from exploding on the griddle. "Some people think we do that so it won't blow up in your face," general manager of fourteen years Pauly Rees told me. "It will still blow up in your face."

The delivery of the burger to your table always comes with a warning. On my first visit to Matt's, former bartender Margaret Lidstone said to me sternly, "You will burn your mouth off if you bite into it too soon. Let it sit."

The phrase FEAR THE CHEESE printed on the waitstaff's shirts was warning enough. I tried to wait, but became a victim instantly. The molten goo was HOT, really hot, and kept the burger moist all the way through. Everyone who ordered the Jucy Lucy got the same stern speech. "I know," a regular responded in singsong, "not my first time." A woman sitting at the next table had no problem saying to me, "You're doing it all wrong. Just nibble at it, take small bites while it cools down."

The Jucy Lucy comes on waxed paper—no plate, no utensils. Onions, fried or raw, are optional and pickles are standard. No tomato, no lettuce. Coke? Sure, no ice. Diet Coke? No lemon. Matt's is bare-bones dining at its very best.

The griddle is positioned behind the bar in full view. The grill cook told me, "We can sell up to five hundred on a good day." The staff, and whoever is available, spend hours a day pinching and stuffing Jucy Lucys. The only menu is the one on the wall behind the bar and it has not changed in six decades (with the exception of the prices, of course). It's on this menu that the "Jucy Lucy" is famously misspelled.

Matt Bristol worked at the bar, then named Mr. Nibb's, before purchasing the quiet corner tavern in 1954 and changing the name to his own. Scott Nelson bought the bar from Matt's daughter in 1998 and changed nothing. Even the crazy '50s wallpaper (which can be viewed on the tavern's website) remains. "It's quite tacky, actually," Scott explained, "but people don't want change." In a time when so many restaurants, and even bars, all look the same from city to city because of franchising, Scott believes that there is a place for Matt's. "Everything looks like a chain. We don't."

Matt's commitment to hamburgers starts with a concept that has its roots in the 1950s, and the simple menu is a testament to the fact that great burgers are immune to fads. Scott said it best when he pointed out, "Burgers and fries don't go out of style, and neither do we."

TENDERMAID

217 4th Ave NE | Austin, MN 55912
507-437-7907 | Mon–Fri 11 am–6 pm | Sat 11 am–3 pm | Sun Closed

The loosemeat sandwich is unquestionably a gastronomic phenomenon of Iowa but in a few instances the iconic crumbly beef, burger-like sandwich has managed to escape the state's borders. It found its way to Wichita, Kansas, at NuWay Cafe, all the way to Ohio at a Maid-Rite in Greenville and just north of the Iowa border at Tendermaid in Austin, Minnesota.

If you've never had the opportunity to eat a loosemeat sandwich, you need to make that happen. It's the only nontraditional burger type in this book, and that's because, on first bite, you'll realize that it tastes basically the same as a classic cheeseburger. The only thing different about the simple combination of pickles, american cheese, and soft white bun is the crumbly steamed beef in place of a burger patty.

To make matters more confusing, the restaurant is called Tendermaid Hamburgers and the menu lists "hamburgers" but none are available. The burgers listed here are actually loosemeat sandwiches. Call them what you want, or just do what the locals do: "They call them 'Tendermaids,'" owner Sara White explained.

"It was Gary's dream to buy this place," Sara told me. Gary and Sara White, high school sweethearts, bought Tendermaid in 1997 and became the sixth owners in the counter's long, eighty-year history. "When I was fourteen," Gary remembered, "I told my parents that someday I was going to buy Tendermaid."

And he did. When it came up for sale there was talk that the counter would close. Gary said no way and sprung to action. "I had thirty days to get it back up and running," he told me. He left his job at nearby Hormel and kept the Tendermaid tradition alive.

The clean, tiny Tendermaid is a lesson in efficiency. Two Formica counters each with seven red leather-topped stools face a small workstation where everything happens. The original 1938 loosemeat cooker is in the center of the action, filled with steaming, crumbled beef. If you order a sandwich, expect to be eating inside of thirty seconds. That's because the assembly of a Tendermaid happens lightning fast. The loose, hot beef is scooped onto a soft white steamed bun, condiments are added and the thing is wrapped up and sent to your spot at the counter. This description is longer than your wait.

Ask for one "all the way" and you'll get ketchup, mustard, chopped raw onion, and pickles. Ask for cheese, and a cold slice is tossed on. But fear not, once wrapped up, the cheese melts perfectly.

People go crazy for loosemeat sandwiches. They are easy to eat, tasty as hell, and deeply nostalgic. They are also great for babies and kids because they are so soft. Some people order plain ones for their dogs. "I used to think that was strange," Sara told me, "but I guess they want good meat for their dogs."

One regular customer, Sander Johnson, ate at Tendermaid twice a day until he was ninety-six. Sara told me "I once asked him, 'What do you eat when you're not here?' and he told me 'hamburgers!'"

Love SPAM? Then you'll love Tendermaid. The loosemeat counter does not serve the iconic American canned meat but the SPAM Museum is located across the street. Plan accordingly.

CASPER & RUNYON'S NOOK

492 Hamline Ave South | St Paul, MN 55116 | 651-698-4347
Sun–Thurs 11 am–1 am | Fri & Sat 11 am–2 am | www.crnook.com

The Nook has been around for a while. First it was Wally's Nook, opened in 1938 by a guy named Wally who turned a gas station into a bar. There were two other owners between Wally and 1965 when grill cook Mickey Brausen took over and called it Mickey's Nook. She successfully ran the bar for thirty-five years until 2000 when two regulars for decades, who had been friends since childhood, bought the bar for their two sons Ted and Mike to run. Willy, manager of seventeen years, told me, "They bought the place for their sons to make sure their favorite bar stayed the same and didn't turn into a taco place, or whatever."

A burger that was invented in the Twin Cities called the Jucy Lucy (correctly spelled) is on the menu at the Nook, although they don't call it that. For those unaware, this cheese-stuffed burger was invented in neighboring Minneapolis called Matt's Bar. The Nook went with the mildly pornographic Juicy Nookie instead, and it's listed under "Stuffed Burgers" on the menu. And unlike Matt's, which only serves the Jucy Lucy, the Nook has an impressive roster of burgers on their menu. You can get everything from a patty melt to a concoction called the Chuck Mitch Ham Hamburger which comes with shaved ham, bourbon sauce, swiss cheese on a one-third-pound burger patty.

When Ted and Mike took over ownership they were not messing with the burger and even brought in Mickey herself to help get them right. The Nook has a butcher that sends them a cut of Angus no one else can get, making the burgers special from the start. The Juicy Nookie can be ordered with either shredded cheddar or american cheese. If you were looking for other cheeses, move on down the menu. The Nookie arrives in a basket ready to consume but WAIT—the danger is out of sight. Hot molten cheese lurks inside this beauty so take it slow. Also, don't make the mistake of pressing too hard because the cheese goo will explode right out the back and onto your lap. There's also a note on the menu saying "All burgers cooked medium," and this is simply because the cheese inside would not melt in a Nookie cooked any less than medium.

When you walked in you probably took note of Ranham Bowling Center next door. It's a functioning basement pocket alley with only eight lanes and is also owned by Ted and Mike and part of the Nook. It was the last manual reset bowling alley in the Twin Cities, going fully automatic in 1958. If you are bowling, you also have access to the full menu. When you place an order, it's sent down a dumbwaiter to the alley.

In 2010, a fire destroyed the restaurant and they lost everything, including the original flattop

griddle. "The firefighters knew enough about the place to start pulling stuff off the walls," Willy told me. Faulty electricity was to blame and the bar was closed for six months to renovate.

So grab one of the substantial stools at bar, which feel like they are designed for some serious not-going-anywhere-for-a-while drinking and eating. Get yourself a sixteen-ounce-tall boy of Grain Belt beer and peruse the burger menu at the Nook. You really should try Mickey's original burger, though it is hard to not fall back on the temptation of the explosive Juicy Nookie.

BILL'S HAMBURGERS

310 North Main St | Amory, MS 38821 | 662-256-2085
Mon–Fri 6:30 am–5:30 pm | Sat 6:30 am–5 pm | Closed Sun

The drive to Amory is quintessential back-country Deep South—miles of two-lane roads lined with cotton fields, cotton gins, and, when I visited, lots of loose cotton all over the road. Amory is a small town and Bill's is a small restaurant at a spot where Main Street bends. Locals affectionately refer to this spot as "Vinegar Bend."

Before it was Bill's, it was Bob's. In 1929, Bob Hill borrowed forty-eight dollars from a local baker named James Toney to open a hamburger restaurant. A stipulation of the deal was that Bob had to buy all of his hamburger buns from Toney's bakery.

One year after opening, Bob hired Bill Tubb to help slice and prep buns with the only two condiments available in the '20s at Bob's—mustard and onion. World War II meat rationing forced Bob's to close, but after the war, Bob reopened and later sold the business to Bill in 1955. Naturally, Bill changed the name to his own, then turned around and sold it in 1957 to another Bill, who then rehired Bill to work there. After a string of Bill's relatives owned and operated the small

burger stand, Bill's was sold to the current owners, Reid and Janice Wilkerson, not a Bob or a Bill.

"I grew up eating here. It was such a big part of my childhood. When it came up for sale, I had to buy it," Reid told me once as he emerged from the back room of the restaurant. Bill's grinds fresh beef there every day for the burgers as it has been done since 1929. Another tradition Reid and Janice adhere to—mustard and onion only—also dates back to the beginning. Toney's bakery closed in 1970, which led Bill's to start using standard four-inch buns, which meant the burgers grew slightly. The new burger size was determined by the size of the buns.

The burgers start as balls of beef that are pressed onto a well-seasoned flattop griddle. They are unbelievably tasty, beefy, and rich with grease flavor. The mustard, onion, beef, and bun combination is heaven. Cheese is unnecessary, though available, but tomato and lettuce are nowhere to be found. If you really need ketchup or mayo, there are packets hiding behind the counter, for take-out orders.

A few things have changed at Bill's all for the better. The restaurant is now open an hour earlier to serve a full breakfast, an innovation thanks to Reid's son, James, who now runs the restaurant. Reid has since become a pastor in Nashville and left the operation of Bill's to James and his new bride, Brittany. They also acquired the space next to Bill's and created a dining room that seats forty. When you add the twenty-three stools at the original counter, the seating has tripled at Bill's. "We had to start serving breakfast with the new dining room," James explained. "That was the only way it was going to work." Everything from Belgian waffles to sausage links can be found at breakfast, but fear not—you can still get a burger for breakfast, too.

On the front of the restaurant is a large painted portrait of the beloved former employee Junior Manasco, a gently disabled fixture at Bill's for over twenty years starting in 1977. On a wall opposite the counter is a framed resolution from the State of Mississippi presented to Junior "for his service to his community." Reid recalled, "He knew and greeted everyone that came in the door."

As I was leaving Bill's once, an old-timer at the counter told me, "The first time I came here the burgers were twenty-five cents." When I pressed for just how long ago that was, he said, "A long time ago."

LATHAM'S HAMBURGER INN

106 West Main St | New Albany, MS 38652
Tues & Wed 10:30 am–2 pm | Thurs–Sat 10:30 am–4 pm | Closed Sun & Mon

One of the most significant contributions to the regional American burger comes from northern Mississippi in the form of the slugburger, or doughburger as they are sometimes referred. As the rural South fell on hard times before and during the Great Depression, burger counters were dreaming up ways to extend their ground beef supply. Bread crumbs from yesterday's bread was the obvious choice and a burger was born. Over the years, cooks making a traditional slug (old slang for a nickel, which is what they cost back then) shifted to ground pork and powdered extenders like soy flour (which was probably even cheaper than bread and beef).

Today, the pork version of the slugburger is available all over northern Mississippi, but if you want a real deal slug, with DNA that dates back almost a century, you need to get to Latham's.

In 1929, Richard Wilson Staggs moved his family from Tennessee to New Albany, Mississippi, and opened the Hamburger Inn. His slugburger was such a success that he opened a second location in town. Staggs kept a daily tally of the burgers he made and between opening day and his retirement in the mid-1950s he made over two million burgers, an astonishing number. The restaurant was run by Geneva Grisham family following Staggs' exit, then to Fairy Latham and her family. The last Latham to run Hamburger Inn (for 15 years) was Fairy's daughter-in-law Vicky, who sold it to a good friend Wally Rakeshaw in

2008. Wally ran it for 8 years before his untimely passing in 2016. The restaurant closed for a while, and briefly reopened by a neighbor Will Neely before Holly and Brad Henry, current owners took over ownership and conducted a massive, much needed renovation.

Through all of the changes Hamburger Inn has witnessed, in name, ownership and location, incredibly the recipe has remained exactly the same. The burger you would have eaten on opening day in 1929 is likely identical to the burger you can get today.

The recipe was passed down from owner to owner but at some point after Vicky sold the place the product seemed slightly altered. Wally kept the recipe but made the burgers smaller and they came out almost black. Will's attempt produced even smaller and darker crisped patties. So when Holly and Brad bought the place they began the process of finding the original recipe and brought back Vicky herself to lend a hand. After some instruction the Henrys were pumping out the most accurate version of this slug burger in years.

The recipe for Staggs' original slugburger is a blood-oath secret that comes with the purchase of the business. It's safe to assume that mixed in with the ground beef is some sort of flour or fine bread crumbs, possibly other seasonings. For decades all of the patties were formed then dropped into a big old cast iron skillet with some beef tallow, or rendered beef fat. The breading content of the burger makes it crisp up and the patty absorbs some of that beef fat.

A regular named Coy Fitts came into the newly renovated Latham's when I was there recently and said to Holly of the return to the original Staggs slugburger, "I want this, not a charred, burnt burger. It should be crisp without being overcooked." The solution was simply a larger, four-ounce burger with a moist center and a very crispy exterior. Served on a classic white squishy bun with nothing more than mustard and pickles this tiny bite of hamburger history is heavenly.

The current location of Hamburger Inn is not the original. In 1974 the Latham family moved the business across the street and brought most of the stuff with them. When Holly and Brad renovated they found the original counter-top underneath a more contemporary one and incorporated it into the restaurant as a shelf on view behind the counter. They also discovered another smaller counter from Staggs' original place and put that to use as well (it's the small counter across from the main counter by the front door). The stools, all 15 of them, are beautifully restored cast iron posts with hardwood seats original to the era of Wilson Staggs. And of course the kitchen received a major overhaul. It's believed that in 45 years the kitchen had never been renovated.

Hamburger Inn is relevant to burger history because the recipe for their slugburger, dough-burger, Latham's Burger, or what ever you want to call it likely one of the most historically accurate versions of the burger that exists today.

PHILLIPS GROCERY

541 East Van Dorn Ave | Holly Springs, MS 38635 | 662-252-4671
Mon–Fri 10 am–4 pm | Sat 10 am–5:30 pm | Closed Sun

Downtown Holly Springs, Mississippi, looks like it may have looked seventy years ago. American flags and freshly painted turn-of-the-century storefronts line the streets. Phillip's Grocery is not here, though. Phillip's is down the road by the train tracks across from a semi-restored 150-year-old ornate train depot, and the area looks a lot like William Eggleston's photography of the South—gritty and real. I got lost trying to find this burger destination, and you will, too.

Phillips serves one of the best burgers in America. Not just because I said so; their burgers have been the subject of many journalistic accolades, including being awarded, "Best Burger in America" twice by USA Today.

The restaurant was first established as Phillips Grocery in 1948 when the Phillips family bought an existing grocery that sold hamburgers. Current owner Larry Davis told me, "The burger's been made here since the '30s." Mrs. Phillips had planned to do away with the burger when they bought the store, but changed her tune when she saw how many they were selling. "She put her kids through college with burger money."

Their success is no accident. The secret lies in the mixture of ground beef and other "secret" ingredients. Adding breading to ground beef was popular in the South during the Depression, and I suspect the burger at Phillips may be a vestige of this lost art. I once arrived at Phillips before opening for the day and interrupted Larry's morning ritual of making the ground beef mixture for the day's burgers.

He actually disappeared behind a closed door and reappeared a few minutes later with rubber gloves and large stainless mixing bowls filled with ground beef. "It's the same recipe since the '30s," Larry said of the secret recipe he purchased with the store in 1989. "I do this every day, sometimes forty to fifty pounds on Saturdays."

A burger at Phillips can be ordered as a single one-third-pound patty, a double with two quarter-pound patties, or a deluxe half-pound patty. That sounds confusing, but not to the kitchen staff who electronically weigh and portion each ball of ground beef. The balls are pressed on a well-seasoned flattop griddle and served on white buns with only mustard, pickle, and onion. Mayo, ketchup, cheese, and bacon are offered (but

unnecessary). The burger is so tasty as is you could eat it with only a bun and emerge contented.

Phillips no longer sells groceries. The business shifted in the '50s when supermarkets killed the corner store. The decor is pure country store kitsch today—Coke advertising from every decade is represented, as well as old grocer's scales, saws, and a vintage John Deere bicycle dangling from the ceiling.

You can sit at one of the random tables offered or find an old school desk to enjoy your burger and one of Larry's homemade fried pies. Look out the window of this 120-year-old building toward the train crossing and savor the sounds of locomotive whistles and the clanking of the active Mississippi Central Railroad rumbling by.

THE SLUG BURGER

Makes 6 burgers

Equipment

A seasoned cast-iron skillet or flattop

A medium-size mixing bowl

A stiff spatula

The Burger

Peanut oil, or other neutral oil

1 pound (500 g) fresh ground 80/20 chuck

1 cup bread crumbs made by hand-crumbling day-old bread or fresh bread, toasted until just dried out

Salt, for seasoning

6 soft white buns

The Toppings

Yellow mustard

Dill pickle chips

1. Preheat the cast-iron skillet over medium heat (or the flat-top to medium) and add a drop or two of oil.

2. Place the ground beef and bread crumbs in the mixing bowl and, using your hands, mix until fully blended. Divide the meat mixture into 6 equal portions (about 3-ounces/90 g each) and roll them into balls.

3. Place the balls of beef on the heated skillet. Each ball should have 3 inches (7 cm) of space around it. (Depending on the size of your cooking surface, you may only be able to cook 2 or 3 at a time.)

4. Use the stiff spatula to give each of the balls a good press until it takes the shape of a patty and sprinkle each with a pinch salt. Let cook, without disturbing them, for 3 minutes or until reddish liquid begins to form on the patty surface.

5. While the patties are cooking, prep the buns by slathering the cut-side of each bottom bun with a swipe of mustard and 2 or 3 pickle chips—the traditional condiments for a classic Slug Burger.

6. Flip the burgers once and cook for another 1 ½ minutes without touching them. They will appear sizzling and crispy on their cooked sides when they're done. Transfer to the prepared buns and serve.

MISSOURI

CARL'S DRIVE-IN

9033 Manchester Rd | Brentwood, MO 63144 | 314-961-9652
Tues–Sat 11 am–8 pm | Closed Sun & Mon

The first time I visited Carl's, I grabbed the best seat in the house, the spot at the counter directly in front of the griddle. I was mesmerized with what I saw and naturally pulled out my phone to snap a photo. The cook turned to me and sternly said, "No photos!" and asked me to photograph only the finished burger. Now I was intrigued.

They had something to hide even though the griddle is in full view of every customer. That's because the burger at Carl's is all about method.

Years went by before I could get back to Carl's again and in that time the iconic burger counter was sold. Whenever a burger joint changes hands and the new owners are not blood related, I get nervous. The new owner was actually longtime customer Mike Franklin and was the perfect choice to take the helm. "I was afraid he was just going to shut it down," Mike said of then owner Frank Cunetto. Frank owned Carl's and worked the griddle since 1986 and was burned out. Mike told me, "twenty-eight years behind a grill like that will wear you down." Then one day he announced from the griddle 'I'm tired - who wants to buy a burger joint?'" Mike told him he might be interested and they negotiated a price, and in 2015 Mike became only the third owner in the restaurant's sixty-year history.

In 1959, Carl Myers turned a filling station into a burger joint and ran it until he sold to Frank in 1986. Apparently this is why the counter setup is so bizarre at Carl's. Two counters face a classic short-order kitchen, but the counters are accessed by their own doors. If for whatever reason you want to go the opposite counter, you'll need to go outside and walk around the building to a different door.

The burger at Carl's is the result of some weird science. 80/20 fresh ground beef is machine por-tioned into wads of beef around three ounces. When fatty beef makes positive contact (by apply-ing aggressive pressure with a stiff spatula) the beef turns almost candy-like with the burger's lacy edge looking like some fancy confection. This is achieved by a very specific move that requires a pro touch. The beef is smashed thin, then with a flat cir-cular move, the edges only of the patty are smashed again paper thin leaving the center thicker. A gla-zier's putty knife is used to scrape the burger off the flattop and flip it. The method is very similar to

Schoop's, a fresh beef mini-chain found in Indiana, and Workingman's Friend in Indianapolis.

American cheese is added at the end and just barely melts. The finished product hangs out of the bun, showing off its "beef candy," the cheese intermingling with the crisped beef. A standard burger order at Carl's adds raw onion, pickle, ketchup to the burger. Lettuce and tomato are also available and the standard white squishy buns are toasted. Be smart and get a double.

Mike was no stranger to the place and has been visiting since 1981 (and knew Carl himself). "I hav-en't changed anything," he told me. Jason at the grill is the connector from the past to the present. He relieved Frank at the griddle during the 2 years leading up to the sale. Jason was inherited from the old ownership, as were a handful of the waitstaff— both Kelly and Pam have been at Carl's for almost twenty years. Mike was wise to keep veteran staff. How else could a place like Carl's survive?

TOWN TOPIC

2021 Broadway St | Kansas City, MO 64108 | 816-842-2298
Open Daily 24 Hours | www.towntopic.com

Most people might drive by Town Topic and see a cute old hamburger stand, an icon of the past, or a relic in a rundown neighborhood. Not me. The people who know better see a vibrant keeper of the flame, a lesson to learn from, and a restaurant that knows its place in history. I couldn't drive by anyhow. Every time I try, I need to stop for a burger.

There are three Town Topics left in Kansas City where there once were seven. Today, only the Broadway location, also known as number three, is open twenty-four hours. At one point all of the Town Topics were open 24/7, as were many other ten-stool midcentury hamburger joints across America.

When I approached the Town Topic for an interview for this book, I had already been there a few times. The night I chose to visit I hit the jackpot—Bonnie Gooch was at the grill. Bonnie should be defined as a hard-boiled sweetheart. She's just what you'd want from a short-order lifer—a woman who takes no crap but takes care of the regulars. "See that guy down there?" she said to me, pointing down the counter to an older man. "He's been like a daddy to me. I've known him since the day I started so I try to take care of him." With that, she slid an unordered slice of lettuce onto his burger and sent it off.

Bonnie started working at the little burger counter in 1965 when she was thirteen. For the next twenty-three years, she worked the night shift alongside her husband, Richard. When he passed away, she switched to the early evening shift. Bonnie has since retired, but not before logging over forty-five years at the Town Topic. Needless to say, she knew how to make a great hamburger.

The burger at Town Topic is a classic thin patty. Small one-eighth-pound wads of fresh ground 80/20 beef are delivered to the restaurant daily. Bonnie pressed the meat thin on the hot, well-seasoned griddle and dropped a small handful of shredded onions on the patty. Not unlike the fried onion burgers of El Reno, Oklahoma, these onions are then pressed into the patty as it sizzles on the grill. The result is a tasty combination of griddled beef and caramelized onions.

Ninety-nine percent order their burgers with onions, and the most popular on the menu is the double cheeseburger. It comes with pickles on a white squishy bun and resembles a burger *Popeye*'s Wimpy might have eaten—a classic American burger.

Fortunately, those of us who understand the significance of a counter like Town Topic need not worry about its future. "The city tried to turn this place into a parking lot," counterperson Keisha once told me, but a grandfather clause spared the restaurant based on its age. "Some people have been coming in here since they were kids," Bonnie reflected once during a lull at the grill. "They just love the place."

WHITE KNIGHT DINER

1801 Olive St. | St. Louis, MO 63103
314-621-5949 | Mon–Fri 6 am–2 pm | Sat 6 am–1:30 pm | Closed Sun

I n a theme you may notice throughout this book the word *white* in a restaurant's name is historically significant. This is simply because the progenitor of the corner burger business model was unquestionably White Castle. Although they fought to protect the name, many burger joints continued to open burger joints similar to White Castle for years. Why? Because at the time they were making the best burgers in America and were a tremendous success. Copycats were inevitable. This is actually *not* one of those restaurants; in fact, the story is much better.

Just after he assumed the family business in 1982, owner Lee Hinds was faced with an eminent domain scenario that would wipe his tiny diner, Super Sandwich Shop, off the map. He spent the next eight years in a legal battle with the city but emerged victorious, and joked, "They say you can't beat city hall. . ." The reason the diner was spared was something right out of a Hollywood plot, literally. As time was running out Universal Pictures chose Super Sandwich as a location for the major motion picture *White Palace,* which was filmed entirely in St. Louis. Lee and his lawyers contended that the property had greater value because of this, a value which did not come close to the offer the city had made to tear it down. Lee legally changed the name to White Knight (the studio refused to grant Lee rights to White Palace) following the filming

for survival and the case was thrown out. "We were abused by the government," Lee told me, "I chose the name because in literature the White Knight is the one that comes and saves your ass."

It started with an empire. In 1938, brothers Leon and Leslie Burrow opened the first of a twelve-diner chain in St. Louis called Courtesy Diner and saw great success. During the Depression and WWII, many other restaurants were going out of business or suffering but the brothers were surviving. This is because Leslie was in the farming business and before the war refused to take government subsidies. This allowed the brothers to get whatever supplies they needed for the restaurants during the war, bypassing imposed rationing, in turn making them millionaires.

The brothers parted ways in the late 1950s over issues of segregation. At the time it was common to see the sign WHITES ONLY on a restaurant door and with the civil rights movement under way Leslie did something about it. Each brother took six diners with Leon retaining the name. Leslie changed the name of his six to Super Sandwich Shops and allowed blacks.

Leslie's side of the business was sold to Ken Keisker, a relative, soon after who sold it to his son-in-law Lee in 1982. When Lee took over there were only two diners left. Then in 1995, a horrific two-car accident completely obliterated one of them. Lee pointed out that both cars were government vehicles, the irony not lost on him. "Ever since I've gotten here they've tried to find ways to get rid of me!"

Today, White Knight still stands, the last diner in the family's six-store chain, a relic of the past that makes some of the best griddled cheeseburgers anywhere. Every morning, for thirty-six years now, Lee arrives 3 a.m. to portion beef and prep for the day, then he's out the door by 6 a.m. I asked him if it's a chore to prep pre-dawn and he told me, "No! It's a way of life, and I'm living the dream."

The interior of White Knight looks like a movie set. It's a tiny, bright and squeaky-clean diner with a few tables and gleaming stainless steel everywhere. Huge picture windows and glass block down to the floor let in a copious amount of daylight. And there's a great little counter that offers the perfect griddle view, always my favorite seat.

All burgers start with quarter-pound balls of beef that are hand-pressed to the shape of a patty

on the flattop. I'm partial to the doubles at White Knight, but manager of twenty-six years Cristy told me, "We sell mostly singles, quarter pound is a lot of meat!" Ask for "everything" and get lettuce, tomato, raw onion, pickles, and mayonnaise.

Most of the customers at White Knight are regulars and you'll hear the all-female staff refer to all of them as "baby." Many regulars don't even need to place an order when they sit down. "We spot them through the large windows and have their 'usual' ready minutes later," Lee told me. It's a very friendly, lively environment, the way a diner should be. I once saw a regular stand up from his spot at the counter and announce loudly in Cristy's direction, "That's the best lunch I've had all day!"

With all that White Knight has been through it's a miracle that it is still with us. It's a testament to a family that wouldn't quit or bow down to anyone. It's also a survival story, which involves art imitating life; a moment that actually helped save an important piece of American history.

WINSTEAD'S

101 Emanuel Cleaver LI Blvd | Kansas City, MO 64112 | 816-753-2244
Sun–Thurs 6:30 am–12 am | Fri & Sat 6:30 am–1 am | Drive-Thru Open 24/7
www.eatwinsteads.com

In the hearts of many Kansas City natives, Winstead's is the only place in the world that serves great hamburgers. Even Kansas City's own Calvin Trillin, food writer and journalist, once said jokingly about Winstead's, "Anyone who doesn't think his hometown has the best hamburger place in the world is a sissy." More than three decades have passed since Trillin made that statement and almost nothing has changed—Winstead's still serves one of the best burgers in America.

Gone are the carhops, replaced by a drive-thru in 1989. On my first visit to the vintage time-warp diner, I was led to longtime employee Judy Eddingfield. Judy started working at Winstead's when she was only sixteen years old, an astonishing fifty-three years ago. "When I was just a kid, my father would take me here for a strawberry shake and a single burger," she told me. Over the decades, her mother, brothers, sisters, and aunts would all work at Winstead's in some capacity.

I asked Judy how she was on skates as a carhop and she quickly pointed out, "No, no. There were no skates back then. Winstead's opened in 1940, which predates skates." True, carhops on skates were a fad and gimmick for the drive-ins of the 1950s and '60s. Winstead's maintained carhops for fifty years until the popular drive-thru was installed (which as of recently is open twenty-four hours at the Plaza location).

Today, there are seven Winstead's restaurants in the Kansas City area but the minichain was actually started in Springfield, Illinois, by sisters Katherine and Nellie Winstead. Their first location in Kansas City, located adjacent to the Midwest shopping mecca Country Club Plaza, remains the flagship restaurant in the chain.

The physical structure of Winstead's is a stunning, well-preserved example of midcentury restaurant architecture. The entire building is sheathed in pastel pink and yellow glazed enamel

brick. The dining room is large and seats 280 comfortably.

The wide, clean, open space is a sea of well-laid-out booths sitting beneath enormous hot pink neon–rimmed ceiling light fixtures. On one of my first visits, an entire elementary school (close to seventy-five kids) had comfortably taken over the restaurant for an early lunch and there was still plenty of room for regulars.

The menu at Winstead's is split—one half lists food items, the other shakes, malts, and drinks, reminding one and all that ice cream is just as important as burgers to drive-in clientele. Winstead's has built its reputation on the "Steakburger," which served with "everything" includes a toasted white bun, a fresh ground two-ounce patty, pickles, a very large slice of onion, and a "secret sauce" that is really just a mixture of mustard and ketchup. Make it a double and add cheese and you have a meal.

The burgers are smashed thin and cooked on a flattop griddle. The result is a moist, loose burger with a salty, crunchy exterior. Order a limeade and fries with your Steakburger to round out the perfect Winstead's eating experience.

Winstead's today does a brisk business and employs over eighty people at the Country Club Plaza location. Judy told me as I took a sip from my ice-cold Mr. Pibb, "There are still a handful of us that have been working here for over thirty years." General manager Cathi Fern told me, "Judy told me she's never going to retire." Cathi herself has worked at Winstead's for over thirty-two years. She told me proudly that many generations of customers come back for nostalgic reasons, and added "The goal is to be able to continue their good memories."

MATT'S PLACE DRIVE-IN

2339 Placer St | Butte, MT 59701
406-782-8049 | Tues–Sat 11:30 am–7 pm | Closed Sun & Mon

Matt's Place is a drive-in on the edge of the boom-bust, Old West, mining town of Butte, Montana. As you approach the hillside town on I-90, you'll notice first the abandoned copper mining equipment and the brick buildings of a somewhat underpopulated downtown. The streets of Butte are lined with vintage neon signage that reflects its colorful past—Irish pubs and Chinese restaurants among many others that existed to entertain

and feed the large number of immigrant mine workers.

Matt's Place opened in 1930 during the peak of copper mining in Butte. Through it all, Matt's has survived. So much so that it can proudly boast that it has a spot on the National Register of Historic Places. Recognized as historically important for its contribution to early American road culture, Matt's also serves amazing, fresh beef burgers and milkshakes made from homemade ice cream. I visited Matt's for all of these reasons, but mostly to sample their fabled "Nutburger."

Of the thousands of burgers I have eaten across America, few piqued my interest like the Nutburger. Maybe it was the remote, beautiful, western locale, or the fact that Matt's has been in existence for over seventy years, but it was the description of the Nutburger that had me planning a trip almost immediately.

In 1930, after a visit to Southern California, Matt Korn returned home and opened a small drive-up burger stand only a few feet from a

busy railroad right-of-way. After a few years of hanging trays on car doors, Matt built a structure twenty-five feet away that would serve as a drive-in, a counter with sixteen stools, and living quarters upstairs for him and his new wife, Betty. That structure still stands today, a vestige of car culture stuck in time that was placed on the National Register in 2002.

In 1936, Mabel Laurence started as a carhop at Matt's, and in 1943, she and her husband bought the restaurant. Many people from "Mae's" family have worked at the vintage burger counter over the decades and for thirty years her son-in-law, Brad Cockhill, ran the place. When Mae passed in 2013, Brad and wife Robin (Mae's daughter) assumed ownership. Brad and Robin are proud of their family's heritage and committed to quality burgers.

Matt's is split in two; one half is a horseshoe counter, the other an efficient short-order kitchen. A server works the counter while Brad flips patties at the freestanding griddle in the kitchen. "This is the original cast-iron griddle from the 1930s," Brad told me, "There's nothing like cast iron." He's right. Very few burger restaurants in America cook on vintage cast iron because they are impossible to find.

Brad uses an ice-cream scoop to make balls out of the fresh, lean ground round. When I asked Brad about the size of the burgers, he shrugged and showed me the scoop. "They're this big. We should probably have better portion control, but we don't." Brad believes the burgers are around a quarter pound each.

The most popular burger at Matt's is the double cheeseburger deluxe, which comes with mustard, pickle, onion, lettuce, and tomato. But do yourself a favor and indulge in a Nutburger.

"We don't really sell many Nutburgers anymore," a former employee told me once. "Maybe six a day?" Just then the phone rang and in came an order for two Nutburgers.

The counterperson spoons chopped salted peanuts from the sundae bar into a coffee mug and adds Miracle Whip. It's that simple. The texture of the nuts and the creamy sweetness of the Miracle Whip synthesize perfectly with the salty, greasy meatiness of the burger. Standard condiments are available to dress up the Nutburger, but why mess with the simplicity? I understand if you are a little squeamish at the concept, but after your first bite, you'll be a convert.

The interior of Matt's is worth the price of admission alone. Grab a seat at the small horseshoe counter and take in the decor. You'll be hard-pressed to find a single fixture not dating back to the 1950s. Everything, from the knotty pine walls to the Coke dispenser, is original. Even the cash register dates back to simpler times—it only goes up to five dollars, so they have to ring up big orders five dollars at a time.

A carhop at Matt's will still take your order from your car if you drive up and toot your horn. "We'll still go out and hang a tray on a window," Brad told me as he dumped out a basket of fresh-cut fries. The carhop service continues at Matt's because as Brad explained, "Some people think it's too fancy to go inside to eat."

THE MISSOULA CLUB

139 West Main St | Missoula, MT 59802
406-728-3740 | Open Daily 10 am–2 am (Grill Closes At 1 am)

The Missoula Club is not the only bar in town. In fact, there are more great bars and vintage neon signage in this western Montana town than I've ever seen in such close proximity to one another. Having ten thousand students at the nearby University of Montana probably helps, but the Missoula Club is a local institution that has been serving beer and burgers to students and regulars, some believe, since 1903.

If you were expecting a cozy, dark pub, you'll be shocked by the Missoula Club's first impression. During the day, the "Mo Club" (as it's affectionately known) looks like any well-worn watering hole, but at night the daylight seems to linger. Thanks to superbright bluish overhead fluorescent lighting, the place is lit up like an operating room in the midst of surgery. There's no hiding at the Mo Club, and the lighting allows one to observe every detail of the bar. The lighting also seems to make patrons overly sociable, so expect to be involved in a random conversation with a stranger almost immediately. The first time I visited the famous burger and beer destination, I walked in with my friend Greg Ennis and we were greeted by a group of rugby players and a boisterous "Hello, LADIES!" It's a rowdy, drinker's bar that serves great burgers. You have been warned.

The burger at the Mo Club is legendary. "The hamburger is the best thing on the menu!" the bartender told me. Of course the joke is that the hamburger is the only thing on the menu, aside from chips and milkshakes.

Tell the bartender what kind of burger you want. The choices are single, double, or the absurd triple known as the "Griz" (named after the University of Montana's sports teams, the Grizzlies). American, swiss, "white," horseradish, and hot pepper cheeses are available and the burger is served with a slice of raw onion and a pickle. The preferred burger at the Mo Club is the double with hot pepper cheese, a tasty pepper jack that doesn't really melt, but softens on the burger. Add some of the Mo Club's signature hot mustard and you'll be in burger heaven. As my friend Greg, a Montana native, squirted copious amounts of the fiery mustard onto his double cheeseburger, grillman Tyler warned, "Whoa, have you had this mustard before?" Greg just laughed, and said, "Oh yeah, the hotter the better!"

Soft white buns are toasted on the tiny electric bar griddle alongside the burgers. I asked Tyler if the buns were buttered and he told me, "No, but the burger grease might work its way over there."

The burgers at the Mo Club are hand-pattied from unmeasured scoops of ground beef. The beef comes in fresh daily from the same butcher they have been using forever. One time while I was at the Mo Club, a man rushed in and dropped

two enormous white paper–wrapped wads of fresh meat on the bar right next to me. They had run low and needed to augment the meat supply before the night crowd showed up hungry.

"Our burgers are over a third of a pound each," former owner Mark Laslovich said of the large, juicy patties. Mark also revealed that the amazing tasting burger has chopped onions mixed into the raw meat before they are pattied. Mark has owned the century-old bar since 2000, but has worked there at some capacity for over forty-five years. One of the recent changes Mark made at the Mo Club was installing a larger griddle. Well, not too much larger. "This one's a burger wider than the old one," Mark said of the tiny two-foot-wide griddle.

In 2016, two brothers, Beau and Colt Anderson, bought the Mo from Laslovich. Bo runs the daily operations while Colt is currently pursuing a pro football career with the Buffalo Bills.

Expect to find all types enjoying burgers and beer at the Mo Club. "We get lawyers, doctors, bums, whatever," Mark once pointed out. There is an old-school sports bar feel to the place, but not the kind that hangs gaudy memorabilia on every usable inch of wall space. The Mo Club's walls are blanketed with decades of UM team photos up to the high ceiling as well as signed sports portraits of Missoula natives who went on to professional fame elsewhere in America.

I asked Mark why the lighting was more conducive to a well-lit truck stop than a cozy Irish pub and he explained, "People come in here and look for themselves in these team photos." He and the other bartenders also believe it keeps people honest and the fights to a minimum. Mark told me that a group of women who frequent the bar once asked him to install a dimmer because they were getting older. His advice: "Have another beer."

NEBRASKA

BOB'S BAR

5205 Main St | Ponca, NE 68770
402-945-2995 | Open Daily 7 am–10 pm

Within minutes of driving west of Sioux City, Iowa, you are into the rolling hills of eastern Nebraska. As corn fields and grain silos whiz past (it's a beautiful drive) you begin to wonder, *Where is this burger joint*? As you turn onto the dusty main street of "downtown" Martinsburg, Bob's Bar is pretty obvious. It's the only functioning business in, what looks like, an abandoned town. The building itself doesn't look like much and is in need of a coat of paint. But as experience has told me this is where great burger discoveries are made.

The first time I visited Bob's, I pulled up to the restaurant at lunchtime. Two farmers getting out of a pickup truck next to me, after spying my rental car's Florida plates, said with a smile, "You're pretty far from home!" Inside I was clearly an interloper. The place has a community center feel with random tables, mismatched chairs, and dim overhead fluorescent lighting. There's a pool table just inside the front door and a very worn wood-grain Formica bar with a handful of stools. Every single patron was a farmer or a mechanic sporting dusty sweatshirts and mesh-backed caps. They were focused on one thing—lunch. Then, as if a bell went off, the men all paid (some by personal check) and left at once, back to work. It was then that Bob's daughter, Bobbi Lamprecht, walked over to say hello. "Got 'em all fed," she said. Bobbi wears a few hats at Bob's but mostly she cooks all of the meals at lunch and, though she downplays it, she's the future owner of Bob's when dad is ready to sell. "I'm like SpongeBob—I'm just a fry cook," Bobbi joked.

The building dates back to the 1940s when it was Dowling's Bar, owned by Bob's in-laws. In 1976, Bob bought the restaurant, changed the name to his own, and put the famous "Big Burger" on the menu.

Simply put, the Big Burger lives up to its name. It's huge. Designed for large appetites, the burger starts as a 10.5-ounce wad of fresh ground beef that is pressed flat and wide on a flattop griddle. It's served with nothing more than raw onion and pickles on the side. The patty-to-bun ratio is part of the shock appeal and looks absurd because the meat hangs way outside the bun. The first few bites are bunless, but then I was told I was doing it all wrong. "A lot of people use the fork," Bobbi told me, "They cut the edge off, eat that first." Now that makes sense, and explains the fork protruding from under the burger.

One curious and tasty item on the menu at Bob's are the Cheese Balls. "I don't think he can take a whole order," Bobbi said to a regular with me listening. She gave me half an order and it was still a pound of deep fried cheese. Apparently two pounds of fried cheese is a perfectly normal order.

The burger has a deeply beefy essence that may be a result of the very seasoned griddle. When I asked Bobbi what she did to the burger to make it taste so good, she shrugged and said, "Nothing. I just cook it."

At nighttime, it's a very different place. The regulars show up as do "city people" and Bob is on the griddle three nights a week. "We get people from all over," Bobbi told me, especially when a bike tour or motorcycle group rolls in. On a Friday night, it's standing room only at Bob's. "It gets crazy," Bobbi told me.

"This is it," Bobbi said of the tiny East Nebraska town. When you roll into town, look for the 7Up sign over the door where the painted BOB'S BAR is barely legible. If you are not from these parts, be brave and get in there for Big Burger. As Bobbi pointed out, "Everyone is welcome."

STELLA'S BAR & GRILL

106 South Galvin Rd | Bellevue, NE 68005 | 402-291-6088
Mon–Sat 11 am–9 pm | Closed Sun | www.stellasbarandgrill.com

When I first found this burger outpost sixteen years ago south of Omaha, it was a ramshackle place on a hill surrounded by a dusty, gravel parking lot. You could barely make out the name of the restaurant haphazardly spelled out in vinyl lettering on the front window. Today, the parking lot is paved and the entire restaurant has received a much needed face-lift. In 2007, Stella's son, Al, and his wife, Mary, sold the decades-old restaurant to their relative, Stephanie Francois. The restaurant is now run by Stephanie with the help of her parents Gene and Pam Francois. Stella's Hamburgers remains in the same family after all these years.

Tiny Stella Francois Sullivan Tobler opened the sunroom at the front of her home to burger lovers in 1936. Within a few years, her home had morphed into a restaurant with a gas station and a general store. She purchased the bar next door, and in 1949, purchased a plot of land a mile away and moved the bar to its current location. The bar became a restaurant, and the house and sunroom went back to being a home.

The burgers have increased in size since Stella's time from 5.2 to 6.5 ounces. Fresh ground beef is delivered to the restaurant, portioned, and made into thick patties daily. Frozen patties are not an option at Stella's and as Gene pointed out,

"We go through so much that it would be impossible for it not to be fresh."

The most popular burger at here is Stella's Staple, which comes with cheese, lettuce, tomato, pickles, onion, mayo, bacon, and a fried egg on top. Because the burger is thick and loaded you'll need to slightly compress it to fit into your mouth. The burger is still delivered, as it has been since day one, on a paper napkin, not a plate. Stella believed that good food didn't need to be fancy.

The menu has expanded since the days of Al and Mary and a new burger "challenge" has been added called the "Stellanator." If you can finish this six-patty burger (which stands over a foot tall), you'll get your name on the "Wall of Fame" and eat for free. If you can't finish, you'll have to pay for your meal. "Over 550 have tried," Gene told me, "but only 26 have finished it so far."

Stephanie knew from a very young age that she would one day own Stella's. "I always wanted it," she told me recently, "since High School." Al said he would never sell the place, but if he did it would only be to family. Along came Stella's great-great niece, Stephanie, at the young age of twenty-four and the rest is history.

The beautiful renovation saved Stella's but did not come without a price. Most of the things that had been grandfathered into the old restaurant were tossed out and Stephanie had to basically start over. "It was a rough time and a huge risk to reopen," she told me, but they made it so on October 30, 2007. "We almost didn't make it," Pam confessed, "I don't know how we made it through the first few weeks and we didn't have a clue what we were doing." As it goes with best laid plans, Al was not feeling well the week Stella's reopened and he had promised to come in and help train the staff. "Al had to train by phone," Pam remembered.

But the customers returned, and today, it's not uncommon to find a line out the door into the parking lot. Stella's is now a vibrant, welcoming place where you'll find families and Little League teams alike. In the old days, it was a more select crowd with not many women around. Stella's today may look very different but rest assured the same cast-iron griddle and practices are in place.

Stephanie may be the living embodiment of the restaurant's namesake. Clearly there is something in the Francois DNA. Stephanie loves to be in the restaurant greeting people. She knows everyone that walks in, which is a trait she apparently shares with the late Stella. Then I met Don, sitting at a stool at the bar. "He gets more free drinks than any pretty woman," Pam pointed out. Don is a World War II vet that comes in for a beer twice a day and Stephanie and the crew treat him like family. Don told me, "I have to come in or they worry about me!"

GILLEY'S PM LUNCH

175 Fleet St | Portsmouth, NH 03801
603-431-6343 | Mon–Sun 11 am–2 am | www.gilleyspmlunch.com

"You can always tell that it's someone's first time here when they pull the door like that," short-order chef Bambi once told me. I had trouble getting in the front door of this six-decade-old diner because the door is not normal. Look for the word *slide* printed on the door and you are in business. It's a pocket door that slides open to reveal one of the most beautiful hidden gems in all of New England.

Gilley's PM Lunch is an old Worcester diner. In the first half of the twentieth century, the Worcester Lunch Car Company of Worcester, Massachusetts, was the premier supplier of mobile lunch carts and prefabricated diners. Their distinct design set the precedent for all diners that followed in America.

Gilley's is now permanently situated on a lot donated by the City of Portsmouth, but prior to 1973 the cart was towed out to the center of town and served food to late-night workers and other hungry people until the wee hours of the morning. There was a time in America, especially in New England, when carts like this were everywhere at night. Many of them were Worcester diners and very few exist today. Gilley's is one of the last.

Though slightly modified, Gilley's retains its barrel-shaped roof and enamel-steel paneled interior, and its kitchen still occupies one narrow end of the car. It's a true step back in time with its tiny griddle and eight stools lining the wood-framed windows. Current co-owner Stephen Kennedy told me, "I had to take two stools out because it gets pretty crowded in here from 11 p.m. to 2 a.m." He says

sometimes over forty people are crammed into the tiny diner waiting for their hamburgers and hot dogs. During the late shift, Gilley's can move over five hundred burgers.

"Isn't that beautiful?" a customer said as he tilted his plate showing off his double cheeseburger. Both hamburgers and hot dogs are served at Gilley's; the hot dogs preceded the burgers by more than sixty years. Starting in 1912, the first owners had a horse-drawn cart with wooden wheels that sold mostly hot dogs. Hamburgers were introduced in the 1970s, and share equal popularity today.

The burger to order at Gilley's is a bacon double cheeseburger. Gilley's uses only fresh ground-pattied chuck loin that is 85 to 88 percent lean. The patties are small, thin, and just under three ounces. Stephen pointed out that it was done that way traditionally for speed, adding, "a smaller burger cooks faster." The white squishy bun is toasted and no lettuce or tomato is offered. The tiny fridge next to the minuscule two-foot-square griddle is really only big enough for the day's hot dogs, hamburgers, and cheese.

In 1996, Stephen and his wife, Gina, attached a construction trailer to the original lunch car to expand the kitchen. This allowed him to add a deep fryer and more refrigeration. Adding a barrel roof to one end of the trailer, mimicked the original structure and preserved the integrity of the restaurant. The last truck to pull the mobile diner is still attached to one end of Gilley's, as are the diner's wheels, now covered by wood paneling.

"Portsmouth is the kind of place where things don't change much," former cook Bambi mused as I ate my burger. That's a good thing, especially when it involves a historically significant slice of Americana like Gilley's. Thanks to people like Stephen and Gina, this tiny lunch cart will likely be around forever.

HOLIDAY SNACK BAR

401 Centre St | Beach Haven, NJ 08008 | 609-492-4544
Open Daily 11:30 am–9 pm | (Memorial Day Weekend To Labor Day)
www.holidaysnackbar.com

The ocean is only three blocks from the Holiday Snack Bar and you can smell it in the salty air. But once you step inside the tiny, seasonal beach diner the smell shifts to burgers. If you arrive at the peak of summer, there's a good chance that all of the stools at the counter will be taken. All of these customers, fresh from the beach, will be eating either burgers or one of the Holiday's signature cakes or pies. High school–aged server Hunter told me, "At lunchtime in the summer this place is packed. There are people up against the wall waiting for a spot." Most likely this is because the burgers are fresh and the bakery is on the premises.

A large, four-sided knotty pine counter takes up just about all of the real estate in the dining area of the Holiday. In the center, proudly displayed, are homemade pies and cakes that all counter patrons are forced to stare at, making a meal without a slice an impossibility. The kitchen adjacent to the dining area is where most of the menu is produced but in one corner of the dining room sits a tiny two-by-three-foot flattop griddle. There's even a stool at the counter that can't be more than three feet from the griddle, a great front-row seat for the burger-obsessed. "In August, the griddle is jammed," owner Glenn Warfield told me. Glenn and his wife are only the third owners of this Jersey Shore landmark that was opened in 1948 by the Whiting family. Glenn bought the restaurant in the '80s and with the purchase gained the Holiday's famous recipes.

Glenn is adamant about preserving the history of the Holiday Snack Bar and is hesitant to change a single thing about the place. One curious phenomenon I noticed at the Holiday was a dual menu system. If you ask for a menu, you are handed one whose contents, for the most part, date to 1948. It includes classics like onion rings and burgers but also a strange old-time favorite, the Tomato Aspic Salad. Glenn has added items to the menu but did not want to add them to the original so he posts these items on a separate menu on the counter. I asked him why he hasn't merged the menus and he told me, "We don't want to stir it up too much."

The classic "Holiday Hamburger" is not the burger to order at the Holiday Snack Bar. Ask for that and you'll end up with an unadorned three-ounce patty on a toasted white bun. Ask for the double cheeseburger and you are getting somewhere. The ratio of meat-to-cheese-to-bun for this burger is perfect. Be sure to add some housemade sweet pepper relish that sits on the counter in plastic tubs.

One item on Glenn's separate menu sells as well as the burgers from the original menu—the "Slam Burger." Lettuce, tomato, and a large onion ring are piled high on a single-patty cheeseburger. A homemade Russian dressing is added and the entire creation is held together with a large toothpick. As you can probably imagine, the additional ingredients dwarf the three-ounce patty so I would suggest a double Slam Burger.

The burgers at the Holiday are made from fresh ground 90/10 lean chuck. A team of two use an ancient manual patty press to make the burgers. It's easy to assume that this contraption predates the electric patty press. I've never seen anything quite like it. A large canister holds fifteen pounds of ground beef that is extruded through a hole in the bottom. One person hand-cranks the press while the other slides a plate back and forth on the bottom that has a cutout the size of the patty, effectively "slicing" off a perfect patty every time. Glenn is clearly in the market for a new, fully automated patty press but I don't think he'll be getting one anytime soon. He told me, "We've paid mechanics to fix it." Glenn does not want to change a thing about the Holiday Snack Bar.

The Holiday is run almost entirely by high school and college kids and this is their summer job. When I asked Hunter if she sees orders for the Tomato Aspic Salad, she winced and said, "Never." Then after a moment said, "The people who do order it go crazy for it. But most people come here for the burgers."

KRUG'S TAVERN

118 Wilson Ave | Newark, NJ 07105 | 973-465-9795 | Mon-Thurs 11 am-10 pm
Fri & Sat 11 am-11 pm | Sun 12 pm-9 pm | www.krugstavern.com

"Before the contest not everybody knew about us," grillman of almost 20 years Rui told me. He was talking about the coveted *NJ.com* Best Burger in the New Jersey award. This under-the-radar bar burger received the award in 2015 and from his vantage at the griddle Rui pointed out, "We are definitely on everyone's radar now!" The 86-year-old tavern is in the multi-ethnic Ironbound neighborhood, so called because this part of Newark, east of downtown, is bordered by train tracks.

The ownership of Krug's has remained in the same family since opening day in 1932. Frank Krug (pronounced "KROOG") ran the Tavern until he passed it onto his daughter Edna in the 1950s. She married Casper LaMotta (a first cousin of the famous World Champion boxer Jake LaMotta, aka "Raging Bull") and they ran the place until the Tavern went to LaMotta's sons Frank and Gary. The brothers both worked full-time as local corrections officers in New Jersey while maintaining the tavern, but when Gary passed in 1998 Frank lost interest in the day-to-day at Krug's. Gary's wife Ellen LaMotta, also an owner, now runs the restaurant with her daughter Joyce.

"I just got engaged!" the bubbly, upbeat Joyce told me. She is in the restaurant just about every day and spends five of those days on the flattop. "I didn't think I'd be flipping burgers for a living," she said smiling, then added, "But this is my full-time baby. My mom keeps asking when she can have a grandchild and I tell her 'Krug's is your grandchild'!"

The famous Bacon Cheeseburger is the way to go at Krug's. It's a beast and uncooked the patty alone weighs in at twelve ounces. Start adding cheese and condiments and this thing will easily get to around a hefty one pound in weight. Krug's gets their beef, fresh ground 80/20, from a local butcher and portions it into round balls the size of grapefruit. The patty is compressed slightly into a burger shape on the beautiful cast-iron skillet which dates back more than fifty years. Surprisingly no seasoning is added to the patty, likely because all of the day's bacon is cooked on the flattop before opening, every day. Joyce pondered,

"If it wasn't for that griddle I don't think they would taste as good."

Ask for cheese and your burger gets three slices because, as Joyce explained, "You have to get the cheese-to-beef ratio right . . . It's a big burger." Yes, it's huge, and good luck eating it. Most likely it will not fit in your face, even after compressing it a bit. Because of its thickness, the burger literally explodes with copious juices, which will run down your arm. Practice the art of the lean to keep your clothes clean. I saw a regular tuck his necktie into his shirt to avoid ruining it. He said to me, "The Krug's Tuck." Then admitted, "I just made that up."

The ultra-efficient kitchen behind the bar, with its flattop, deli slicer, fridge, and dishwasher, can handle the entire menu at Krug's. It takes up half of the real estate behind the beautiful and original hardwood bar, which when busy is staffed with four. "We do it all," Joyce said of the bar staff, where they engage in a sort of dance back there, constantly avoiding collision. It's an open kitchen where there are no secrets. "You can see what we are doing," Rui pointed out. Clearly there's nothing to hide.

"We were an old dive bar," Joyce told me, "but when we remodeled a few years ago it really took off." So thanks to their new wave of fame expect a 1½ hour wait for a seat at night or on weekends. And once you've sat and ordered the menu warns of a half hour wait for the burgers themselves. Of course, the wait is well worth it. Belly up to bar, grab a beer, check out the signed Jake LaMotta boxing glove behind the bar, and by all means stay hungry.

ROSSI'S BAR & GRILL

2110 Whitehorse-Mercerville Rd | Hamilton Township, NJ 08619
609-890-2004 | Mon–Sun 11 am–11 pm | www.rossisbarandgrill.com

"Now we'll see if he knows how to eat a Rossi-burger!" Sharon Jemison, now-retired owner and Rossi family member, was heckling me and warned, "If you cut it in half, you're a wuss." As I stared at the enormous, inch-thick burger, I did the smart thing—I put the knife down.

Most great burger joints have their share of multigenerational family pride, but few are as proud as Rossi's. Throw in an Italian American pedigree and you have a recipe for a burger born of unrelenting pride.

In the early 1930s, Michael Alfred Rossi bought a corner soda fountain in the Italian neighborhood of Chambersburg in Trenton, New Jersey, and lived upstairs. When prohibition was repealed in 1933, Rossi promptly turned the fountain into a bar. "Back then," Sharon told me, "they just had a meatball sandwich [on the menu]." Rossi eventually expanded the menu to include other Italian fare and made a dining room out of the family's living space. But it was Michael's son, Alfred Michael Rossi, who would bring their now-famous burger to the menu in the early 1960s.

Al Rossi had a promising career in professional baseball and played for the Washington Senators farm team for eleven years. Just as he was offered a spot on the Philadelphia Athletics roster, his brother shipped off to fight in World War II.

Al's dad told him to leave baseball, come home, and help run the restaurant. In this family, that's just what you did.

Maybe if Al Rossi had continued on his path to be a major league ballplayer there would be no Rossiburger, a thought most would probably not like to entertain.

There's only one burger to order at Rossi's and it is very large and only comes in one size. "That's the million-dollar question, 'Can we get a smaller burger?'" Sharon told me once years ago, "Nope."

Don't be put off by the enormous mound of meat in front of you, though. Despite its size, the burger at Rossi's is moist and loosely packed, its center almost pebbly. It's actually a breeze to eat, especially if you are hungry.

Rossi's gets a delivery of fresh ground 87/13 chuck daily and can go through 250 pounds over the weekend. The burgers are unmeasured but are around a half pound. They are loosely hand-pattied and cooked by indirect heat in a steak broiler called a Salamander. Nothing is added, no salt, no pepper, and it's served on a freshly baked kaiser roll with nothing but a slice of raw onion.

Just about everyone involved at Rossi's is family. Sharon told me once, "When we run out of family, we pull in other people." Today, Rossi's is run by

Al's son, Michael, and Sharon has retired but still visits often.

If you are wondering why the place looks so new it's because in 2014 Sharon and Michael Rossi sold the original location and built a freestanding restaurant ten minutes away in Hamilton. "Most of the Italian families and restaurants have relocated to Hamilton Township," Michael explained. Chambersburg has changed over the years to a vibrant Hispanic neighborhood so the Rossi family sold to a couple who opened an Argentine restaurant. The new version of Rossi's is much larger but the layout is similar. The four-sided bar is the first thing you

see when you walk in the front door but instead of the original 70-seat dining room the capacity has grown to 240. The capacity of the Salamander changed as well, from the original that could cook eight at a time to now thirty. The burger made the move intact and nothing about it has changed. And a great touch, right inside the front door, the family re-created the original front window of the old location complete with painted lettering, red-and-white-striped awning and the signature red neon flourish.

Thanks to his involvement with professional baseball, Al Rossi had an impressive roster of buddies. Joe DiMaggio was a frequent visitor, as were Mickey Mantle and Ted Williams. Joe D

didn't go to Rossi's for the burger, though, he went to see his good friend Al and have a bowl of his lentil soup. The restaurant is filled with authentic baseball memorabilia and the bar evokes a time when baseball greats might have mingled freely with their fans. For years, a pair of Mickey Mantle's cleats that were given to Al hung in a corner of the dining room.

Al worked at Rossi's right up until the day before he died in 2007. "He loved it," Sharon recalled of her father. "People came here just to talk to him." Al was involved with the business his entire life and, according to Sharon, "He'd see a pasta dish go out that wasn't right and he'd send it back."

WHITE MANNA HAMBURGERS

358 River Rd | Hackensack, NJ 07601 | 201-342-0914
Mon–Wed 8 am–9 pm | Thurs–Sat 8 am–11:30 pm | Sunday 10 am–6 pm

White Manna is, beyond a doubt, one of the most historically important burger joints in America. As the burger business began widespread franchising in the 1960s, most of the tiny burger counters across America were wiped out. Amazingly, White Manna survives and thrives, even with a McDonald's directly across the street.

There was a time in America when the burgers you ate were small and came from a tiny stainless-steel or white porcelain–paneled diner. Thanks to the success of White Castle in America, most burger counters used the word *white* in their names to convey cleanliness. In the case of this diner, the biblical word *manna* is used, as in bread from heaven.

White Manna is a vintage Paramount diner that still proudly serves the early-century American classic "slider" burger. The diner is the descendant of the 1939 World's Fair "Diner of the Future" that was built to represent the future of fast food. The original White Manna was purchased by Louis Bridges and brought to Jersey City, where it remains today. Louis built four other White Mannas around northern New Jersey, but only the Hackensack and Jersey City locations survive. Inside and out, the tiny diner remains true to its original design. The structure is sheathed in stainless steel, has vertical white porcelain panels beneath the windows, and includes Paramount Diner Company's signature use of glass block throughout.

The interior cannot be more than 130 square feet. Behind a small horseshoe counter surrounded by stools, a short-order cook takes one order after the next, never putting pen to paper. You sit patiently, taking in the thick oniony aroma, until the cook makes *eye contact* with you. When you place your order, the cook reaches into a pan below the counter, grabs golf ball–sized balls of meat, presses them onto the tiny griddle, and places a wad of thinly sliced onion on top. If you ask for a double, two of the small balls of beef get pressed together. The cook uses a right-to-left system on the griddle to keep track and miraculously keeps all of the orders straight. Similar to the original White Castle system, buns are placed atop the cooking burgers to steam and soak up the onion essence.

The sliders are served on soft potato rolls on a paper plate with a pile of pickle chips. If you order cheese, expect not a picture-perfect burger, but a glorious pile of tangled beef, onions, and cheese that is barely contained by its bun. The burgers at White Manna may not look pretty, but they sure are delicious. You'll need more than a few sliders to fill you up. Order doubles to accomplish a better beef-to-bun ratio.

Ronny and Ofer Cohen bought the Hackensack White Manna in 1986 as a business venture, but were also seduced by its charm. "You just fall in love with this place," Ronny told me. They have changed very little about the White Manna, but admitted an attempt to add potato salad and coleslaw to the menu early on in their ownership. "People walk into White Manna to buy burgers." Ronny feels the crush of commercial fast food all around him in Hackensack, New Jersey. "The only way I can survive is to do things the old-fashioned way."

Before walking into White Manna, strip down to the least amount of clothing. Not because it's hot in there, but because after you leave, your clothes will be infused with the unmistakable fragrance of grease and onions. There'll be no hiding the fact that you just dined at the famous White Manna.

SLIDER VS. THE MINIBURGER: THERE IS A DIFFERENCE

Chances are you've heard of both the slider and the miniburger, and probably wondered what the difference was, if any at all. Hamburger cognoscenti have argued the topic ad nauseam, and the conclusion is that, YES, of course there is a difference! The time has come to set the record straight.

A miniburger is exactly what it sounds like—a tiny version of the classic American patty-cheese-and-bun combination. It's a scale-model reproduction that could even be called "cute" due to its shrunken proportions. Miniburgers are usually found at fancy parties, where they're served as passed hors d'oeuvres; they are rarely any good. By the time a miniburger has been fussed over in the catering kitchen, placed on a tray, and paraded around a party, it has become cold and lifeless. Few have figured out the science behind the perfect miniburger, and some of the best I've had were served at high-end restaurants as an appetizer. They are usually served three to an order, which calls into question their usefulness: Why not just get a full-sized burger and call it a day? Miniburgers are difficult to produce because the cook must work in miniature—all of the proper elements are a fraction of their normal size, including cooking times.

A slider is far more than the sum of its parts, and is arguably the most historically significant burger ever created. It is a confluence of method, history, and flavor. It bears the weight of one hundred years of proletarian sustenance—a simple comfort food for the wage earners of America. It is considered the original hamburger, the one that begat all that followed. Yes, this is that burger, and it crushes the influence of the miniburger to bits.

For starters, the slider is a small burger. To qualify, its patty size is a diminutive 1.5 to 2 ounces. Ask for "double meat" at a classic burger joint, and you'll get just that—two tiny balls of fresh ground beef pressed into approximately one three-ounce patty. The slider bun is an uncomplicated, white squishy bun that, in most cases, finds itself on or near the griddle, warming to a supple softness. Sometimes the buns are actually placed directly atop the sizzling patty to steam directly. Which brings me to cooking method: Sliders are cooked only one way—smashed thin on a flattop griddle. The most authentic sliders have thinly sliced or diced onion pressed into the patty at the outset, usually applied with a stiff spatula and some muscle. As the onion cooks, sweet liquid is released directly into the patty, min-

gling with the rendered beef to create a flavor profile unique to the roots of American gastronomy.

There are various accounts of the slider's etymology; one common one points to their ability to "slide" down your throat. Another version I've come across is that in the early days of hamburgers, short-order cooks at tiny burger joints would "slide" a plate of burgers down the counter to a waiting customer, a flourish that helped define the nature of fast food.

Today, authentic sliders that contain the DNA of the original can still be found all over America at places like Power's Hamburgers in Fort Wayne, Indiana; the Cozy Inn in Salina, Kansas; and White Manna in New Jersey, among others. Walking into these places is a complete time warp because things rarely change in real slider emporiums.

Sorry I didn't give equal space here to the miniburger. Frankly, it doesn't deserve it. To call yourself a true American, put down that miniburger and go find a slider.

WHITE ROSE SYSTEM

1301 East Elizabeth Ave | Linden, NJ 07036
908-486-9651 | Mon–Sat 5 am–4 pm | Closed Sun

At one time in north Jersey the slider reigned supreme. As the homogenization of burger culture in America swept over the tri-state area, the tiny slider emporiums started to disappear. Many of these gleaming, stainless-steel-and-porcelain diners had the word *white* in their names no doubt as a nod to the most famous slider joint of them all—White Castle. Places like White Diamond, White Manna, and White Tower were all trying to share the limelight with the more successful Wichita chain. What's incredible is that after all of these years, unlike White Castle, the places that survived have remained virtually unchanged and still serve the same classic slider that they always have. So if you really want to see what White Castle was like back in the day, you'll need to drop into a place like White Rose System in Linden, New Jersey.

The idea of a "system" in hamburgers was basically started by White Castle as a way to promote the uniformity of the product. Today, there are a few White Rose Systems in north Jersey but they are all owned separately. The Linden White Rose, according to the authority on Jersey sliders, Nick Solares, may be the best example. The first time I ate there with him I heard him quietly exclaim, "This is a great fucking hamburger," and he is absolutely right.

The White Rose sits on the edge of residential Linden on an industrial stretch that used to be dotted with automotive shops. "This used to be body shop row," Rich said. Rich has owned the White Rose since 1992 when he purchased the diner from Jack and Bobby Hemmings, the family that started the minichain. The White Rose was moved to this location at some point in 1967, its origins unknown.

The menu has expanded slightly since Rich took over, but the original griddle still sees its share of sliders. Rich uses the same local butcher that he has for years, whose 75/25 ground beef comes from steak trimmings. They arrive in two-ounce wads of beef that Rich presses thin on the flattop. You can order a "slider," which is one wad, or a "large," which is two wads pressed together. There is also a quarter-pound burger on the menu (three wads) that's served on a very soft Kaiser roll. Although it tastes amazing, I go to White Rose for the large slider, which has the best beef-to-bun ratio. The burger is served with a pile of pickle slices on the side on a small porcelain plate.

After the wads have been pressed, Rich tosses some thin-cut onion onto the patty. When the patty is flipped, the onions cook into the burger and both halves of a white squishy bun are placed on top to steam. The result is

a soft, hot, simple burger that explodes with onion flavor.

The burgers at White Rose, with caramelized onions and gooey cheese, basically melt in your mouth. It really makes you concentrate on the simplicity of these elements and wonder why so many chefs overthink the hamburger. This slider, for me, is hamburger perfection.

Rich grew up in the restaurant business and you could say that owning a classic lunch counter was his destiny. "After college I was looking for something other than sitting in an accounting office," he told me with a smile. But his father, who had owned five luncheonettes in north Jersey, may have been a major influence. Rich told me that when he was a kid, "Every chance I got, I worked there. I loved it."

In 2010, White Rose became the subject of a *CBS Sunday Morning* episode with Bobby Flay. After the show aired, the tiny, out-of-the-way diner started to get visitors from near and far. Rich was so perplexed by the influx of new customers that he started keeping a log. "We have been getting people from all over." He then pointed to a regular at the counter named Teddy and continued, "But these are my friends. Teddy has been coming here for eighteen years," and Teddy nodded quietly. "I think that's why I have been successful."

NEW MEXICO

SANTA FE BITE

311 Old Santa Fe Trail | Santa Fe, NM 87501 | 505-982-0544 | Tues–Fri 11 am–9 pm
Sat 8 am–9 pm | Sun 8 am–8 pm | Closed Mon | www.santafebite.com

The Bobcat Bite is no longer, another sad victim of selfishness and greed, but I'm happy to report that the spirit of the Bobcat has been salvaged thanks, of course, to New Mexico's first couple of the Green Chile Cheeseburger, John and Bonnie Eckre.

The Bobcat used to be a destination burger on the long, lonely Old Las Vegas Highway miles from Santa Fe proper. The tiny adobe structure sat on a rocky washboard incline at the foot of what once was a large quarter-horse ranch. The interior was cozy with a low viga ceiling and a large picture window that looked onto the rolling hills of New Mexico and a very active hummingbird feeder. The place was perfection, and they just happened to serve one of the greatest burgers in the world.

But as we know, all good things must come to an end. For most of us this one ended far too soon. A rent hike and an ownership disagreement forced John and Bonnie into a very tough decision, and in 2013 they shut down the sixty-year-old Bobcat and reopened a few months later as the Santa Fe Bite.

The cute eight-stool restaurant with five tables out in countryside has been replaced by a 130-seat restaurant right in the heart of Santa Fe. The thrill of the long drive out to the little adobe joint is gone, but thankfully their famous, award-winning Green Chile Burger survived intact.

John and Bonnie were dating when he, a contractor at the time, was doing some work with the then owners of the Bobcat Bite Bob & Judy Amos. One day "Big Bob," who was always on the griddle, had a heart attack and Judy asked John to jump in and cook. A few months passed, and John, realizing that he had to get back to contracting, convinced the Amos family to hire his girlfriend. Nine years later, Bob and Judy wanted to sell and looked to Bonnie. She and John were married at this point and they jumped at the chance. John left his life in construction and never looked back.

The first big change John made to the menu was to improve the quality of the burger. "Big Bob used cheap beef," John told me. "I wouldn't eat it." He told Bonnie he planned to make the best burger in America and set out to do so. The rest is history and today John's Green Chile Cheeseburger is arguably the best one out there. Almost two decades of "Best of" awards and tens of thousands of happy customers have proven this point.

Green Chile is indigenous to New Mexico and some of the best comes from Hatch, a town in the southern part of the state. It's a pepper similar to, but far more complex than, the Anaheim pepper. When roasted, the skin falls away revealing a unique flesh that when stewed and placed on a cheeseburger is absolute ecstasy.

The Green Chile Cheeseburger at the Santa Fe Bite is a beauty. Roasted and diced green chiles are held in place atop a ten-ounce patty by a slice of melted white swiss/american cheese. John uses naturally raised antibiotic- and hormone-free beef from Clovis, New Mexico, for his burgers. The well-seasoned cast-iron griddle creates a crunchy exterior and leaves the interior perfectly moist. John is also a master of cooking temperatures, so if you ask for your burger medium-rare it'll be medium-rare. He employs a complex system of bacon weights to manage the different temperatures of the burgers.

I beg of you, please do not pollute this burger with ketchup and mustard. The simplicity of the Green Chile Cheeseburger should not be tampered with. The chiles, hot and flavorful, enhance the beefiness, creating one of the greatest marriages of flavors and textures in the burger world.

The Santa Fe Bite may not be the cute little diner it once was but the new location can't be

beat. In addition to eighty seats inside, the Bite has a fifty-seat porch with a view of the river and hubbub of beautiful downtown Santa Fe. And their new kitchen is enormous, "It's at least ten times larger," John told me. And with two seasoned cast-iron griddles (one brought over from Bobcat), they now have the ability to cook up to fifty burgers at the same time, and in most cases need to.

The Bobcat had a strange closing time of 7:50 p.m., which was related to an imposed curfew from decades ago, which gave you ten minutes to get home by 8 p.m. Today's Santa Fe Bite has normal, rounded-up closing times. John said the decision to make that change was easy because, "It mostly just pissed people off."

BOBCAT BITE COLESLAW

Makes a lot of coleslaw (this is a day's worth for the Bobcat)

1 head cabbage, shredded

1 green bell pepper, seeded and finely chopped

½ cup sugar

⅔ cup distilled white vinegar

¼ cup canola oil

¼ teaspoon salt

½ teaspoon ground black pepper

½ teaspoon celery seed

1 tablespoon ground mustard

1. Place the shredded cabbage and chopped pepper in a large bowl. Pour the sugar over the cabbage and pepper.

2. In a small saucepan bring the vinegar, oil, salt, black pepper, celery seed, and mustard to a boil. According to Bonnie, the smell of the boiling vinegar concoction will drive you out of the kitchen. Boil for 5 minutes and then pour the hot brew over the cabbage and peppers. Don't stir it yet! Allow it to cool before stirring. It will appear as if there isn't enough liquid to transform all that cabbage into the saucy coleslaw of your dreams, but trust me, it'll work.

3. When the bowl of slaw and dressing has cooled, mix the contents, cover, and refrigerate for at least 2 hours. Bonnie suggests allowing the slaw to marinate overnight for optimum flavor.

OWL BAR & CAFE

77 US 380 | San Antonio, NM 87832 | 575-835-9946 | Mon–Sat 8 am–8 pm
Closed Sun | (Drive-Thru Open Mon–Fri 7 am–12 pm) | www.sanantonioowl.com

The Owl Bar & Cafe seems an unlikely candidate for producing a world-famous burger. The bar sits at a crossroads deep in the dry desert of central New Mexico. Its adobe structure has barely a window and is one of only a handful on the main drag in the tiny town of San Antonio. Even though you have to wait until your eyes adjust after entering, and there is a large supply of booze behind the bar, the Owl is a friendly place, a family saloon with an excellent burger on the menu.

The Owl Burger is what many call the "other great green chile cheeseburger in New Mexico."

The first time I visited I drove 280 miles to eat this burger. Needless to say my expectations were high. I sat at the bar at 11 a.m. and watched as burger after burger was dispatched to the booths opposite the bar. Thankfully, mine showed up in only four minutes—the green chile aroma wafting through the air was making me very hungry.

All of the burgers are served on plastic plates with a napkin between the burger and the plate. Their famous green chile cheeseburger starts as a patty of fresh ground beef that has been pressed flat on a flattop griddle (the Owl grinds its own beef daily). Cheese, onion, tomato, mayo, and pickles are standard, and the green chiles pack a punch. They come from Hatch, New Mexico, and are lovingly prepared by Pinto, the kitchen prep cook. Pinto has been preparing the green chile for the Owl Bar for over forty-five years. "I think he's finally getting the hang of it," Owner Rowena Baca joked.

The clientele is a mix of silver-haired motor-home enthusiasts and servicemen in fatigues. The bar's entrance celebrates its proximity to the infamous Trinity Site, the spot where scientists tested the first atomic bomb only twenty-five miles away. Large photos of the mushroom cloud and other missile-site ephemera are proudly displayed. Frank Chavez opened the Owl Bar in 1945, just in time to accommodate the entertainment-starved scientists who were frequenting the area. At the request of these scientists, a griddle was installed and the Owl Burger was born.

The shelves of the bar are covered with hundreds of donated servicemen's uniform patches from all over the country. Rowena, Frank Chavez's daughter, started the collection years ago. "I told a cop I liked the patch on his uniform so he ripped it off and gave it to me," Rowena told me. "Since then, we get patches from everywhere."

Another item tacked to the walls is money. Tourists are encouraged to sign and donate a bill of their choice and pick a spot on the wall. Once a year the money is taken down, counted, and given to charity. The walls at Owl Bar have amassed sometimes over $5,000 a year, with the exception of the occasional late-night robbery. Rowena told me once, "I don't know how they got it off the walls so fast—it takes us forever."

THE PANTRY

1820 Cerrillos Rd | Santa Fe, NM 87505 | 505-986-0022
Mon–Sat 6:30 am–8:30 pm | Sun 7 am–8:30 pm | www.pantrysantafe.com

Any visit to Santa Fe, New Mexico, would not be complete without a stop at the Pantry. The small adobe structure on busy Cerrillos Road, with the vintage blue-and-yellow neon sign, is one of the oldest New Mexican diners in the state and serves totally authentic regional comfort food. The morning is when the Pantry hits its stride with legendary breakfast burritos smothered in green or red chile sauce. They serve excellent pancakes, huevos rancheros, and traditional New Mexican dishes like stuffed sopapillas and Frito Pie. But my favorite thing to order is their take on a local creation called the Tortilla Burger.

Legend has it that the Tortilla Burger showed up first around the corner at Maria's, another authentic institution that has been serving New Mexican food forever. The version at the Pantry is served all day and works well as breakfast, lunch, or dinner.

Red and green chile is indigenous to New Mexico and parts of neighboring states. It graces nearly every single menu in the state, and rarely found elsewhere. It is a defining ingredient in New Mexican cooking and is served either green or red. Green chile has a subtle earthy flavor whereas red chile (left on the vine to ripen after the initial fall harvest) has a deep, smoky essence. It is one of the most unique natural flavors in America.

New Mexican chile is not native to New Mexico and the story of how the pepper found its way to the region is fascinating. As Spanish Conquistadors colonized the Southwest in the sixteenth century they found the Native American diet bland. They brought peppers from Spain to spice things up and the course of the region's gastronomic fabric was forever altered.

The Tortilla Burger is one of the only burgers I'll eat with a fork and you'll have to as well. That's because the burger is served on a plate smothered in smoky, mildly spicy red chile sauce. It's not a traditional burger that you'd pick up with your hands; in fact, that would be impossible and you'd look ridiculous.

At the Pantry, a fresh beef patty is cooked over an indoor flame grill. The patty is then transferred to a waiting soft flour tortilla that has been prepped with a gob of shredded cheddar cheese and refried pinto beans. The tortilla is wrapped or folded, placed seamed-side down on a plate, smothered with a generous amount of housemade red chile sauce and more shredded cheddar. The plate then takes a trip to the broiler to turn the cheddar into gooey goodness. Sounds tasty? It's downright heavenly.

The Pantry was opened in 1948 by George Myers, who actually used what is now the back dining room as his residence. Today, the seventh owners of the Pantry are Stan Singley and his son, Michael. They consider themselves stewards of tradition and have changed very little about the place.

Tortilla Burgers are available all over the state today but I'm a big fan of the version at the Pantry. And it's not just because the burger tastes great, it's because you can tell that it's made with love. Sit at the counter and meet passionate locals who are proud of their state's official question, red or green (chile)? You may want to move to Santa Fe just to be closer to this authentic regional burger experience.

THE BLAZER PUB

440 Ny-22 | North Salem, NY 10560 | 914-277-4424 | Mon–Thurs 11 am–10:30 pm
Fri & Sat 11 am–11:30 pm | Sun 12 pm–10:30 pm | www.theblazerpub.com

Blazer Pub is up in the northern part of Westchester, where things are a little more spread out. The classic roadhouse is by itself on a stretch of Route 22 just south of Purdys, New York. Regardless of its semi-remote location (with zero foot traffic) if the restaurant is open the parking lot is often filled. "We're busy all of the time," waitress of thirty years Dina Tompkins told me recently. They come for the burgers mostly, or to hang at the bar with bartender of thirty-six years Tommy Hunt.

The Blazer has a reputation for being a very friendly place and that comes from the all-female waitstaff, many of whom have been at the pub for over twenty-five years. "We come, and we stay," waitress of 'only' twenty-two years Lisa Montini told me. "It's not only nice for the customers here," Dina added, "it's nice for us too."

After a string of businesses dating back over one hundred years the Blazer Pub opened in 1971 by Tom and Emer Heavey. The pub is named after group of Irish fox hunters dating back to the 1700s called the Galway Blazers. Legend has it that on one of the many hunts a celebration followed at a hotel in Dooley, Ireland. The revelers decided to commemorate the occasion by setting the hotel "ablaze," and the name Blazers stuck. The etymology for the men's coat with the same name likely comes from The Blazers, who still wear red coats when they hunt.

In 1988, Richard and Rita O'Leary bought the pub and changed very little. The O'Leary's have passed and today Alice O'Leary Kerrigan, part owner with her six siblings, runs the restaurant day-to-day.

The pub has a cozy, old-world Irish feel. It's a large rambling restaurant with separate rooms covered in dark-stained wainscoting, school pennants on the walls and Tiffany-style stained-glass lamps hanging from the ceiling. It's the kind of place a dad might take his son or daughter for their first real burger (and get a beer and watch the game).

Since opening day the pub has served an eight ounce fist of fresh ground 83/13 served on a no-nonsense white squishy bun, nothing fancy.

They are cooked on a flattop perfectly to temperature, delivered juicy. There are a few options, but head for the Celsus Burger (original owner Tom's mother's maiden name) and add grilled onions. The simple confluence of that fist of beef, caramelized sweet onion, bacon, and a cascade of gooey melted swiss is hard to beat. And once you start eating the thing, do NOT put it down—it's only a matter of time before the copious combination of elements go their separate ways and end up in your lap. The signature Blazer Burger comes on a harder Kaiser roll and you can ask for one for the Celsus too, but Dina told me, "People like the smaller bun. The hard roll takes away from the experience, you know?" She's right, embrace the struggle.

I wasn't going to have the soup (I rarely eat anything but burgers during "research"). Then I heard the magic words come out of Lisa's mouth, "Our cream of tomato and bacon soup is award winning, you really should try it!" The soup was so ridiculously good that I literally laughed out loud, hard, in disbelief. It was that good. In the beginning it was only on the menu one day a week. "People kept asking for it," Dina told me so they offer it every day now (though it's still not listed on the menu).

The bar is a beaut, a compact horseshoe surrounded by barstools, some vintage video games and a juke box. "There's nothing on that juke past 1986—that's Tommy for you," Mick, bartender on Sundays told me. Dina described the bar scene, with the Blazer Pub's diehard regulars in mind, as "like watching something out of [the TV sitcom] *Cheers.*"

Longtime bartender Tommy runs a benefit for a local charity leading up to St. Patrick's Day so expect to find the entire ceiling to be covered in hanging paper shamrocks, each one representing a cash donation. "He's raises over fifteen thousand dollars every year," Alice told me.

Because of its friendly family vibe and consistently good comfort food The Blazer gets its share of famous regulars like David Letterman and Martha Stewart, both of whom live nearby. But don't go there for star sightings. Go there because you know the burger, and the company, (and that damn *soup*) will be memorable.

BRENNAN & CARR

3432 Nostrand Ave | Brooklyn, NY 11229
(718) 769-1254 | Open Daily 11 am-12 am

Old-school Brennan & Carr looks out of place on the busy South Brooklyn corner of Nostrand Avenue and Avenue U. That's because it predates everything on the corner. When Brennan and Carr, both carpenters, built their roast beef sandwich restaurant in 1938 there was not much else around. But there it stands, eighty years later, as a testament to hard work and good food.

Walking into Brennan & Carr is a trip because you basically enter through the kitchen. The full-frontal assault of kitchen activity, the deep aroma of roast beef, and the visual beauty of sandwiches being dipped in a trough of hot beef

au jus is incredible. Every restaurant should be set up like this. "I love it," general manager Eddie Sullivan, who sits at his perch up front taking orders and greeting everyone who walks through the door. "We get to meet everybody." Eddie is the son of owner John Sullivan, who bought the place with wife Ursula in 1969.

In the late 1940s, John worked for Brennan & Carr then found work as a police officer. Twenty years later he heard that the Carr Family (Brennan was bought out sometime in the 1950s) was looking to sell the place so the Sullivans became only the second owners in the restaurant's long history. The Carrs and Sullivans lived on the same block in Brooklyn and Eddie told me, "They are like family."

Most stop into Brennan & Carr for their famous roast beef sandwiches and eat in the cozy Civil War and Bicentennial themed rooms. The (real) wood paneling, tables, chairs and wooden light fixtures hanging from the ceiling are all the color of roast beef. But they also come for the burger, or more important, the "Gargiulo Burger."

The burger starts with a quarter-pound patty of fresh beef cooked on a flattop. The beef is ground in-house using the clean trim from the boneless top rounds before they become roast beef. When flipped, a wad of thin-sliced roast beef goes on top with a handful of sautéed spanish onion and two slices of american cheese. The pile of beef and cheese is transferred to a substantial, hand-sliced, locally made kaiser roll and brought to the "dipping" station.

In the center of the kitchen, in full view of the walk-up window and customers inside, is an array of decommissioned vintage kitchen equipment, artifacts from a time before health inspectors. "Roasts used to hang from here!" Eddie told me pointing to a thick pipe over an old charcoal fireplace. There is one piece of the past still being used however —the deep, free-standing trough filled with gallons of glorious beef broth, or *au jus*. It's here the Gargiulo Burger is fully immersed, like a burger baptismal. "Some want them double-dipped," Eddie told me. The impact hot au jus has on this burger is mind blowing. It soaks into the the roll turning the bun into a flavor

component, not just a delivery system for meat and cheese.

The namesake of the burger belongs to Gargiulo's of Coney Island, the high-end Italian restaurant. For decades, the staff and owners make their way to Brennan & Carr for every Sunday dinner. "Years ago we'd put out trays of burgers and roast beef for them," Eddie told me. "They used to bring their family's own Italian bread and one day they put the two together."

The waiters all wear ties and pressed white coats and take their jobs very seriously. If someone shows up for the day without a tie, they are sent home. "And pens!" Eddie told me, "they have to come with a pen." The Sullivans have tremendous loyalty toward their staff, and waiter Rich Egan has been at Brennan & Carr for thirty years. Maxine

"Eduardo" Vincent has worked in the kitchen prepping roasts for an astonishing forty years.

Eddie started working with his father full time in 1978 and bucked the family trend to go into the military, fire or police departments like the rest of his six siblings (two of which are currently army colonels). He told me with complete sincerity, "I like doing this, I like people, and I like being with my father." And he is very hands-on, which for forty years at the restaurant is an amazing feat. He is still involved with every aspect of the business from quality control to ordering supplies. "We do things very old-school here," Eddie explained as he told me of his family's long-standing relationships with vendors, many of whom have never changed in fifty years. "The service that comes with that, the trust . . . it's all important."

CORNER BISTRO

331 West 4th St | New York, NY 10014 | 212-242-9502
Mon–Sat 11:30 am–4 am | Sun 12 pm–4 am

For two decades the Corner Bistro in Greenwich Village, New York City, served my "hometown" burger. It's the burger that became the standard by which all others would be measured. I've eaten over a thousand burgers at the Bistro in different states of intoxication or sober, for lunch and dinner, and a few times I even ate them with friends at 3 a.m. on a Tuesday. For five of those years I lived a block away and secretly wondered if my motive for moving

had been burger proximity. I knew the right times to visit to avoid the crowds, and their phone number is in the speed dial of my cell phone. I placed phone orders and used the quiet side door to sneak in, grab my waiting hot paper bag, and make a swift exit. My burger quest started here and ends here as well. I went forth into Hamburger America, ate well, returned, and was confident that the "Bistro Burger" really is one of the best in the nation.

Up until a few years ago the Corner Bistro looked the part of the casual New York City Irish pub. Carved-up wooden tables, well-worn, wide plank floorboards, and a long bar with a noticeable dip in the center created your lasting first impression. "The building is still settling," former owner Bill O'Donnell once said in defense of the sloping bar. Bill was an icon of the burger business for decades and in 2016 he passed away after a battle with cancer. His family stepped in to run the place and Bill's daughter, Elizabeth, made a handful of much-needed improvements, including fixing the deep slope in the bar. She kept with the dark bar theme, threw up a coat of paint, and the place still looks amazing . . . and very clean.

The building housing the Corner Bistro dates back to 1827 and before it was a bar it was an inn. The existing decor surrounding the bar (stained-glass cabinetry and mirrors), as well as the brass-foot-railed bar itself is said to date back to 1880. After Prohibition was repealed, the bar became Barney McNichols and attracted mostly the longshoremen who populated the neighborhood. After its short stint as a gay bar, in 1961 a Spanish woman bought it and attempted to put a European spin on the old tavern by calling it the Corner Bistro. It didn't last and went back to being what it has been for well over a century—a cozy dive with a great jukebox.

In 1977, Mimi Sheraton, the well-known food critic from the *New York Times*, wrote a favorable piece on the Bistro Burger that kickstarted the surge of popularity that has not slowed since. "I came in the next day and the

place was packed," Bill once told me. "I was shocked." Bill himself admitted that there's nothing special about the burger and nothing has changed in over fifty years. Bistro still uses the same butcher around the corner and get a chuck/sirloin blend. Two hundred and fifty pounds of the fresh ground beef gets walked over by hand cart from 14th Street to the Bistro every day. This was the way all restaurants received their meat in the first half of the twentieth century, delivered by hand from a local butcher.

The Bistro Burger doesn't try to be anything but a great hamburger. It's a thick, eight-ounce burger whose only flourish is three crispy strips of bacon that have been flash-fried in the deep fryer (ever wonder why those fries taste so damn good?). It's now served on a toasted Martin's Potato Roll (this change came without notice in 2017!) with lettuce, tomato, and a thick onion slice hidden beneath the burger. It's cooked in a tiny, postage stamp–sized kitchen staffed by two. They cook the burgers to your preferred temperature in a salamander broiler, a small, specialized oven that cooks the burgers slowly by indirect, overhead heat. Bartender turned general manager of forty-five years, Harold, explained, "It keeps the burgers soft and juicy."

Hard-working Louis arrived in 1980 and has been the head chef and chief of burger operations at the Bistro for over thirty-eight years (though he thinks it's only been thirty). He is a man of few words but will always get your order right. Louis is in charge of the line that builds most nights for people waiting for a table and will take your order. The infamous line starts at the phone booth and can go all the way to the front door, so grab a beer at the bar first.

Many people try to bad-mouth this burger because they are embarrassed by its simplicity. In a city with no tangible burger identity (you really can find any type of burger in New York City, from the bloated wallet busters to tasty sliders), the Bistro Burger stands out as an unflappable success grounded in modesty. The success has spread to other bars in the neighborhood that claim to "know the secret of the Bistro Burger" and have even hired cast-off Bistro kitchen staff to boost business. "There are no secrets," Bill once told me in his gentle NY accent. He added, laughing very hard, "The recipe is 'good meat,' you idiots."

DONOVAN'S PUB

57-24 Roosevelt Ave | Woodside, NY 11377 | 718-429-9339 | Mon–Thurs 11 am–12 am
Fri & Sat 11 am–1 am | Sun 11:30 am–12 am | www.donovansny.com

Regulars, God bless 'em, show up at this Woodside, Queens, Irish pub at 11 a.m. daily to slowly drink their Guinness and just talk. The bar is an impressive one—long, dark, solid and with the type of patina that only comes with age. It's a great bar to sit at, drink a Guinness, and just talk, but even better to enjoy a burger, one of the best classic pub burgers in New York City.

I asked now-retired bartender Robert how big the burgers were and his only response was, "They are pretty big." He was not far off. This pub has been serving half-pound burgers since 1970, and a lot of them. Artie Kardaras, was head chef at Donovan's for over forty years before retiring and told me they hand-patty four hundred pounds of quality ground shell steak (New York strip) a day for their burgers.

The Donovan's burger is a lesson in how a large burger should be prepared. It's cooked in a way that few burgers are in America—in a broiler used for cooking steaks. The loose-pattied burger is broiled to the temperature of your choice with little attention paid to it by the chef. And like a great steak the best burgers are left alone and touched the least.

When you bite into the inch-thick Donovan's burger, the first thing you notice is how loose the meat is. The delicate exterior char can barely contain the tender, steamy beef inside. A half-pound burger may sound tough to tackle, but the meat-to-bun ratio is nearly perfect, making the entire experience incredibly beefy and satisfying.

Other than a bar, burgers, and regulars, Donovan's also has an impressive dining room and a great menu loaded with comfort food. Go during the colder months and enjoy your burgers by the cozy fireplace in the dark-paneled dining room with Tiffany lamps hanging overhead.

For years, the pub was owned by Joe Donovan and his father, Joe, who for almost thirty years threatened to sell the place. They were all false alarms until one day Joe actually did put the place on the market. Part-time bartender Jimmy Jacobson, who started in 1985 as a busboy, heard the news but had already considered buying the restaurant. He and brother-in-law Dan Connor (who grew up at Donovan's) had been talking about a plan to

partner for twenty years and in 2013 it became a reality. "We were ready and waiting for the opportunity," Dan told me.

Jimmy and Dan were wise not to change much about the legendary pub with the exception of getting more business in the door. Using their status as an award-winning burger destination they began entering and winning burger competitions, generating press and awareness that the Donovan's burger was still as great as ever. Both Dan and Jimmy have full-time jobs outside of owning the bar and consider the place a labor of love and a community center for their friends and family. "I have a massive family," Dan told me, "and at any given moment there's a Connor in the restaurant either working or not."

Most of the staff has been at Donovan's forever. Theresa Ashton has been a waitress for thirty-nine years and met her husband at the bar. "He was dancing on the bar with his pants down,

and I said 'look at this asshole,' and then I married him!" She remembers when Jimmy started at Donovan's. "He was my first busboy," she told me. And even though Jimmy is now her boss he says that Theresa is really the one in charge.

The most obvious landmark you'll notice outside Donovan's Pub is the undeniably old-school New York elevated number seven train rumbling overhead every few minutes. What you may not pick out is the tavern's odd proximity to a church only a few feet away, directly across the street. "This place was here before the church so they were allowed to stay," regular Don Moran told me once from his spot at the bar. According to New York City zoning law, no drinking establishment may be operated within five hundred feet of a place of worship. So this may be the closest to a church you'll be able to drink and eat great burgers in New York City—in fact, the stained-glass windows in the bar area do give the place a church-like feel.

And if you are a Mets fan, you know that hardcore believers do two things before the first game of the season—make a stop at Donovan's for a few early morning pregame drinks (open at 9 a.m. that day), and then head across the street to St. Sebastian's to say a prayer before heading to the stadium. If anything, Jimmy and Dan saved this very special tradition.

HILDEBRANDT'S

84 Hillside Ave | Williston Park, NY 11596 | 516-741-0608
Tues–Thurs 11 am–8:30 pm | Fri & Sat 11 am–11 pm | Sun 10 am–4 pm | Closed Mon
www.hildebrandtsrestaurant.com

Densely packed suburban Long Island, New York, is a place where new malls and homes are constantly springing up and, unless protected, the past is unceremoniously swept away. In a part of the country where it's getting harder to find genuine nostalgia, locals embrace Hildebrandt's Luncheonette. This early-twentieth-century landmark soda counter, confectionery, and ice cream parlor offers a glimpse into the past. The counter, though, is not a washed-up has-been. It's as vibrant as ever and happens to serve some of the tastiest burgers this side of Manhattan.

Hildebrandt's opened in 1927 and was the only business in the newly developing dirt road suburb of Williston Park, twenty miles from New York City.

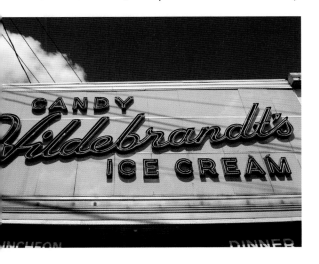

Today, Hildebrandt's is owned by Joanne Strano and her son-in-law, Bryan Acosta. Joanne and her late husband, Al, bought the vintage luncheonette in 1974 when longtime owner and chocolate maker Henry Schreiver was looking to retire. The Acostas learned the chocolate-making trade from Schreiver and made a major improvement to the existing burger on the menu—fresh ground beef.

This classic luncheonette, with its checker-tiled floor and long marble counter with thirteen stools, maintains a vintage look by making use of the soda fountain trappings of a bygone era. The seltzer and syrup dispensers are not vintage props. They all function daily, as does the long bank of ice-cream chests behind the counter. Ice cream is a big draw at Hildebrandt's because it's made right at the restaurant.

But according to Bryan, most come for the food, which is a mix of classic diner fare and Italian specialties added by the Acosta family in the 1970s. Surprisingly, this amazing burger has been exiled to the bottom of the menu. Look for your cheeseburger in a section marked "sandwiches" at the bottom of the list, just after the meatball hero.

"We have the greatest burger," Bryan told me without pause, and added, "I've never really had a better burger. I really haven't." He can boast all he wants. It really is a great burger. The burgers

at Hildebrandt's start as fresh ground sirloin the restaurant receives from the butcher down the street. Bryan himself hand-patties the four-ounce burgers just before the lunch crowd shows up. The burgers are offered at the four-ounce size, or ask for the eight-ounce and get twice the meat. "We just take two four-ounce patties and smoosh them together on the grill," Bryan explained. On the flattop griddle, Alfredo presses the burger flat and places a bacon weight on top. It's served on a classic white bun with tomato, sliced onion, and a wedge of iceberg lettuce. Bacon is available, but not necessary (this meat is so good you won't want anything to hide the flavor). Ketchup is king at Hildebrandt's (there's a bottle every few feet on the counter) but mustard has to be coaxed from the countermen in small pouches.

Hildebrandt's fries are a great addition to your hamburger lunch. They are large, hand-cut, deep-fried slices of potato that, if ordered well-done, resemble homemade potato chips. Order a milkshake, listed on the menu in Long Island vernacular as a "frosted," and you'll get a tall glass and the obligatory metal cup the shake was made in. Since the ice cream is homemade, the shakes are superb.

The clientele at Hildebrandt's ranges from little old ladies to large families with kids. Bryan, waiting tables in the back, makes jokes as he takes orders. "These are the best seats in the house," he tells two older ladies looking for a table, "unless, of course, I'm waiting on you!"

In the vicinity of New York City, Hildebrandt's is not alone. The long-gone business model for this type of soda fountain survives at places like Hinsch's in Bayridge, Brooklyn, and Bischoff's in Teaneck, New Jersey. They, too, make their own chocolates, and in the case of Bischoff's, countermen still wear white paper caps and striped shirts. At all of these vintage soda fountains of German descent, you can take home hand-packed ice cream by the pint or quart, but the similarities end there. Only Hildebrandt's makes a top-quality burger. That, and the mocha frosted, will keep me coming back.

JG MELON

1291 Third Ave | New York, NY 10021 | 212-744-0585 | Mon–Wed 11:30 am–3 am
Thurs–Sat 11:30 am–4 am | Sun 11:30 am–1 am | Holiday Weekend Sun 11:30 am–3 am
www.jgmelonnyc.com

The Upper East Side of Manhattan is known more for its high cost of living and less for good old places like JG Melon. The humble, dark, no-nonsense tavern should have been in the first edition of this book, and was prevented only by scheduling conflicts. When Mayor Mike Bloomberg saw my book, he told me, "JG should be in here. They make a great burger." He should know. The mayor lives only a few blocks away and is crazy about hamburgers.

Jack O'Neill and George Mourges (the J and G of JG Melon) were working at midtown restaurant Joe Allen when they decided they wanted to open a place of their own. In 1972, they leased Bar Central on 74th and 3rd and changed the name to JG Melon. The building dates back to the 1920s when the tavern was built by a local brewery to dispense its own products following Prohibition. Almost immediately, JG Melon became a watering hole for socialites and politicians, as well as locals and Wall Street types. Every sitting mayor for the last forty years has felt comfortable at the tavern and the burger is at the center of it all.

Both Jack and George have since passed and the restaurant is now owned by a handful of Mourges and O'Neill family members. JG Melon retains its friendly broken-in pub ambiance thanks to Jack's widow, Jaine O'Neill, who handles the day-to-day and oversees the delivery of hundreds of burgers daily to her regulars at JG Melon.

JG Melon's burgers start as a special blend of cuts ground by the same butcher they've used for years. The burgers are portioned into seven-ounce balls then gently flattened on a large, very hot griddle. They are left untouched until they are flipped once, then gently transferred to a waiting, toasted bun. The result is a substantially thick two-fister whose construction is perfect. No crazy toppings here, just a basic, beefy, uncomplicated burger that is truly satisfying. Because of the high heat and the steak-treatment, the exterior of the burger is seared to a serious griddle char that helps retain all of the moisture. You'll need a napkin—this one is juicy.

Equally famous at JG Melon are the cottage fries that have been on the menu since the beginning. At one point, Jack and George decided to switch to shoestring fries. "There was a complete revolt!" former manager Shaun Young told me once. "We had to switch back immediately."

Do not leave JG Melon without having a Bloody Bull. A drink you don't see often that hails from New Orleans, the Bloody Bull is like a Bloody Mary but half of the tomato juice is replaced with ice-cold beef broth. What could go better with a beefy burger than a cool beefy drink?

There are a few tables in a rear dining room and sixteen coveted seats on the sidewalk, but grab a stool at the bar if possible and listen to the burgers sear on the flattop adjacent to the bar. The sound is heavenly.

JOE JR. RESTAURANT

167 3rd Ave | New York, Ny 10003
212-473-5150 | Mon–Sun 6 am–11:30 pm

You'd never know from the looks of Joe Junior that the classic New York City diner is in peril. Not Joe Junior itself, but diner culture in general is losing the real estate battle in Manhattan. The atmosphere at Joe is quite the opposite. A constant stream of New Yorkers walk in and out the door to grab a seat at the counter or pick up an order to go. The mix is pure New York with construction workers in reflective gear and hard hats to business men to students to the elderly and everyone in between. The lunch crowd at Joe Junior may be even more diverse than a car on the number-six train. At any given moment (there's never a lull), the tiny diner on the busy corner of 3rd Avenue and 15th Street is very busy.

Greasy spoon would be an unfair moniker to attach to this icon. Sure, it's a diner, but unlike fast-food America (where some chains are truly gross and greasy), Joe Junior still does things the traditional way. All of their food is prepped on-site, including the turkey (roasted in the tiny kitchen), the salads and soups are housemade, and of course the burgers start with fresh ground beef. Also, there's no computer system running inventory or taking orders, just a single, manual cash register that looks to be about fifty years old and all orders are written by hand. As longtime manager Armando pointed out, "It's really old-fashioned."

The burger at Joe Junior is pure and simple. They use the same meatpacker as the beloved Corner Bistro across town and it arrives ground in bulk. When a burger order comes in, the line cook reaches into a refrigerated drawer underneath the griddle and grabs a portioned wad of beef that looks be around six ounces. In a flash on the way up to the flattop, the cook shapes the wad into a patty and slaps it on the griddle. Once one side has acquired the appropriate griddle crust and is flipped, the cook places a bacon weight on top to speed up the cooking process. You'd think this move would kill the burger, but every time I've ordered mine "medium" the resulting patty is pink throughout and incredibly juicy. Nick Solares, host of *The Meat Show* and a regular at Joe Junior for almost two decades, orders his without the bacon weight step. "I like mine rare, and thicker," he told me. "And it still gets that amazing maillard crust." It's true, and this burger hits the flattop unseasoned, which means that griddle crust is seasoned by whatever the cooks put on that griddle (which is most likely the result of cooking bacon all day).

Ask for a Deluxe and you'll get lettuce and tomato on the side, a thimble of coleslaw, fries, and a dill pickle spear. If you order a cheeseburger, the cook will put a slice of american on both top and bottom of the seeded white squishy bun and toss it into the broiler to melt. It's a good move to make this

a separate step because it allows the cook to finish the burger to the appropriate interior temperature without having to worry about the melting point of cheese. I order mine with cheese only and it comes with nothing more than the side of coleslaw. At Joe Junior, that's the best way to enjoy the burger.

The decor at Joe Junior is not the reason to visit. The mirror strips and thick ornate hardwood give the place an '80s dental office look. You came for the food.

Sit at the counter and watch Armando work. He mans the phone breakfast and dinner and has an incredible capacity for multitasking, answering calls for orders, and making change at the register at the same time. It's the frenetic pace of NYC embodied in a singular moment at Joe Junior, handled beautifully, with grace and a smile.

P.J. CLARKE'S

915 Third Ave | New York, NY 10022 | 212-317-1616
Open Daily 11:30 am–3 am | Bar Closes At 4 am | www.pjclarkes.com

There are few taverns in America as steeped in history as P.J. Clarke's. All at once a neighborhood bar, broken-in dive, and a celebrity hang for decades, it's also a great place to find high-quality pub fare. Among that fare is the world-famous P.J. Clarke's hamburger. P.J.'s has not been affected by its own celebrity status. It remains a comfortable place in the heart of a sometimes cold city—a friendly pub with a welcoming staff and a remarkably unpretentious hamburger on the menu.

The iconic corner saloon, in a two-story brick tenement-style structure, looks totally out of place surrounded by the tall glass and steel office buildings of midtown Manhattan. Irish immigrant

Patrick J. Clarke started working at the corner bar in 1902, and in 1912 he purchased the business and changed the name to his own.

Before the skyscrapers, the neighborhood surrounding P.J.'s was mostly breweries and slaughterhouses. And those who are old enough will remember that the Third Avenue subway was elevated, giving the area a radically different feel. By 1960, the elevated tracks were down and the slaughterhouses were long gone. P.J.'s neighborhood has undergone a profound transformation in the last century but the tiny saloon remains, dwarfed by its neighbors.

The tin ceilings, faded mirrors behind the bar, and stained-glass windows in front remind the casual observer of the saloon's rich past. Sinatra made P.J.'s his last stop on nights out and even had his own table (number twenty). General manager Patrick Walsh once told me, through his Irish brogue, "If there was anyone sitting there when Sinatra came in, they'd get the boot." Buddy Holly proposed to his wife here and Nat King Cole once called the hamburger at P.J.'s "the Cadillac of burgers." Even the famed 1970s sports painter LeRoy Neiman put brush to canvas to create a portrait of the bar in full swing that proudly hangs in the dining room.

The meat for the burgers comes from cattle that are handpicked for P.J.'s. They grind their own chuck steaks and the fat-to-lean ratio is kept secret. The seven-ounce burgers are hand-pressed one by one, cooked on a flattop griddle, and served on a classic white squishy bun. Don't be surprised to find a slice of onion underneath your burger—it's there to soak up the juices and protect the heel of the bun from disintegrating.

I've been going to P.J.'s for decades and the burger has always been perfect. The bun-to-beef ratio, the slight griddle crunch, and the moist, meaty flavor are what burger dreams are made of. There are a few burger choices at P.J.'s, but my favorite for years was the "Béarnaise Burger." Imagine the simplicity of the elements—the perfect burger, a soft white bun, and a healthy dose of pure, buttery béarnaise sauce. A few years back, the burger was unceremoniously dumped from the menu but new manager Michael Long told me, "We still keep béarnaise in case it's requested."

The dark dining room walls are covered with an amazing collection of New York City ephemera (including P.J.'s death certificate) and old photographs of past patrons. The one-hundred-year-old men's urinals are as famous as the burgers and must be seen to be believed. (They're over five feet tall with thick porcelain embellishment.) Sinatra once said they were "big enough to take a bath in."

P.J.'s has been part of the collective unconscious of literally millions of former and present New Yorkers. Just like your favorite jacket or an old pair of shoes, the tavern has always been a familiar, unchanging place that many rely on for hearty comfort food, a drink, and good company. The burger at P.J.'s is part of that legacy of comfort and hopefully will be forever.

TARA INN

1519 Main St. | Port Jefferson, NY 11777 | 631-828-5987 | Mon & Tues 11 am–2 am
Wed & Thurs 11 am–3 am | Fri & Sat 11 am–4 am | Sun 12 pm–2 am

There's an important rule that I live by—if I'm taking the Port Jeff ferry to OR from Connecticut I need to stop at Tara Inn for a burger and 2 beers. I've been doing this for years and very little has changed about my routine, or this broken-in locals-only pub, except a sudden price hike in the burger. It sounds ridiculous but true—The Tara Inn serves a great burger that is only 2 dollars. But for years that same burger was only one dollar!

"Joe said he'd never raise the price," Melinda, manager of almost 40 years, told me. Joe Higgins and his wife Pat bought the bar and renamed it Tara in 1977 (so named after one of their 8 children). He has always been able to serve burgers cheaply because they are

subsidized by the bar sales. Melinda explained, "Joe wanted to make sure whoever you were, down-and-out or whatever, that you could come and get a good burger."

There's a tendency to think cheap equals low quality. Not so here. It's a stunt that may have ties to the dawn of bar culture in America. Bartenders would offer some sort of sustenance to keep regulars from wandering off in search of food, and a hamburger is the perfect solution.

Just one glance at the extensive menu on the chalkboard wall behind the bar will tell you the sort of quality the kitchen at Tara is dealing with—filet mignon sandwich, peel and eat shrimp, scallops, a porterhouse steak…they are not messing around. The burger, although served with zero

pretense on a styrofoam plate with potato chips, is a very high quality item.

Fresh ¼ pound patties come from a local butcher shop, daily, and are cooked over an indoor flame grill. Add melty white American cheese and bacon and the price soars to $2.75. And new last year—you can now order a double and get a ½ pound burger, for only $5, which is an insane bargain. Ask for 'everything' and get lettuce, tomato, pickles and a slice of raw onion (included in the price). Other condiments like ketchup and mustard are available but unnecessary because this burger so damn juicy.

Over the years the building has had quite a history. It has been the home of several bars, including the Anchor Club and Al's Ten Pin Inn. That's right, there used to be bowling in the basement at Tara Inn. "It was just a 2-lane thing where you had to manually resent the pins," Melinda told me.

Today Tara is run by Joe and Pat Higgins' children Tara and Kate, and Melinda. On game days the 10 screens at Tara Inn are on, and the beer flows freely. "We easily go through a barrel of Miller Lite a day," bartender Katie told me. Tara Inn also frequently raises money for charities, many of them local beneficiaries. They recently held a fundraiser for a regular that died at work to help his wisdow cope. When I hear these stories I'm moved and reminded of how strong the ties are between families and pub culture. And it warms my heart to know that a 2-dollar burger can be at the core of good will.

MY FAVORITE NATIONAL BURGER CHAINS

In the corporate burger world, all burgers are created equal by design. Most are frozen, then shipped for miles to their intended fast-food outlet. Increasingly however, a handful of hamburger chains have chosen to buck the system and offer burgers made with fresh ground beef. Here is a short list of my personal favorites. All make excellent substitutes for the classics listed in this book:

STEAK 'N SHAKE
Locations throughout the Midwest and the South
www.steaknshake.com

This classic drive-in burger stand opened its first location in Normal, Illinois, in 1934. Since then, Steak 'n Shake has expanded to over 544 locations and still serves burgers made from fresh ground strip steak, sirloin, and T-bone. A seat at the counter offers excellent views of the white paper-capped grillperson preparing your "Steakburger." A wad of beef is smashed thin and seared on a superhot flattop griddle. Within just a few minutes, a moist yet crispy patty is placed on a toasted white bun and delivered to you on a porcelain diner plate. Get a double with bacon for an unforgettable meal.

SMASHBURGER
Locations throughout the United States
www.smashburger.com

How could I not love a burger chain that smashes fresh ground beef the old-fashioned way? In 2007, there was one Smashburger, in Denver. Today, there are over 370 locations in nine countries and thirty-seven states. Smashburger was the brainchild of Tom Ryan, a longtime food industry rockstar with a PhD in flavor chemistry and a deep love of the American burger.

FIVE GUYS
Locations throughout the United States
www.fiveguys.com

This no-frills fresh beef chain has made quite a dent in corporate burgers. One college student I spoke to told me he'd never visit a Mickey D's if there was a Five Guys nearby. What's all the fuss about? Great burgers made in large portions from excellent, consistently good fresh ground beef (not to mention free refills and a bottomless bag of fresh-cut fries). Corporate burger biggies are in trouble when even drunken students can tell the difference between fresh and frozen burgers.

NORTH CAROLINA

BROOKS' SANDWICH HOUSE

2710 North Brevard St | Charlotte, NC 28205 | 704-375-7808
Mon–Fri 7 am–3 pm | Closed Sat & Sun | www.eatbrookschili.com

At first glance, this nondescript cinderblock box painted deep red does not seem like a place one might find food. It looks more like an equipment storage structure for a highway crew. But you'll know you've arrived at one of the most talked about burger joints in Charlotte when you spot the line snaking out the door and down the hill.

Inside, twin brothers Scott and David Brooks run the show, with each sharing grill duties every other day. One works the register while the other sends out an astonishing five-hundred-plus burgers at lunch. Brooks' is only open for breakfast and lunch, five days a week, and closes sharply at 3 p.m. To the twins that's plenty. Including prep time in the morning, a day for them is eleven to twelve hours. "That's enough," David once told me.

Brooks' is a true burger and hot dog joint which exists for one purpose: to feed people good food quickly. Don't look for plates, or seating inside, "Unless you want to sit on the floor," Scott told me. I would recommend eating in, or on, your car, or seek out one of the picnic benches in the parking lot. I like to simply stand in the parking lot and consume my burger at Brooks'. The entire act takes roughly two minutes.

The menu at Brooks' is short, with the most popular items being their chili dog and burger, with a few truly Southern old-time favorites—fried bologna and liver mush. Order their signature burger and it will arrive wrapped in waxed paper. Ask for yours "all the way" and you'll get mustard, chopped onion, and their amazing beef chili sauce. It is a beautifully sloppy burger, with a dominant beefy flavor. Add their house-made slaw and turn yours into a Carolina Slaw Burger (not on the menu). And you should know, there is no cheeseburger on the menu. For that, you'll have to ask for a burger, with cheese.

The burgers start as balls of fresh ground 81/19 ground round that are pressed onto a hot flattop griddle that sits in the center of the kitchen, in full view of the ordering counter. The balls are not really measured but as Dave put it, "I've been doing this so long that I don't make mistakes."

The Charlotte area is the home of NASCAR and race teams frequent Brooks'. "Joe Gibbs's team is here every Thursday," Scott told me. "A great bunch of guys."

When the twins' father, Calvin T. Brooks, opened his hot dog and burger stand in North Charlotte, the neighborhood was a very different place. Textile manufacturing dominated the area, and an experimental "Mill Village" was created. As the factories started closing down, the area went into decline. C.T., an automotive painter, saw potential in the changing neighborhood and hand-built the 480-square-foot stand with a friend. Artists began to discover the old buildings and renamed the area NoDa,

for north of Davidson Avenue and today, it is a vibrant community with a new light rail stop and planned high-rises on the way. Somehow the brothers remain unfazed by the change. Offers are made on a weekly basis to purchase the prime piece of real estate upon which the classic burger joint sits, but the family remains steadfast. "We are not going anywhere," Scott told me. Music to my ears.

The twins have been at it for over thirty-four years, and both started working in the stand full-time after their mother passed away. They seem to truly love their jobs even though it is backbreaking work. Dave pointed out once, "I don't think I could find a job now . . . that's kinda scary!"

CHAR-GRILL

618 Hillsborough St | Raleigh, NC 27603 | 919-821-7636 | Mon–Wed 10 am–12 am
Thurs 10 am–1 am | Fri & Sat 10 am–2 am | Sun 10:30 am–11 pm
(Nine Other Locations In NC) | www.chargrillusa.com

Racing to catch a flight, I was sure to miss out on Raleigh, North Carolina's, own vintage burger minichain, the Char-Grill. Fortunately, I did stop, but would have missed the flight had the service not been super fast.

The setup is pure 1950s drive-in, but the ordering process is peculiar. No honking for service here. You park your car, walk up to the window, and fill out a cryptic order form. Once you have marked your choices, you shove the slim piece of paper into a thin slot in one of the large plate glass windows. Your order form slides down a stainless chute to the waiting grill cook. The lack of indoor seating and a glass-enclosed kitchen creates a sort of public hamburger laboratory—as you wait, you can peer inside and watch your burger being constructed according to the condiments you checked off on your order. Within minutes, your number is called and you are rewarded with a white paper bag full of hot food by a smiling employee.

The burgers are grilled over a flame and come in three sizes, the largest being the half-pound hamburger steak sandwich. Any combination of mayo, lettuce, tomato, onion, pickle, cheese, and bacon can be created. The staff all wear white paper caps and aprons and work at stations to keep this model of efficiency chugging along. The beef comes in fresh daily, as square pre-formed Angus chuck patties, and all of the lettuce, tomato, and onion come from a local farmers market.

Bruce Garner opened Char-Grill in 1959. In 1975, two fraternity brothers, Mahlon Aycock and Ryon Wilder, assumed ownership and forty-three years later are still partners in the business. They have expanded from the one Raleigh location they purchased in 1975 to six additional locations around Raleigh-Durham with two others near Fayetteville and Charlotte.

By design, not much has changed at Char-Grill. The Hillsborough location is a piece of American architecture stuck in time. The deliberately oversized, overdesigned structure is almost sculpture—the enormous white wavy roof looks as if it could crush the floor-to-ceiling windows supporting it. The other Raleigh locations also serve their well-known Charburgers, but it's the original location that has that great drive-in feel. And for over fifty years Char-Grill has continued to serve the same tasty, flame-grilled burgers and creamy shakes.

All walks of life visit Char-Grill for a dose of nostalgia. Mahlon told me, "We get everybody from the governor of North Carolina to construction folk and anybody in between."

DUKE'S GRILL

1114 Concord Ave | Monroe, NC 28110
704-283-4960 | Tues–Sat 6 am–8 pm | Closed Sun & Mon

"I don't think about what I'm doing, but I love it," Duke's owner Dennis Parker told me when I caught him in a rare slow moment between breakfast and lunch. And I believe him. Dennis has an air of confidence and composure at the griddle, even when the orders are coming fast and furious. His calm radiates and affects the entire staff who buzz around the sixty-five-year-old burger joint with smiles for the regulars. And I, clearly an outsider, was treated like an old friend from the moment I first set foot in Duke's.

The interior of Duke's has the look of a place that has seen decades of minor renovations to accommodate changing tastes and dining styles. When it first opened, the restaurant had curb hops and not many seats inside. Today, the hops are gone and all dining takes place in a quaint array of random nooks and side rooms that can accommodate a seemingly impossible fifty-five patrons. One room, a tiny one with just a few seats named the Johnny Cash room, is the best room in the house. "Especially in summer," Dennis told me, "that room has great air-conditioning. It's a great place to hide."

The kitchen is in full view and if you are placing an order to go, you can watch all of the magic unfold from the register. Duke's burger is one that could only be born in the South, and what outsiders refer to as the Carolina Slaw Burger (and referred to here as simply a "burger all-the-way"). Dennis starts with fresh ground beef and mixes in egg and bread crumbs. "Duke would use stale bread instead," he pointed out, but switched to finer crumbs because people didn't want big chunks of bread in their burgers.

The Slaw Burger is just that—a burger with a layer of creamy, housemade coleslaw. In North

in a car accident and his uncle Henry Dewey "Duke" Parker stepped in to help the family. "He was like a father to me," Dennis told me. His first job was curbhopping at his uncle's restaurant in 1967. Dennis stuck with it and in 1993 bought the business from his uncle.

Other than amendments to the restaurant's layout, nothing much has changed at Duke's since opening day in 1953. "I did change Duke's original chile sauce," Dennis confided, "but I made it better." The sauce during Duke's time was made with nothing but ketchup, chile powder, and a trace of beef. Today's sauce is similar but there's much more beef.

Carolina, it's safe to assume that coleslaw made its way to the burger following its success on the pulled pork sandwich (arguably the official state sandwich of North Carolina). The result is pure brilliance. Someone once asked me why this hyper-regional burger style has never left the Carolinas and I wish I knew. The combination of vinegary mayo, beef grease, and the crunch of cabbage is pretty stellar. Ask for yours all-the-way at Duke's and Dennis adds his mild chile sauce and diced onion. You are thinking correctly—this burger is a handful.

Dennis started working at the restaurant when he was nine years old. Two years earlier his father, a brother, and sister were killed

Be forewarned before your first visit to Duke's: Dennis and his team have a very strict cell phone policy. If you are caught yabbering away on your phone, you may be asked to leave. The first warning will come from one of the servers, and if they get "the hand," Dennis steps in. "I will scoop up your lunch and show you the door," he told me with a smile. He means it, though. "It bothers me that people come in here with kids and they are on their phones. I want people to enjoy the food and enjoy who they are eating with." Who can argue with that? Dennis went on, "Call me old-fashioned, I guess."

HUB GRILL

1350 US-74 | Wadesboro, NC 28170 | 704-694-5330
Tues–Sat 5:30 am–2 pm | Closed Sun & Mon

North Carolinians take their breakfast very seriously. So does the Hub, which happily serves a hearty breakfast crowd that ranges from hunters and loggers to "crackheads and politicians!" Scott Drye told me. Scott's family owns and runs the Hub and he should know. "I'm here every day," he told me. Scott can be found at the griddle behind the counter, which handles pretty much the entire breakfast menu. "Breakfast is long," he told me, but only because at the Hub breakfast starts at the crack of dawn, 5:30 a.m.

The Hub was opened by Clegg Thomas in 1961 on the outskirts of Wadesboro when he turned a small ice-cream/snack shack into a tiny breakfast and burger joint. In 1967, Clegg's nephew Sandy Drye left his job at Eastern Airlines and started working at the Hub. Sandy saw opportunity, he also noticed that Clegg had lost interest in running the place. "At one point he just walked out," Scott told me. "He was done." In 1969, Sandy was given the option to buy the place and he did. And by 1974 he was the sole owner of the Hub.

Today, the Hub is packed the entire time they are opened. "Most of the time you can't get in the parking lot," Scott told me. The building can handle it, which is a collection of dining rooms added over the years. "When I bought in 1969 there were no indoor bathrooms," Sandy told me. He spent decades adding to and tweaking the Hub to what it has become today. Scott told me, "My dad is the Hub."

There are two ways to enjoy burgers at the Hub. The menu lists hamburgers and cheeseburgers, which are actually Carolina Slaw burgers. This includes a quarter-pound patty griddled with a fantastic crispy exterior, a toasted bun, cheese, coleslaw, pickles, and a dollop of beef chili. It's an incredible combo found in other parts of North Carolina. But ask for the Big H for something a little more on the classic side, where Scott squishes two patties together making one large half-pound patty which comes with lettuce, tomato, and pickles. "Honestly, you can have whatever you want on the burger," Scott told me.

The burgers start as fresh ground 80/20 beef but salt, pepper, egg, and breading is mixed into the meat. This is likely a holdover from hard times in the South when cooks used things like bread crumbs extend their ground beef supply. Familiar tastes and nostalgia always prevail and this method has remained. A large part of its appeal is what happens to the bread crumbs when they mix with rendered burger fat on the griddle—a crispiness to die for.

Even though the breakfast is long, don't look for it past 10:30 a.m. Also don't expect to order a burger during breakfast. Scott explained, "At 10:30 we switch to cafeteria line," which means that the buffet is open and you grab a tray, a plate and some lunch. Scott told me, "We won't fix 'em [burgers] for breakfast because it messes with the griddle." Scott is correct—burger grease and pancakes don't really mix well.

So if you do the math, since the place close at 2 p.m. you have a 3½ hour window every day to enjoy a burger. Don't mess around.

Also if you arrive too early for a burger, have a livermush sandwich (only available at breakfast) as an appetizer. For those not familiar with this old-timey Southern treat, it's basically pig liverwurst mixed with cornmeal in a patty form. For years Sandy cooked the livermush patties on the griddle with middling results. "One day the delivery guy suggested that we throw it in the deep fryer," he told me and success was at hand.

I know Scott works hard but I still had to ask him why the Hub closes at 2 p.m., which to me always seems like the middle of the lunch rush. He told me flat out, "If you close at two you can still get eighteen holes in." It's hard to argue with that logic.

SNAPPY LUNCH

125 North Main St | Mount Airy, NC 27030 | 336-786-4931 | Mon–Wed & Fri 5:45 am–1:45 pm
Thurs & Sat 5:45 am–1:15 pm | Closed Sun | www.thesnappylunch.com

The Snappy Lunch sells one of the best pork chop sandwiches in America and it is "World Famous" according to the menu. But this is a hamburger book, and the restaurant does its part to offer a bit of hamburger history as well. Popular with the locals, the Snappy Lunch sells a curiosity called the "Breaded Hamburger." Sometimes referred to as the "No-Burger" or the "old-fashioned," this throwback to the Great Depression was invented when meat was scarce. At the Snappy Lunch, the breaded burger still outsells the regular burger on the menu 3 to 1.

"I don't even get into it with out-of-towners," said Mary Dowell, widow of longtime owner and local food celebrity Charles Dowell. "I don't even like them!" she told me with a smile. I tried my first Depression-era burger at the Snappy Lunch and really liked it. It kind of resembled a bland crab cake with ground beef inside. "What do ya think?" Mary asked. I told her it tasted like a biscuit and she informed me that I had named the main ingredient.

The breaded burger, referred to as just a "hamburger" by the staff (a nonbreaded burger is a "burger with meat") starts as a blend of ground beef, crumbled cooked biscuits, and day-old bread. The blend, which leans mostly toward bread, is then formed into patties and cooked on the flattop griddle. A finished burger "all the way" has on it coleslaw, mustard, onion, tomato, and chili.

The chili, a tasty, sweet, and chunky concoction, is ladled onto both the pork chop sandwich and the burgers. It was created by Charles by accident in the 1950s. He was trying to make up something to put on the pork chops and the recipe has not changed since then.

Charles was a fixture at the Snappy Lunch since 1943 when, at age fifteen, he was paid ten dollars a week. Eight years later, his father, a local grocer, helped Charles negotiate the purchase of a share in the restaurant and in 1960 he became the sole owner.

The name Snappy is fitting for the turn-of-the-century post office turned lunch counter because the doors close most days at 1:45 p.m. Oddly on Thursday, closing time is 1:15 p.m. "As part of the war effort," Charles told me years ago, "restaurants were asked to choose a day to close early."

Mount Airy, North Carolina, exists in the minds of *The Andy Griffith Show* fans as the inspiration for Mayberry, the setting of the popular 1960s TV show. Not only did Andy grow up in Mount Airy, he also ate at the Snappy Lunch frequently as a child. Because of this, and his massive fan base, you may want to avoid the restaurant in late September when thousands descend on the small country town for Mayberry Days.

Mary and Charles met years ago when someone tried to set her up with Charles's son at the restaurant. Charles, who passed away in 2012, was at the restaurant daily, even though he had retired, and the energetic Mary ran the day-to-day. Today, Mary holds down the fort at the busy restaurant and a recent visit left me with the notion that in Mary's hands the future is secure at Snappy Lunch.

SOUTH 21 DRIVE-IN

3101 East Independence Blvd | Charlotte, NC 28205 | 704-377-4509
Tues 11 am–3 pm | Wed & Thurs 11 am–9 pm | Fri & Sat 11 am–9:30 pm | Closed Sun & Mon

Traveling along Independence Boulevard just east of downtown Charlotte, North Carolina, you'll notice a vintage red neon sign that blinks with the words "curb service" and beckons you to pull in and float back in time. Slip into one of the many stalls, check out the menu, and push the order button. You are on your way to a classic South 21 Drive-In experience.

Since 1959, very little has changed at this Charlotte institution. Owned by the same family of Greek immigrants since the beginning, South 21 serves the same fresh, thin-patty burger that has come from the same local meat supplier for over fifty years. In 1955, George Copsis and his two brothers decided to open a drive-in on South Boulevard in Charlotte. The business boomed and the brothers opened another nearby in 1959. They leased the original location and made the Independence location their flagship. Over the years, the family would open and sell off other drive-ins across town, but offspring Maria and her husband, George Housiadas, have held on to the flagship icon.

You've heard the story before but it bears repeating—Greeks in the hamburger business. The Housiadas family is not alone. Many proud Greek families still own classic burger stands across America, namely the famous minichains of the Billy Goat of Chicago, Burger House of Dallas, and Crown Burgers of Salt Lake City. Or the one-offs like Helvetia Tavern near Portland, Oregon. All of these restaurants were the result of hard-working Greeks finding their way in America.

Not surprisingly, most stories of Greek burger entrepreneurism in this country start the same way. "They came here with nothing," Maria told me. "They didn't know what else to do so they started flipping burgers and didn't stop!" She told me that in the beginning the brothers would sell a few burgers, take the cash, run down the street to the Winn-Dixie supermarket, and buy another few pounds of ground beef. "Can you imagine if we did that today?" Maria pondered.

South 21 is the real deal. Expect carhops, window trays, and tasty, classic burgers. The burgers start as pre-formed fresh ground four-ounce patties and can be ordered as singles or doubles. Make it a "Super Boy" and you will get two patties on a toasted white bun with chopped lettuce, onion, mustard, and tomato. If you want cheese, you'll need to order the "Jumbo." The burgers show up on your window tray with a large pickle speared to the top bun.

The fries at South 21 are great, but it's the onion rings that have received decades of accolades. The kitchen at South 21 slices and breads fresh onion rings daily, tasty circles of deep fried goodness.

You'll also notice an item on the menu that sounds almost cartoonish but is anything but—the

"Fish-O-Burger." Imagine two pieces of fresh (not frozen) lightly breaded and deep-fried trout served with tartar sauce on a toasted white bun. It's a heavenly sandwich, especially for those who want to partake of the drive-in culture without the red meat.

One thing you may find odd about South 21 is the black fedora your carhop will be wearing as he clips the tray to your car window. It was part of a uniform that was retired about twenty years ago according to Maria. "The uniforms used to be absolutely ridiculous." For years, carhops were required to wear what looked like a period carriage driver's getup—a long red coat with two gold buttons and heavy black pants. "They looked nice," Maria remembered, "but the carhops hated to wear them. The heavy material was really only comfortable in the three colder months of the year."

South 21 still employs a hard-working staff of four; some have been at the drive-in for decades. And Nick, the Greek cook who has been flipping perfect patties at South 21 since 1971, finally retired in 2014 logging an impressive forty-three years at the griddle.

Maria is at the drive-in every day to take orders and manage the staff. She seems confident in the quality of their fare and understands why people continue to patronize South 21. She told me once, "Diehard fans tell people, 'If you haven't eaten there, you haven't eaten.'"

WHAT-A-BURGER DRIVE-IN

210 South Main St | Mooresville, NC 28115 | 704-664-5455 | Mon–Sat 10 am–10 pm
(Five Other Locations In Kannapolis, Greensboro and Concord, NC)

This is not the well-known Texas burger chain you are thinking of. In fact, this What-A-Burger actually opened in 1950 in Virginia, the same year as the seven-hundred-store Whataburger chain, but both owners were unaware of the existence of the other. After a lawsuit brought more than fifty years later, the two chains agreed that they would not expand into each other's territory and that was that. Today, the Texas based burger chain has expanded into eight states and Mexico but has stayed away from North Carolina and Virginia where a handful of What-A-Burgers still exist.

Eb Bost opened the first What-A-Burger in North Carolina in 1955. At one point, through the ownership of many members of the Bost family, there were up to fifteen locations in the Charlotte area. Today, Eb's son Mike Bost is the president of the company and there are now five locations that still retain their original number in the chain (for example, the Mooresville location is still called number eleven). Some of the locations still offer curb service.

Built in 1965, the What-A-Burger of Mooresville is an authentic artifact of the drive-in era that sits just south of the main drag. Twenty-eight curb service stalls sit under a retro corrugated shelter and the dining room inside can hold up to a hundred hungry burger lovers.

The burgers at What-A-Burger are very wide, cooked on a flattop, and are made from fresh ground beef. "The patties come in every morning from a butcher in town," employee and manager of thirty-three years Diane told me. They are served on soft white buns that have been toasted on a large press. The thin patty and the squashed, toasted bun make for a very flat but satisfying burger. If you are hungry, go for the "Double

What-A-Burger." Priced at around six dollars this half-pound burger could be the best deal going. There's also a kid-sized What-A-Burger, a smaller version of the original.

You'd have to be a local to understand the baffling burger combinations that What-A-Burger offers. The signature "What-A-Burger" comes with shredded lettuce, sliced tomato, mustard, and onion. The "What-A-Cheeseburger" adds cheese, but mysteriously takes away the mustard. The "What-A-Salisbury" has no mustard, either, and no cheese and, follow me here, the "What-A-Hamburger" comes Southern Style with mustard, coleslaw, and chili. In reality, you can get a burger any way you want it. Just ask.

On my first visit, I was compelled to order a crazy-sounding drink on the menu called the "Witch Doctor." When I asked what was in the drink, through the muffled vintage drive-in speakerphone, I could not make out what the kitchen was telling me. All I could hear was, "Wah, wah waah, wah waaah." When the drink appeared at my car, I took a sip and tasted cherry and lime soda, and something savory. Then I opened the lid of the Styrofoam cup to find a wedge of lemon and three pickle slices floating in ice. The Witch Doctor, a drink that goes back almost six decades at What-A-Burger, is made by filling a cup with a little bit from each soda on the fountain. "There used to be a raw onion ring in there, too," employee Jeff told me. Diane added, "Some people still ask for the onion. Yuck." Mike Bost told me, "The customers dreamed that one up a long time ago." The drink was amazing with a flavor that was complex and refreshing. Just don't make the mistake I made and take a sip hours later after the ice had melted and the pickles had marinated.

The Witch Doctor is a great drink, but the bestseller at What-A-Burger is the "Cherry-Lemon Sundrop." It's so popular that Mike told me, "If we couldn't sell those and burgers, I think we'd go out of business."

Each curb stall is set up in twos and you'll need to follow curb service etiquette to park correctly. Imagine two gas pumps and you'll get the idea. In a row of two curb stalls, pull through to the second one so that someone can pull in behind you. I did not do this the first time I visited and received some quizzical looks from regulars.

For many years, the curb service at the Mooresville location was not up and running. A lack of qualified carhops led Mike to shut down the talkback speakers and send all of the business indoors. But after pressure from regulars, three years ago the curb service returned. Thanks to that pressure you can now enjoy your What-A-Burger and Witch Doctor curbside.

DAKOTA DRIVE-IN

211 6th St SW | Hankinson, ND 58041 | 701-242-7620 | Open Daily 11 am–8 pm
(Summer Hours: Memorial Day to Labor Day 11 am–10 pm)

Often I'll spot a tiny ice-cream stand on a quiet country road and imagine that they also serve a classic burger worthy of being in the book. What seems to be the case most of the time is that these places serve frozen, lifeless burgers as an afterthought, their glory days decades behind them. But every once in a while, I come across absolute gold.

This is exactly what happened as I was driving from Fargo, North Dakota, to Sioux City, Iowa. It's a long drive, and I needed a break. Google told me there was an antique shop nearby so I ventured into the quiet, dusty farming town of Hankinson, North Dakota. I drove past the Dakota Drive-In, turned around, passed again. . . . I must have looked insane because after three trips driving past slowly I cruised into the parking lot, all eyes inside the tiny stand were on me.

When I approached the window, there was an older guy picking up an order to go, a double cheeseburger. I asked him, "How's the burger?" and he answered simply, "The best," and walked off.

That was enough for me. When I asked the person taking orders (who turned out to be the owner's mother) if the beef was fresh not frozen, she cocked her head, looked at me with annoyance and said, "Of course it's fresh!"

The seasonal burger and ice-cream stand opened in 1952 and today is owned by local farmers Brandon and Amber Wahler. Brandon manages the family corn and soybean farm and Amber runs the seasonal stand, which is open from April to October, Seven days a week. The town of Hankinson gets very excited when spring rolls around. Amber told me, "They are waiting for us to open." When I happened upon the stand it was thirty-two degrees out and they had only been open two days for the season.

The burgers at Dakota come in a few sizes depending on how many patties you want. They start as what looks like slightly misshaped four-ounce patties made from 85/15 fresh ground beef. "It's what we are known for," Amber explained. "I don't like the taste of the prepackaged frozen stuff. . . . I can tell the difference." The buns are toasted with a copious amount of butter and a burger with everything comes with ketchup, mustard, pickle, and onion. Get a double cheeseburger and an "insert" bun is included (basically a piece of buttered toast in the center). The Cali Burger adds lettuce, tomato, and Miracle Whip.

My first bite of a simple single was pure bliss. Standing in the parking lot with the buttery bun, beef, and cheese combination in my hand was classically American, and it was gone within seconds. I was back for a double cheeseburger.

The endless list of deep-fried veggies, cheese, and potatoes (even chicken gizzards) is the stuff state fair dreams are made of so go nuts. And of course don't walk away without getting a soft-serve cone dipped. They are one of the only ice-cream stands I've been to in America that offers a *peanut butter* dip, a sweet departure from the standard chocolate dip.

After my visit, a flurry of activity on social media told me that I had accidentally discovered a hidden secret, as if I had solved a scavenger hunt riddle. One wrote, "So glad you found it!" and another, "None of us can wait until it opens each spring. . . . Don't tell anyone. It's our secret."

And no, I never made it to the antique shop.

OHIO

BOB'S HAMBURG

1351 East Ave | Akron, OH 44307 | 330-253-2627 | Mon–Thurs 7 am–5 pm
Fri & Sat 7:30 am–6 pm | Sun 9 am–12:30 pm | www.bobshamburg.com

The famous local burger drive-in chain Swenson's seems to have a lock on vintage burger popularity in the Akron area so I was happy to discover Bob's Hamburg. From the outside the squat structure sort of looks like a streetcar because that's exactly what it was in the beginning. In 1931, Bob Holbrook turned a streetcar into a diner and started selling smashed patties made from fresh ground beef. "The wheels are still down there," owner Aimee Buckeye told me.

Over the past eighty-six years, many modifications to the building have clearly altered the original integrity of the streetcar, although the low-ceilinged interior definitely gives the place the feeling as if you are standing up in a moving vehicle.

Bob only ran his namesake burger joint for a few years before Walter Ridge purchased it from him and ran it for almost half a century. After that, a few owners over the last thirty years ran the place until Aimee came along. She managed a local TGI Fridays but was laid off, and found work at Bob's. Soon after, the owner wanted to sell the place so Aimee bought the iconic burger counter.

"I bought the business, which came with a box of archives and all the recipes," Amy told me.

The menu offers double and triple cheeseburgers (and at just north of five bucks for a triple it's a helluva bargain) but the most popular burger is the single with everything. This includes a craggy-edged smashed patty, mustard, pickle, onion, shredded iceberg lettuce and Bob's "special" sauce (which seems to be a ketchup-based concoction).

Aimee picks up the beef for her burgers herself. "I go to the butcher every morning," she told me. Quarter-pound balls of fresh beef are pressed thin on the ancient cast-iron griddle which is jet black from years of use. The griddle is the center point of the diner, surrounded by beautifully dented, perfectly aged stainless steel. It's apparently also the original griddle from opening day. Bob's predates all other burger joints in the area making the griddle the oldest, continually used burger flattop in Akron. In case you are wondering, the answer is yes—much of the flavor of Bob's burgers comes from that griddle.

When Aimee is in the restaurant, which is always, she does it all—works the griddle, makes change, and answers the phone, and she does it all with ease and moves at her own pace. She does have a small staff to relieve her once in a while. And since Bob's is an open kitchen diner Aimee talks to everyone in the tiny place as she works. I once saw her turn from the griddle and say to a regular at the counter, "I have an extra patty, do you want it? I won't charge you for it." Aimee knows she is a steward of hamburger history and treating regulars like family is part of the deal.

CRABILL'S HAMBURGERS

727 Miami St | Urbana, OH 43078 | 937-653-5133 | Mon–Fri 10 am–6 pm
Sat 10 am–5 pm | Closed Sun | www.crabillshamburgers.com

Crabill's is very, very small. What's amazing is that the original Crabill's was much smaller. Eight stools sit bolted to the floor at a small counter and there is barely enough room to pass behind them. "The old place was five times smaller," owner and grill cook Andy Hiltibran told me. Andy is married to third-generation owner Marsha Crabill, the granddaughter of Forest Crabill, who opened this heartland burger stand nearly one hundred years ago.

Crabill's started as a hamburger counter in Norman Rockwell–esque downtown Urbana. Two men, Crabill and Carpenter, opened the minuscule six-stool counter in 1927. After only three days, Crabill bought out Carpenter for seventy-five dollars. The counter remained in operation, run by Forest's son and daughter-in-law, David and Joyce, until it closed in 1988.

Marsha and Andy decided to restart the family business soon after with the help of Marsha's parents. They were eager to leave their factory jobs (she worked at Honda, he worked at Bristol-Myers) so they purchased a small motor home and dubbed it "Crabill's on Wheels." They made the rounds of county fairs and horse shows, and after three years on wheels the couple decided to go brick-and-mortar. Crabill's was reborn on the west side of town, just a few blocks from, and not much larger than, the original location.

The first time I visited the reincarnation of the burger counter, I sat next to a white-bearded regular named Will Yoder who for decades played the annual town Santa. Will had recently had his teeth removed and was on a soft food diet. The tiny burgers at Crabill's, with their pillowy, fresh-baked buns and healthy dose of burger grease, actually do melt in your mouth.

The burgers at Crabill's are cooked in a wide, shallow griddle. The griddle is filled with about a half inch of grease. "The griddle in the old place was much smaller," Andy told me, and showed me with his hands only a foot apart. "It was also much deeper." Small balls of fresh ground beef are tossed into the grease, then pressed once with specially made spatulas. The grillperson uses two of these spatulas at a time to systematically press and flip the dozens of patties resting in the grease.

Chopped raw onion, spicy mustard, and relish are standard, but cheese and ketchup are also available (both unnecessary). There is a sign on the wall menu that explains that ketchup was introduced in 1990. That's right, it took ketchup sixty-three years to be accepted at Crabill's.

On a busy Saturday, Crabill's can move up to three hundred burgers in thirty minutes. When someone walks in with an order for twenty doubles, the griddle is quickly filled with the balls of meat and the spatulas start whacking away.

The aroma inside Crabill's is intoxicating. The rendered beef grease permeates everything and has a rich smell not unlike brownies or baking cookies. Leave your jacket in the car if you plan to be presentable the rest of the day.

Don't waste your time with singles; go for doubles. Twice the beef, twice the grease, and half the bread. If you are feeling brave, do what some regulars do—ask for yours double-dipped and you'll get the top of your bun dipped in the grease. A double, double-dipped anyone?

Andy and Marsha's children have all done time in the restaurant. Their youngest, Meredith (age twenty-one), currently works hard for the family business and when I asked her how long she had been working at Crabill's she told me, "My whole freaking life!" She is likely to assume ownership at some point, not that Marsha and Andy are retiring. Marsha, within earshot of Meredith, told me with a smile, "We are at least ten years from that."

GAHANNA GRILL

82 Granville St | Gahanna, OH 43230 | 614-476-9017 | Mon–Thurs 11 am–9:30 pm
Fri & Sat 11 am–10:30 pm | Sun 11 am–9 pm | www.gahannagrill.com

"This used to be all farm fields out here," former owner of the Gahanna Grill Jimmy Staravecka told me, waving his arm. He pointed to a photo that shows the bar in 1900, not surrounded by much of anything. Looking at the restaurant today in this busy suburb of Columbus, it's hard to imagine its former surroundings. No one seems to know the age of the building, but supposedly the business dates back to the days of mud streets and horse-drawn carriages. This means the tavern has been pouring drinks for well over a century and makes the Gahanna Grill one of the oldest restaurants in the area.

In 2005, brothers Gary and Jimmy Staravecka bought Gahanna Grill and made a few improvements. The kitchen received a needed upgrade and Jimmy, formerly a Gracie Mansion chef under NYC mayor Rudolph Giuliani, added steak and pastas to the menu. And in 2014, Gary, who had been acting as a silent partner, bought out his brother and assumed day-to-day operations. Jimmy now owns another restaurant across town.

The nondescript exterior of the tavern yields to a comfortable interior. The wood-paneled walls are covered with photos of the tavern's past (one depicting the former Gahanna Lanes, a bowling alley on the premises) and the large bar is surrounded by televisions. The surface of the bar is a potpourri of advertisements for local services—from real estate to a hair salon—laminated directly into the finish. One corner of the bar is dedicated to the Beanie Burger Hall of Fame. Floor-to-ceiling photographs show the brave souls who have ingested the burger that has made the Gahanna famous—the "Double Beanie Burger."

The regular Beanie Burger itself is a monster, with its patty of fresh ground beef weighing in at about half a pound. The Double gives you two half-pound patties, a photo on the wall, and a free T-shirt for your efforts. But the Beanie Burger, named after the cook who invented it decades ago, does not just contain a perfectly griddled patty. The burger is also piled high with lettuce, tomato, grilled onions, bacon, cheese, and a hearty scoop of homemade coleslaw. The burger is a sloppy, tasty mess that is barely contained by its toasted, soft kaiser roll. For that reason, the kitchen staff takes great pride in stabbing the vertical burger with a large steak knife. I know of no frilly toothpick that could keep this beast together.

Beanie Vesner retired in 2013, after suffering a stroke, but the kitchen still turns out hundreds of burgers for the lunchtime crowd consisting mostly of construction workers and faithful regulars. Jim Ellison, a local friend who alerted me to this hamburger destination, calls the Beanie Burger "A good, manly lunch," referring to the nearly 100 percent male population at noon.

I once asked Beanie how long he had been making burgers at Gahanna and he refused to give me a straight answer. Smiling, with a toothpick in his mouth, he told me, "Maybe twenty years, maybe?" But by other accounts, by the time he retired, the figure was more like thirty-five years.

To make the burger, the grill cook grabs a half-pound wad of ground beef measured by hand and presses it flat, also by hand, onto the hot griddle. The burger is flipped once and a bacon weight is placed on top. I ordered my Beanie Burger cooked to the chef's specs and ended up with a medium-well, but moist, burger.

"Beanie still comes in three times a week," longtime manager Tiffany Workman told me. Tiffany is responsible for the latest decor and feel of Gahanna. A few years ago she told Gary, "This place looks like a cafeteria," and she then began to make this cozy bar even cozier. "I said, 'Give me some dimmers, anything!' I wanted to make it comfy."

HAMBURGER WAGON

12 East Central Ave | Miamisburg, OH 45342 | 937-847-2442 | Mon–Sat 10:30 am–6 pm
Sun 11 am–6 pm (Labor Day to Memorial Day) | Mon–Sat 10:30–7 pm
Sun 11–7 pm (Memorial Day to Labor Day) | www.hamburgerwagon.com

Every day of the year, two dedicated employees of the Hamburger Wagon open a small garage door and drag a tiny spoked-wheel lunch cart fifty feet to a spot across the street. "It's pretty awkward to pull," an employee told me once, "but if you get a running start it's okay." The wagon has been selling burgers in roughly the same spot for over one hundred years to faithful regulars from the center of this picturesque town south of Dayton. I asked former owner Michelle Lyons if the Hamburger Wagon would be around for a while and she told me, "I think there would be civil unrest if they tried to get rid of the wagon."

Born of necessity, the Hamburger Wagon was started by Sherman "Cocky" Porter just after the devastating Dayton Flood of 1913. Miamisburg was evacuated and in shambles, left without power or water. Cocky served burgers from a cart

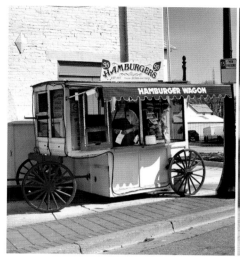

to relief workers and locals who were put to the task of rebuilding the town.

Today, the Wagon still sells the one thing it has sold for almost a century—hamburgers. It's as basic as you can get. The burger comes one way only, on a bun with pickle and onion, no cheese. You can always tell when someone in line has never been to the wagon when they ask for cheese. Various cranky old men have owned and worked on the Wagon through the decades and one was known to yell, "If you want cheese, get yer ass over to the McDonald's!"

The small patties, around three ounces apiece, come as singles or doubles on tiny buns from local Nickles Bakery. Chips and pop are offered, but that's about it. If you were looking for variety, you came to the wrong place. Current owner Jack Sperry told me that when Michelle added pop and chips, "There was a mini revolt." Jack bought the Hamburger Wagon in 2008 and changed virtually

nothing, except that now the Wagon is open year round. Jack told me, "Unless there's a ten-foot snow drift, we're dragging out the Wagon." This is a big change from the previous owners who would close down for the month of February much to the dismay of the regulars.

The burgers at the Wagon are unique. The thing you'll notice upon first bite is the extraordinarily crunchy exterior and the pleasantly moist interior. Think chicken-fried burger. You also probably watched your burger being deep-fried in the enormous twenty-inch skillet through one of the Wagon's windows. The reason for the super-crunch of the burgers is kept secret, but I'd venture to guess that one of the ingredients is some sort of breading. Adding bread to ground beef was a government-sanctioned method for stretching food during the Depression and hard times. It's a method that a few old-time burger stands in America still operate successfully with.

An average order at the wagon is four burgers. A customer of over sixty years named Glenn makes the forty-mile round trip twice a week for four of the tasty deep-fried burgers. One day when I was there he added a Diet Coke to his order. Rubbing his belly, he told me, laughing, "I'm watching my figure!"

Two employees work at lightning speed to prep, cook, and bag hundreds of burgers an hour. One stands at the skillet managing the tiny bobbing and bubbling patties while the other preps buns and makes change. This sounds entirely ordinary except that it is accomplished in a space that is no more than four by five feet wide. The illusion

of the small cart is perpetuated though by a large commercial kitchen across the street where the meat, onions, and buns are prepped and stored.

Jack's kids have been put to work at the wagon—sixteen-year-old Alex just started in the wagon, "She's joining the crew!" Jack told me enthusiastically and his younger daughter, Emma, works in the kitchen part-time rolling balls of beef.

Sales today are incredible at the Wagon and Jack stays very busy all year round. He told me with confidence, "I'd put my sales-per-square-foot up against anybody." It's true . . . two-hundred-plus burgers an hour out of a space that is no more than twenty square feet has to be a record.

JOHNNIE'S TAVERN

3503 Trabue Rd | Columbus, OH 43204 | 614-488-0110
Mon–Thurs & Sat 11 am–10 pm | Fri 11 am–12 am | Closed Sun

On my first visit to this semi-suburban burger destination, I was invited into the kitchen to interview the chef and I was sort of shocked by what I found. Although Johnnie's is a tiny out-of-the-way tavern, they do manage to crank out a ton of burgers during the lunch hour and all of those burgers are prepped, cooked, cheesed, and placed on buns by the one-man hamburger machine Joe Lombardi.

"When I get real backed up it can take me a while," the young fourth-generation Lombardi told me. "I'm alone back here." As he jumped from griddle to prep surface and back again with lightning speed, the band Phish poured out of a beat-up boom box. The only other employee during lunch, the bubbly server/bartender Brittney, burst into the kitchen with the next large order of burgers and announced, "You're gonna HATE this order." The order contained about nine burgers, all with different types of cheese and different toppings, not to mention that the order was hard to read. When I asked why she thought Joe would hate the order, she told me, "Just because it's a bunch of mumbo-jumbo."

Joe's grandfather, Dominic, opened the comfortable, broken-in bar in 1948 by turning his family's local grocery store into a tavern. Joe's great-grandfather emigrated from Italy to open the grocery store around the turn of the century. Johnnie's sits near a busy freight rail crossing in the old-world Italian neighborhood of San Margherita, an attractive spot to Italian immigrants at the time due to its proximity to a large, nearby marble quarry.

As I stood talking to Joe in the kitchen at Johnnie's, I saw him reach somewhere and toss what looked like perfectly pressed frozen burger patties on the griddle. My heart sank and I shouted out in disbelief, "Are your burgers frozen?" Fortunately, my trip to Johnnie's was not in vain and Joe explained with a chuckle, "No, that's fried bologna." The fried bologna, which is clearly linked to the strong Ohio roots in European sausage making, is a local central Ohio favorite.

The "Super Burgers" are the only burger on the menu and they come in one size—huge. Every morning Joe and other family members

hand-patty enough burgers for lunch and dinner. Joe told me, "I usually don't weigh them but they are around a pound." These burgers are beasts and after cooking they are still just north of three-quarters-pound. The fresh ground chuck comes from two local sources and blended in the kitchen. Why two sources? "That's just the way it's always been done," Joe told me with a straight face. I love those answers.

A burger with everything comes on a seeded white squishy bun with your choice of cheese (six to choose from), raw onion, a slice of tomato, and lettuce. The regular's cheese of choice is Pepper Jack, which has a decent kick and is the perfect cheese for the Super Burger. Fried onions are also available, but you'll have to ask for them.

On my first weekday visit to Johnnie's, the place was full by 11:30 a.m. and there were beers on every table. A pool table dominates the dining area, leaving only enough room for about twenty-eight hungry patrons. The bar is also an option with its thirteen stools but a wait seems inevitable after 11:45. On one wall is a poster of Grandpa Dominic standing at the bar, a mug of beer in front of him with a strange contraption protruding. I asked local friend and burger expert Jim Ellison about the beer and he explained that more than once Johnnie's has been awarded the "Coldest Tap Beer in Columbus." The thing sticking out of the beer? A thermometer.

People who love Johnnie's really love the place. A guy in the booth next to me announced, unprovoked, "I've been coming here for twenty-five years." That's the kind of burger-love I'm looking for across America. Jim pointed out that for most people who live in Columbus a trip to Johnnie's is not serendipitous because it's way out by itself in a quiet part of town surrounded by homes with perfectly trimmed lawns. "If you are coming here, you are making a choice to be here."

Joe plans to keep Johnnie's in the family and eventually buy the place from his dad. When his dad asked him to step into the business, Joe told me, "I took about a month to decide." Let's hope a Lombardi runs this American icon for at least another four generations.

K'S HAMBURGER SHOP

117 East Main St | Troy, OH 45373 | 937-339-3902 | Mon–Fri 6 am–9 pm
Sat 6 am–7 pm | Closed Sun | www.kshamburgershoptroy.com

K's is an American treasure and it's the sort of place that should be in the Smithsonian. This is not to say that it is a relic, in fact, it is anything but. The vibrant 83-year-old burger restaurant acts as if it opened yesterday, still packing the place on a Saturday and pushing out the same burger that has been on the menu since opening day.

Time has caught up to K's and what's old is new again. The restaurant is an anchor in historic downtown Troy, Ohio, and a stop for every tourist that rambles through. A vintage neon sign hangs over the front door that simply reads "EAT." Inside the walls and ceiling are sheathed in white enameled steel sheeting which has proven to withstand decades of use and they make the place look almost new. And one glance at the diner menu reveals what seems like throwback pricing—not one single item is over five dollars.

In 1935, Paul and Doris Klein opened K's, a tiny, boxy white burger joint directly across the street from its current location. Their lease expired in 1940 so the Kleins bought some land and, with a borrowed tractor, dragged the building to a its new home. The Kleins added a dining room next to the existing counter layout in 1958.

What's incredible, Paul and Doris ran the restaurant for sixty years. At that point their

History repeating itself—K's circa 1940 and 2017

daughter, Marcia Bodmer who started working in the restaurant at age thirteen, was already a large part of the day-to-day at K's.

K's opened in the height of the Great Depression but they've always been successful. A major factor was that during WWII, as many other burger joints were closing due to lack of supplies, K's survived because the government asked Paul to stay open twenty-four hours to feed nearby wartime factory workers that had shifts around the clock.

The cooking method for the burgers at K's is as much of a throwback as the decor. Like many burger joints of the 1930s instead of using a flame grill or flattop griddle burgers are basically deep-fried in what is called a "wet grill" with astonishingly tasty results. Today, K's uses vegetable oil to fry in but in the old days it was rendered beef grease, or tallow. "Back then we rendered our own," Marcia told me. And there's definitely a skill in cooking this way. Marcia remembered the words of her father, "On a dry grill you can cook a shoe," which I took to mean that anyone can operate a flattop griddle.

Michael Scheib operates the wet grill with ease and stands in the center of the action just inside the front door behind the counters. K's grinds their own chuck steaks for the burgers and use a scoop to portion the beef. When you order, Michael grabs a few balls of beef and presses them in the tank of oil. They bob around and when cooked he drains of some grease and marries it to a soft slider bun. Ask for cheese, and a square of yellow american goes on cold after cooking (the cheese in the tank would make a mess for sure). But all burgers at K's are served wrapped in thin deli paper so the insulating effect melts the cheese in seconds. The double cheeseburger is the most popular, and Michael pointed out that the classic combo at K's is one with mustard, pickles and diced onion. "Some ask for everything but they don't know what that means," he told me. Ask for everything at K's (please don't), and you'll get mustard, pickle, onion, ketchup, mayo, lettuce, and tomato. Just stick with a few classics for surefire happiness. "Some also want their bun dipped in there," Michael told me, "and that's just gross." In the days of rendered beef fat that would make sense.

The first time I met Michael I was sort of taken aback. His outfit that day was almost a costume—he was wearing (and does every day) a nearly pitch-perfect uniform that placed him at K's in the 1940s. The thin black tie, clean white shirt, black apron, and his paper cap askew gave him the look of a vintage Paul Klein himself. Then I discovered that Michael is the heir apparent to K's Hamburgers. He's a young man with an old soul and started working at the diner at age seventeen. Marcia told me, "We've spent eight years together here. I wish I could adopt him!" Eventually Marcia will start to hand over the business to Michael, who looks more prepared for the challenge than anyone. Marcia told me that according to his teachers, he talked about about owning K's one day as early as the first grade. Michael, leaning on the counter during a rare lull, said to me "I love old things," and looking around, "This place is beautiful."

KEWPEE

111 North Elizabeth St | Lima, OH 45801 | 419-228-1778
Mon–Thurs 5:30 am–10 pm | Fri & Sat 5:30 am–11 pm | Sun 3 pm–10 pm

In the center of Lima, Ohio, sits a slice of Americana that is impossible to ignore. A well-preserved art-deco restaurant with a big history, this 1920s hamburger tradition once existed throughout the Upper Midwest with over two hundred locations that competed with White Castle and outlived White Tower. Today, there are only six Kewpees remaining, and of those, three are in Lima.

Owner Harry Shutt hasn't done much to his enameled-brick burger restaurant that was built in 1938 (and replaced a version built in 1928). "We have tried to maintain our image and not change much." That's a good thing because this Kewpee has been turning out tasty square-patty burgers for over eighty years.

Yes, the burgers at Kewpee are square, not round. Sound familiar? In 1969, Dave Thomas, the founder of the ubiquitous Wendy's chain, introduced a square burger to America. It may have been a new concept to some, but both Kewpee

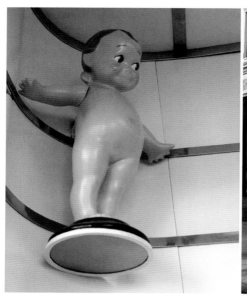

and White Castle have been serving square burgers since the 1920s. Dave was clearly influenced by the local Kewpee in his hometown of Kalamazoo, Michigan. But unlike both White Castle and Wendy's, the burgers at Kewpee are made from fresh ground beef, not frozen.

Step into the Kewpee of downtown Lima and instantly step back in time. Very little has changed from the food to the 1930s fast-food decor. The restaurant's original curved white enamel-steel wall and ceiling panels look as clean as if it were opening day. Newish orange plastic booths, a low counter with stools, and random tables fill the small terrazzo-floored restaurant. In the dining area, two large Kewpee dolls stand watch over customers enjoying their burgers and thick shakes. Fortunately, Harry has held on to these icons of a forgotten age and has even had the priceless dolls refurbished

recently. The Kewpee name comes from the popular early twentieth–century doll of the same name (but different spelling), the Kewpie doll.

The burgers are fresh. "I buy boneless carcass beef and grind it here," Harry told me. The beef comes from a Lima meatpacker that processes only local cows. Harry said it best when he explained, "The worst thing you can do to meat is haul it. These animals have never been more than forty miles from Lima." This makes Harry and Kewpee an anomaly in fast-food America. The hamburger überchains today, with their cross-country shipments and city-sized warehouses, could not even begin to imagine this sort of localized business plan.

Two separate griddles work full-time during the lunch rush; one services the drive-thru and the other walk-up customers inside. A few of the women working behind the counter slinging patties and dressing burgers have been at the Kewpee for almost forty years.

The burgers are super thin and so fresh they are almost falling apart. The usual condiments like mustard, ketchup, and pickle are available, but most order "The Special," which is a burger with mayonnaise, lettuce, and tomato. The produce for Kewpee comes from a local farmer and is hydroponically grown. One menu item, the vegetable sandwich, appears to be a late addition for a health-conscious America, but this is not the case. On the menu for decades, the sandwich was probably added during World War II to make up for the lack of available burger meat. "We've had a vegetable sandwich for over seventy years," Harry pointed out. Harry has been at Kewpee for almost sixty years and owns the rights to the franchise as well as two other "contemporary" Kewpees in Lima. He started flipping burgers at the downtown Kewpee when he was twenty-five and became the owner in 1980. Harry has a lot to say about the "Walmarting" of America. He feels the crush of commercial fast food and the lack of support for small business in America. Coincidentally, one of his Kewpees is threatened by highway expansion designed to accommodate . . . a new Walmart! Regardless, Kewpee does a brisk business and is hardly fazed by the seven McDonald's restaurants in Lima.

You owe it to yourself to visit Kewpee. It's a part of American hamburger tradition that remains vital in the face of a homogenizing fast-food culture. Pay homage to a burger chain that preceded Burger King and Wendy's by almost forty years. Look for the wide-eyed smiling Kewpee doll over the front door and remember the Kewpee slogan, "Hamburg pickle on top makes your heart go flippity-flop."

MAID-RITE SANDWICH SHOPPE

125 North Broadway St | Greenville, OH 45331 | 937-548-9340
Mon–Thurs 10 am–10 pm | Fri & Sat 10 am–11 pm | Sun 11 am–10 pm
www.maidrite-greenville.com

Loosemeat sandwiches are a midwestern invention and technically an import from Iowa. Starting in 1927 in Muscatine, Iowa, Fred Angell started steaming crumbled beef and scooping it onto burger buns and called them Maid-Rites. The name itself has gone on to become a fast growing restaurant chain that serves the tasty, pebbly beef sandwiches midwesterners have come to love, but deep in the sandwich's past can be found a few of the original outposts that serve an authentic piece of food history. Maid-Rite Sandwich Shoppe is one of those outposts (and has no affiliation to the corporate chain of the same name).

Some of the best examples of the loosemeat sandwich can be found at NuWay in Kansas, Tendermaid in Minnesota, and of course Canteen Lunch and Taylor's in Iowa. Other than the lack of a formed burger patty, the flavor profile is very similar to a classic American burger that's served with nothing more than pickles, onion, and mustard. Maid-Rite Sandwich Shoppe in Greenville, Ohio, is no different and is beloved by generations of locals.

Maid-Rite opened in 1934 by Louise Maher with the help of her brothers Tom and Gene. Later, more family would get involved and become owners like Louise's brother-in-law "Big" Jim Koontz, his son Little Jim, and currently Dave Trimble. All these names belong to the same family making Maid-Rite a family-owned business for over eighty years. Mark Koontz, the son of Little Jim, has a full-time job as an art therapist in the local school system but still returns to help out, often, with the family business. Mark has spent his life at Maid-Rite, working there though high school and after college. He told me, "I grew up in the building."

If you've never experienced a loosemeat sandwich, you are in for a treat. Soft crumbly beef served on a burger bun is hard to beat. At Maid-Rite, fresh beef is cooked and crumbled at a high temperature with water in a large trough behind the counter. Some "secret" seasoning is added, and contrary to rumor no beer. "People say we use cola, or beer," Mark told me. "We don't." The beef is scooped onto a steamed bun that has mustard, two pickles and diced raw onion. You can opt for less condiments, but not more. Maid-Rite (thankfully) is a very traditional place, although you can get cheese. If you want something slightly different and unique at Maid-Rite, go for the Big Jim Sandwich, created decades ago by Mark's grandfather. A slice of ham and american cheese are added to the bottom of a steamed sesame seed bun, then crumbled beef on top of that.

In 1942, the original building was sold, and moved off the property so that the family could build the substantial brick structure that remains today. In the early years, you walked in the front door and went straight down a flight of stairs to a subterranean dining room. "There was even a tiny dance floor down there," Mark told me. Maid-Rite was a hot spot following WWII and was granted one of the first licenses to sell beer to go in Darke County. "Sometimes fights would break out in the back lot," Mark told me, "and Grandpa would have to go and break it up." Big Jim kept a list of the instigators and would boot people for thirty days. "He was. . . ," Mark said, laughing and searching for the right word, "cantankerous!"

Easily the most recognizable attribute to the exterior of the Maid-Rite Sandwich Shoppe, other than the glorious neon sign over the front door, is the chewing gum that seems to cover the brick walls of the entire restaurant. Mark told me it started at the back door, years ago but has now spread to all four walls. "People would stick their gum on the wall outside the door instead of throwing it on the ground." Today, it has become a tradition to stick your gum on the building as much as it is to make a pilgrimage for a Maid-Rite sandwich. "Some people draw hearts, spell their name with gum, whatever. . . ." Mark told me. I asked if the gum tradition is an issue for the restaurant and he joked, "It's holding the building together so I'm okay with it!"

THE SPOT

201 South Ohio Ave | Sidney, OH 45365 | 937-492-9181
Mon–Sat 7 am–9 pm | Sun 8 am–9 pm | www.thespottoeat.com

The Spot has been a fixture in the center of downtown Sidney, Ohio, for over a century. The large, gleaming neon sign over the front door is a beacon to those in search of genuine diner food and one of the best burgers in the country—the "Big Buy."

The first time I stepped into this updated time-warp diner with its two-tone leather booths and vintage Coke signage I thought the place may have lost its way. Then an old-timer got up from his booth, approached the vintage jukebox, and put on Little Anthony's "Tears on My Pillow" and the whole place was transformed. The ownership had not fallen prey to '50s kitsch. They had merely embraced it. A major remodeling effort in 1976 updated the interior of the Spot to a wood-paneled "country kitchen" look and it took sixth owner Michael Jannides to rescue the diner and restore it to its original character. "I wanted to bring the place back to the way it looked in

was growing up, and this most likely influenced Michael's decision to buy the Spot.

There are many diner favorites on the menu like the BLT, the tuna salad sandwich, the seasonal mincemeat pie, and a housemade tenderloin sandwich. Michael confessed, "We've added things to the menu over the years but people come in for the burgers." For sure, the burger remains the number-one seller at the Spot. The restaurant can go through up to one thousand on a busy Friday.

I had blinders on when I saw the best seller on the long burger menu—the "Big Buy." Advertised as a triple-decker, the Big Buy is actually a double patty burger with one of those bun inserts in between the patties (like you'd find on a Big Mac). Cooked on a flattop griddle, the Big Buy is served on a toasted white squishy bun with shredded lettuce, pickles, american cheese, and a housemade tartar sauce. The taste of this thing is phenomenal, although you'll find lifting the Big Buy to your face a challenge. The two quarter-pound square patties slip and slide in the tartar sauce and make a mockery of the bun. If you can manage to get a solid bite that includes all of the ingredients, you are in for a treat. The tartar, tangy and sweet, plays to the beefiness of the burger with the cheese lending a salty hand.

The Spot grinds and patties their own burgers and have done so for years. Michael showed me the patty maker he inherited with the purchase of the restaurant, a strange looking contraption with many parts. From what I could tell, the burgers are not "pressed" or "stamped" like most patty

the '40s," Michael explained, and he did so with amazing detail.

Don't let the sock hop decor fool you. The Spot actually dates back to a time well before Elvis was King. In 1907, Spot Miller was selling food from a cart on the location where the restaurant now sits. The cart eventually became a permanent structure that burned down in 1940. A year later, the second owners rebuilt the Spot in the art moderne style that remains today.

Michael was no stranger to the Spot when he assumed ownership of the Ohio hamburger icon in 1999. In 1989, Michael took a part-time job at the Spot and liked what he saw. His grandfather owned an ice-cream parlor in Sidney when he machines, rather they are extruded sideways through a narrow opening and cut into squares. The patty, when cooked, stays loose and almost crumbly, most likely from not being pressed in the patty-making process.

Grab a booth or a spot at the counter along the window, then place your order at the register in the rear of the restaurant. When your order is ready, listen for your number to be called over a loudspeaker and pick up your burgers at the counter. At the Spot you can also enjoy traditional carhop service in one of the restaurant's twenty-one parking spaces. Regulars have enjoyed carhop service for decades and as Michael put it, "It never went out of vogue here!"

After six owners, I have a feeling this place will be around for a while (and this year the Spot celebrates its 111th year in business). Almost everything at the Spot is fresh and made to order, which is a tough claim for most diners today.

SWENSON'S DRIVE IN

658 East Cuyahoga Falls Ave | Akron, OH 44310 | 330-928-8515 | Sun–Thurs 11 am–1 am
Fri & Sat 11 am–1:30 am | (Six Other Locations In Akron, Canton, and Cleveland)
www.swensonsdriveins.com

I was happy to find that classic carhop drive-in culture is alive and well in Ohio. Anyone who has ever visited the Cuyahoga Falls Avenue location of Swenson's can tell you that. There are other large burger chains in the United States that employ carhops but I've never seen anything like the energy displayed by the carhops at Swenson's. For these carhops, delivery of a burger to your car is a true sport.

My first impression of Swenson's, with its young men and women in white polo shirts darting back and forth, was that something was wrong. These carhops were moving way too fast for college-age kids. A half-dozen carhops crisscross with trays of burgers and drinks at lightning speed, often running into each other entering and leaving the kitchen area. When a car pulls up to the sixty-six-year-old drive-in, the driver barely has to flash lights before a carhop is sprinting in their direction. And when a regular pulls up, the carhops all shout out their name in singsong fashion, "Angela's here!" or "Omar's here!" It's pretty incredible to witness and a great show to watch. Swenson's hires only college students for their youth and their flexible schedules. "It's a rigorous, hard job," Patty Palmer from Swenson's main office told me. "It takes a special person to do that."

The Cuyahoga Falls Avenue location is the oldest physical structure dating back to 1952 but the local chain now boasts seven locations in Akron, Canton, and Cleveland, all drive-ins with

and the Sloppy Joe, but the burgers are the star attraction, headlining the top of the menu. The signature burger at Swenson's is the "Galley Boy," a double cheeseburger with two special sauces. I deduced that one sauce was tartar and the other was barbecue sauce. "You are sort of right but not quite," Patty told me. Clearly the sauces are a secret. There are many condiments available at Swenson's, but if you ask for everything, you'll get mustard, pickles, and raw onion. But the Galley Boy, with its two sauces, two three-ounce patties, and cheese, is perfect.

All of the burgers are served on buns that are a special recipe and been made exclusively for Swenson's by the local Massoli's Italian Bakery. Fresh ground beef is delivered daily to each of the locations in the chain, pattied and shipped out from their central commissary location in North Akron.

Swenson's is also known for its shakes and the incredible chocolate peanut butter is one of the most popular. There are eighteen flavors to choose from with "limitless combinations," Patty explained. Swenson's also offers seasonal flavors, like the immensely popular pumpkin shake in the fall.

People are crazy about Swenson's and the restaurant has a solid legion of fans. "It's bizzaro!" Patty explained of the lengths some fanatics go to enjoy their Swenson's burgers. "We just sent two burgers to a wedding for the bride and groom," Patty explained. That's right, the newlyweds ate Swenson's burgers, and the guests ate the catered food. That is my kind of wedding.

carhops, or "curb-servers" as they are referred to at Swenson's. Wesley "Pop" Swenson opened his first drive-in in 1934 after he had success selling burgers from his station wagon to high school students as classes let out.

The Swenson family sold the business in the late '50s to the Phillips family who in turn sold it to current owner Steve Thompson in 1974 (a former curb server himself at Swenson's in the '60s). He was responsible for expanding the business by adding five additional locations, as well as rebuilding the original 1934 West Akron drive-in. The Phillips family probably ran the drive-ins well, but Steve had an added advantage. Friendly with Pop's granddaughter, Steve was able to get the original Swenson recipes making the drive-in today as authentic as it could possibly be.

The menu at Swenson's is large and offers Ohio classics like the fried bologna sandwich

THE THURMAN CAFE

183 Thurman Ave | Columbus, OH 43206 614-443-1570
Sun–Thurs 11 am–12 am | Fri & Sat 11 am–1 am | www.thethurmancafe.com

The quaint, historic German Village in Columbus, Ohio, with its low, ancient buildings and streets paved with red brick, is the perfect setting for this broken-in, dark and cozy tavern. The menu at Thurman Cafe is loaded with great food from decades-old family recipes like the Coney sauce for the hot dogs and terrific french fries. But it's the burger you came to eat, so settle into one of the odd-shaped booths and prepare to feast on one of the tallest burgers in the land—the "Thurman Burger."

Thurman Cafe has all the trappings of a typical time-tested favorite local hang—walls covered with the obligatory license plates, beer ads, and old photos. But look a little closer and discover the amazing ceiling covered in vintage Budweiser wallpaper and the thousands of signed dollar bills dangling over the bar area like party decorations. Chances are, while you are waiting for your Thurman Burger to arrive, one will pass by on its way to another customer. Your first glance at the famed burger will result in an audible gulp that signals either fear or hunger. This is because the Thurman Burger is enormous.

Macedonian immigrants Nancho and Dena Suclescy opened the Thurman Cafe in 1937. Today, eighty-one years later, the café is still in the Suclescy family, run by third-generation siblings Mike, Paul, and Donna. There are many different burgers on the menu, but it's the Thurman Burger that outsells them all. The creation starts with a three-quarter-pound patty of griddled fresh ground beef that is topped with (follow me here) grilled onions, lettuce, tomato, sliced sautéed mushrooms, pickle, jalapeño slices, mayonnaise, and a half-pound mound of sliced ham. The pile of ingredients is then covered with both mozzarella and american cheese, capped with a toasted bun, and speared with extra-long toothpicks.

When I say tall, I'm guessing this burger stands no less than seven inches high. Get your mouth ready. "The best way to eat this thing," local burger expert and friend Jim Ellison told me, "is to press it down and flip it over. The juices have

already destroyed the bottom bun." He was right, and flipping worked, but after the first few bites something went wrong, and my burger imploded. The combination of ingredients and sheer size beg for your patience. Take your time and enjoy this pile of goodness. It's a sloppy burger.

On a busy Saturday at Thurman, the kitchen will prepare and serve up to five hundred of the famed burgers. "We go through over 1,500 pounds of beef a week," Mike Suclescy told me. Good meat, too. Mike buys only top-quality 85/15 ground chuck and told me, "We ran out once and went over to the Kroger Supermarket for ground beef. The taste just wasn't the same."

The "Blue Cheeseburger" (for which the Suclescys go through over eight gallons of blue cheese dressing a week) is also a big seller as is the "Macedonian," served on Texas toast with sweet red peppers. Or try the "Thurmanator," a Thurman Burger on top of a cheddar cheeseburger. You heard correctly, it's basically a double Thurman Burger. A regular cheeseburger has been banished to the bottom of the menu, clearly a lightweight choice at this tavern.

My favorite-sounding concoction was the "Johnnie Burger." Invented by a chronic tequila-quaffing regular, the Johnnie is a three-quarter-pound burger with bacon and blue cheese that's drizzled with a shot of top-shelf 1800 tequila. No lettuce, tomato, or mayo is offered because, as Johnnie once explained, "If I wanted a salad, I'd order one!"

WILSON'S SANDWICH SHOP

600 S. Main St | Findlay, OH 45840 | 419-422-5051
Mon–Sat 7 am–11 pm | Sun 12 pm–8 pm

It's hard to miss Wilson's as you roll through downtown Findlay, Ohio. The restaurant is on a busy crossroads in the center of town with the word *WILSON* spelled above the front door in large black letters. Across the street sits the impressive former Marathon Oil world headquarters: a beautiful glass, steel, and concrete monument to the automobile age.

Wilson's has walls of windows on three sides. From inside, the sun-drenched space makes you feel like you're in a huge fishbowl.

Grab a stool at one of the long counters lining the windows, watch small town America unfold, and enjoy a fresh beef double cheeseburger and a chocolate malt.

The building is the second constructed in the restaurant's long history. The first, built in 1936, was a stunning example of enamel-steel road food culture. It was replaced with a greatly expanded Wilson's in the midsixties. During construction of the new Wilson's, the tiny yellow restaurant was pushed to the back of the parking lot and remained open. The original Wilson's was as narrow as a subway car and held only 32 people. Today's newer building seats over 130 hungry patrons in a wide dining room filled with a combination of booths, tables, and counters. Expect to find a line out the door at lunch and dinner.

Stub Wilson opened Wilson's Sandwich Shop in 1936. A few years earlier, Stub had opened two Kewpee restaurants in nearby Lima, Ohio, and decided to open another in Findlay. Finding another Kewpee already in Findlay (the restaurants were independently owned), he chose to name the new restaurant after himself. When Stub Wilson died, he passed all three restaurants on to his managers—the Kewpees in Lima went to Harrison Shutt and Wilson's went to three managers, Woody Curtis, Wilber Fenbert, and Lance Baker. Today, Wilson's is part-owned and run by Lance Baker's widow, Pat. After a few years of declining sales, Pat stepped in to take charge of the situation. "I got everybody back on track and back in uniforms." She was wise not to change the menu and she told me, "The burgers are still hot, juicy, and good!"

There's no question that the burgers at Wilson's are fresh. Three times a week the restaurant receives a delivery of six hundred pounds of beef from a meatpacker in Lima. Every morning the staff grinds and patties enough for the day's burgers. A patty machine attached to the grinder forms them into square patties, a shape that Wendy's popularized in the late 1960s but actually hails from the original Kewpee chain.

The basic, three-and-a-half-ounce griddled burger comes with mustard, pickle, and onion. Make it a "Special" and you'll also get lettuce, tomato, and mayo. And new to the menu, if you are looking for a burger for breakfast at Wilson's, you can now add an egg between 7 and 10 a.m.

Similarities between the Kewpees of Lima and Wilson's still exist, but the most notable is the historically significant vegetable sandwich. Listed on the menu as the "Veggie," this meatless sandwich (a Special without the burger patty) is a product of the World War II years when meat rationing forced many burger stands to adapt or shut down. White Castle temporarily embraced the grilled cheese sandwich, many others went to fish sandwiches, and Wilson's (and the Kewpees of Lima) introduced the vegetable sandwich.

People come from all over to eat the burgers they ate growing up in Findley. Mark Metcalf, an actor from this western Ohio town best known for his role as the ROTC commander Neidermeyer

in the film *Animal House*, recalls Wilson's burgers fondly. He told me by phone, "My grandfather used to go down to Wilson's and bring back bagfuls of hamburgers." Pat is aware of the restaurant's popularity and its place in the memory of anyone who was raised on Wilson's burgers. And I for one am overjoyed that she had the good sense to step in to basically rescue the place.

ZIP'S CAFE

1036 Delta Ave | Cincinnati, OH 45208 | 513-871-9876 | Mon–Thurs 10:30 am–11 pm
Fri & Sat 10:30 am–11:30 pm | Sun 11 am–11 pm | www.zipscafe.com

This tiny slice of history in the Mount Lookout neighborhood of Cincinnati celebrated its 90th anniversary in 2016, though the exact date is unknown. The place was opened by Zip Kirchner in the height of Prohibition, and details seem hazy in the shadow of potential illegal activity of the era. Was it a speakeasy? Was there illegal gambling? No one's talking, but as the story goes, "If the blinds were open, the books were open," Zip's owner Mike Burke told me.

Mike is the sixth owner and steward to Zip's illustrious and long history. If you arrive at the restaurant during daylight hours, it may take you a minute for your eyes to adjust to the dark interior. The floorboards date back almost 100 years as does the dark wood paneling on the walls. At first you'll see families of all ages eating underneath a model train that circles the dining room on a high shelf. Then you'll pick out the "Code Room" at the rear of the restaurant, with its out-of-place swinging saloon doors.

The burger at Zip's is nothing special and that's the point, and it's delicious. The classic cheeseburger that wins awards nonstop is simplicity personified. Mike enjoys the accolades but winces when he hears about some of the other winners in town, "A lot of them are sixteen-dollar burgers," he told me, "Ours are six bucks." The unfair advantage is not lost on me. Fortunately there are enough people out there that understand that if you've been making burgers for almost a century you must be doing something right.

Mike gets a daily delivery of fresh beef from beloved local butcher shop Avril Bleh (it's the kind of shop that could make a grown man weep it's so beautiful). They have been getting the same blend for years which has some prime and dry aged trim thrown in for flavor. The beef is formed into one-third pound patties and cooked on a flattop, and Mike pointed out, "If you can cook something in its own fat you should." The burger is served open-faced on a local Klosterman's bun with nothing more than some pickles, crisp lettuce, tomato and raw onion. On a busy Saturday Zip's will sell hundreds and hundreds of burgers.

If you thought the front room was dark, wait until you push through the swinging doors and enter the bar. The segregation of the front dining area from the back bar harkens to a time of bookies and illegal booze. It was a place where women and

children did not go (this is why, you'll notice, that the women's room is still in the dining room and the men's room in the bar). The nine-stool pocket bar is a gem and apparently never crowded. This is where you should eat your burger. The atmosphere is palpable—you can really feel the history in this room. The bar is also used as the pickup point for to-go orders. Bartender Casey told me that some people show up too early for their orders on purpose so they can grab a beer or two at the bar while they wait. The only problem with this logic is then I'd never want to leave. And if it were the 1920s all over again, I'd probably bet on a few races too.

CLAUD'S HAMBURGERS

3834 South Peoria Blvd | Tulsa, OK 74105 | 918-742-8332
Tues, Wed & Sat 10:30 am–4 pm | Thurs & Fri 10:30 am–8 pm | Closed Sun & Mon

The hours posted in the window at Claud's are correct but slightly loose depending on the number of people waiting outside for the fifty-six-year-old hamburger counter to open. "Depends on how I feel that morning," Robert Hobson said with a smile after opening a few minutes early. "Every day is different."

Robert owns the tiny, bright diner in the neighborhood of Brookside, just south of downtown Tulsa. In 1985, Claud Hobson passed the business to his sons, who had already put in plenty of years behind the counter. "I was four months old when he moved to this location [in 1965]," Robert told me. "I guess you can say I've been here all my life."

The interior of Claud's is clean and utilitarian, with white walls and a long counter lined with short green and chrome swivel stools. Robert has only the absolute basics behind the faux-wood Formica counter: a flattop griddle, refrigerators, and a deep fryer, everything in gleaming stainless steel. Large picture windows allow ample daylight to stream in and passing cars on South Peoria send flashes down the counter.

The burgers at Claud's are a lesson in simplicity. When Claud was at the griddle, your options were only mustard, pickle, and onion. Today, Robert has expanded options slightly to include lettuce and tomato. American cheese reigns supreme but as Robert told me with a sigh, "We also offer pepper jack cheese, but I think I made three yesterday." Robert is a man after my own heart. "Our main focus is the meat," he told me, standing at the griddle. "When you cover it up with all that stuff, you lose the taste."

The burger to get at Claud's is the double cheeseburger with onions. The onion is not just a slice tossed on cold or grilled to limp. When you order yours with onions, watch what happens. To the right of the flattop is a small piece of white marble embedded in the countertop. Robert takes a patty, slaps it onto the marble, and works a handful of chopped raw onion into the patty with the back of a stiff spatula. He then takes the flattened patty and plops it, onion-side down, onto the hot flattop. If you require a double, Robert takes two patties and stacks them on the marble and works them together with the spatula. The result is a very flat, wide burger that hangs far outside the white squishy bun, a style that has been Claud's for decades.

The only change Claud's burger has seen over the years was an increase in the size of the patty from two to three ounces and a switch from balled-beef to pre-formed patties. After two decades of balling ground chuck to smash into patties, Claud finally purchased a patty machine in the early seventies. "He used to say," Robert told me, "if someone is smart enough to make a machine to make my life easier, I'm smart enough to buy it."

Before it was Claud's, the burger counter was well known as Van's Hamburgers, part of a minichain in Tulsa. Claud opened his original burger joint in 1954 east of downtown Tulsa on the corner of Admiral and Sheridan, but moved to the Van's on South Peoria in 1965. "He was actually 'chosen' to take over this location," Robert told me. The busy thoroughfare has its share of burger joints with the nearly ninety-year-old Weber's Root Beer Stand directly across the street and a Sonic Drive-In just two doors down from Claud's. Amazingly, the Sonic has not affected their business.

Robert is fifty-three years young and plans to run the business for a while. "I plan on being here until our seventy-fifth anniversary!" he told me with a chuckle, which would be in 2030. "Maybe longer."

FOLGER'S DRIVE-INN

406 East Main St | Ada, OK 74820 | 580-332-9808
Mon–Fri 10:30 am–3 pm | Closed Sat & Sun

If you didn't know what you were looking for, you could drive right by Folger's. The unassuming little '50s prefab on the east end of downtown Ada has only two neon signs in the window—one that reads FOLGER'S, the other OPEN. A short flight of red concrete steps leads directly into hamburger heaven. Inside you'll find a bright, sunny, clean restaurant filled with the friendliest people. I'm not kidding. Within fifteen minutes of my first visit to Folger's, I knew everyone in the place.

Folger's is definitely a family-run business. In October 1935, G.G. and Christine Folger opened a hamburger concession in the local movie theater just up Main Street. They opened the current location in 1950 and eventually turned over operations and ownership to their two sons, Jim and Jerry Folger. Today, Jim and Jerry spend the better part of their day behind the large flattop griddle and Jerry's wife, Wanda, works the tiny twelve-stool counter. Orders to-go come in on the pay phone by the front door and Jim makes change at the register between burger flips.

"We have a few other things on the menu but hamburger baskets are 90 percent of our business," a very busy lunchtime Jim told me. I stood and watched him methodically flip and manage twelve quarter-pound burgers on the griddle at the same time. The Folger brothers engage in a sort of silent culinary dance in their open, narrow kitchen—Jim flips burgers, Jerry dresses them, and Wanda delivers. The dance is repeated over and over again for hours at lunch until hundreds of burgers have been dispensed to happy customers.

Folger's has been open for eighty-three years, and Jim explained, "We have quite a bit of loyalty and now five generations of families are coming in." A regular customer named Mike, smiling and rubbing his belly joked, "You can tell I've had a bunch of them." The burger at Folger's comes with mustard, onion, lettuce, and tomato. Ask for an "Educated Burger" (not on the menu), and you'll get a burger that replaces the onion with mayo. Make it a "basket" and you'll get to experience the other reason you came to Ada—for their outstanding fries. Every day, Folger's manages to go through over two hundred pounds of potatoes for their fresh-cut fries.

"The produce and meat are fresh, every day," Jim told me as he flattened another hand-formed patty on the griddle with a long spatula. Jim uses large Wonder buns that are perfectly toasted on the griddle. The finished product is a wide, flat burger that is bursting with greasy goodness and flavor.

"The grill used to be right behind the counter, and was smaller," Bill Peterson, the former district attorney in Ada, told me. If it had not been for Bill and mutual friend Tom Palmore, I may never have found Folger's. Both Bill and Tom grew up in Ada and were classmates of Jerry Folger's. They agreed that Folger's was not to be missed on the hunt for great burgers in America—they were right.

HAMBURGER KING

322 E. Main St | Shawnee, OK 74801
405-878-0488 | Mon–Sat 11 am–8 pm | Closed Sun

Legend has it that there used to be two Hamburger Kings in Oklahoma, one in Shawnee and one in Ada, and the Ada location was lost in a craps game. The owners of both were George "The Hamburger King" Macsas and his brother, Joe. The Macsas brothers emigrated from Beirut to Oklahoma and opened the successful hamburger venture in 1927. Today, more than ninety years later, the Hamburger King still stands in Shawnee and proudly remains in the Macsas family.

Dusty downtown Shawnee, Oklahoma, feels proudly American. A restaurant named Hamburger King is almost required in this setting, along with the Rexall drugstore, the furniture store (with layaway plans), and the enormous

Colleen Macsas told me. Colleen is the restaurant's manager and met her husband, owner Michael Macsas, at the Hamburger King in 1975.

The burgers at Hamburger King are fantastic. Fresh 80/20 patties are delivered to the restaurant daily and cooked on a large, well-seasoned flattop griddle. Quarter-pound singles and doubles are offered. Order a double and you'll get double the cheese as well. On my first visit, waitress Beverly pointed out, "Most men order the double meat burger." I was not about to let my manhood be challenged and naturally ordered a

grain elevators on the edge of town. The Hamburger King exists in its third location in Shawnee; the other two were only steps away and the previous one burned down in a grease fire in 1965.

Soon after the fire, the Macsas family rebuilt a much larger version of their burger restaurant a block up Main Street. Today's Hamburger King is a large, airy diner awash in pastels. The walls are pink-and-white-striped Masonite panels. Two long rows of booths and a small counter in the rear service customers and there are the constant sounds of sizzling burgers and the whir of the milkshake machine. Since 1965, at least, nothing has changed. "We switched to Pepsi once and the people rebelled,"

double, a half-pound burger loaded with lettuce, tomato, onions, pickles, and mustard on a toasted white squishy bun. This burger is not small. Order a "basket" and you'll get deep-fried potato wedges or tater tots, not fries.

The method for ordering your burger at Hamburger King is one of the most unique in America. If you sit at the counter, expect normal interaction with a counterperson. Sit at one of the many booths and you'll need to place your order by phone. That's right, each table is equipped with a red phone and a single button—your lifeline to the kitchen. On the other end of the red food phone is a switchboard operator who relays your order to the grill cook. The funny thing is, the restaurant is not so large that you can't just call out your order, but the quirkiness of the phone system can't be beat.

Regulars in a place like Hamburger King are as expected as good burgers. "See those guys over there," Colleen said to me, pointing to a group of older men at a booth in trucker hats, overalls, and plaid shirts, "they come in here every day and they bring in their wives on Saturday." Naturally, I had to approach and ask them the obvious, "Do you guys phone in your order?" One guy, smiling, told me, "Naw, they know what we want."

HARDEN'S HAMBURGERS

432 South Sheridan Rd | Tulsa, OK 74112 | 918-834-2558 | Mon–Fri 11 am–8 pm
Sat 10:30 am–8 pm | Sun 11:30 pm–4 pm | www.thehamburgerstore.com

As I savored the first bite of my "Men's Burger" at Harden's, owner Rick West said in his quiet Oklahoma drawl, "That's what you want, isn't it?" This smiling, intense burger man with piercing blue eyes wasn't asking about the specifics of the burger in my hand. And he wasn't asking my opinion of this glorious pile of beef and cheese either. I could tell by the tone in his voice that his question had a larger meaning, as if to say, "Isn't this what everyone really wants?" Oh yes, most certainly.

Rick started his career in burgers at the age of twelve working at the long-gone Tanner's Drive-In on Admiral Place and Garnett Road. "I knew that I wanted to be in the hamburger business after working for Tanner," Rick told me. But it wasn't Tanner that had the largest influence on Rick. In 1987, after spending many years outside the restaurant business, Rick bought the decades-old burger joint from the hamburger icon Johney Harden. Johney taught Rick the secrets to his success.

As my friend (and local hamburger expert) Joe Price clicked off names of past and present Tulsa burger flippers, Rick said with a serious tone, "Johney trained a lot of those guys." His influence today is far-reaching and can probably be felt in every corner of Tulsa. At one point, Johney even consulted for Wendy's founder Dave Thomas and designed his first hamburger kitchen.

A large sign hanging underneath the menu at the register says "We cook 'em with a light pink center." The burgers come in four sizes. The Girl's Quarter Pound, the Men's Double, the Triple, and the four-patty, one-pound B.O.B., which stands for "Big Old Burger." "If you are a guy and order a Girl's Burger, you're gonna get flack," Rick warned, "but I love it when a girl orders the Men's Burger."

The most popular burger on the menu is the Men's Burger, two quarter-pound patties neatly stacked on a toasted white squishy bun. The burger is cooked on a flattop and is actually cooked with a bit of pink in the middle. The large, well-seasoned burger explodes with flavor and is incredibly moist. Just after the patties of fresh beef hit the griddle, they are sprinkled with a top-secret seasoning. Rick is one of the only people who actually know what is in this seasoning and the company that blends the spices for Harden's has strict orders to keep it to themselves. "People actually call the spice company all the time for the recipe," Rick told me.

The onion rings at Harden's are legendary. Size alone would be a reason to order and ogle these rings. They are so large that they resemble bangle bracelets. They taste amazing. Where most battered onion rings separate on contact, these stay together. Whatever process Rick uses has the batter sticking to the onion like glue.

In 1997, Rick moved Harden's from its second location, setting up shop in a former truck rental business that he owned. This incarnation of Harden's is a virtual museum of midcentury Americana. Authentic enameled-steel gasoline and soda signs are everywhere and display cases are full of vintage scale-model cars. Large, detailed model airplanes hang from the ceiling and Rick's collection of restored pedal cars are spread around the dining room. You could spend hours in Harden's and still not see everything.

When you place your order at the register, you are handed an oversized playing card as your "number." Listen for your suit to be called out over the loudspeaker (i.e. "King of Hearts!"). There is a drive-up window on the north side of the building but Rick dissuades most people from just driving up. "We prefer that you call an order in to pick up at the window." He explained that he can't guarantee how the experience will go and recommends that you park and come inside to order. It's a drive-up, not a drive-thru.

Burger making is part science and part art, and Rick West is clearly at peace with both. He told me, "I watched what Johney did and do it exactly the same way." Okay, part fear, too, I guess.

J&W GRILL

501 West Choctaw Ave | Chickasha, OK 73018
405-224-9912 | Mon–Wed 6 am–2 pm | Thurs–Sat 6 am–9 pm | Closed Sun

"Just down from the courthouse in Chickasha there's a little place that makes a great burger," was the advice Bill Peterson gave me. Bill was the district attorney for the area, and a man to be trusted with hamburger knowledge. It was Bill who had led me to the amazing burger at Folger's in Ada, so hopes were high. Not only was the burger at J&W first-rate, but unbeknownst to Bill, I had stumbled upon one of the most historically important burger joints of the Oklahoma onion-fried burger phenomenon.

Onion-fried burgers are to this part of Oklahoma what cheesesteaks are to Philadelphia. The epicenter of the onion-fried burger world is thirty-five miles north from Chickasha in El Reno. This small town near Oklahoma City boasts three of the best burgers in America, served at counters that are only a few hundred feet from each other. The onion-fried burger craze, started in the 1920s, was created in an effort to stretch meat and feed laid-off railroad workers cheaply.

Restaurants serving the tasty local burger popped up all over town and competition was fierce. But in 1957 a man named Richard Want moved down to Chickasha to open the J&W Grill. He was not alone in his venture, though. Johnnie Siler, already successful with Johnnie's Grill in El Reno, helped to finance the new onion-burger counter.

In an effort to avoid confusion when attempting to figure out the rich histories of these Oklahoma burger joints, let's just say that they are all connected in some way. Many owners and employees

of the remaining burger stands have all worked at one another's stands, though most worked for and learned from Johnnie Siler. Current owner Darren Cook seems to be the only burger man in this part of Oklahoma who did not work in El Reno. "I started at J&W when I was twelve years old washing dishes," Darren told me, "I had to use a milk crate to reach the sink." When he was nineteen, he purchased a share in the restaurant, and in 1981, when he was only twenty-three, bought the restaurant outright. Understandably, J&W is his life and he has been at the burger counter for over thirty-five years.

The J in J&W stands for Johnnie, the W for Want. "I think it was supposed to be 'S&W' for their last names but the sign people made a mistake," Maryann Davis, wife of past owner Jim Davis, told me.

J&W has everything you'd want in a burger joint—meat ground fresh on premises, onions hand-sliced in back, a basic menu, and fast service. The concept is simple. Order a "hamburger"

and it comes with onions. A quarter-pound wad of fresh ground beef is pressed onto a hot flat-top griddle and sprinkled with a large amount of sliced (not diced) onions. The stringy onions go limp, and the result is a mess of beef and caramelized onions that create a moist burger with an intense onion flavor. At J&W, if you want a double, two wads of beef are pressed together and twice the amount of onion is dispensed.

The restaurant sits on the busy thoroughfare of Choctaw Avenue near downtown Chickasha. It's a very visible red and white cinder block structure with bright red picnic tables out front and a large American flag painted on one side. The long, low, wood-grain Formica counter has sixteen swivel stools that are never empty at lunchtime. "It gets crowded in here at lunch. The line goes out the door," manager Brandi told me. The good news is that the average time at a stool is ten minutes and, Brandi said with a smile, "We can move them in and out of here in fifteen."

Brandi has been at J&W for nineteen years. She knows just about everyone who walks in the door and calls out their order to the grill cook before they even take a seat. Biscuits and gravy are a big seller in the morning, but she told me some customers order burgers first thing. "We'll start making burgers at 6 a.m. if someone wants one."

When I visited J&W, there was no music playing, just the sounds of the exhaust fan, regulars talking about just getting off a night shift, and the sizzle of burgers on the griddle. It was refreshing to enjoy my burger without music for once, just the mesmerizing sounds of America.

JOHNNIE'S GRILL

301 S Rock Island Ave | El Reno, OK 73036 | 405-262-4721
Mon–Thurs 7 am–9 pm | Fri & Sat 6 am–9 pm | Sun 11 am–8 pm

Steve Galway is a dedicated man. The first time I visited Johnnie's to taste an onion-fried burger, the pride of El Reno, Oklahoma, Steve was not there. "He comes in every day at two," a counterperson told me. But it was 3 p.m. and he was nowhere to be found. That's because Steve comes in every day at 2 a.m. to prep the restaurant for the day and is gone by 11 a.m. Now that's dedication to burgers. When I finally caught up with him, we had a long talk about what it takes to keep a restaurant successful. "Give the best you've got and the people will come back," are the words he lives by. He must be doing something right because every time I've been there the place has been packed—the people most definitely come back.

Don't be fooled by the fairly nondescript exterior of Johnnie's Grill. Located on one of the main drags in downtown El Reno, the simple, brick-faced restaurant is set back from the street by a small parking lot. The only windows are the glass in the front door and a small drive-up on one side of the building. The inside is bright and clean with a sea of tables and booths, a fact you could not imagine from a parking lot assessment. There's also a short counter with seven stools and a clear view of the large flattop griddle that's usually loaded with onion-fried burgers.

This version of Johnnie's is new as of 2005. Prior to that, Johnnie's was a narrow burger joint at the same location with a counter on the left and four booths on the right. Prior to that, the original location was across the street, but, collapsed under the weight of snow in 1986. Today's Johnnie's could easily seat up to a hundred. There's even a "party table" in the new Johnnie's that seats twenty.

But for all its newness, Johnnie's remains one of the most historically important purveyors of the El Reno Fried Onion burger, important because it seems that all roads lead back there. Sid and Marty Hall from the popular Sid's (only two blocks away) both worked at the counter and Johnnie himself brought the Fried Onion Burger south when he opened the J&W Grill of Chickasha in 1957.

Order a hamburger at Johnnie's and it comes standard with onions smashed in. In the old days, onion was used in a burger to stretch the day's meat and to add flavor, but Steve told me, "Back then it was a lot of onion and a little meat."

The grillman takes a ball of fresh ground chuck, slaps it on the grill, covers it with thinly sliced onions, and starts pressing the patty until the onion and red meat are one. The thin patty cooks on the hot griddle until the beef has a crunchy char and the onions are caramelized. As it nears doneness, a white squishy bun is placed on the burger, softened by onion steam. The burger is served with pickles on the side only. All other condiments are self-serve.

Steve started working at Johnnie's for then owner Bruce Otis at age twelve, over fifty years ago. He and Marty Hall (from Sid's Diner) worked at the grill at the same time and have remained friends. "It's not like it used to be," Steve said, referring to the cutthroat competition in the early days between rival burger stands in El Reno. "If I need some sacks (paper bags), I'll call Marty. We try to help each other."

If you really want to experience El Reno at its peak, show up in town on the first Saturday in May. That's when this proud town just west of Oklahoma City celebrates Burger Day.

Thirty-thousand people descend on El Reno for live music, a car show, and a public construction of the "World's Largest Fried Onion Burger." The three main burger outposts, Sid's, Robert's, and Johnnie's, all within a block of each other, operate at beyond capacity. "That day we'll have a six-block line for burgers and forty employees," Steve told me.

Steve has three sons and plans to bring them up in the business if they are interested, but makes a point to tell them his secret to success. "I tell them if you are going to own one of these you have to come down and talk to the people." But he doesn't plan on ceding control to anyone just yet. "If I'm going to do something the rest of my life, I want it to be here." Like I said, Steve Galway is a dedicated man.

LINDA-MAR DRIVE-IN

1614 West 51st St | Tulsa, OK 74107 | 918-446-6024 | Mon–Sat 10:30 am–9 pm
Closed Sun | (One Other Location across Town) | www.facebook.com/lindamardrivein

Oklahoma has no shortage of great burger joints and Tulsa is no exception. It was very difficult to choose from the bounty of burger options in Tulsa but this tiny, bright yellow-and-red painted cinderblock box stood out. That may be because their signature burger, "The Westside," a double-meat double cheeseburger served on Texas Toast, is a sight to behold.

Linda-Mar sits just outside the cloverleaf where I-44 meets Route 75 in a neighborhood called the Westside. The place is spotless and the decor is Nascar-themed with an image of Winston Cup champion Rusty Wallace's Blue Deuce taking up one entire wall of the dining room. There are also framed shots of dirt track racecars everywhere, some bearing the Linda-Mar logo. Owner Mike McCutchen, who at one point was an owner at Tulsa Speedway, used to sponsor a Sprint racecar team. Not coincidentally, his brother, Danny, was the driver and the entire McCutchen family worked on the team. Today, Mike owns two bars, an automotive shop, and Linda-Mar, and he opened a second location with a drive-thru west of downtown Tulsa in 2015.

The restaurant was first called Warren's in the early '60s and around 1970 was sold to the bun supplier, Walt Cook. He named the restaurant after his two daughters, Linda and Margaret, and eventually sold it to his son-in-law, Jerry McCutchen. Various members of the McCutchen family have owned and run Linda-Mar over the past forty years, with Danny nearly running it into the ground. In 2009, Mike stepped in to take the reins at the restaurant because, as he put it, "He was sick of it. He had let it go downhill." Under Danny it had been open for business only two hours a day, five days a week. "Everywhere people were bitching about the hours and asking why it was not open on Saturdays," Mike told me, "So I said, 'To hell with that,' and took it over from Danny. I went in, gutted it, and cleaned it up." Mike also expanded the menu, the hours, and changed the work ethic in the kitchen. "I always tell the kids [working at Linda-Mar], 'Every time you cook something, make it like you would for yourself.'"

Linda-Mar uses fresh beef from Tulsa's favorite meatpacker Tulsa Beef and they make quarter-pound patties at the restaurant every morning with their own patty machine. The machine makes the patties wide and flat so on the well-seasoned flattop they cook quickly. "The Westside" comes with tomato, shredded lettuce, pickles, mustard, and mayo by request. It also

comes with diced onion that is cooked next to your patties on the flattop.

The Westside is a colossal pile of cheesy, greasy goodness. The major difference between a regular double cheeseburger and the Westside is in the Texas toast. The thick-sliced, regional favorite is brushed with butter on both sides and toasted directly on the flattop with the patties. A burger bun only gets toasted on one side whereas the Texas toast gets toasted on both sides. The Westside also comes with not two but four slices of gooey american cheese. It's a lot to handle but not as much of a mess as you would think. If the half-pound grease and cheese intake from the Westside doesn't frighten you, indulge in Linda-Mar's deep-fried sides, like fries, tater tots, onion rings, cheese balls, and mushrooms. They are all great, but the real winner here is the jalepeño chicken—deep-fried bits of chicken in

a buttermilk jalepeño batter. Mike told me, "We marinate the chicken in the batter overnight. Makes a huge difference."

One curious element to the Linda-Mar experience is a small television that plays episodes of *The Andy Griffith Show* nonstop. "My mom loved Andy Griffith and that sumbitch would play until I whistled myself to sleep," Mike told me. It has become an integral part of the restaurant, so much so that when an employee recently tried to put on something else (*The Addams Family*) the customers rebelled.

I was tipped off to Linda-Mar by friend and local burger expert Joe Price. As we were leaving we spotted an ancient milkshake mixer behind the counter and almost fell over. "Do you still use that?" I asked, not because it looked like its best days were behind it but because I was fully aware of its historical significance. "We use it every day," Tiffany told me as she reached over to start it up. The mixer slowly came to life and I could hear the whir of the friction-driven mechanics inside. This was the same mixer, the Multimixer, that Ray Croc sold as a traveling salesman in the '40s, the same mixer that led him to McDonald's for the first time and the rest was history.

"Have a very Linda-Mar day!" former manager Tiffany shouted to me as left my first visit there. "That's just what we say here." I wish I could have a Linda-Mar day more often.

THE MEERS STORE & RESTAURANT

Highway 115 | Meers, OK 73507 | 580-429-8051
Mon, Wed, Thurs & Sun 10:30 am–8:30 pm | Fri & Sat 10:30 am–9 pm | Closed Tues
www.meersstore.com

The Meers Store is way out in the country. About two hours from Oklahoma City and four from Dallas, the "Meersburger" had better be good because it's the only reason you got in the car this morning. The burgers are better than good, they are excellent, and the drive is beautiful. Joe Maranto, the owner of the 116-year-old burger destination, put it best when he told me, "We're out in the middle of nowhere, but the good thing is we're the only thing in nowhere." Meers is not as desolate as it sounds. The restaurant is a short drive from the entrance to the Wichita Mountains Wildlife Preserve and the next town over is Medicine Park, former hideout of Bonnie and Clyde and turn-of-the-century resort for Oklahomans.

The restaurant is made up of a bunch of cobbled-together old buildings from 1902 and newer ones built over the last century. The older ones were abandoned when Meers did not produce the copious amounts of gold it promised. Remnants of the tiny post office have been incorporated into the newer buildings, all of them strung together like a bunch of shoeboxes. Joe is responsible for the larger additions. The expansion is a result of the popularity of his Meersburger and the need to accommodate the five hundred–plus daily burger seekers, bike tours, and other backcountry tourists.

It's no secret what goes into a Meersburger. Joe proudly displays, inside and out, the key ingredient to his success—the lean Texas longhorn cattle. What's better, Joe raises the longhorns himself (with the help of his stepson, Peterhood) at a ranch nearby, and they are free of antibiotics and hormones.

During the summer, Peterhood and Joe send at least 2,500 pounds of longhorn to slaughter every six days. "We sell A LOT of Meersburgers. They wait in line for the burgers," one of the grill cooks told me. On a busy day, Joe can sell over four hundred burgers. That's quite a feat, considering the burger is a half pound of lean Texas longhorn beef served on a specially made seven-inch bun.

Joe claims, and is correct, that longhorn beef is lower in cholesterol than chicken or turkey, especially since he is raising them the old-fashioned way—on grass, not grain, and contains yellow fat, which is actually really good for you.

Recently, Joe decided that the Meersburger was not large enough to feed his hungry patrons. The "Seismic Burger" was created to fill this need. The Seismic is a gut-busting one pound of ground longhorn beef on the same seven-inch bun, topped with cheese, onions, lettuce, tomato, sweet relish, pickles, jalapeño slices, and bacon. I finished one without trouble, just some sweat and a full belly. The grease was in the bacon, not the burger.

The store's proximity to the Wichita Mountains Wildlife Preserve, where the Texas longhorn was saved from extinction in the 1920s, is a little odd. But the cattle in the preserve and on Joe's ranch have quite the life. Joe said it best when he told me once, "These are happy cows. Happy cows taste better."

ROBERT'S GRILL

300 South Bickford | El Reno, OK 73036 | 405-262-1262
Mon–Sat 6 am–9 pm | Sun 11 am–7 pm

Step into Robert's and step back in time. Much like the Texas Tavern in Roanoke, Virginia, or the Cozy Inn of Salina, Kansas, very little has changed at Robert's Grill in the last ninety-two years. Maybe the stools and the red Formica counter are new, or the front door was moved about a half-century ago, but Robert's is a perfect example of what all hamburger stands looked, felt, and smelled like in the 1920s. Robert's is, historically speaking, one of America's most important treasures.

Don't expect warm hellos, pictures on the walls, or a large menu. Robert's is a tiny, clean, utilitarian place—a counter with fourteen stools facing a flattop griddle surrounded by a wall of stainless steel. It's the kind of counter where you don't linger long, and the burgers come fast and go down even faster. The exterior is sparse as well. The building is a bright white box with small windows and red trim—the visual effect may be off-putting to the untrained gourmand but believe me, you have come to the right place.

Robert's menu is limited to Coneys (chili dogs), grilled cheese, fries, tater tots, and the burger that made El Reno famous, the onion-fried burger.

Located in the burger belt of El Reno, Robert's is only a few hundred feet from Johnnie's and Sid's, and across the street from the spot where the onion-fried burger was born. "The Hamburger Inn was right where that bank is now," owner of three decades, Edward Graham, told me. It was at the eight-stool Hamburger Inn that a man named Ross Davis tried to stretch his burger meat by pressing in sliced onions, appealing to cash-strapped, out-of-work railroad men. The

Hamburger Inn was situated on old Route 66, an outpost at the onset of the auto age, so you can imagine the brisk business. Imitators were born and a legendary burger was embraced.

The hamburger at Robert's, as it is all over town, is an onion burger. Edward smashes a ball of fresh ground chuck on the hot griddle with a sawed-off mason's trowel, and a pile of shredded onions is placed on top. The onions are pressed hard into the patty. The contents fuse, creating a beautiful, caramelized, onion-beef mess. Edward places a white squishy bun on the patty as it finishes so that the bun soaks up the onion steam. The result is a flat, odd-looking burger that tastes incredible.

When Robert's opened in 1926, it was called Bob's White Rock. The front door was on the Route 66 side only steps from a trolley stop. Edward told me, "People could get off the trolley here, get burgers at the window, and jump back on again. The grill used to be in the front window." Edward started working at Robert's in 1979 and purchased the counter in 1989.

For locals, there is an abundance of great onion-fried burger options in El Reno. When I asked a regular named Troy at the counter why he chose to patronize Robert's, he seemed to fall back on brand loyalty. "I've been coming here for fifty years. I remember when they were eight for a dollar." Now that's a good customer.

MY FAVORITE SIDES

On my eighteen-year journey to the best hamburgers in the nation, I came across a few regional treats that I just could not pass up. Here's a short list of the not-to-be-missed sides you'll find while burgering your way through America. I didn't include fries because most burgers come with them anyway. These are the sides, drinks, and desserts you would likely miss out on if I didn't alert you to their greatness.

Steak Fingers
Harden's Hamburgers, Tulsa, OK
Owner Rick West made me do it. After polishing off his double cheeseburger, he presented his battered steak fingers and I somehow managed to finish them, too. The best I've ever had.

Frickles
The Meers Store & Restaurant, Meers, OK
Joe Maranto is constantly adding things to his menu and this one is a winner. I sat with him once, a basket of his new deep-fried pickles between us and he said, "I can't stop eating them!" Neither could I.

Banana Cream Pie
The Apple Pan, Los Angeles, CA
This is the king of all banana cream pies. Reserve your slice with one of the countermen before you bite into your burger.

Cheese Curds
Dotty Dumpling's Dowry, Madison, WI
These are a must-have on a burger tour of Madison. Skip the fries and get some curds, a treat whose distant cousin is the overprocessed mozzarella stick. You'll never look at hot cheese the same way again.

Flan
El Mago De Las Fritas, West Miami, FL
This is, unquestionably, the BEST flan I've ever eaten, period.

Onion Rings
Crown Burgers, Salt Lake City, UT
Made by hand in a private, windowless basement room. Amazing dipped in Utah's favorite fry sauce.

Fried Pies
Phillips Grocery, Holly Springs, MS
Basically a skillet-fried, fruit-stuffed pie-crust. Owner Larry Davis is tired of making these tasty Southern treats—so get them soon before he gives up.

Witch Doctor
What-A-Burger Drive-In, Mooresville, NC
A sweet and savory soda drink that is topped off with sliced pickles. Sounds so gross but it's actually good.

Peanut Butter Chocolate Shake
Sid's Diner, El Reno, OK
After inhaling two of Marty Hall's beautiful onion-fried burgers, this would be the last thing I need. I always manage to finish one, though, knowing that it will be a while before I'd taste something this great again.

Cinnamon Coke
Zaharakos Ice Cream Parlor and Museum, Columbus, IN
Mixed by a real soda jerk at this perfectly restored ice cream parlor, this drink has no equal.

Onion Rings
Bobo's Drive In, Topeka, KS
Lightly greasy oniony goodness. In a word—sublime.

Raspberry Lime Rickey
Mr. Bartley's, Cambridge, MA
A mix of seltzer, sugar, raspberry, and lime syrup. Refreshing, crisp, and cool, it's the perfect accompaniment to Bartley's large, flavor-packed burgers.

Lemon Ice Box Pie
Rotier's Restaurant, Nashville, TN
Just try and say no to Eddie. It's like a Key Lime Pie, but creamier and better.

Cup of Chili
Zip's Cafe, Cincinnati, OH
Cincinnati is known for chili and Zip's is known for both burgers and chili. Get a cup, it's amazing.

Fried Clam Bellies
The White Cottage Snack Bar, Woodstock, VT
Given the option between clam bellies and strips, go for the bellies. No burger joint serves them, though, but White Cottage does and they are the best, from Ipswich, Massachusetts.

Blueberry Milkshake
Paradise Pup, Des Plaines, IL
It may look like just another Chicago hot dog stand (which it's not) but they serve up a fresh blueberry shake when in season that rocks.

Cream of Tomato Soup with Bacon
The Blazer Pub, North Salem, NY
I wasn't going to, but glad I did. Quite possibly the best soup ever.

SID'S DINER

300 South Choctaw | El Reno, OK 73036
405-262-7757 | Mon–Sat 7 am–8 pm | Closed Sun

"Do you know what the definition of a diner is?" Marty Hall, part owner of this El Reno burger destination asked me years ago in his gentle Oklahoma drawl. "It's a place where the grill is in view and I can turn around and talk to the people." And he does, making Sid's one of the friendliest places I have ever set foot in. But it doesn't stop there—Marty also makes one of the best Fried-Onion Burgers anywhere.

Sid's is named after Marty's father, who passed away just before the restaurant opened in 1989. Marty had planned to work side by side with Sid, a retired highway employee. When he died, Sid's brother, Bob, asked if he could take his spot. This sounds like a customary role

for a family member to play, except that Bob left a six-figure job at Chevron in Houston to flip burgers. El Reno, Oklahoma, is famous for one thing—onion-fried burgers. Invented just across the street from Sid's at the long-gone Hamburger Inn.

Sid's is not alone in El Reno. At one point there were over nine onion-fried-burger joints within five blocks of downtown. Today, Sid's, Johnnie's, and Robert's, the three remaining diners, are just a few hundred feet from one another.

If you choose a seat at the counter, you'll have a great view of the construction of a Fried-Onion Burger. Marty grabs a ball of fresh ground chuck from a beautiful pyramid of beef balls at the side of the griddle. A gob of thinly sliced sweet onion is piled onto the ball of beef on the large flattop griddle. The ball is pressed thin and the onions are worked into the soft meat. The burger is flipped, and after a few minutes, the caramelized onions have fused to the griddle-charred beef. Prepare your mouth for a taste explosion.

The burger is served on a white squishy bun with the meat and gnarled onions hanging out of it. Nothing is served with a regular burger except pickles (on the side) but you may find condiments unnecessary. If you require lettuce and tomato, ask for a Deluxe. Make yours a King Size and the meat and onions are doubled. The King is the most popular burger and makes for a perfect meal, especially if enjoyed with Sid's excellent hand-cut, homemade fries. "I learned how to make fries down at J&W," Marty told me, referring to another not-to-be-missed onion-fried burger further south in Chickasha (see page 271).

One of the more unique features of Sid's is their impressive decoupage countertop, sealed in poured resin. "The history of El Reno starts on that end," Marty told me, pointing to the far left side of the counter. The patchwork of vintage El Reno photography includes everything from early shots of downtown to color photos of local baseball teams. "I wanted people who came in who weren't from here to know something about my town."

Even though Sid's is technically a newcomer to the Fried-Onion Burger phenomenon, Marty has been involved his entire life.

"I used to work at Johnnie's and my father helped out there as well." Sid's, he told me, was modeled after the old Johnnie's.

In 2012, we lost Bob, and Marty's son, Adam, stepped into his position at the griddle. "He loves it," Marty said of his son's interest in the business. "In a few years, I may turn it over to him," Marty mused recently. "Would be nice to take it easy for a while."

Marty and Adam take turns flipping and pressing a lot of onions into the burgers. When the pyramid of beef balls next to the griddle gets low, a new, perfect pyramid miraculously appears courtesy of the efficient staff at Sid's. Every once in a while Marty will turn and dispense life lessons with a smile to anyone at the counter. "Be good to your daddy," he says to some teenaged girls picking at their fries. "I should know. I have three daughters."

GIANT DRIVE-IN

15840 Boones Ferry Rd | Lake Oswego, OR 97035 | 503-636-0255
Mon–Sat 10 am–9 pm | Closed Sun

Hooray for the mom-and-pop hamburger stand. Giant Drive-In is quite literally a mom-and-pop—owned and operated by a husband-and-wife team that is dedicated to bringing quality comfort food to the neighborhood and have done so for thirty-seven years.

Bill Kreger and his wife, Gail, bought Giant in 1981 after Bill had burned out on a mechanical engineering career. "We had planned to fix it up and flip it, but here we are!" Bill told me enthusiastically. The odd looking A-frame ski chalet structure was originally part of a failed '60s chain called Mr. Swiss. In 1970, it became Giant and was open for ten years until a Burger King opened across the street. "The previous owner just gave up, locked the doors, and walked away," Bill told me. But today, the Burger King is gone. When I asked Bill what happened, he just smiled and shrugged. I gathered there's only room for one burger stand in this stretch of suburban Portland.

Starting the business was not easy for the Kregers. "You have to keep your hand in it or you are not going to have it," Bill explained. "We spent

seventeen hours a day, seven days a week for the first seven years to get this place up and running." The time invested shows—the burgers are excellent.

The list of hamburger concoctions is vast. You can order a standard quarter-pound burger or choose from an eclectic selection of burgers like the "Teriyaki," the "Hawaiian," or an "Avocado Burger." But the burger that gets its own neon sign is the enormous "Filler." The Filler is almost too big to put in your mouth, but I managed. Its contents are similar to nearby Stanich's signature burger, but the Filler contains two quarter-pound patties instead of one. The burger also contains a slice of ham, cheese, a fried egg, bacon, lettuce, onion, pickles, tomato, and mayo. All this piled neatly on a locally baked seeded sourdough roll. I was speechless (and dazed) for hours after I consumed this thing. Amazingly, Gail told me it was her burger of choice, but said, "Believe it or not, I actually put an extra patty on it."

The fresh hamburger patties are delivered daily and come from local grass-fed Angus sirloin. The Kregers request a 90 percent lean grind. "Any less fat and the burger breaks up on the griddle. Any more and the burger shrinks to nothing." The cheese is also local Tillamook, purchased in forty-pound blocks and sliced on premises. Bill explained, "We try to only use local, fresh ingredients." He added, "In the summertime, Oregon

tomatoes can get to be this big," making a shape with his hands the size of an invisible grapefruit.

The interior of the Giant is a classic retro burger drive-in. Bright, clean, and inviting, the Giant has floor-to-ceiling windows on three sides, booths for seating, and a yellow-and-brown checkered linoleum floor. Hanging over the cash register is a photo of a half dozen UPS trucks lined up in the Giant parking lot. "Once a week the local UPS guys converge on Giant," Bill explained. "Sometimes there are over fifteen trucks out there."

I watched the Kregers greet familiar faces, pleasantly take orders, and flip burgers. "We've had the same clientele in here for thirty-seven years," Gail told me. They make the business of selling hamburgers look easy as if anyone could do it. But years ago Gail gave me some sage advice, "Keep your sanity and stay out of the restaurant business!"

HELVETIA TAVERN

10275 NW Helvetia Rd | Hillsboro, OR 97124 | 503-647-5286
Sun–Thurs 11 am–10 pm | Fri & Sat 11 am–11 pm

Nestled in the rolling farm country of western Oregon, a short distance from Portland but a world away, sits a restaurant and bar that amazingly turns out over a thousand burgers on a busy Saturday. The restaurant is the comfortable Helvetia Tavern (pronounced Hel-VAY-sha) and is way out in the country. Regardless of how far it is from anything, burger lovers gladly make

the trek to the Helvetia for their signature "Jumbo Burger" and great selection of microbrews on tap.

"It's a pretty simple menu and nothing has changed since we opened," owner Mike Lampros told me. "We did add salads, though, two years ago." There are a few sandwiches on the menu and a grilled cheese, but I looked around and saw mostly burgers being consumed. A lot of them,

too—the grill stayed full the entire time I was at Helvetia. They easily served over two hundred burgers in the hour that I sat at the counter.

The Jumbo is just that—two thin quarter-pound patties of fresh ground beef are cooked on a large flattop griddle and served on a toasted six-inch bun with bacon, cheese, lettuce, onion, tomato, and the ubiquitous and tasty Pacific Northwest condiment, "Goop" (see sidebar on page 380). The bun is larger than the patties, which are arranged slightly overlapping so the burger is presented wider, not taller. "That's the way we've always done it," Mike explained. "The single patty is served on a smaller bun." As a finishing touch, the Jumbo is stabbed in the center and delivered with a plastic knife, as Mike explained, "to keep the contents from sliding around." The burgers are moist and exploding with flavor, thanks to the

mustardy-mayo Goop holding the large burger together.

The building that houses the Helvetia first opened in 1914 as a general store. In 1946, a bar was added to one side and burgers were served. Mike's father, Nick Lampros, bought the tavern in 1978 and changed nothing until the late 1990s when he and his son turned the old general store into a dining room. "Up until then it was a twenty-one-and-over bar crowd," Mike told me, taking a break from the grill. "The dining room allowed us to start attracting families." And they do, and those families have the benefit of dining at Helvetia with a picture-perfect view of the sheep grazing across the street. The dining room tables are actually enormous foot-thick blocks of timber with a high-gloss finish. Mike pointed out, "They came from a tree that fell in a neighbor's yard."

The tavern side of Helvetia is a comfortably dark, broken-in bar with a 1950 Brunswick pool table that still costs only fifty cents to play. A strange collection of baseball caps hangs from the ceiling, some signed by pro athletes. Mike explained that the thousand of caps were up there to hide the ugly ceiling. "We take them down twice a year to clean them."

If there was any doubt as to how accommodating this place was to regulars, just take a counter seat at the last stool in the back of the restaurant. That's Grant's seat. Then look over the food prep area directly in front of you. Hanging on an air duct is a mirror positioned perfectly to read the TV behind you in reverse. "He comes in here at three every day, like clockwork," the grillman told me. Then Mike explained, "We blocked his view of the TV across the room with a new sign. This was his solution."

STANICH'S TAVERN

4915 NE Fremont St | Portland, OR 97213 | 503-281-2322 | Closed Mon & Tues
Wed & Thurs 11 am–10 pm | Fri & Sat 11 am–11 pm | Sun 11 am–9 pm | www.stanichs.com

Once upon a time in America, the "sports bar" was merely a neighborhood bar where you could guarantee that the game you wanted to watch would be on the TV hanging in the corner over the bottles of booze. If there were two games on at the same time, the TV at the other end of the bar would be tuned in. At some point, the sports bar concept went corporate and today it is not uncommon to find many with stadium seating and games on up to thirty screens, some of them full-sized movie screens. The sports bar became a soulless, unfamiliar place where the only reason to go was to ensure you'd see your game. Stanich's is a real sports bar, one that is oozing soul. It's an unquestionably comfortable, welcoming place that also happens to make one of the tastiest burgers I've ever eaten.

"Sometimes the wait for a burger can be an hour, but we have a great jukebox," Steve Stanich told me. Steve is the owner and son of the couple who opened the tavern in 1949. Serbian immigrants Gladys and George Stanich opened this Portland tavern and put a burger on the menu. In the old days, Gladys cooked and George would be out back playing pinochle. It was Gladys who invented what the menu still today bills as the "World's Greatest Hamburger," the sloppy two-fister "Special."

The Special is large. Gladys must have had the very hungry in mind when she dreamed up this burger. The grillperson swiftly assembles the impressively diverse ingredients that go onto the Special, which include a quarter-pound patty of fresh chuck, an egg, bacon, ham, cheese, lettuce, red onion, and tomato. All of this is piled high on a large five-inch toasted bun with the obligatory mustard, mayo, and "burger relish" that seems to adorn all burgers in the Northwest.

There's a two-napkin limit per burger, so use them wisely. The moment the juices, hot cheese, and mayo start running down your arms (and they will) resist the urge to reach for a napkin. "We don't like to hand out napkins," a bartender told me once, "but if you really need one, okay."

When you first walk into Stanich's, you'll be shocked by the decor. Every inch of the walls at this decades-old tavern is covered in those felt triangular pennants and pretty much nothing else. There could be a thousand, and all were donated by regulars. The bar is one of the deepest I've ever seen, lined with cozy leather swivel stools that take some practice getting into. There is no way to look cool getting into one of these seats, and someone pointed out, "It's kind of a 'slide 'n' twirl' move."

Steve Stanich, an ex-pro football player for the 49ers, believes in giving back. Among the sea of pennants that lines the walls of his tavern are more than a few accolades of his philanthropic efforts. On the fiftieth anniversary of Stanich's, Steve brought the price of his family's signature burger back to its original twenty-five cents for a day. The proceeds built a gymnasium for a local school. He also sponsors numerous local teams and every year gives out scholarships to college-bound kids. Steve told me, "It comes back to you tenfold."

When Thrillist called "Nick's Burger," with red relish, mustard, mayo and sautéed onion, the best burger in America in 2017, the busy restaurant just got busier. "We had people flying in just for the burger, from all over," Steve told me. It was too busy and Steve kindly asked, jokingly, "Please get out, we can't take care of all of you." The sentiment goes back to his dad's time when in 1970 Stanich's was voted the Restaurant of the Year. "My dad screamed 'Get the hell out! I want my regulars back,'" Steve remembered.

After over thirty years in the business, Steve is trying to figure out his next move. There have been lucrative offers to buy the burger icon out, but Steve told me recently, "I'm not just selling it to anyone." And he's even considering a return to the 49ers as a local Portland scout, and he's serious. "They asked me and I said 'I'm ready, Coach!'"

PENNSYLVANIA

CHARLIE'S HAMBURGERS

336 Kedron Ave. (Academy Ave at Kedron—Route 420) | Folsom, PA 19033
610-461-4228 | Mon–Thurs 11 am–9 pm | Fri & Sat 11 am–10 pm | Sun 12 pm–7 pm

If you prefer your burgers with ketchup, Charlie's is the place to go. A "loaded" burger at this decades-old hamburger spot comes with onions, ketchup, pickles, relish, and cheese, creating a sweet burger experience that is hard to find among the more staid and traditional burger stands of America. "Pretty much everyone orders them that way," a teenaged prep girl told me. She wasn't kidding—just about every person who walked in during the hour I spent at Charlie's ordered burgers with ketchup. Of course the burgers can also be ordered with mustard and tomato, but not lettuce.

Charlie's is a real place with real food. A menu of hamburgers, hot dogs, and milkshakes keeps things simple. Some may see a greasy spoon. Others see a haven for grease lovers. You get the point—this is not health food. Fortunately, the burgers are made from fresh ground chuck (pattied in the kitchen with a small patty former) and the shakes are made with great ice cream and real milk. In fact, people frequent Charlie's more for its shakes then for its burgers.

The milk for the shakes still comes out of a large vintage aluminum milk dispenser.

The crowd is a mix of airport employees from nearby Philadelphia International, kids from the local schools, and a blend of salty regulars. When I visited, the better part of a girls volleyball team had landed in search of nourishment.

Charlie's location is relatively new, though the business dates back to 1935. Charlie Convery operated the restaurant nearby at an intersection of the Baltimore Pike until 1984, when an expansion of the road spelled the end of Charlie's. Through a confusing set of purchases and sales, the restaurant relocated a mile away to a former fruit stand next to a defunct miniature golf course (the concrete skeleton of the weeded-over course is still visible behind the restaurant).

Colorful character and part-time manager of eleven years Mike Goodwin once explained to me, "After they moved, changed owners, and reopened, they still went back to Charlie's original butcher." The small burgers are cooked on a very seasoned flattop griddle, smashed thin, and cooked in the bubbling grease of previous burgers. They are served on a toasted white squishy bun. "No lettuce, no bacon, no tofu, no pineapple," Mike joked, emphasizing the simplicity of the burgers at Charlie's.

One important note: for many years Charlie's was closed on Tuesdays. In a vestige of wartime America, the restaurant once observed "meatless Tuesdays," a day that most burger joints closed during World War II for meat rationing. "Are you familiar with Wimpy?" Mike asked me. "I'll pay you TUESDAY for a hamburger today?" A lightbulb went off in my head—Wimpy was a lot smarter than I thought.

CONEY ISLAND LUNCH

3015 Buffalo Rd | Erie, PA 16510
814-899-0339 | Mon–Sat 6 am–3:30 am | Sun 2:30 pm–7 pm

Coney Island Lunch is not really known for burgers. They are best known, for ninety-five years now, for their wieners loaded with housemade chili sauce. "Outside of here they are called chili dogs," part owner Bob Ventura told me. "Here in Scranton we call them Texas Wieners." The wiener may be king at Coney Island Lunch but their under-the-radar chili burger is awesome.

The first thing you'll see when you step into Coney Island Lunch is Bob (or his brother, Pete, depending on what day it is). That's because the cooking station is right inside the window at the end of a ridiculously long counter. The restaurant is deep and seats many, but the best spot is right up front near the griddle by the action. Bob is a character, outgoing and personable and his vantage at the front allows him to interact with every single customer walking through the front door.

Steve Karampilas opened Coney Island Lunch in 1923 and his son, Jack, followed in his footsteps and ran the place next. In the late 1960s, "Boss Jack's" sons started working at Coney Island and the third generation was set. A landlord dispute in 1988 caused the family to seek a new space and the business moved around the corner. "The landlord never put a dime into the place," Bob told me, so the brothers decided it was time to buy their own place.

Bob recently celebrated fifty years working at Coney Island. Pete came home one day with fifty cents and Bob asked, "Where did you get that??" Pete had helped out his dad and grandfather at the restaurant. Bob went right down and asked to help and has worked at Coney Island ever since. He was thirteen.

This is not a normal burger. So much preamble and prep goes into this thing I wondered if it could be any good. Step one, yesterday's buns are soaked in water and mixed into fresh ground beef with salt and pepper. The beef is an odd mix of 75 percent ground round and 25 percent chuck. Step two, the hand-pattied beef mix is fried in a pan then refrigerated. Step three, the cold patties are marinated in a "special sauce" in a pan warming on the flattop at the front of the restaurant. When someone orders a burger, Bob grabs a soft, marinated patty from the pan and slips it onto a steamed bun and adds the famous chili sauce, mustard, and chopped onion. The taste is out of this world. It's intense. And they are small, you'll definitely need more than one. The tiny hand-sliced buns, the same for decades, are actually sized for the wieners, although they are closer in shape to a burger bun.

Bob has been the keeper of the chili sauce recipe for nearly half a century. "It's up here," Bob told me tapping his temple, "and it's not going anywhere." Bob learned the secret method to making the beef-based chili sauce from his grandfather and since he was sixteen has been the only one who makes it every morning.

When Bob was hospitalized for cancer a few years back, Pete took over chili duty, but when he recovered he was back at it. And for over forty-five years, the chili at Coney Island has been incredibly consistent. "I joke that even if I were in a coma, I'd still make the chili the same way."

Bob is not particularly menacing looking but does wear cutoff tees to reveal a few arm tattoos. "I'm famous for cutting off my sleeves to show off my guns," Bob joked the first time I met him. One day I was there when there was a tattoo convention in town. He turned to two tat-covered dudes at the counter and said, "You in for the convention?" When they replied yes Bob said to a waitress, "Give 'em ten percent off."

TESSARO'S

4601 Liberty Ave | Pittsburgh, PA 15224
412-682-6809 | Mon–Sat 11 am–11 pm | Closed Sun | www.tessaros.com

For years, the incredible ground beef that Tessaro's used for its burgers came from a butcher shop directly across the street called House of Meats. When the shop closed one day, Kelly Harrington, former part owner of this Pittsburgh burger destination, did what seemed the most sensible—he hired the butcher.

Dominic Piccola, a retired Pittsburgh fireman, is now employed by Tessaro's as their in-house butcher. He has become their link to hamburger perfection. Six days a week, at 7 a.m., Dominic grinds hundreds of pounds of chuck shoulder for the day's burgers. "Since I'm the only one grinding, the consistency is always the same," Dominic told me through his classic fireman's bushy handlebar mustache.

I was interested in Tessaro's because of its stellar reputation among hamburger cognoscenti, but it was the method of cooking the burgers that put me on an airplane to Pittsburgh. I had to see for myself the fabled hardwood grill that many had talked about. Unique to the burger world, the hamburgers at Tessaro's are grilled over a fire made from west Pennsylvania hardwoods, not the charcoal or the blue propane flames that seem standard for indoor flame grilling. Tessaro's uses a mixture of yellow maple, red oak, and walnut, all indigenous to the area. "We stay away from hickory because it's too strong," Kelly pointed out, "and no fruit trees because they are loaded with pesticides." Hardwoods produce a flame that is far hotter than gas or charcoal. Grillman of thirty years Courtney McFarlane told me, "The fire can get up to six hundred degrees in there."

Courtney invited me into the grill area, a section of the restaurant adjacent to the bar that was once the dance floor and is now a small room with a big picture window. I stood about three feet from the grill and the heat was so intense it felt like my eyebrows were burning right off my face. Every few minutes, Courtney tossed a small cup of water onto the flames and told me, "That's just to slow the heat down a bit."

The burgers at Tessaro's are unmeasured but somewhere near a half pound. Courtney grabs a wad of Dominic's fresh ground beef and tells me, "After a while it's easy to guess the size." He then swiftly forms the ball into a patty, slaps the beef onto a stainless-steel surface next to the grill, and does this move where he spins the patty to form an edge. The entire process takes seconds. He is a master burger maker and the finished product strangely resembles a large, machined-pressed patty.

The burgers are served with many cheese options and just about any condiment you can think of from barbecue sauce to three types of mustard. To be honest, this burger is so amazing it'd be idiotic to cover it with anything. Served on a soft, portuguese-type roll from a bakery down the street, the hefty burger is a sight to behold. It's perfectly charred on the outside and juicy and moist on the inside. And thanks to the hardwood, the burger has a taste like no other—a woodsy, backyard barbecue essence that manages not to overpower the flavor of the high-quality beef.

In 1984, Kelly, his sister, Ena, and their mother, Tee, bought the bar and restaurant from Richard Tessaro. It was Richard who began the tradition of flame grilling burgers that the Harringtons perfected. He started by grilling on the street in front of the bar on a makeshift barbecue made from halved fifty-five-gallon drums. He eventually moved the operation to the backyard, once starting a fire that burned part of the building and finally moved the grill indoors.

The restaurant is dark and cozy with a long vintage bar running along one side. The walls

are wood paneled and the aroma of the burning hardwoods is arresting. The building has been a bar for over seventy-five years, but previously housed a dry goods store and a nickelodeon as far back as the turn of the century.

In 2009, Kelly passed away due to complications from cancer. His imprint on the burger business was enormous and he will surely be missed. Within thirty-six hours of Kelly's death, Tee's husband passed as well. It was a tragic moment for the Harrington family, but they persevered. Tee called on daughters Michele (nicknamed "Mike") and Moira, who at the time were not involved with the business. "She said 'get down here to work' and we did," Moira explained. And a year later, Ena retired in 2010 because she, too, was battling cancer. When Tee passed away in 2015, Mike and Moira became the owners. Moira credits the incredible staff at Tessaro's, most of whom have been there for over thirty years, with their ability to deal with the onslaught of family crises. Moira told me, "If it weren't for the great staff, I'm not sure we could have stayed in business."

RHODE ISLAND

STANLEY'S HAMBURGERS

535 Dexter St | Central Falls, RI 02863 | 401-726-9689 | Mon–Thurs 11 am–8 pm
Fri & Sat 11 am–9 pm | Closed Sun | www.stanleyshamburgers.com

Stanley's is an absolute gem of a burger destination in a neighborhood about ten minutes north of downtown Providence. The tiny restaurant is so picture-perfect that it looks completely out of place in an area that has clearly seen better days. From my experience there's usually only one reason burger joints like Stanley's survive—someone came along and saved the place. That's exactly what happened, and we should all be thankful.

In 1987, Gregory Raheb bought the fading diner and didn't simply grab the keys and continue making burgers. He actually gutted the entire place at one point and rebuilt to exact specifications and amazing detail, sending the decor back to opening day in 1932. "When I took over it was rundown," Greg told me years ago. "It had dark wood paneling and old vinyl floor tiles. But the food was great so I knew it had potential." The centerpiece of the menu then as it is now is the prewar American standard in hamburgers—one that is loaded with onions.

The "Stanley Burger" is a classic and something closer to the original American hamburger. In the beginning, burgers were small. The patties were anywhere from one to two ounces and almost always loaded with steam grilled onions. The Stanley Burger is a perfect nod to the past and a primary example of burgers from the first half of the twentieth century. As you step out of your car in the lot next door, you are immediately enveloped in the intoxicating essence

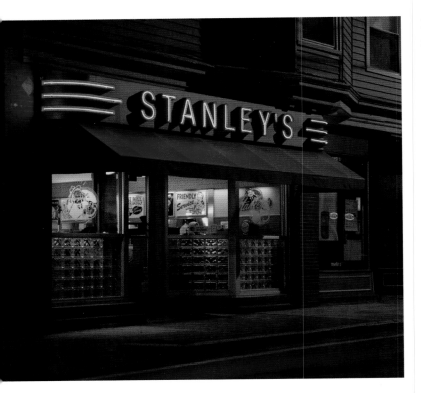

personally it is one of my favorite way to enjoy a hamburger. Places like the White Manna, Cozy Inn, and Town Topic as well as all of the burger joints in El Reno, Oklahoma, are still making burgers this way.

If you ask for a double, watch what happens. The grillperson takes two wads of beef and presses them together on the griddle. Cheese is available and it seems that ketchup rules the counter at Stanley's, but neither is necessary. This little burger, thanks to equal amounts of beef and onion, absolutely explodes with flavor. "Some people ask for extra onions," longtime manager and counterperson Nancy told me.

of grilled onions pouring from the restaurant's exhaust. It is a sign of good things to come.

The burger to get is the double Stanley Burger, or two of them. The burgers start as fresh ground beef that is machine-formed at the restaurant into "plugs," or tiny two-ounce tall patties. The wad of beef is tossed on the flattop and a pile of paper-thin spanish onion is thrown on top. With great force, the onions are smashed into the burger and the whole commingled mess cooks to perfection. When the patty is flipped, the bun is placed on top to steam. The same practice of smashing onions can be found at primary source burger joints across America, and

The menu is not limited to burgers and offers a vast selection of diner favorites, all of it homemade from the freshest ingredients.

Polish immigrant Stanley Kryla opened the burger counter back in 1932 in the early days of the Depression. Most burger joints failed during this time in American history and if they didn't, they were wiped out by meat rationing during World War II. It's a miracle that Stanley's survived.

After almost thirty years at Stanley's, Greg sold the restaurant to former manager of ten years Louie Augusta in 2016. He added beer and wine, but the Stanley Burger is still at the top of the menu.

NORTHGATE SODA SHOP

918 North Main St | Greenville, SC 29609 | 864-235-6770
Mon–Fri 11 am–8 pm | Sat 11 am–3 pm | Closed Sun | www.northgatesodashop.com

Just up the hill on Main Street in Greenville, South Carolina, where the high-rises give way to trees and homes, I discovered an excellent spot to enjoy a Southern favorite—the "Pimento Cheeseburger." Longtime owner of forty-one years Jim DeYoung was looking to retire, and sold the shop to a lawyer with an office just twenty feet away named Catherine Christophillis. A few years later, she sold it to one of Jim's friends, Iris Hood-Bell, in 2009. I was sitting at Jim's round table once (that the former owner installed for daily visits with his friends) when Jim told me, "I wanted to sell the shop

to someone who would keep everything almost the same." That sounds like a simple request, except that just about every square inch of the Northgate is covered in four decades of collectibles. It resembles an antique shop that happens to have a soda fountain, with signed eight-by-tens, extensive bottle, can, and cigar box collections, beer and soda neon, a vintage Ex-Lax sign, and an impressive church fan collection. This is the real deal—no fake made-in-China reproduction crap here. When Catherine bought the shop, she bought the stuff, too. "Where was I going to put it?" Jim said of his antiques. "It belongs here anyway." And when Iris bought Northgate, the stuff was again part of the deal.

The menu at the Northgate is classic soda shop diner fare—tuna, peanut butter and jelly, hot dogs, grilled cheese, and egg sandwiches, but the big seller is their fantastic Pimento Cheeseburger. "You'll either love it or hate it," longtime waitress Brenda warned me before I bit into my burger. I have to admit I had never had one, even though my mother is from South Carolina. Fortunately, I fall into the "love it" category.

The pimento cheese for the Northgate's sandwiches and burgers is a tangy mix of mayo, cheddar, and diced pimentos. "We make it right here, fresh every day," former waitress Maudie told me once of the fifty-year-old recipe. The beef is also fresh, picked up daily from a butcher just up Main Street (this fact is also proudly announced on the menu, complete with the butcher's name and address).

The burger starts as fresh ground beef that is pressed in a vintage burger press. The press produces a three-and-a-half-ounce patty that is cooked on a flattop griddle. The burger comes to you on a toasted bun with tomato, lettuce, and a large dollop of pimento cheese. I also had a cherry smash, a drink made from cherry syrup and soda water, dispensed from the Northgate's venerable soda fountain. A few years ago, Jim's cherry syrup supplier stopped making the syrup, so he started making it himself. "I found some extract so we started making it in-house."

Today, Iris's husband, Ren, works at Northgate and nothing has changed much since the days when Jim owned the soda fountain. "Same burgers, same sodas, same butcher." And Jim still comes in to hang out at his round table. Ren told me, "He's here every day!"

ROCKAWAY ATHLETIC CLUB

2719 Rosewood Dr | Columbia, SC 29205
803-256-1075 | Open Daily 11 am–11 pm

I swear I drove by the place five times before accidentally turning into the parking lot. There are no signs of life from the street side of the Rockaway Athletic Club, an imposing brick structure with armored windows. As I was pulling out of the lot after checking the map, I noticed a small piece of cardboard by a back door with the words *Boiled Peanuts Tonight* scrawled in black Sharpie. I figured this must be the place.

"We've always been sort of low-key," part owner Forest Whitlark said, describing the thirty-six-year-old hangout in this quiet neighborhood in Columbia. The fortresslike building is a somewhat recent addition in the history of the Rockaway. "The original burned to the ground," Forest told me. In 2002, it was the victim of a faulty air conditioner. The Rockaway opened in 1982 by brothers Paul and Forest Whitlark and friend David Melson. The original bar occupied three storefronts of a 1940s strip mall at the same location. My guess is that when they rebuilt they wanted to make sure that the Rockaway could withstand anything.

I was there to sample their often talked about "Pimento Cheeseburger" (pronounced "pimena" in these parts). The Rockaway Pimento Cheeseburger has so much gooey cheese on it that it's almost impossible to pick up. Fortunately, the burger comes cut in half, and each half has a large toothpick to keep the contents together. The second you pull the toothpick, get a good grip on your burger as the contents have a tendency to slip and slide.

Pimento cheese is a Southern staple and is traditionally made with only three ingredients— cheddar cheese, mayonnaise, and diced pimentos. In his book *Hamburgers & Fries*, burger scholar John T. Edge points out that the marriage of pimento cheese to the burger may have actually happened in Columbia by J. C. Reynolds at the now-defunct Dairy Bar. I believe the claim. There are more pimento cheeseburgers available in this town than anywhere else on the planet. And the Rockaway claims to have been the first in town to create the beloved Pimento Cheese Fries.

The burgers at Rockaway start as eight-ounce hand-formed patties of fresh ground chuck. They are cooked on a flattop and the large seeded buns are warmed nearby on the griddle until they are soft as a pillow. In keeping with tradition, Rockaway only uses the three basic ingredients to make their pimento cheese and it's amazing.

In 2005, George W. Bush visited Rockaway on a swing through South Carolina. He ordered two burgers and two pimento cheese fries to go, then made a point to shake a few hands. Forest remembered, "I think he spoke to everyone in here." A comfortable bar will do that to you.

Rockaway is huge. With the University of South Carolina only five minutes away with its thirty thousand students, it's a good thing they have a capacity of almost three hundred. There are booths and tables everywhere, an air hockey table, a pool table, and a very long bar.

So if you can actually find the Rockaway and make it through the throngs of students, you will be rewarded with a great pimento cheeseburger. The Rockaway Athletic Club did not invent the pimento cheeseburger but they are doing something just as important: perpetuating a great Southern food tradition.

NICK'S HAMBURGER SHOP

427 Main Ave | Brookings, SD 57006 | 605-692-4324 | Mon–Fri 11 am–7 pm
Sat 11 am–4 pm | Closed Sun | www.nickshamburgers.com

Nick's Hamburger Shop sits in the center of bustling downtown Brookings, South Dakota, and looks as if it were placed there by a film crew to "complete the scene." Step inside and you'll be immediately consumed by the intoxicating aroma of beef grease, a rich smell like no other. That's because the burgers at Nick's are cooked the way they have been for almost one hundred years—deep-fried in a secret blend of beef tallow and spices.

The tiny burgers at Nick's are cooked in a low-sided "tank" of rendered beef tallow. Small measured balls of fresh beef are pressed into the shallow grease, bobbing for a few minutes before they are removed and placed on special rolls made from a secret recipe just for Nick's. The restaurant can serve up to seven hundred per hour when it's busy.

Longtime owner Dick Fergen passed away in 2013, and his son, Todd, stepped in to assume operations and ownership. When his dad was sick with cancer, he returned to Brookings from his home in Montana, ended up staying for the funeral, and subsequently jumped in to run Nick's

in his father's absence. Since that time Todd has moved to Brookings to run Nick's full-time. "It has been a very scary but exciting time to move back home," Todd explained. "I hadn't planned to move back . . . yet." In keeping with his father's

wishes the tallow, relish, and bun recipes remain very secret.

Dick was one helluva guy. He left a job in farm management in Texas to return to his hometown of Brookings, South Dakota. Upon his arrival, he inquired about the landmark burger joint, Nick's, and soon after purchased it from the notorious and sometimes volatile third owner, Duane Larson. In his nearly three decades at the grill, Duane was known to close early because he ran out of buns, and refused to sell the business to just anyone, saying that he'd burn the place down before he sold it to the wrong person. Duane was also involved in a spat between the Coca-Cola Company and Nick's that led to a dramatic photo in *Time* magazine of Duane pouring Coke into the street.

Nick's was started by Harold and Gladys Nikalson in 1929 and was later passed on to their son, Harold Jr., in 1947. When Duane Larson bought Nick's in 1972, much to the dismay of the old-timers,

he added the cheeseburger to the menu. The small burgers come with a secret relish whose recipe goes back to the beginning. It's a mustard-based pickle-and-onion relish that has "other seasonings," a waitress once told me.

Orders are not taken, they are yelled. "We just holler [to the grillperson] what we need," former waitress Laurie told me. First, you tell the counterperson what you want. When your burgers are ready, you tell them what you want on them, which is limited to relish, ketchup, mustard, pickles, and raw onion. Lettuce, mayo, and tomato are not available at Nick's so don't even ask. The little burgers arrive at your counter spot on a square of waxed paper (Nick's "fine china") and can be consumed at a rate of roughly one every twenty seconds, which is good, because you will need to make room for the thirty people waiting for your stool.

In 2008, Dick bought the barbershop next door and doubled the size of Nick's. The new counter wraps around the griddle, which is in the center of the restaurant, and the burger joint can now seat many more hungry burger lovers.

A man named Stewart sitting next to me at the counter once told me that he had been coming back to Nick's every time he visited his alma mater, South Dakota State University. "I've been coming ever since I graduated in '52." Old-timers refer to their visits as getting their "Nick's fix."

"If you are not from South Dakota, then you wouldn't understand," Dick once pondered seriously the first time I met him. "There's something about these people. I wouldn't trade them for anyone in the world."

TENNESSEE

ALEX'S TAVERN

1445 Jackson Ave | Memphis, TN 38107 | 901-278-9086
Mon–Sun 11 am–3 am

I will walk into literally anyplace on a hot burger tip, regardless of the locale. Sure, Alex's Tavern is a scrappy dive, and it's not trying to be anything but a dive. It's a place where a handful of regulars probably feel more at home here than at their actual homes and where every stranger that walks immediately becomes family. And fortunately for me, they also serve up an excellent under-the-radar bar burger.

Alex's is not downtown, or near anything really in Memphis. And from the outside, it's hard to tell if the place is safe to enter. Note to first-timers: take the leap of faith and get in there—it's one of the best bars in town. The window shades have never been opened (with the exception of when we filmed *Burger Land* and our producer opened them for more natural light—whoa). The only light sources in the bar are beer signage, a string of old Christmas lights, and a multitude of large screen TVs. The Formica on the bar is chipping in places and the ceiling tiles are warped and discolored but you did not come here for the decor.

Likely the first person you'll meet at Alex's is Rocky Kasaftes. Rocky's dad, Alex, opened the bar in 1953, a few years after family friend Charlie Vergos opened the now-famous BBQ joint

Owner Rocky Kasaftes

Rendezvous in downtown Memphis. Alex was young and clueless but Charlie gave him some sage advice, "You are Greek. You'll figure it out."

Rocky grew up in the bar and actually started working there at age four. "My dad used to give me a knife and make me scrape gum off under the tables," he told me. Rocky ran the bar with his dad through his teens, and back then Alex had waiters in white coats to help out. He gets emotional talking about his dad but describes Alex as "tough as nails."

In the beginning, the only food offered at Alex's was a ham sandwich. Rocky's mom, Eugenia, baked the ham at home so Alex could shave ham for sandwiches right behind the bar. In the late 1970s, Alex began to experiment with burgers

and they were a hit. Alex passed away while Rocky was at college, and at twenty-one decided to run the bar with his best friend John McCormick. "My mother was like 'Oh no, I'm going to have to live through this shit again??'" Rocky remembered, laughing.

Today, Rocky serves more than just burgers. There's Rocky's famous gumbo (which is incredible), his ribs (which are smoked right outside the back door), and of course his burgers. For almost forty years, the 80/20 chuck Rocky uses for the burgers has come from the same butcher. The six-ounce, hand-pattied burger is cooked in a skillet sized for one burger only. The burger gets a generous sprinkle of a "secret," Greek seasoning, which includes garlic powder, pepper, and oregano. It's served on a toasted white squishy bun with american cheese, mustard, pickle, tomato, and raw onion. The griddle char is pronounced and the cheese is super melty.

You'll notice something peculiar about Alex's, side-by-side jukeboxes and naturally there's a story. "There used to be one," Rocky told me, "but we figured out which songs weren't being played and switched out Dad's music [for Motown hits, etc.] without changing the labels." Brilliant move, until one day Jimmy Buffett's "Why Don't We Get Drunk And Screw?" came on the juke. "We were busted," Rocky said with a big smile. His dad diplomatically solved the problem by getting a second juke.

The neighborhood changed dramatically after Rocky took over the bar, but as he put it, "I'm too stubborn to quit." They said he wouldn't make it and he most certainly has. And now that the neighborhood is changing again, it seems that Rocky's stubbornness has paid off.

BROWN'S DINER

2102 Blair Blvd | Nashville, TN 37212 | 615-269-5509
Mon–Sat 11 am–11 pm | Sun 11 am–9 pm | www.brownsdiner.com

It may not look like much, but Brown's may be one of the most historically significant burger joints in this book. The fact that it survives is a miracle, and a testament to the power of hamburger culture in this country. It has lived through more than one fire and withstood many face-lifts.

To the untrained eye, Brown's appears to be a dump—an unimpressive double-wide with a drab gray/beige exterior. An enormous defunct radar dish on the roof gives the entire structure the look of a scientific outpost on Antarctica. But for lovers of American cultural history, it is a treasure. There was a time in this country when hamburgers were not king. They were considered dirty food for wage earners, and were served in establishments much like Brown's. The only difference is that

places like this, which once dotted the American landscape in the thousands, and were mostly found in close proximity to factories and urban areas, are just about gone.

Charlie Brown demonstrates the new "electric" coffeemaker, circa mid-1930's.

What makes Brown's Diner special is that its core is made up of two retired trolley cars, mule-drawn cars that were left at the end of the line in the early 1920s as the automobile became ubiquitous in city life. The trolleys are arranged in a T shape, one making up the bar, the other serving as the kitchen. Terry Young, the bartender and manager, told me, "The wooden wheels are still on it, though I wouldn't suggest going down there." The practice of converting trolleys and diner cars into eating establishments was so popular in the early part of the twentieth century that

companies emerged to fabricate the restaurants without the wheels—and the modern diner was born.

Today, Brown's is a beloved spot in Nashville and has numerous regulars, famous and not. Vince Gill loves the burgers, as do Marty Stuart and Faith Hill, among other members of Nashville's country elite. Johnny Cash dedicated an album to the place and John Prine was as comfortable there as you will be. According to a regular, Prine was at the bar one night when someone recognized him and put one of his songs on the jukebox. Apparently, Prine stood up and mimicked himself continuing to sing along to his own music and giving the bar patrons a twisted, impromptu karaoke performance.

And good luck navigating the bar stools, designed for long-term drinking. I'm sure at one point these upholstered chairs on low poles were mighty comfortable, but today they are lumpy and lopsided—you may feel instantly drunk as you settle into one. "That one is like a rodeo," a regular said as he watched me struggle.

Randy, a twenty-five-year veteran of Brown's, told me, "This is a good anti-anorexia place." I'm assuming he was referring to the gloriously unhealthy menu that includes, beyond burgers, grilled cheese, Frito pie, hush puppies, and a catfish dinner. The only salad on the menu is coleslaw. The burger at Brown's has been on the menu since it opened in 1927. It's made from a daily delivery of fresh chuck, hand-pattied to around five ounces. A cheeseburger comes with mayo, tomato, lettuce, and onion on a white squishy bun with pickles speared to the top. If you ask for a cheeseburger, you don't get mustard. If you ask for a hamburger, you do. I'm confused, too—just read the menu and have another Budweiser.

DINO'S BAR

411 Gallatin Ave | Nashville, TN 37206 | 615-226-3566 | Mon–Fri 4 pm–3 am
Sat & Sun 12 pm–3 am | www.dinosnashville.com

At first glance, Dino's does not seem like the kind of place that would serve up fine food. The fairly nondescript, squat, red brick storefront bar has large picture windows with painted lettering and one reads DINO'S FINE FOOD. So there you have it. Why would the window lie?

At its core Dino's is an East Nashville dive bar, one of the most beautiful dives in America. Nashville is known of course for late night honky-tonk bars but Dino's is outside the tourist mainstream and a favorite haunt of locals (who would probably never be caught in a bar downtown). The interior is pure comfort, dark and mysterious, and just the right size. During the day, the large windows let in some light, and at night, the place is low-lit and packed with a chill, tattooed twenty- to thirtysomething drinking crowd. There is a refreshing no-bull-shit vibe about the place.

Today's Dino's is a bit different than the Dino's of just a few years ago. Manager Jeremy is a constant at the bar and has been there his entire life. "This is the first bar I ever drank a beer in," he told me as a brunch crowd started filing into Dino's. Jeremy would bring in all of his underage friends in the days when the drinking policy was a little looser. He pointed out that was a very different time back then. "The picnic table out back was actually stolen by a few regulars from Shelby Park in the 1980s," he told me. "They wanted a place to smoke pot."

No one seems to know the history of Dino's but it is rumored to have opened in the 1970s (in a building that dates to the '30s) by a guy named Dino. "All we know," Jeremy told me, "is that he was a short man with curly hair that had a way with the ladies." He rattled off the names of past owners for me, "...Dino, John, Travis, Rick, Alex...". Current co-owner Alex Wendkos bought the place in 2014 with restauranteur Miranda Pontes and there was a general uneasiness among Dino's regulars about the purchase. Alex had zero interest in changing a thing about the ethos of Dino's and when it reopened in 2015 regulars were pleased to discover that their Dino's survived. The menu received a huge upgrade and smoking was banned, which

are positive things, and the beloved cheese-burger remained as did the cold-ass, cheap beer. A few months after opening, the classic beer-only bar added hard booze and that too was a welcome change.

Before Wendkos and Pontes bought Dino's the late nite menu consisted of deep-fried frozen crap like jalapeño poppers and cheese sticks. The new menu has a pedigree from some of the best new restaurants in Nash-ville, with an aggressive brunch as well as real food like Frito Pie, a chicken sandwich and an excellent BLT.

But it's the burgers they all come back for. Cooked on the very seasoned original flattop right behind the bar, the burgers start as fresh ground beef hand pattied to 5.5 ounces. The cheeseburger with everything comes with the best in non-fancy condiments—iceberg lettuce, raw onion, a thick slice of tomato and a few dill pickle chips. It's a classic burger package and a very welcome sight after a few beers. And at six bucks it's a steal. You can also add bacon or a fried egg (or both), and the only cheese avail-able is cheddar. I added fries to my order and Jeremy responded, "Always, baby." Order at the bar, grab a seat and dig the music selection which will likely be an eclectic mix of old-timey country and rock.

"I liked it before too," a regular at the bar mentioned the last time I visited. It's very diffi-cult to upgrade a beloved classic. Major kudos to the heroes that have the guts to at least try, and succeed.

DYER'S BURGERS

205 Beale St | Memphis, TN 38103 | 901-527-3937
Sun–Thurs 11 am–3 am | Fri & Sat 11 am–5 am | www.dyersonbeale.com

No hamburger restaurant in America flaunts the method of deep-frying a burger quite like Dyer's in Memphis, Tennessee. There are other burgers out there that are cooked in skillets of bubbling proprietary, blended grease, but Dyer's goes to the extreme and employs a two-foot-wide skillet that I'm guessing holds more than three gallons of grease. But that's not all. Dyer's claims the grease has never been changed since the restaurant opened 106 years ago.

I know this sounds nuts, but according to previous manager Tom Robertson, the grease has never been changed, just added to. "We'll top off the grease but never throw it out and start over," he told me as I interviewed him for my film, *Hamburger America*. As I sat there in disbelief, he produced one photograph after another documenting the police-escorted bucket of grease being relocated from the old location to the new. On some news footage I obtained for the film, you can hear someone say, "As soon as the mayor gets here, we'll go inside and make some lunch!" Now I've really seen it all.

The burgers are not deep-fried in just any old grease. Dyer's uses beef tallow, or rendered beef fat to add to the decades-old skillet. You'd think your burger would emerge from the grease a sludgy disaster, but quite the opposite occurs. The grease, of course, adds flavor, but the burger turns

out being no greasier than a regular, griddled burger. It's probably because of this that some regulars ask to have their bun dipped, which is where the top half of the bun is returned to the skillet for a dip in the grease.

The method for cooking a burger at Dyer's is the most peculiar of any burger counter in America. A quarter-pound wad of fresh ground beef is placed on a marble surface. The cook then uses a large spatula and a mallet to pound the meat into a paper-thin patty nearly eight inches wide. The flat beef is then scraped off the surface and slid into the nearby skillet of bubbling, brown grease. Within a minute, the patty floats to the top and it's done. Ask for cheese and watch what happens. The cook lifts the patty out of the grease with the spatula, places a square of american cheese on it, and the patty is quickly dipped back into the grease to melt the cheese.

Mississippi native Elmer Dyer opened Dyer's Restaurant in 1912 in the midtown section of Memphis. The burger shack proudly served both blacks and whites, though in the Southern tradition before the civil rights movement, they had to enter though separate doors. At some point, Dyer's moved around the corner to Poplar and North Cleveland and that's when John Robertson, Tom's brother, bought the place.

Soon after the historic move of the fabled Dyer's grease to Beale Street (complete with police escort, media coverage, photo ops, and proud politicians), John passed away and ownership of Dyer's went to his wife, Sandy. Today, Dyer's is run by Sandy and her son, Kendall, who has worked at the iconic burger joint since birth. "I knew I'd be doing this [running Dyer's], for sure," he told me recently. Kendall takes his role as a steward to a burger legend very seriously and the future of Dyer's is strong. And Beale has changed recently with the addition of both new basketball and baseball stadiums within just a few blocks walking distance. Kendall told me, "We always fill up before and after games." On weekends, when the tourist and party crowd wanders, Beale Dyer's stays open until 5 a.m.

The Dyer's of Beale Street is not the shack it once was years ago. Today's version comes off as upgraded and slick, but maintains the fabled grease and uses only fresh ground beef for the burgers. The fabled grease even has its own slogan, printed everywhere: "Have You Had Your Vitamin G Today?" Naturally, the G stands for grease.

FAT MO'S

2620 Franklin Pike | Nashville, TN 37204 | 615-298-1111 | Tues–Sat 10 am–11 pm
Mon 10 am–10 pm | Sun 10 am–9 pm | (Twelve Other Nashville Metro Locations)
www.fatmos.com

Ask any current or former Nashville area college student about Fat Mo's and most likely they'll tell you they've been there. That may be because in the Nashville metro area there are thirteen Fat Mo's locations. It also may be because people in Nashville love burgers and Fat Mo's makes one helluva burger.

At first glance, anyone of the Fat Mo's outposts look like a standard roadside burger joint, some of them nondescript, brightly painted cinderblock boxes near highway interchanges. But to those who know Fat Mo's, there is something entirely unique at play here. Opened in 1991 by Iranian husband and wife Mohammad Ali and Shiva Karimy, the burgers at Fat Mo's have a very distinct flavor that is unmistakably Middle Eastern.

The story of how Mo and Shiva came to found a burger empire in Nashville is right out of a storybook. After the Shah of Iran was deposed in 1979, the lives of any remaining supporters of his regime were in danger under the new ruler Ayatollah Khomeini. "After the revolution, I escaped," Mo told me, "I was for the Shah and if I had stayed I'd be killed. They had no mercy." Mo was a prominent businessman in Iran prior to the revolution and owned a number of restaurants, four of them burger joints. Inspired by the success of McDonald's in his country, Mo saw potential in the burger business. He opened his own burger joint and called it "Mamad Topol," which translated from Farsi means "Fat Mo's." "The Iranians loved American culture," Mo explained, "and they still do! Don't believe what you see on the news."

Mo and Shiva have made their name with a unique twist to the all-American hamburger. The basic construction of the burger is the same but a very important step in the cooking process sets these burgers apart from the rest. When you bite into the half-pound Fat Mo, you'll be struck by the subtle spices at work. Black pepper, salt, and garlic are all present as well as other spices, but none of this overwhelms the beef-and-cheese

profile of the burger. The secret is in the marinade, an old family recipe.

All of the burgers at Fat Mo's come from bulk fresh ground beef that is hand-pattied daily. "We weigh it on a scale, then flatten into patties on a hard surface," Mo explained. The burgers are cooked on a flattop griddle, and just before they are finished, the patties are dipped into the marinade then returned to the griddle. "That's how we do it," Mo explained proudly. "But the marinade is a secret. I cannot tell you what is in that." Whatever it is, it makes the Fat Mo one unique, tasty burger.

The menu is vast but the burger options are pretty basic at Fat Mo's. The biggest seller is the "Fat Mo," which is a half-pound patty on a toasted sesame seed bun. Unless you specify what you want on your burger the Fat Mo comes with everything, which is shredded lettuce, tomato, raw onion, pickles, mustard, ketchup, mayonnaise, and american cheese. Mo's personal favorite burger on the menu (and coincidentally mine as well) is the half-pound Double Mo. Instead of one large half-pound patty, the Double Mo comes with two quarter-pound patties, more griddle char, and an extra slice of cheese. There's also the Little Mo, a quarter-pound burger that Mo says, "Most of the ladies get that one." If you are feeling adventurous (or really hungry), go for the Super Deluxe Fat Mo, a twenty-seven-ounce patty that comes with everything plus grilled onions, barbecue sauce, bacon, and jalapeños. It may be your only meal of the day.

Fat Mo's locations are a mixed bag of restaurant types because each location is an independently owned franchise. A handful of them are sit-down restaurants with drive-thrus, a few are sit-down with no drive-thru, and some are tiny roadside drive-up windows. Five of these have a curious double drive-up system with two lanes, one on either side of the building. When you pull up to the large menu in the parking lot, there is no speaker asking you for your order. You make a selection and drive up to a window to order, or an employee will emerge from the rear of the restaurant to take your order to bring to the kitchen. It's all very low-tech but everything is made to order and very fresh.

Although most of the locations have been franchised, Mo and Shiva have retained the Smyrna location for themselves. They spend much of their time in the restaurant because as Mo put it, "People in Nashville want to see me, see that I'm alive, that I exist." Mr. Mo, as he is affectionately known, most definitely exists and so do his amazing burgers.

ROTIER'S RESTAURANT

2413 Elliston Place | Nashville, TN 37203 | 615-327-9892 | Mon & Tues 10:30 am–9:30 pm
Wed–Fri 10:30 am–10 pm | Sat 9 am–10 pm | Closed Sun | www.rotiersrestaurant.com

Nashvillians are proud of Rotier's and the burger that is served there on french bread. At first glance, the burger looks impossible to eat, a tower of edible elements that defy gravity, thanks, only to feathery sandwich toothpicks. And that bread—why the big loaf of french bread? "My father ordered some loaves of french bread from Sunbeam one day in the '40s to serve with our spaghetti," owner Margaret Crouse told me. One thing led to another and the famous Rotier's cheeseburger on french bread was born. Despite how tall the burger looks, it's a breeze to eat and the supersoft bread cradles the burger patty and condiments perfectly.

It should be a good burger. It has been on the top of every best burger list in Nashville for decades. Loretta Lynn, Tim McGraw, and Faith Hill are all fans of the cozy dive. Jimmy Buffett used to sit at the bar and write songs and eat burgers regularly back in the late '60s when he lived in Nashville, prompting many to assume that he penned the famous "Cheeseburger in Paradise" at Rotier's. Alas, he did not (see page 66).

Evelyn and John Rotier opened their tavern and restaurant in 1945 just steps from Vanderbilt University. Today, the giggly, effervescent Margaret Crouse, daughter of the Rotiers, owns the dark, comfortably broken-in tavern with her brother, Charlie Rotier. "I've worked here for forty-four years," she told me, which seems impossible because she looks to be under forty-four years of age. Many of her employees can boast similar claims; Pamela has been in the kitchen for twenty-six years. Her mother gave her the job after *she* had flipped burgers there for over thirty years, starting in 1951.

There are three burgers on the menu at Rotier's and the descriptions can be somewhat confusing. The well-known "cheeseburger on french bread" is self-explanatory, but order a grilled cheeseburger and it comes on white or wheat toast. Order just a cheeseburger and you'll get the same patty on a white squishy bun. The six-ounce burgers are hand-pattied every morning from over one hundred pounds of fresh ground chuck. A burger with everything comes with lettuce, onion, and tomato. Order a "half & half" and you'll get a plate with both fries and onion rings.

Other than hamburgers and the surprisingly good spicy fried pickles, Rotier's is also known for its plate dinners that come with Southern sides, like lima beans, broccoli casserole, and fried okra. And don't miss Eddie Cartwright's Lemon Ice Box Pie, a tangy, creamy dessert similar to key lime pie with a buttery graham cracker crust. Jack-of-all-trades Eddie and the pie recipe have been at Rotier's for over twenty years. (Eddie is married to grill cook Pamela.) Every single time I'm in Rotier's, Eddie comes around taunting me with his pie. He's knows I'm weak,

and also knows that I have more burgers to eat that day. But no matter what, I somehow make room for Eddie's incredible pie.

My good friend from Nashville, Vadis Turner, told me once, "My dad took me here for my first burger. It is the kind of place where you bring your kid to get them their first real hamburger." Last time I was there an old-timer sat down and enjoyed a full meal, complete with Eddie's Lemon Ice Box Pie. When he was through he looked at the bartender and sighed, "Man, I love this place."

ZARZOUR'S CAFE

1627 Rossville Ave | Chattanooga, TN 37408 | 423-266-0424
Mon–Fri 11 am–2 pm | Closed Sat & Sun

Zarzour's is one of the places I visited where I had wished this book wasn't just about hamburgers. In addition to serving up one of the best burgers I've ever had, Zarzour's also provides a meat-and-threes menu that the locals love. But even if burgers were the only draw, it's worth a trip to this South Chattanooga food gem.

Until recently, Zarzour's burgers were not even listed on the menu. Local lunch patron Blythe Bailey told me, "I came here a few times before I realized they even made burgers." I asked Shannon Fuller, fourth-generation owner, grill chef, and master of ceremonies, why the burgers were not advertised. "Because I hate making them!" she said laughing hard. "Just kidding! But

in the summertime, it gets real hot in here because of the burgers."

It couldn't be a friendlier place. Everyone knows one another and some descendant of Zarzour is always in the restaurant either eating or working. "They come here to eat and I put every damn one of them to work—go clear that table," Shirley Fuller once told me. Shirley was the third-generation Zarzour but passed away in 2015 and her son, Joe, and daughter-in-law, Shannon, became owners. Shirley's grandfather, Charles Zarzour, a Lebanese immigrant, opened the café in 1918.

The burgers are large. How large? Shannon made an air patty with her hands "about this big" and burst out laughing. "And the large burger is this big!" and she made a bigger air patty. Each burger is pattied to order. Shannon scoops ground chuck out of a Tupperware dish next to the grill, hand-forms a patty, and places it on the small, flattop griddle in the front part of the restaurant, surrounded by customers.

No burger is the same, though she gets pretty close. If you ask for grilled onion, a thick slice is cooked like a burger patty on the griddle. A cheeseburger with everything comes with pickles, lettuce, tomato, onion, mayo, and mustard on a bun that comes

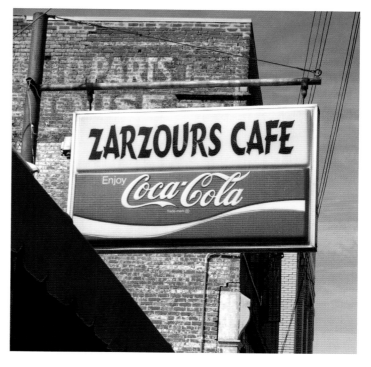

from a bakery across the street. But wait, the condiments are not just tossed on there. Shannon takes the construction of the burger very seriously and explained that the mustard must touch the burger. "I don't know why but it definitely makes the burger taste better."

From the outside, Zarzour's doesn't look like much. Look for the small painted-brick structure with heavily fortified windows. The only warmth on the exterior is the red-checked curtain hanging in the window of the front door. Inside you'll find just the opposite—a warm country café with tables of all sizes covered with the same red-checked fabric and a capacity crowd happy to be there.

Besides burgers, I watched plates of great Southern food be dispatched to tables. Butter beans, collard greens, and skillet corn bread are on the menu, as is the local favorite, lemon ice box pie.

The tables all have clear bottles filled with odd science experiments: things like homemade chow chow relish and pickled okra. One bottle's contents even the waitress could not identify, but I'm sure it was tasty.

It would be easy to miss out on a lunch at Zarzour's if you showed up, for example, after 2 p.m., or on a weekend. And this year the restaurant celebrates its hundredth year. Shannon is proud to be the generation that brings the restaurant into the next century and plans to be there for a while.

TEXAS

105 GROCERY & DELI

17255 Texas 105 | Washington, TX 77880 | 936-878-2273
Mon–Thurs 11 am–7:30 pm | Fri & Sat 11 am–8 pm

This is not a burger joint. It's not really even a well-stocked grocery store. 105 Grocery is a tiny country store, a place to meet and buy beer, lotto tickets, and a bag of chips. They also happen to serve one of the best burgers I've ever had in Texas.

105 Grocery is way out there. Far beyond the sprawl of Houston and a healthy eighty-mile drive northwest is a burger spot that is barely on the map. Inside and out, the 105 is a friendly, classic, functioning rural country store. Mismatched chairs and tables fill the area by the register and people come and go, paying for gas and hauling away beer by the twelve-pack. At the 105 Grocery, the beer in the coolers far exceeds the space allotted for soda.

The best-looking seat in the house is a community table in the rear of the store near the beer coolers. The table is surrounded by a bunch of random chairs and one comfortable, high-backed leather office chair on wheels. As I eyed the chair at the empty table, I heard a voice say, "Nobody better sit in that chair." One of the grill cooks, Sherrie, explained to me that, like clockwork, the owner's brother, Sam, shows up every day at 8 a.m. and 4 p.m. to sit in that chair. Sure enough, at exactly 4:01 a guy in a dusty John Deere hat walked in, helped himself to a can of Miller Lite and slipped into the chair. A friend in suspenders, jeans, and cowboy hat joined him with a Bud in hand and all I could think of was how fortunate I was to be in this authentic joint. Most people never get to see this side of the country.

Your choices for burgers are with or without cheese and single or double patty. As tempting as a double sounds deep in the heart of Texas, beware. The fresh, hand-pattied burgers seem to be close to half a pound, making a double-meat burger one full pound of beef. I opted for the half-pound single patty and that was sufficient. The girl on the grill, Beaujolais, told me, "Some folks come in and order double meat with bacon . . . that's big." A burger with everything comes with mayo, pickles, mustard, iceberg lettuce, a slice of tomato, and raw onion. The whole package is delivered on a toasted, buttered, soft white bun in a plastic basket and is an absolutely tasty belly bomb.

The flavor is peppery and I'm assuming that Beaujolais (named by her mother, who worked in a wine store) sprinkled a liberal amount of seasoning on the patties. Everyone who works at 105 does it all, and Sherrie said it best: "Cook, cashier . . . whatever." The tiny flattop griddle can be seen though a small pass-thru behind the register and on busy days there's a wait due to the limited capacity of the griddle.

An older, outgoing regular named Donald, sitting at a table sipping a beer, told me that the 105 has been around forever and remembers the place from his youth, when it was called Jensen's Store. "I damn near own the place," he declared. "I'm here every day!"

The actual owners are Betty and John Eichelberger, who own a ranch nearby. Betty's aunt and uncle Minnie and Melvin Jensen opened the grocery many decades ago. The progression of ownership still exists in the signage outside, making the 105 look like it has an identity problem. One sign reads B&J's GAS and another across the parking lot calls the place D&K GENERAL STORE. When you call, they answer the phone, "105." My favorite sign, though, is on the front door and lists two rules—NO SMOKING CIGARS—NO SAGGING PANTS. I wonder if they are enforced.

As Sam sat in his leather office chair and watched the activity at the register, he told anyone who would listen, "Can't get a bad burger here." He then turned to me. "I eat burgers here every day," he said, then added with a chuckle, "I eat all my meals here."

ADAIR'S SALOON

2624 Commerce St | Dallas, TX 75226 | 214-939-9900
Mon–Sat 11 am–2 am | Sun 12 pm–2 am | www.adairssaloon.com

Down in Deep Ellum, a section of Dallas just north of downtown known for its honky-tonk nightlife, is a comfortably broken-in bar called Adair's Saloon. If you walk in off the street out of the blazing Texas sun, it'll take a while for your eyes to adjust to the darkness. But when they do, you'll find a place that is hard to leave. There are happy hour specials all day, old-timey country tunes on the jukebox, instant friends lining the bar, and they just happen to serve one of the best burgers in Texas.

Adair's is full of beer neon and other signage but most noticeable is the graffiti, which is everywhere. It's on the floor, walls, and tables, and there's a lot of it. A tattooed bartender once told me, "We encourage it," and handed me a few black Sharpies. Adair's is the perfect spot if you need to let loose with a pen after a few beers. Just ask the bartender for a marker.

Settle into a booth or belly up to the bar and order a burger and a local favorite beer (one of my favorites), Shiner Bock. If you need a menu, there's one posted behind the bar but the choices are limited. You can order a cheeseburger or hamburger, and at Adair's they only come in one size—huge.

This classic Texas burger is a thing of beauty. It comes in a plastic basket, wrapped in checked wax paper and speared with a fat, whole jalapeño pepper. The contents are bursting from its wrapping, begging you to grab hold and take a bite. A

burger with everything comes with a thick slice of tomato, shredded lettuce, a slice of raw onion, pickles, and mustard. They also offer grilled onion, available upon request. The whole thing is sandwiched between two halves of a soft white squishy bun that has been warmed in a steaming tray. A bite that includes all of these elements is blissful.

Like all classic Texas hamburgers, the burger at Adair's weighs in at a half pound. The way the grill cook arrives at this measurement is one of the more unique methods I have ever seen. Fresh ground beef arrives at Adair's in long tubes that just happen to share the same circumference as Mrs. Baird's enriched buns. Sergio Perez, who has manned the griddle at Adair's for two decades, lays out the beef tube and slices, with the plastic still on, half-pound patties. Each slice is identical (thanks to years of practice) and when the plastic is peeled off—voilà!—perfect patties! There's an art to slicing the patties and as bartender Tarah put it, "If I had to do it, it'd be a mess."

The burgers are cooked on a flattop in a spotless kitchen that in no way resembles the rest of the grungy bar. "I keep it very clean in here," Sergio told me with a smile. The only piece of graffiti in the spartan kitchen is over the door and reads, "Sergio's burgers are the best!" When he showed me the bun steamer, I remembered that the bun on my burger had been toasted. "Only for special people," Sergio pointed out. Everyone else gets a steamed bun. The fries are peculiar, long potato wedges that resemble truck stop jo-jos. Even though they are frozen and come out of a bag, they are not bad. There is no deep fryer in Sergio's kitchen so the jo-jos get tossed onto the flattop to cook, making the exterior very crunchy.

Seven nights a week patrons enjoy live music at Adair's with no cover charge. There is a full-sized tabletop shuffleboard that is addictive and will allow you to channel your inner-Olympic curler. The walls are covered with framed photos and one very large one stands out. Look for the enlarged snapshot of Elvis Presley in a deep embrace with former owner Lois Adair. Apparently, during a live show in the '50s Lois broke through security to lay a big hug on the King. Thankfully, someone had a camera.

Friend and local burger expert Wayne Geyer led me to Adair's when I told him I was looking for a quintessential Texas burger in Dallas. I caught him mumbling to himself as we enjoyed our burgers, "There's something about a Texas burger. . . ." And he's right. There is something special about burgers in Texas, and it's not just because Texas is the land of beef. I think it's because a true Texas burger is a simple thing, but it's large. Simplicity and size are what make a burger a Texas burger, and Adair's has it right.

BELLAIRE BROILER BURGER

5216 Bellaire Blvd | Bellaire, TX 77401
713-668-8171 | Mon–Sat 11 am–8 pm | Closed Sun

As you approach Bellaire Broiler Burger from the parking lot, the first thing you'll see are flames. In fact, to get into the restaurant the front door is just beyond the window where burgers are being flame grilled. If there are a lot of burgers being flipped, there is so much flame that it could seem dangerous. The scene seems theatrical, and shocking, but comforting as well because all customers can witness firsthand where their burger originates.

Once inside, find the register near the door to place your order. But be ready to eat because this food comes *fast*. The kitchen, in full view of all who order, runs like a well-oiled machine. The ultra-thin patties seem to cook in seconds on the insanely hot flame grill. Cooked patties are transferred to a station where the burgers are literally thrown together and dispensed to customers in record time. What you'll get will look like a sloppy disaster but it will taste amazing.

The most popular burger on Bellaire's extensive menu is the #4 Chili Cheeseburger, which is served on a big, floppy toasted bun, with housemade chili, diced onion, and soft, shredded cheddar spilling out of the sides. But just before the patty is bunned and dressed it's *dipped in barbecue sauce*. Between the soft cheese, the chili, and the barbecue sauce, you'll have a hard time trying to look cool eating this thing.

The dining room at Bellaire is strange and beautifully dated, think circa 1978. It's so outdated that it's definitively cool again. I sure hope no one messes with this room because with its low, recessed-lit ceiling, large mirrors, wood paneling, and orange/beige pleather booths, it could have been a location for *Boogie Nights*, or better *Dazed and Confused*. Amazing framed photos of '60s and '70s American muscle cars (showing hoods up, and down) complete the scene.

Since 1972 Bellaire has been owned by the Daneman family and it seems many family members have worked behind the counter over the years. Manager Pam, who is related to the owners, told me, "The only secret to this place is that grill," while pointing as flames nearly enveloped the grill cook.

The first time I visited, on a tip from burger friend Billy Kramer, I spoke to two different devoted regulars that had been coming to Bellaire for fifty years! One told me, "It used to be all woods and deer out here." Very hard to imagine as I looked out on the current urban strip mall sprawl of Houston.

BLAKE'S BBQ AND BURGERS

2916 Jeanetta St | Houston, TX 77063 | 713-266-6860 | Mon–Sat 10:30 am–9 pm
Closed Sun | www.blakesbbqandburgers.com

I can always count on my good friend and Houston food critic Robb Walsh to dig up the obscure. Robb thankfully put this burger joint on my radar and I am forever grateful. Robb also introduced me to Don Blake, the man behind the burger. Don't call him Don, though. I tried a few times and he didn't respond. Finally he told me quietly, "My mom called me Don. Everybody else calls me Blake."

Blake didn't always serve the best, freshest burgers in town from his dream-come-true barbecue joint on the west side of Houston. "When we first started we were serving frozen," Blake admitted, but he knew the burger could be better. As fate would have it, when a truck didn't show with frozen patties one day, Blake ran to a local grocery store to buy fresh ground 80/20 chuck and the rest was history. "It was like a phenomenon," Blake told me. "Word got out and people were asking 'What are you putting in there?'" There was no turning back, and after thirty-six years Blake is still using the same 80/20 chuck for his burgers that he picks up from a local butcher.

I had my first burger at Blake's with Robb Walsh and noticed right away that it seemed loaded with butter. "You have a problem with that?" Robb shot back. No, I most certainly did not. The burger to get at Blake's is the cheeseburger with everything. The griddleperson takes a measured eight-ounce ball of ground chuck, presses

it between two sheets of wax paper, then plops it onto the well-seasoned flattop. A liberal amount of "secret" seasoning (which looked like salt and pepper) is sprinkled on top and the burger is pressed again. A very complicated bun-toasting procedure ensues where a five-inch white squishy is sent through a buttering toaster press and then transferred to the griddle to finish. "The key is the bun cooking on that griddle," Blake pointed out. The bun is prepped with pickles, mayo, mustard, shredded lettuce, and tomato. It ain't a picture-perfect burger, with its squashed bun and erupting contents, but don't let that fool you. The butter, beef, mustard, pickles, and soft bun make for an enormously satisfying burger experience. (I added bacon and grilled onions, too.) Add some jalapeños to remind yourself that you're in Texas.

There's a curious burger on the menu called the "Kick-Burger," designed by one of Blake's biggest fans, Houston megadeveloper Vincent Kickerillo. The Kick comes with pepper jack cheese, jalapeños, and a splash of barbecue sauce. Even Frank Sinatra became a fan (thanks to his good friend Kickerillo) and had Blake frequently ship raw patties to his home in Malibu. "He and Kick loved the seasoning so I'd overnight fifteen to twenty pounds to them."

There are many other things on the menu like sandwiches, baked potatoes, and burritos, but I've never tried them. I have not even tasted the world-class barbecue that Blake is known for. I've only indulged in his amazing burgers.

There is no signage indicating a drive-up window but at Blake's you can order from your car. Look for the tiny window on the right side of the building and place your order. "Twenty-five percent of our business is drive-up," Blake told me.

The idea for a barbecue and burger restaurant was born of necessity. As a young salesman for an office supply business, Blake was constantly on the search for decent, affordable barbecue and decided to open his own place. Blake's sales beat had him in on the west side of Houston daily and he discovered his current location by accident while taking a shortcut. "This street was a two-lane dirt road back then," he told me, which is hard to imagine

given the unstoppable urban sprawl of Houston. It turned out to be the perfect location.

Blake's stands out on Jeanetta Street thanks to its design. "I wanted it to look 'cowboy,'" Blake told me, and pointed out the horse hitch that completes the Alamo-esqe facade. The dining room has a floor-to-ceiling painted mural depicting a dusty Old West version of his hometown of Brownwood, Texas. "That's not really what it looks like," Blake confessed. He grew up in a town where being black was an anomaly. He showed me his high school reunion picture and said with a chuckle, "See if you can find me!" As I scanned the sea of white faces, it was not hard to spot Blake.

Every year, just before Thanksgiving, Blake smokes one hundred turkeys and donates them to underprivileged families and a shelter for homeless vets in the neighborhood. Blake explained, "I grew up poor and know how it feels to get food during the holidays."

BOOTS BURGER

701 Austin St | Rockwall, TX 75087 | 972-722-5802
Tues–Sat 11 am–1:30 pm | Closed Sun & Mon

You have to *want* this burger. And you must follow my advice herein or you most likely will *not* get this burger. In fact, it's entirely possible that you'll head all the way out to Rockwall, Texas, and walk away empty-handed. That's because you didn't listen to me. Have I scared you? Good. Pay attention and you will be rewarded with a stellar hamburger experience.

Boots is not where you would expect to find a burger joint. It's actually in a quiet residential neighborhood, in a private home about a thirty-minute drive from downtown Dallas. "It's always been right here, behind the house," owner Russell Mooney told me. Russell's grandfather Boots started it in 1968 after losing his job when the Dallas Ford Motor Company plant closed.

Most orders are called in, and you should call yours in, too. On most days, Russell sells out before closing, pushing over 240 burgers out the window in just a couple of hours. "It goes by pretty quick," Russell told me. The day I visited for the first time he had sixty orders for burgers fifteen minutes *before* opening. Fifteen minutes after opening, they had only fifty burgers left. By 12:30, Russell will unplug the phone, especially if they are running low. "People say 'I come down here and it's all gone,'" Russell told me. "I tell them 'get up earlier.'"

Order at the small window (just past the vintage 7Up machine) and Russell will give you the same warning every customer gets—the wait will likely be long. Just be happy you are getting one. Russell takes orders and builds the burgers and his uncle Dave (Boots's son) flips the patties. Customers seem to be content with the wait and Russell has an air saw mounted in the kitchen with the sign "Complaint Dept."

Russell is intense, friendly, and bearded with a long ponytail, and he is committed to making great burgers for his dedicated regulars. "It's as simple as it gets," he told me. "Just throw it out there, get it down the road." Russell stays focused and works diligently to get those burgers out. That's because he has to go back to work at a nearby custom embroidery company. You read that correctly—this is Russell's lunch break.

The burger to get is the double meat cheeseburger with everything. This includes chopped iceberg lettuce, slice of tomato, pickles, onion, and hot relish. The relish is a great touch and is a mix of chopped Cajun Chef pickled jalapeños, onion, and carrots. If you ask for a cheeseburger, you'll also get mustard. Order one without cheese and you'll get mayo, not mustard. It's served wrapped in waxed paper, speared with a tooth pick. I asked Russell why the toothpick and he answered, pointing at the one in my mouth, "For that reason right there. It's a throwback thing so you wouldn't have to ask for one."

The resulting burger is an enormously satisfying Texas two-fister that was well worth the wait and the drive. But do not eat your burger on the premises, even though there are seats everywhere (these are for people waiting). Tailgating is allowed but a visit to a park a block away is recommended.

This burger experience is not for all, and Russell would agree. For me, though, the challenge made the adventure worth every moment.

BURGER BAR

109 North Anglin St | Cleburne, TX 76031
817-645-9031 | Mon–Sat 9:30 am–3 pm

"Cute" is your first impression of Burger Bar, a former wagon yard office that dates back to the late 1800s. This impossibly small burger joint in downtown Cleburne actually has seats inside but there's only enough room for three people at the counter. If you walk in and all of those seats are taken, you are eating elsewhere (or at the picnic table outside). I lucked into one of the stools the first time I was there, and the next customer that walked in joked, "Well, mine's a to-go order, obviously."

Burger Bar was opened in 1949 when Miss Landman and Dorothy Baze converted the brick box into a functioning burger joint. Mike Elmore bought the business in 2003, and today the place is run by daughter Katy and her husband, Caleb Grantges. "My father-in-law was the second owner," Caleb told me. "We'll be the third."

The small griddle at Burger Bar is a thing of beauty, and in full view of anyone standing or sitting at Burger Bar. "That's half the hamburger right there," an older woman sitting at the counter offered. She's correct, because it's obvious that the ancient griddle, with a beautiful black patina and a slick of grease, lends a flavor like no other to every burger patty.

The most popular burger to get is "mustard, all the way." This means shredded iceberg lettuce, slice of tomato, pickles, and mustard. Mayo

is available but not included, and it's served on a wide, soft seeded bun that has been toasted on the griddle. Fresh beef is delivered and Caleb turns the ground chuck into one-third-pound thin patties.

Burger Bar is easily the smallest burger joint with the largest parking lot. Between functioning as a wagon yard and a restaurant the lot was apparently used as a Ford dealership during the days of the Model T. "We let the guys at the plumbing shop use our lot," Caleb told me, "and they let us use their toilet."

For whatever reason, Burger Bar recently added a frozen veggie patty to the menu but to anyone who is paying attention the veggie burger patty is cooked right alongside the beef patties, luxuriating in rendered beef grease. A young girl working the griddle told me, "Sometimes people point that out and I just say . . ." And she

shrugged. It has to be hands-down the best-tasting veggie burger in America.

The large picture window at the front of Burger Bar used to slide open when the place had walk-up business. Now a single pane of glass helps the impossibly small interior feel less claustrophobic. Jordan, an Elmore cousin working the grill, said with a smile, "You see lots of interesting things though this window."

BURGER HOUSE

6913 Hillcrest Ave | Dallas, TX 75205 | 214-361-0370 | Open Daily 11 am–9 pm
(Other Locations around Dallas) | www.burgerhouse.com

Any visit to Dallas, Texas, warrants a stop at this tiny, beloved burger stand. Impossibly small and showing its age, Burger House (aka Jack's from a previous owner) serves excellent, fresh meat burgers to hungry college students and locals in this wealthy Dallas suburb. Constantly topping best-of lists, Burger House, opened in 1951, has been a favorite of Dallas natives for generations.

Jack Koustoubardis built Burger House and worked at the Hillcrest location flipping burgers for over thirty years. Even though there is no mention of his name anywhere in the restaurant's signage, dedicated regulars still refer to the restaurant as "Jack's" Burger House. In 1982, friends of Jack's, Angelo Chantilis and Steve Canellos, bought the burger stand and the recipe for its now famous "seasoned salt." The salt goes

House gets a delivery of large, flat quarter-pound patties of 80/20 chuck. Angelo told me, "We buy from a local purveyor of meat and they only give us the best." The burgers have been cooked on the well-seasoned, original griddle from opening day at Burger House, a griddle that's almost sixty years old. A wide, toasted sesame-seed bun is standard, as are shredded lettuce, tomato, onion, pickles, and mustard. The double with cheese is a large, two-fisted wad of greasy goodness that will fill you up and have you dreaming about your next visit even before you take your last bite.

The seasoned salt, a garlicky secret recipe invented by Jack's brother, Jerry, is so popular that in the 1990s Angelo and Steve decided to bottle and sell the stuff. "People would walk off with the shakers of the salt that we put out," Angelo told me, "so we figured we should just start selling it." Now you can attempt to re-create Jack's burger at home.

Today, Burger House is a minichain with four locations around Dallas. The enormous Mockingbird location (with its large dining room and drive-thru) does the most business, but it's the original Hillcrest location with its red, white, and blue neon sign that burger lovers visit to get their dose of Americana. I asked Angelo if there were plans to keep expanding, and he responded with an emphatic. "Hell yeah."

onto all of the burgers and fries and creates the taste that regulars crave.

The restaurant is split in two—one part a tiny, fluorescent-lit diner (no more than two hundred square feet) with a few stools and a narrow counter, the other an alleyway dining room with a sloped concrete floor and carved-up picnic tables. Of curious note, the stand closes every night at 9 p.m., but the dining room side stays open all night. Manager Nicholas once told me, "That's just the way it was. Jack kept it open all night." Angelo, aware of the extremely low crime rate in this suburb, confirmed the policy, but said of would-be thieves, with a chuckle "Let 'em walk in instead of breaking the damn glass."

The most popular burger at Burger House is the double cheeseburger. Every morning Burger

CASINO EL CAMINO

517 East 6th St | Austin, TX 78701 | 512-469-9330
Open Daily 11:30 am–2 am | www.casinoelcamino.net

Casino El Camino is not a burger joint. It's a dark punkabilly rock bar with tattooed and pierced patrons that maintains one of the best jukeboxes just about anywhere. People go to Casino to drink and listen to great tunes at this bar on the 6th Street party strip in downtown Austin, Texas. I was in a rock band for ten years so I feel at home in a place like Casino. But it wasn't until my third visit that I realized they offered amazing burgers to the buzzed clientele.

I was informed of Casino's burger prowess by a friend who begged me to give it a shot. In a town whose burger culture is dominated by Hut's and Dirty Martin's, and in a state enormously burger-proud, I was skeptical. My friend even commented, "It's not the kind of place you'd expect to find good food."

I approached the tiny opening in a dark back corner of the bar to place my order. The small kitchen is manned by a staff of one. A solitary chef takes orders, preps buns, and grills the burgers. When the chef on duty that night was through tending to burgers on the grill, he reluctantly sauntered over to take my order. I waited over half an hour, but for my patience I was rewarded with a heavenly burger.

The burgers at Casino el Camino start as fresh ground 90 percent lean chuck that's hand-formed into three quarter-pound patties. They are cooked on an open-flame grill, placed on a bun, halved, then the two halves are placed back on the

grill again, cut side down, to achieve a decorative grill brand on the cross section of your burger. It should be noted that cooking over a flame and achieving decent results don't often go together. Most grill cooks, especially those working from a Weber in their backyards, manage to overcook and ruin burgers. Every time I've been to Casino, the burger has been cooked perfectly. Casino el Camino cooks their burgers to temperature. If you ask for rare, get out the napkins and listen for that mooing sound. The cooks know what they are doing. Even a medium-well comes out juicy.

The menu lists burger concoctions that use the three-quarter-pound burger model and add condiments. There's the "Buffalo Burger," which is not

★ 329 ★

actually buffalo beef, but a regular burger topped with hot wing sauce and blue cheese. Or try the "Amarillo Burger" with roasted serrano chiles, jalapeño cheese, and cilantro mayo. My favorite is the standard bacon cheeseburger with cheddar, listed as the "Chicago Burger."

Casino el Camino is both a bar and a person. Casino el Camino, the stage name for this rocker and bar owner, came to Austin for the famed South by Southwest Music Festival in 1990. He was impressed with the forward-thinking Texas town and told a friend back in Buffalo, New York, that it would make a great spot for a bar. "Before I went I thought Texas was all tumbleweeds and fucking cowboys," the Long Island, New York, native admitted. Casino el Camino, the bar, became a joint venture in 1994 between Casino and the Buffalo restaurateur, Mark Supples.

In the beginning, there was a substantial wait for your burger, sometimes forever. And on busy nights the wait used to be over an hour. Not anymore. Grill cook of six years Zach Volta told me, "We cut it down to fifteen to twenty minutes now, even during SXSW." The speed is in part due to a new grill that almost doubled capacity and can cook twenty-four burgers (up from fifteen). Even if there is a wait remember, *you are in one of the coolest bars in America.* Enjoy the music, gawk at the crazy piercings, and get a drink. If you complain, you may make it worse.

CHRIS MADRID'S

1900 Blanco Rd | San Antonio, TX 78212 | 210-735-3552
Mon–Sat 11 am–10 pm | Closed Sun | www.chrismadrids.com

Chris Madrid was like no other hamburger icon that I've met. If you were searching for him in the vast, sprawling forty-plus-year-old burger joint, you were looking for the guy with jet-black hair smiling and hugging customers. He was hands-on from opening day in 1977, but unfortunately, we lost him too soon in 2012. His imprint on the burger world was indelible however.

In the late '70s, Chris bought a tiny burger stand in San Antonio on the corner of Blanco Road and Hollywood called Larry's Place. Fresh out of college, he saw potential in running a taco and burger stand. He renamed the place Chris Madrid's Tacos & Burgers but dropped "tacos" from the name (and menu) in 1980 because the burgers were selling so well.

Originally, there were three burger sizes to choose from—the Baby, the Mama, and the Papa, but the menu was streamlined. In 1980, inspired by the Village People's hit song "Macho Man," Madrid's decided to call the larger eight-ounce burger "macho"-sized. The smaller four-ounce "regular" sells well, but the macho is hard to resist. You can keep it simple and order the Old-Fashion

Hamburger, a Texas classic with mustard, pickle, lettuce, onion, and tomato, but there's a better reason to eat at Chris Madrid's—the "Tostada Burger."

The Tostada Burger at Chris Madrid's is legendary. Madrid's did not invent this staple of San Antonio burger culture but he most definitely made improvements on the classic. The original version, called the "Beanburger," was apparently invented at the now-defunct Sill's Snack Shack in San Antonio in the '50s and was soon copied by many other burger joints. A traditional Beanburger consists of only four basic elements—a hamburger, refried beans, Fritos, and Cheese Whiz. That's it, with no lettuce, pickle, or anything else to get in the way. Chris changed the name and altered the ingredients slightly for his version but has kept the basic integrity of the original intact. The Tostada Burger uses refried beans, but replaces the Cheese Whiz with cheddar and uses housemade corn chips instead of Fritos.

The macho Tostada Burger is a sight to behold. As you contemplate how to eat this enormous pile of heavenly goo, take a moment to appreciate what is in front of you. The bun, toasted on the grill, can barely contain the brown-and-yellow hues of its contents. The burger patty itself, a thin-pressed wonder made from fresh 75/25 beef, is hidden beneath a layer of refried beans and cascading cheddar.

The burger is impossible to pick up. I found that cutting it in half made things slightly easier. My first bite of this legend sent me soaring. As I easily made my way through the macho, I wondered why this burger was not replicated in every corner of America. The beans and chips worked

so well with the beef, and the cheddar tied it all together. Chris said it best when he told me years ago, "It's like a hamburger and an enchilada plate in one." What an amazing invention.

Chris Madrid's is enormous and has grown slowly over the years. They bought the icehouse (the Texas version of a deli/package store) next door years ago and eventually put an awning over the large gravel parking lot between the two buildings and added more tables. The awning was replaced by a glassed-in structure and seating capacity increased to over three hundred. Today, the core of the restaurant is the connecting structure, a high-ceilinged dining room filled with mismatched tables and chairs. The icehouse side of the restaurant contains a beautiful recycled bar that was purchased from a closed convent in the '80s and the original thick refrigerator doors from the icehouse are still functioning.

Grab a local Texas favorite beer, Shiner Bock, while you wait for your burger. It'll come wrapped in "pickle paper," or waxed paper, to keep your hands dry from the bottle sweat. "That's the way they used to do it back in the icehouse days," bartender for decades Jimmy told me. Every once in a while a mariachi group will wander through the restaurant entertaining customers downing their Tostada Burgers. They are not hired musicians, they just wander in and play for tips. The music and the Tex-Mex flavors help to create an excellent burger experience.

CHRISTIAN'S TAILGATE BAR & GRILL

2000 Bagby St | Houston, TX 77002 | 713-527-0261 | Sun–Wed 11 am–12 am
Thurs–Sat 11 am–2 am | (Three Other Locations in Houston)
www.christianstailgate.com

It's been a few crazy years at Christian's Tailgate but it seems the dust has settled and most everything worked out just fine. I say most everything because unfortunately third-generation family member Steve Christian had to close his iconic roadhouse out on Washington Avenue. It was there that Billy Gibbons would surprise the crowd with impromptu karaoke, and it was the place where I had my first Jalapeño Cheeseburger.

Road expansion and city officials that would budge caused Steve to shutter the place. "I would have lost all of my parking," Steve told me recently. No parking at Christian's would have equaled certain death because there is zero walk-by traffic out there. Fear not, however, recall that back in 2004, Steve began an expansion of his solid brand and opened a few versions of Tailgate around town. Those still exist.

And now for the next big change—Steve sold the restaurant! But fortunately for all involved the sale was to the right people. When he started to pursue the sale of his local burger and bar mini empire, he had many suitors. Steve was hounded by corporate entities that saw the value in his enormous roadhouse-style bars and restaurants with excellent service and tasty food but held out for the right buyer. "I knew it just wouldn't be the same if I went in that direction," Steve told me recently, "I'm proud of this name."

"We could have easily removed his name," new co-owner Chris Alan of a local restaurant group told me, Steve within earshot. "He's our Colonel Sanders, he's the personality." The group bought the handful of very successful roadhouses and changed very little.

Steve Christian was the third-generation owner of a roadhouse burger joint just off I-10 west of downtown Houston. Steve's grandfather opened Christian's Totem in the early '40s as a convenience store and icehouse. Before refrigeration and air-conditioning, icehouses were integral to daily life in warm climes. Steve told me, "Guys would come down here to get ice for their wives and end up staying and drinking beer for a while." The beer fridge used to sit in the parking lot with a padlock on it. "My grandfather would leave for the night and toss the guys the key. Eventually, Christian's became a bar."

Steve's grandfather and father ran Christian's as a convenience store and a roadside bar for over fifty years. Steve told me, "In the '40s, this was a dirt road out here," he said, pointing to the impossibly busy Washington Avenue, large trucks rumbling in every direction. After a stint as a DJ in a topless club and a job as a crane operator, Steve told his dad he wanted to be the third-generation owner of Christian's. When he took over the business he had plans for expansion. Part of his plan was to put a great burger on the menu, and that burger wins "Best of Houston" awards annually. In 2004, Steve changed the longtime name of the bar from Christian's Totem to Tailgate Bar & Grill for purely logistical reasons. "We were not really a 'totem' any longer (Texas vernacular for the convenience store) and we were getting too many calls from people thinking we sold religious books."

The burger to get is the Jalapeño Cheeseburger—a fresh ground, half-pound, griddled two-fister that comes in a plastic basket on a toasted white bun with lettuce, onion, tomato, pickle, mustard, and mayo. The jalapeños are snappy and hot and complement the large portion of meat well.

Years ago, Steve experimented with deep-frying of bacon. "It's awesome!" he said as he once dragged me into the kitchen to witness firsthand. A strip of bacon is dipped into a batter and tossed

into the fryer. The Fried Bacon Burger was born at the old Washington Avenue location and remains on the menu.

The new owners did make a few improvements to the menu, adding salads for one. "We wanted to get more ladies and couple in the restaurant," Chris explained. And the long lines and waits for burgers is over, replaced with food runners that bring burgers to your table. In the old days, you had to wait for your number to be called. "It's just the way we always did it," Steve told me. "But I like the new method."

Steve still visits the restaurants regularly, has a few beers, and hugs regulars. He's proud of the business he built and I'm glad he has the good sense to sell to people that understood him and his iconic burger. And he pointed out recently that personal service is the endgame for any restaurant. Christian's has that down. "These places will always be a powerhouse."

DIRTY MARTIN'S KUM-BAK PLACE

2808 Guadalupe St | Austin, TX 78705
512-477-3173 | Open Daily 11 am–11 pm | www.dirtymartins.com

irty Martin's does not serve thick, gourmet burgers. Dirty Martin's serves excellent, greasy, thin-patty burgers to Austin locals and students from the nearby University of Texas. Alongside these famed grease bombs, Dirty's also serves a guilty pleasure of yours and mine—the deep-fried tater tot.

Opened in 1926 as Martin's Kum-Bak Place by John Martin, the burger counter earned the nickname "Dirty's" for the dirt floor that remained until 1951. The original counter had

just eight stools inside and most of the business was conducted in the parking lot with carhops. Today, the carhops are gone and the dirt floor has been covered for half a century, but Dirty's is still cranking out great burgers over eighty years from opening day.

The menu at Dirty Martin's is loaded with great bar food geared to pre- and post-party revelers in search of nourishment. The lunch crowd looks to be on the other end of the spectrum, nursing hangovers or old-timers looking for their friends. There are many choices on the menu, but the burgers are king at Dirty's.

The burgers start as fresh ground, thin patties. They are cooked on a flattop griddle and slid onto waiting, toasted, gloriously buttered sesame seed buns. Have fun trying to interpret the somewhat cryptic burger options on the menu. Ask for a hamburger, and you'll get a single patty with mustard, onion, pickle, tomato, and a generous sprinkle of seasoned salt. Ask for a large hamburger, and you'll get the same but twice the meat (two patties). Then there's the infamous "Sissy Burger," which replaces the mustard and onion with mayonnaise. Years ago I asked the grill team about the definition of a Sissy Burger and was directed to a man named Wesley sitting at the end of the counter. Wesley Hughes (who passed away in 2009) flipped burgers at Dirty's for forty-five years. He bluntly explained to me, "Mustard is strong and not for sissies." I deduced that mayo is for sissies and left it at that. If you need a double-patty burger with mayo, be prepared to tell your waiter you need a "Big Sissy."

Few restaurants in America have the guts to put tater tots on their menus. This trashy little potato treat somehow has the ability to get crispier than fries and retains more grease (or flavor). You can go to the freezer aisle of your supermarket, buy a bag of tots, and cook them in your oven, but we all know how that tastes. Tater tots are best enjoyed deep-fried at places like Dirty Martin's. And what could be better than tater tots? How about the ultimate guilty pleasure—cheese tots. "We actually have Truffle Tots," longtime general manager Daniel Young told me recently, adding, "but those are almost too fancy for us."

If you find yourself hungry and near the University of Texas, don't hesitate to stop at the oldest burger stand in Austin. Look for the white boxy drive-in that still has bars on the windows, clearly a nod to an earlier time. Sit at the counter for a real treat and watch the two grill cooks Will and Darren at work. It's like a nonstop standup routine and they know everyone that walks in the door. "These two banter back and forth all day," Daniel told me, "and they get more excited the busier it gets." Just then Will dispensed some philosophy, excitedly, "I don't wake up unless I'm ready to go!"

Grill cooks Darren and Will

ED'S PLACE

209 W 3rd St | Taylor, TX 76574 | 512-352-9050
Sun–Fri 10 am–9 pm | Sat 10 am–4 pm

I love barbecue (the noun, not the verb), and if it's beef I'm in Texas. On a recent barbecue trip to visit the iconic Louie Mueller Barbecue in Taylor, Texas, I was tipped off to a burger spot named Ed's that was just through the parking lot, behind Louie's. I wasn't going to miss out on Wayne Mueller's beef rib so visited both, naturally. Win-win for me.

Ed's is an old place, a real Texas dive somewhat untouched by time or trend. The building, a sturdy brick structure with a bright white facade has a sign over the door with its hours, simply stating OPEN 'TIL CLOSED—CLOSED 'TIL OPEN. And that is pretty accurate. Inside, find a cozy yet utilitarian bar with a pool table in the rear and the unmistakable aroma of Texas burgers wafting through the air.

The building was originally a soda water factory at the turn of the century. Following Prohibition, Walter Gonsenbach bought the factory and turned it in to a bar and domino hall, and in 1959 Ed Mucha became the second owner. The place used to be filled with domino tables and players, and "sweaters." "A sweater was someone standing around watching dominos but not playing," Dave Mucha, Ed's son, told me. There's an excellent vintage sign in back that reads SWEATERS—DO NOT BLOCK PASSAGEWAY TO REST ROOMS.

Dave, who bought the bar from his dad in 1983, put a burger on the menu in 1995 just after a locally beloved burger joint called Diamond Inn shut down. Someone who worked at Diamond was in the bar soon after and Dave told me, "I asked him how did they make those burgers over there," and the handoff was in motion. Dave followed the method this guy was telling him exactly and it was a success. "Most people

say they taste just like Diamond," Dave told me. "Some say they're better!"

The short-order smash method is employed at Ed's where Dave uses a custom smashing tool to create the perfect patties. The thing looks like a substantial barbell missing one end. Dave uses fresh ground 73/27 beef and fresh veggies every day. When I asked him what size the patties were, he cupped his hand and said, "Well, this is about a quarter pound."

The single is great, but the double is the way to go. This classic Texas two-fister is served with American cheese, onion, pickle, lettuce, tomato, and "slop" (actually written on the ticket to designate ketchup, mustard, mayo), on a perfectly griddle-toasted bun which has soaked up some burger grease. "I don't like hamburgers," employee Holly told me. "This is the only place I'll eat one."

Grab a Shiner Bock at the bar and look for the two remaining heavily worn domino tables, identifiable by a low ridge around the edge to keep the dominos off the floor. The domino player generation has all but died off so honor their past and eat your burger at one of these tiny pieces of American history.

HERD'S HAMBURGERS

407 North Main St | Jacksboro, TX 76458
No Phone | Mon–Sat 10:30 am–9 pm | Closed Sun

About an hour and a half northwest of Fort Worth, deep in rolling Texas ranch land dotted with oil rigs and cows, is a family-run burger joint in the tiny town of Jacksboro. They have no phone and the place is only open five days a week. But if you hit it just right, you'll get to experience one of the more unique burgers in Texas, the amazing "Herdburger."

What you won't get at Herd's is a big, juicy, classic Texas-sized burger, one that you can barely fit in your face and, like many other Texas burger joints, a thick patty weighing in at over a half pound. Instead what you'll find at Herd's Hamburgers is one of the flattest burgers in America,

cooked to perfection by third-generation owner Danny Herd.

When I say flat, I mean flat. The method for cooking burgers at Herd's is one that I've never witnessed anywhere else in America. When I told the fortysomething, mustached Danny this, he replied, "Others don't do this?"

Erase any notion that a burger should start as a patty. Picture a beautifully seasoned flattop griddle from the '40s that has a three-pound pile of ground chuck sitting on the upper left corner. To make a burger, Danny slices an appropriately sized wad of beef from the pile with a concrete trowel, and then with a lightning-fast move, under the

★ 338 ★

under the weight of the trowel, turns that wad into a flat patty six inches wide that is so paper-thin you could see through it. Danny works fast to fill, empty, and refill the griddle every few minutes, warming the buns on the flipped patties. The finished product is transferred to a station where most burgers are dressed "all the way," which is mustard, pickle, chopped onion, tomato, and lettuce. If you ask for a "double meat, double cheese," expect a glorious burger that weighs in at just under a half pound and whose loose, crumbly meat is falling out of the waxed paper bursting with a jumble of ingredients.

There are no plates at Herd's. There are also not many seats (except for a few upside-down soda crates and a strange, long row of old school desk chairs). And thankfully, there aren't many other food options, either. Burgers are the focus at Herd's so don't come here looking for things like fries or malts. Danny's father, Claude, who owned and ran the place with his wife, Orlene, from 1971 to 2008, told me, "This was the way it was back in 1916 when my aunt started. I thought about [adding fries] but it's easier to pull a bag of chips off the rack." I asked Danny why there was no phone and his answer was perfect. "We really don't need it. That way we don't have to take phone orders." He's absolutely right—why take phone orders when the line is out the door most days by noon?

Claude and Orlene moved Herd's to its current location just north of downtown Jacksboro. They bought a small two-story apartment house and turned the garage downstairs into the restaurant. But this was not the only move in Herd's one-hundred-year history. From what I could glean from conversations with Claude and from inspecting photos on the walls, Herd's may have actually moved over seven times. Claude's first response when I asked about the moves was, "Gosh. I don't know." What we do know was that Herd's started as a tiny canvas shack downtown by Claude's aunt Ella Gafford. Apparently, in one hundred years, the method for making burgers at Herd's has never changed.

When Danny got word that his dad was planning to retire, he knew he was the only one who could continue the tradition. "I worked here as a kid," Danny explained, and after twenty-one years in Denton, Texas, as an employee at UPS he moved home to run the business. Danny likens work at Herd's to a vacation compared to his life with the shipping giant. "I think I'll get more mileage out of my body here than I would at UPS."

HUT'S HAMBURGERS

807 West 6th St | Austin, TX 78703 | 512-472-0693 | Sun–Tues 11 am–9:30 pm
Wed–Sat 11 am–10 pm | www.hutsfrankandangies.com

Hut's Hamburgers is not on the party drag in downtown Austin, Texas, where the crowds migrate to East 6th Street. This out-of-the-way burger restaurant is on the residential west end of 6th Street, which is recent years has become very trendy with new high-rises and a new eighty-thousand-square-foot Whole Foods flagship store. Look for a vintage green and red neon sign and follow the arrow on the sign to the odd-shaped 1930s red, white, and blue building.

The history of Hut's is so convoluted that I'll spare you the details and give you the skinny version. Basically, Homer "Hut" Hutson opened Hut's Hamburgers on South Congress in 1939. Across town the same year, Sammie Joseph opened Sammie's Drive-In on West 6th Street. In 1969, after numerous owners, Sammie's became Hut's.

The Memorial Day Flood of 1981 devastated downtown Austin. A witness to the aftermath described it as looking like a week of hurricanes had rambled through town. The west side of town, particularly where Hut's is situated, was destroyed. A local newspaper noted that through all the death and destruction, Hut's remained standing, prompting the phrase "God Bless Hut's."

Since 1981 Hut's has been owned and run by Kim and Hutch Hutchinson. Kim told me, "Since we bought Hut's very little has changed. We make everything from scratch." The Hut's they purchased was still selling burgers and chicken-fried steak, but the Hutchinsons updated the menu. The restaurant now offers salads and daily blue-plate specials like fried catfish on Fridays, but every time I've been to Hut's, I'm there to consume one of their award-winning burgers.

If you are looking for variety, you have come to the right place. Hut's serves high-quality, fresh meat burgers with just about any topping you can think of. The menu is loaded with cute names for the burgers like the "Alan Freed" (with hickory sauce) and the "Beachboy" (with pine-apple). Stick to the basics like the "Hut's Favorite," a bacon cheeseburger, or the "Buddy Holly" with "the works" and be rewarded with an unforgettable burger experience.

A rarity in the burger world, Hut's gives you the option to choose the type of meat for your burger. Hut's offers traditional fresh ground beef, buffalo, or Texas Longhorn. "We added buffalo and Longhorn to the menu for health reasons," Kim told me. Both Texas Longhorn beef and buffalo meat are super lean, and in the case of Longhorn beef, low in the type of fat that causes bad cholesterol. The one-third-pound patties are cooked on a well-seasoned flattop griddle. The Longhorn beef comes from Don and Debbie Davis's ranch nearby as it has for almost two decades. "Debbie brings the meat to us," Kim told me. How about that for ranch-to-table?

By noon most days, the restaurant is packed. On game days (the University of Texas is nearby) expect to be waiting on line or at the bar surrounded by fans decked out in UT orange. Use the time you'll spend waiting for a table to admire the taxidermy on the walls—they all have stories and come from the ranches that have supplied Hut's with the burger meat you are enjoying. Also make sure to browse the flood photos on the walls and learn a bit about Hut's history. By the time you bite into your burger, you'll be glad Hut's was saved, too.

KELLER'S DRIVE-IN

6537 East Northwest Hwy | Dallas, TX 75231 | 214-368-1209
Open Daily 10:30 am–10 pm

The sign in front of this vintage relic of Dallas hamburger culture says it all—KELLER'S HAMBURGERS BEER. That's what you'll find here and not much more. Personally, I don't require much else so at Keller's I'm always in heaven.

During the day, Keller's doesn't look like much. The low, faded green, beige, and brick central structure that houses the kitchen sits in the middle of a huge parking lot surrounded by long parking shelters that can accommodate up to one hundred cars. Lunch seems to be moderately busy but at night, Keller's comes alive. The parking shelters light up with flashing neon and pickup trucks line the drive-in with tailgating Texans. On most Saturday nights, owners of classic cars still cruise into the drive-in to stage impromptu shows and beer flows more than soda. At Keller's, they'll not only bring your burger to your car seat, they'll bring you a beer, too.

But Keller's is not just another roadside hamburger joint. Jack Keller opened his first drive-in in 1950 after working for the Big Sam Company. Big Sam developed drive-in restaurants and is credited with opening the first in America, the Pig Stand in Dallas in 1921. Jack wanted to open his own drive-in and saw that there was a need to serve beer with the burgers. As Jack once explained to me in his gentle Texas drawl, "Beer, hamburgers . . . that's all you need really." Cheers to that.

My first visit to Keller's was around 4 p.m. on a Tuesday and I was a little shocked to find people pulling up in pickups and motorcycles ordering beer and skipping the burger. Most seemed to just have one and move on, a post-work cold one before the ride home that made perfect sense to me. "Some come for the beers because they are only $1.75 here!" carhop Rachel told me. Rachel, a sweet, salt-of-the-earth, sun-baked Texan wearing an oversized T-shirt, told me she has been at Keller's for over twenty-eight years and loves her job. "The tips are excellent. That's why I started here."

The burger selection is totally confusing with random, specially numbered burger combinations that are strangely out of sync. The number nine is a double meat with chili and the regular cheeseburger gets no number. I once asked Jack about the reasoning behind the numbered burgers and he replied, "Lack of a good sign painter, I guess." Avoid confusion and order the number five, a double meat and cheese with tomato, shredded lettuce, and "special sauce," which my taste buds identified as Thousand Island dressing. Tater tots are on the menu at Keller's and when tots are on the menu, I always skip the fries.

The thin-patty burgers at Keller's are cooked on a large flattop griddle and served on toasted, soft white poppy seed buns that have been delivered daily by a local baker for over seventy years. The drive-in gets a shipment of fresh 80/20 beef daily and they come in as patties just over three ounces each. Your order is delivered to your car wrapped in waxed paper, creating a perfect package of cheesy, beefy, greasy deliciousness. I can eat one of their doubles in three bites and go back for more.

The carhops are all female and range in age. There doesn't seem to be an enforced dress code for the carhops at Keller's and the outfits go from baggy tees to tight tank tops. One side of the drive-in is frequented by bikers and is affectionately known as the Zoo Side. This section of the parking lot, to the left of the main structure, also has a few mismatched benches that look like church pews. Here, the bikers can rest, have a burger, and sip a beer. "These guys are mostly weekend bikers, you know, doctors, lawyers," Rachel pointed out. She didn't want me to get the impression that the Zoo Side was a hangout for some dangerous biker gang. From what I've seen there day and night, Keller's attracts a pretty docile biker crowd.

To order at Keller's, find a spot, check the menu posted on the main structure, and put on your hazard lights. (Or as the window says, "turn on your blinkers for service.") Soon after, a carhop will approach to take your order. Your meal will arrive on the classic drive-in tray that hooks on your window and your beer will be wrapped with a napkin to prevent beer sweat—a nice touch.

If it were not enough that you can get an amazing burger, tots, and a beer brought to your car, you can also buy cases of beer to go. Keller's doubles as a package store, which means you can go on a beer run and reward yourself with a burger at the same time.

In 2016, Jack Keller passed and Jack Jr. assumed the business. We sat on the hood of my car at Keller's recently talking about his father's legacy, and Jack Jr. told me that at home all they talked about growing up was food and service. Jack Jr. was no stranger to the business and had worked alongside his father at Keller's for years. He's not a day-to-day guy at the drive-in, but told me, "If I walk in [the kitchen] and there's fifty tickets up, I'll jump on the griddle to help." And his father's burger ethos is safe with his son, who told me, "If you don't start with everything fresh, you can really screw things up."

KINCAID'S HAMBURGERS

4901 Camp Bowie Blvd | Fort Worth, TX 76107 | 817-732-2881 | Mon–Sat 11 am–8 pm
Sun 11 am–3 pm | (Various Other Locations around Fort Worth,
Southlake, Arlington, and Weatherford) | www.kincaidshamburgers.com

A visit to Kincaid's is a must on the burger trail in America. The restaurant is a revamped corner grocery that today is profoundly dedicated to the American hamburger. Most burgers found in Texas fall into the half-pound category and a hamburger at Kincaid's is no exception. The good word spread in the early 1970s that Kincaid's was serving up a stellar burger in the rear of the store. It was only a matter of time before burger sales eclipsed grocery sales and the rest is history. Today,

Kincaid's grinds and patties up to eight hundred pounds of fresh beef daily (you read that correctly). For groceries, you'll have to go elsewhere.

Kincaid's is located on a corner on the edge of a quiet residential neighborhood in Fort Worth, and the atmosphere inside and out is laid-back and comfortable. Inside, the long, original stock shelves remain in place, their tops sawed off to act as surfaces to stand at, unwrap your burger, and dig in. It was O. R. Gentry, a meat cutter and manager at the grocery store, who bought the business from the ailing Charles Kincaid in 1967. It was O.R. who cut down those shelves and created countertops out of old doors he found for one dollar. And it was O.R. who created one of the greatest burgers in America, a burger whose fame is so widespread that it can claim fans from every corner of the globe.

"He started with a twenty-five-dollar grill," Lynn Gentry said of her father-in-law. "O.R. would take the prime meats that didn't sell and grind them to make hamburgers the next day," Lynn explained. As the need for the corner grocery faded in America in the 1970s (spurred by the proliferation of the supermarket), O.R. began to focus more on burgers and less on groceries. When his son, Ronald, took over the business in 1991, he and wife Lynn did away with the remaining groceries for good. "We pulled out all of the produce bins and refrigeration in the front and replaced them with picnic tables," Lynn told me. "We needed the space."

Kincaid's is a gigantic place. Today, it's a clean, functional, bright restaurant where the integrity of the old grocery has been preserved. The concrete floors are polished to a high shine, and the original neon grocer's sign continues to glow red over the front door. The interior walls are still painted seafoam green and Lynn told me, "The local hardware store calls this color Kincaid's Green," and today it's actually listed in the Sherwin-Williams catalog. The restaurant can accommodate up to 280 burger enthusiasts, either standing or sitting, in over 3,500 square feet of space.

Every day Kincaid's grinds the meat for their half-pound burgers. They use only chuck steaks from All-Natural Texas beef that is free from hormones, antibiotics, and steroids. The burgers are cooked on two six-foot flattop griddles. You can cook a lot of burgers with twelve linear feet of griddle space.

The burger is served on a toasted white bun with tomato, shredded lettuce, pickles, yellow mustard, and thinly sliced onions. The elements of this burger are so well balanced that, taken as a whole, they create a nearly perfect burger experience and in turn, a euphoric first bite. Curiously, the burger's condiments are placed underneath the burger instead of the standard above-the-patty placement. "We do that for speed," Lynn explained, pointing out that the buns are prepped before the burgers come off the grill. The inverted burger actually allows the juices from the meat to drip into the condiments and Lynn told me, "We think it makes the burger taste better."

Kincaid's is a family business. The Gentrys' two sons, Christian and Jonathan, work at the restaurant and Lynn's father was the manager of Kincaid's for over a decade before he passed. In the last decade, the Gentrys have opened a few new locations around Fort Worth, including a five-thousand-square-foot version of the original complete with grocery shelves for eating and "Kincaid's green" painted walls.

Many refer to the burger at Kincaid's as the best in Texas. That's a mighty claim in this burger-proud state. It is a claim that the Kincaid's burger lives up to and a challenge the Gentry family takes in stride.

KUBY'S

6601 Snider Plaza | Dallas, TX 75205 | 214-363-2231
Mon–Thurs 6 am–5 pm | Fri & Sat 6 am–9 pm | Sun 9 am–2 pm | www.kubys.com

Kuby's is one of the most authentic outposts of the German American experience in Texas that I've come across. Inside, the Snider Plaza business is split in two, with a casual old-world German family restaurant on one side and an extraordinary butcher shop and delicatessen on the other. The meat in the glass cases are beautifully displayed like some of the finest old world European markets with endless varieties of bratwurst, knockwurst, weisswurst ,and every cut of meat imaginable. The shop is a window onto the freshness of Kuby's burgers.

Step into the restaurant side and slip back in time. The decor is dated, amazing, and has not changed since opening day in 1977. German crests, cuckoo clocks, and beer steins line the walls and wood details and warm walls send you right to yesterday's Europe. First glance at the menu and you'll notice there is no burger listed. That's because you are at Kuby's for a "Frikadellen," or German-style hamburger. Unlike a classic American burger made from nothing but fresh ground beef the Frikadellen is basically a loaded, flattened, griddled meatball which includes beef, pork, parsley, egg, and onion.

The Frikadellen served at Kuby's is significant to the history of the American burger because it's likely that this is close to the recipe

that made its way from Hamburg, Germany, to the United States arriving as the "Hamburg Steak." In the second half of the nineteenth century, a wave of immigration to the United States brought many Germans to New York City and with them came this minced beef dish served on a plate. At some point a total *genius* put the squashed, spiced meatball on bread and the rest was history.

The restaurant and market first opened as Kuby's Sausage House in 1961 . . . in America. But the history of Kuby's meat market goes back an astonishing fourteen generations to Europe. Kuby's opened as a butcher shop in Kaiserslautern, Germany, in 1728. Thirteenth-generation family member Karl Kuby immigrated to South Texas in 1956, met up with an uncle there, then made his way to Dallas and found work at a sausage company. A friend urged to open his own shop and in 1961 Karl set down roots on Snider Square. "It was dead here," Karl remembered, "nothing but a hardware store and a drug store." Kuby's changed all of that.

Today, Karl's son, Karl Jr., runs the business, which along with the market and restaurant includes a large, twenty-five-employee processing facility for hunters. In the short four-month season, Kuby's can process up to 14,000 deer.

Kuby's easily has the largest selection of cheese choices for your burger because of the full-service delicatessen next door. You can choose from twenty-plus different cheeses but the recommended cheese for the Frikadellen is Finnish Lappi. It's a perfect, melty cheese that is almost a cross between american and swiss. The Frikadellen contains pork so obviously this burger is not served rare. Your first bite will reveal a patty cooked through but fear not; the onion, parsley, and rendered beef fat help to keep the burger moist. The flavor is distinctly meatball, and German, with smoky bacon, lettuce, and tomato to complete the package.

On weekends, Kuby's sees an influx of Germans and other Europeans in the market. "My dad calls them 'old-timers,'" Karl Jr. told me, "but he's older than they are!" Karl Sr. at eighty-six years old is still a presence at Kuby's and comes in a few days a week to hand out gummy bears to kids.

Make sure to time your visit to take in the authentic glockenspiel on the outside corner of the building, which goes off every half hour. Karl Jr. had it shipped over from Germany and fought hard to get the enormous, animated, musical cuckoo clock approved by the city. The original permit was denied because it had "moving parts," to which Karl Jr. replied with a good laugh, "But that's what a glockenspiel is!"

LANKFORD GROCERY

88 Dennis St | Houston, TX 77006
713-522-9555 | Mon–Sat 7 am–3 pm | Closed Sun

"There's nothing better than a good burger," was the first thing out of Eydie Prior's mouth when I told her about the book I was working on. Eydie is the owner of Lankford Grocery, a breakfast-and-burger destination opened by her parents, Nona and Aubrey Lankford, in 1939. From 1939 to 1977, the Lankfords operated the business as a grocery store before turning it into the café it is today. The only visible evidence of the store's past is the original Coca-Cola grocer's sign out front.

Lankford's is a funky place with a lot of heart and soul. The floor is impossibly slanted and creaky, the ceiling is low, and Eydie heavily decorates the restaurant depending on the season. My first visit was just before Halloween so you can imagine the decor. "We just took down our summer theme," Eydie's brother, Jimmy, told me, "We had beach balls and stuff hanging from the ceiling."

Jimmy, who has since passed, used to work at Lankford making change and small talk at the end of the counter. He said to me once, referring to the much-debated *GQ* magazine Best Burger list, "What do these swanky men know about good hamburgers anyway?" True. A real man would do well to put one of these burgers down—a Texas-sized, fresh meat, two-fister.

Burgers at Lankford's are cooked to perfection on a flattop griddle, juicy on the inside and crisp on the outside. They start as hand-pattied fresh ground meat and are roughly eight ounces. Order a double and you are getting a pound of meat. The burger to order is the Bacon Double Cheeseburger (the bacon single works just fine, especially if you plan on eating again that day). The burgers come with shredded lettuce, red onion, pickles, tomato, cheese, mayo, mustard, and copious amounts of crisp bacon. All of this is served on a large toasted bun with a single toothpick straining to keep the contents vertical. I'm a hamburger professional and can deftly maneuver the sloppiest of burgers with ease, but this one got the better of me. "Uh, would you like a fork?" Jimmy said, sensing my struggle with the unruly pile of ingredients.

There are other burgers on the menu that sound excellent, like the "Soldier Burger," explained best by waitress Robin. "A man walked in one day and asked for a burger with an egg on it, so I did it!" Or try the "Fire House Burger" that contains a homemade habanero paste. "It is REALLY hot!" Eydie warned me as she approached with a mason jar containing an orange paste. "Just try a little . . . do you have water?" The paste contained radishes, onion, mustard, and habanero peppers and was hot as hell. It was a deep-down hurt, though, not a sharp pain, with lasting heat. Would I spread this on a burger? Absolutely. And recently a new burger creation has become a big seller, the "Grim Burger," which is topped with mac and cheese, bacon, an egg,

and jalapeños. "One of our customers dreamed that one up," Eydie told me.

Lankford's is only open for breakfast and lunch, so don't plan on having dinner there. Burgers are served all day, though, starting when they open at 7 a.m. "People order burgers for breakfast, right when we open," Eydie told me.

The small, sleepy café looks slightly out of place in this neighborhood very close to downtown Houston. "We used to be able to see the buildings downtown. These were all vacant lots," Eydie pointed out. Those lots are being quickly transformed into condos and other large construction projects. Eydie plans to be around for a while, though. She wants to leave the business to family one day but told me, "I plan on being here as long as I can flip that burger." Eydie's husband, Cotton, now works the register, and when asked about retirement he said, "We can't even spell that word!"

LONGHORN CAFE

17625 Blanco Rd | San Antonio, TX 78232 | 210-492-0301 | Sun–Thurs 11 am–9 pm
Fri & Sat 11 am–10 pm | (Five Other Locations in The San Antonio Metro Area and Beyond)
www.thelonghorncafe.com

One of the keys to the success of the Longhorn Cafe is the amazing attention to the quality of the ingredients. Everything that goes into the burgers at the Longhorn is visible in a bank of glass-front coolers behind the counter. The burgers are cooked on a flattop griddle in a big, open kitchen and prepped at a station adjacent to the griddle. It is all out in the open, and as an employee proudly pointed out with a wave of his arm, "Everything we do is right here."

What they do is burgers and they do them expertly, and have been for thirty-four years now. The original griddle from opening day in 1984 is still in place and sees thousands of burgers a week. A former manager once told me that the beef is always fresh, never frozen. "If someone brings in frozen, I'll have to slap them!" he proclaimed enthusiastically.

The sign outside of the restaurant exclaims that the Longhorn Cafe is the "Home of the Big

Juicy." I asked someone what was on the "Big Juicy" and they explained, "All the burgers are Big Juicys," which is basically a one-third-pound, wide, flat patty on a large, toasted white squishy bun. There are many burger options at Longhorn Cafe but the most popular is the double meat, double cheese. Ask for everything, and you'll get a burger piled high with shredded lettuce, raw onion, mayo, mustard, and pickles—a true Texas classic.

The kitchen area is an incredible study in efficiency. Everyone has a task to complete and during peak times the kitchen works like a well-oiled assembly line. A griddleperson slaps patties on the flattop and toasts buns alongside the burgers while another employee preps buns with condiments. Completed burgers are delivered to the counter in plastic baskets lined with waxed paper.

One employee spends his time only at the deep fryer. Get the "Half & Half" with your order and choose two of the three deep-fried sides: onion rings, fries, or tater tots. The onion rings are not to be missed (they are cut and battered in-house) but it's also hard to pass up on tater tots.

At Longhorn Cafe, you place an order at the counter, then find a seat and wait for your name to be called. Grab a pickled jalapeño at the counter to munch on while you are waiting. At the Blanco Road location, you can sit in either the large dining room filled with booths and picnic tables, or check out the equally large outdoor patio with its big homemade slide for kids to play on.

It's a big, clean, easygoing place that caters to all types. The first time I was there it was lunchtime and the place was mostly filled with dudes in auto mechanic uniforms and families, a mixed clientele that changes as the day progresses. Nighttime brings local high school and college students (and sometimes players from the San Antonio Spurs). There is usually a line out the door and the place is packed on game day weekends.

The restaurant apparently opened in the '50s as a taco stand at what is now the Blanco Road location. In 1984, a Sooner (a graduate of the University of Oklahoma) and an Aggie (a graduate of Texas A&M) bought the stand, started selling hamburgers, and changed the name to the Longhorn Cafe. Two high school buddies, David Wynn and Paul Weir, came along and purchased the business in 1995. The duo is responsible for the Longhorn's expansion into a six-store chain.

What I also love about the Longhorn Cafe is that my favorite Texas beer, Shiner Bock, is available by the pitcher. I couldn't think of anything better to do in Texas than eat a roadhouse burger while drinking one of the best beers in Texas at a picnic table. What more do you need?

Directly across the street from the Blanco Road location (the original) is a Sonic Drive-In that is obviously not affecting business in the slightest. "We've been here so long that our customers are pretty loyal," Director of Operations Karen Turner told me. Be smart and go where the locals go.

MORRIS NEAL'S HANDY HAMBURGERS

200 South Mill St | Cleburne, TX 76033
817-556-6464 | Mon–Sat 9:30 am–3 pm | Closed Sun

Morris Neal's ain't fancy, but it is most definitely not trying to be. Actually, it's not really trying to be anything but a great burger restaurant for local burger lovers who have been coming to this place for decades. That's it.

There is no background music at Morris Neal's, only the din of lunchtime chatter and the natural sounds of sizzling burgers and orders being wrapped and bagged. It's a tiny, utilitarian place off the main drag in Cleburne where most of the orders are to-go and everyone knows each other. The griddle stays filled to capacity with patties for the entire lunch rush and it is all handled with ease by owner Johnnie Jordan and her crew.

Johnnie builds and wraps every single order and takes breaks to hug customers and say hello. She runs the show, quietly, and when she asks one of her many employees something, the response is a respectful, "Yes ma'am." It's the Zen of burgers in Texas, much like the environment at the iconic Louis' Lunch in New Haven.

Every morning the crew at Morris Neal's hand-rolls four-ounce balls of fresh beef for the burgers. If you order a double meat burger (denoted as "DM" on the wall menu), two balls are pressed together in the griddle to make an eight-ounce patty. Some order the "Real Treat," a Jumbo that somehow includes four balls of beef and is still under eight bucks. "That one will make you want to nap after," Johnnie joked.

The Slim Jim combo is what to order at Morris Neal's, which comes with fries and a drink. The burger is the perfect Texas package wrapped in waxed paper and bursting with fresh, crunchy lettuce, tomato, onion, pickle, mustard, and a tasty double-meat patty with a slice of american cheese. The cheese goes on cold, but is placed in the center of the action and melts in

the wrapping. The bun, toasted on the griddle, picks up some burger grease and tastes buttery. "The flavor is in that griddle," Johnnie told me. "People ask me 'What do you do to these burgers?' and I tell them it's because that griddle came from the original stand."

That griddle has seen some action over the years and started its life downtown when Morris Neal opened a burger stand in the 1930s in an alley nearby. "It was just a lean-to," Johnnie told me. She is the fourth owner, started working at Morris in 1979 and bought the place in 2000. After divorcing her husband, the place closed

for a short time, much to the dismay of her regulars. In stepped good friends Rick and Wanda Malone to help Johnnie get Morris Neal's renovated and reopened.

The best seat in the house is an odd nook far right of the order counter. It's a single-seat table, complete with a setup of napkins, salt, pepper, etc., and it is where you are going to want to sit. From this vantage, you'll have a front row seat on the action and can watch all of the orders built and wrapped up. "People call that the 'in trouble' seat," Johnnie told me. I call it the "hamburger heaven" seat.

BEST SEAT
IN THE HOUSE

In the world of mom 'n' pop burger joints, no two are alike. In many cases across America if a burger spot has seating it's a charming jumble of random seats and tables wedged into available spaces in the dining room. My default for the classic burger counter is at the stool closest to the griddle action; always the best call. But a handful of these places have some pretty unique places to enjoy burgers.

Anchor Bar, Superior, WI
The Library: a tiny, private, single-table room filled with books just inside the front door.

Hodad's, Ocean Beach, CA
The VW Microbus "booth."

Morris Neal's Handy Hamburgers, Cleburne, TX
The single-seat "counter," a tiny nook to the far right of the order counter.

Louis' Lunch, New Haven, CT
The two-person, windowed "booth" just to the left of order counter.

P.J. Clarke's, New York, NY
Table number twenty (Frank Sinatra's favorite table). Cozy and private.

The Apple Pan, Los Angeles, CA
The last stool, far right. Amazing view into pie room.

Tune Inn, Washington, DC
The second booth on the left (then Senator JFK's favorite seat).

Helvetia Tavern, Hillsboro, OR
Grant's Seat: the last stool at counter, far left. Look for the mirror in the ceiling—you can see the TV reflected (in reverse).

Solly's Grille, Milwaukee, WI
The stool on left of the left horseshoe counter, labeled *George Motz, Hamburger America*. *wink.

MELIOS BROS CHAR BAR

2026 Greenville Ave | Dallas, TX 75206
214-826-8800 | Mon–Sat 6 am–9 pm | Sun 7 am–9 pm

It's hard not to love a place like Char Bar. The Dallas neighborhood Greenville is quickly changing and new shops and restaurants are moving in, and there's Char Bar in the center of it all. The large, freestanding almost Nordic-looking restaurant painted robin's egg blue, seems beautifully out of place. Inside, the dining room has the look of a tourism office with images promoting travel to Greece, but the air is rich with smoke from the open kitchen by the register.

Char Bar is not quite a diner, and not quite a steakhouse, or even a burger joint. But it is a place that serves good, honest comfort food with a meat-centric menu. Steak is at the core of the business and the sound of searing beef is constant. Char Bar is owned and run by Tom and Costas Melios, two brothers who immigrated to the United States from Greece in search of opportunity. "I'm from a town that had only two roads," Tom told me, gesturing with his hands, "One went this way, one went that way." In 1968, the brothers left their tiny hometown of Nafpaktos, Greece, landed in Houston and made their way to Dallas and a job at Char Bar. "We had no education," Tom told me through a thick accent that seems unaffected by fifty years in America. "All we know how to do is cook." In 1971 the owner died and the brothers bought the restaurant, at the time one of four units in Dallas. "I should have bought

them all," Tom told me, "but your head is all full of garbage when you are young."

The Melios brothers are part of a breed of Greek Americans that are becoming harder and harder to find. In the beginning, Greek immigrants dominated the burger business and today deep roots can still be discovered at places across the US from Capitol Burger in Los Angeles to South 21 Drive-In of Charlotte, North Carolina and many in between.

Tom does all of the cooking and Costas works the register and takes orders. When Tom has an order ready, he drops the plates on the counter and shouts to the dining room "Number SEVEN!" To order, first approach the counter, pay, and find a seat. When your order is complete, which seems lightning fast, Costas will deliver it to your table on an old-school plastic cafeteria tray.

The burgers at Char Bar start with fresh ground, quarter-pound patties that are cooked over a flame grill in full view. There's a classic burger loaded with condiments and a few other options but you really need to stick to my favorite—the #2, which is served with nothing more than a copious amount of hickory-flavored barbecue sauce and a handful of shredded, soft cheddar cheese. The sweet sauce, melty cheddar, and smoky essence are a powerful trio. And the big, Mrs, Baird's local white bun is of course toasted because if not I guarantee it would disintegrate well before it arrives at your table.

"I love to cook," Tom told me when he had a break. He's tired from forty-five years at the grill but keeps going, day after day. "Cooking is what makes me happy. You have to do something in life that you want to do."

STANTON'S CITY BITES

1420 Edwards St | Houston, TX 77007 | 713-227-4893 | Mon Closed
Tues–Thurs 11 am–8 pm | Fri & Sat 11 am–9 pm | Sun 11 am–4 pm
www.stantoncitybites.com

The first time I set foot in Stanton's I was on camera for my Travel Channel show *Burger Land*. It was a stunt for the close of the show where a local expert, in this case esteemed Texas food critic Robb Walsh, takes me to a burger joint I'd never been. Much had been said of Arthur "Art" Fong's grocery-store-turned-burger-destination, and the burgers, which were the result of his wife Theresa's hard work. Things have changed since

that day unfortunately. About three weeks after we filmed the episode, the affable Art suddenly passed away, taken too soon at age sixty-three.

After fleeing Hong Kong as refuges in the early 1950s, Art and his family immigrated to San Francisco. Art's father wanted to own a business and "Texas was open," as Theresa put it. When Art was twelve the family relocated to Houston and opened a grocery store in the First Ward

downtown. It was a classic setup with stocked shelves, produce in the back, and a butcher counter. The family lived upstairs and Art helped his father with the meat and learned how to be a butcher. Then on a return trip to Hong Kong, he met his future wife Theresa. "Art asked me to marry him on our second date," she remembered.

During a cold winter in the early 1990s, Theresa was bored of working the register ("I used to fall asleep," she told me, "that's how boring it was!") and ventured into the kitchen to make some spaghetti. Workers from across the street smelled the food and came asking if they could buy some. She began to offer daily specials—beef stroganoff one day, oxtail soup the next, as part of a rotating menu. Then one day Art pointed out, "This is America, we need to sell burgers." Theresa didn't like burgers but Art had become a skilled butcher after years

behind his father's meat counter in the store. She reluctantly added a burger to the rotating menu and it was such a hit that customers demanded it daily. And after two years as a weekly special, the burger was available every day. Eventually Stanton's slowly morphed from a grocery store to a restaurant. The first time I visited we ate among a small selection of dry goods and groceries. But today the groceries are gone and the family is focused on making and selling great food.

The big secret behind this burger is what's in it. "A lot of love," Theresa joked, "and a lot of pain." But truthfully what goes into Theresa's burgers is a family secret. She adds some seasonings to fresh 80/20 chuck and forms it into half-pound patties. "Art wouldn't allow anything smaller than a half-pound burger," Theresa remembered, "He would say 'This is Texas, either you want a burger or not.'" The patties get a good sear from the flattop griddle and go onto big, pillowy, seeded challah rolls the Fong's have been using for years. Get the bacon cheeseburger (my favorite) and it comes with crispy bacon, american cheese, romaine lettuce, red onion, pickles, mayo, and mustard. It's a glorious combination of flavors and textures that must be eaten using both hands.

"I'm a worrier," Theresa admitted, and that her worry stems from getting it right. "The quality of the food is first, before money," she told me recently. When Art passed away, he left Theresa and her children with a burger joint and a big hole in their lives. Good news is they've picked up and kept Stanton's the way it was, if not better. Their daughter Samantha left her job at Chevron to work at the restaurant, and son Jonathan left behind a career in finance to do the the same. Art is not around anymore but he'd sure be proud of the legacy he has left behind.

TOOKIE'S HAMBURGERS

1202 Bayport Blvd | Seabrook, TX 77586 | 281-942-9334
Sun–Thurs 11 am–10 pm | Fri & Sat 11 am–11 pm | www.tookiesburgers.com

A burger friend once told me that Tookie's is "near Houston," so I'm guessing that by Texas standards a seventy-mile round trip from downtown for lunch is no big deal. Regardless, I'd drive a hundred miles or more to eat at this classic Texas roadhouse, the home of the Squealer.

Years ago, food writer and burger savant John T. Edge informed me that no trip to the Houston area would be complete without a Squealer in my belly. Houston food critic and friend Robb Walsh backed up the claim and I was off.

Seabrook, Texas, is sort of midway between Houston and Galveston and is home to astronauts and scientists employed by nearby Johnson Space Center (the home of mission control for NASA space missions, which employs over 3,000 Texans). Tookie's sits near a crossroads of the main drag in Seabrook and a road awkwardly named NASA 1 Road. For those working at the Space Center, Tookie's is only a short drive down this road. For everyone else, it's a destination.

Tookie's has an excellent selection of burgers but it's the Squealer that'll have you planning your next trip back to Seabrook. Imagine fresh-ground beef mixed with ground bacon, pattied, griddled with some melted cheddar and placed on a bun. The taste is expectedly sublime and easily ups the ante on the traditional bacon cheeseburger. John T. described this unique burger creation best when he told me, "If a mule is the result of a donkey mating with a horse, then the Squealer is a kissing cousin of a similar marriage of a pig to a cow. The resulting beast is better for it."

The Squealer is basically a wad of bacony beef with a smoky flavor profile and a salty, crunchy exterior. In short, heaven. The bacon definitely gives the patty a reddish color and there's even a warning on the menu about the color shift.

Daily, the kitchen crew hand-mixes fresh ground beef with ground bacon. The bacon-to-beef ratio is so classified that years ago a neighboring restaurant once sent their son to work at Tookie's with a mission to snag the famous recipe. "It didn't work," former owner Jim Spears once told me, "the kid was just a dishwasher and didn't really know what was going on."

Before it was a hamburger destination, it was a soft-serve ice-cream business. It then became a location for the now-defunct local burger chain Bonus Burger. And in 1975, Jim Spears opened Tookie's. Jim was the sole proprietor for thirty-three years before disaster struck in the form of Hurricane Ike. The restaurant took on four feet of water which effectively destroyed the entire kitchen and bar. I stayed in touch with Jim for a year or so about his plans to rebuild but nothing materialized. "I'm old," he told me, and said he had no family to step in. He was looking to sell the iconic burger joint instead of starting over.

Enter Barry Terrell, three long years later, in 2011. Barry saw value in resurrecting Tookie's and worked hard to reopen. He maintained the ethos of the original restaurant, including what he could salvage from the storm, but had to rebuild the entire kitchen. "The recipes came with the purchase of the restaurant," Barry told me on the show *Burger Land*. That was great to hear. There was one big (positive) change however—the size of the Squealer increased from one-quarter pound to one-half pound. Barry knew there should be more Squealer to love.

The interior of Tookie's has a homespun rambling feel. Over the years, Jim added many additions to the structure, including a back porch, so that the restaurant has plenty of places to hide out and eat a burger. Each room is filled with all sorts of authentic bits of road culture and Americana. A barber pole, a large ceramic mermaid, street signs, and an impressive collection of stained glass hangs everywhere. A waitress once told me, "Every time you look up you notice something different."

Another must-eat at Tookie's are the amazing lightly battered fried onion rings. They arrive at your table as a perfectly balanced pile of bracelet-sized deep-fried beauties. On most days, Tookie's can sell well over three hundred orders averaging fifty or more orders an *hour*.

When I first visited Tookie's in 2005, it was the only bacon-in-patty burger I had heard of in America. But over the years, I've noticed a number of restaurants around the United States and beyond have attempted to replicate this famous burger. Of the ones I've tried, though, none have even come close to the Squealer at Tookie's.

And when you visit Tookie's, make sure to take note of the Kilroy-esque drawing just inside the front door to the right. He's peering over a green line that represents the high water mark from the flooding caused by Hurricane Ike. Had it not been for the vision and perseverance of Barry Terrell, there would likely be no Tookie's today.

TOP NOTCH HAMBURGERS

7525 Burnet Rd | Austin, TX 78757 | 512-452-2181
Open Daily 11 am–10 pm | www.topnotchaustin.com

Top Notch is a well preserved American icon, saved by what I consider to be an American hero. That hero is current co-owner Kelly Chappell. Kelly hung out at Top Notch as a kid, then as an adult watched the drive-in slip slowly into decline. Today, Kelly owns other restaurants with partners Chris Courtney and Jay Bunda and stepped in to save Top Notch from its imminent demise.

You may recognize Top Notch from the classic Texas teen coming-of-age film *Dazed and Confused*. Director Richard Linklater used the drive-in as a location and it has become arguably the most recognizable in the film, with some memorable scenes filmed here (like Matthew McConaughey's line, "I love those redheads!").

My guess is that Top Notch looks pretty much the same way today as it looked in the film, and for that matter, since opening day in 1971. *Dazed and Confused* was a period film set

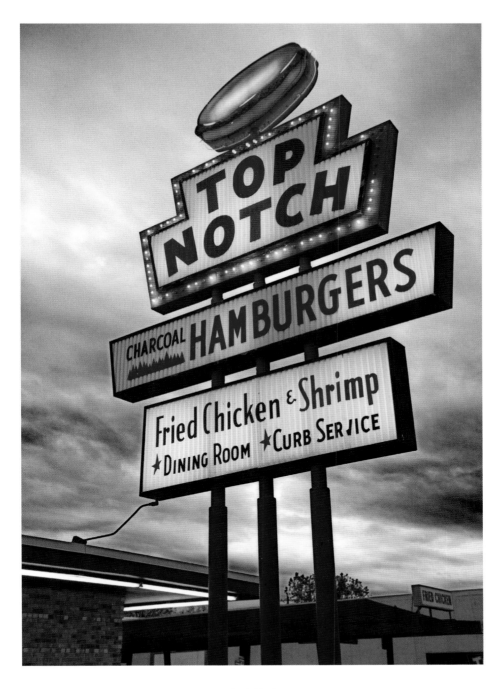

in 1976 making the location historically accurate. And following Kelly's purchase in 2010 he kept the menu exactly the same at it was from opening day 1971. Before it was a burger drive-in the location was Burkhart's Barbecue, opened in 1959.

If you choose to eat inside at one of the many tables instead of in your car with carhop service, you may be shocked by what you see as you walk in the door—flames. The fresh, thin patties cook ultra fast over an indoor charcoal grill just behind the counter. When the grill cook flips a bunch of patties, the rendered beef fat causes huge, dramatic flames. Needless to say, that smoky outdoor grilled burger taste is part of the flavor profile.

The most-ordered burger on the menu is the Top Pick number three, and it's not an ordinary burger, especially by Texas standards. Most likely sharing some DNA with the previous barbecue business, the number three comes with a hickory barbecue sauce, a house "special" sauce, onions, and grated cheddar cheese. The combination of the tangy barbecue sauce, smoky beef, and cheddar made this burger a standout option. Or try the number four Longhorn Special, which some local college students take issue with. Manager Kyle Schaefer told me, "I've had [Texas] A&M students who refuse to call it the Longhorn, and call it the number four instead."

Should you find yourself in the Austin area around April 20 (4–20, get it?), grab a lawn chair and make your way to Top Notch for their annual screening of the film that made them famous.

UTAH

CROWN BURGERS

118 North 300 West | Salt Lake City, UT 84103 | 801-532-5300
Mon–Sat 10 am–10:30 pm | Closed Sun | (Multiple Locations) | www.crown-burgers.com

Behold the "Crown Burger." At first you see what appears to be a pastrami sandwich, then, upon closer inspection, realize that your wildest fantasies have just come true—you are gazing at a cheeseburger stuffed to bursting with warm, thinly sliced pastrami.

Unique to Salt Lake City and its neighbors, the pastrami cheeseburger is a beloved Utah burger that, according to some locals, is best represented at the Greek-owned Crown Burgers chain. The Crown I visited was the second built (in 1979) in Salt Lake City. I was assured that the other six Crowns were similar, which is hard to believe given the almost indescribable decor of the interior of this restaurant. "Back in the '70s my family was in the Greek nightclub business," Mike, son of owner Manuel Katsanevas, tried to explain. Gargoyles, stuffed quail in flight, large chandeliers, Greek statuary, lush wallpaper, and a huge working fireplace round out the phantasmagorical setting. "We know we are fast food but we wanted to create an upscale dining experience," Mike told me.

It's true—don't be put off by the large staff in uniform behind the counter working at warp speed, multiple registers, numbers being called over a loudspeaker, and a general feeling of ordering food at one of the superchains. As you wait for your number to be called you stand between an ancient nine-foot-tall ornately carved wooden hutch and a grandfather clock, both salvaged from a hotel in France. "People ask all the time if this stuff is for sale," Mike said, pointing to the clock. "No, it is not."

The genius behind Crown is their business plan, which could only be pulled off by an intensely proud Greek family (they are actually from Crete). Each restaurant in the chain is independently owned by a family member. They share recipes and suppliers to maintain sameness and quality.

The burgers come in fresh as quarter-pound patties "every morning," Manuel explained. The menu is large and eclectic and includes hot dogs, tuna sandwiches, a fish burger, and, you guessed it, some of the best souvlaki and gyros in town.

The Crown Burger, charbroiled over an open flame, comes wrapped tightly in waxed paper and includes lettuce, tomato, chopped onion, american cheese, and, of course, gobs of pastrami. My warning to you—do not remove the waxed paper prior to hoisting this beast to your lips. It will explode and the pastrami will end up in your lap.

The idea for pastrami on a cheeseburger was imported from Anaheim, California, by a relative of the Katsanevas family. "Uncle James had a restaurant called Minos Burgers and served a pastrami burger," Mike explained. When he moved to Salt Lake, he brought the idea to his family.

The burger also includes a Utah curiosity called fry sauce. For those unfamiliar with the fast-food habits of Utahans, fry sauce is basically ketchup and mayo mixed together. Mike told me, "We make our own fry sauce in house, made of seven ingredients, most of them secret." The sauce is mainly used as a dip for fries.

The Katsanevases have been approached more than once with offers to franchise but have resisted. Fear that the quality of their product would decline was not their only reason. "We make a comfortable living and we're happy with the way things are," Mike told me. "We have worked very hard for everything we have. Besides, this couldn't be a franchise; everything is made to order!"

DOT'S RESTAURANT

3 East Main St | Wilmington, VT 05363 | 802-464-7284 | Sun–Thurs 5:30 am–8 pm
Fri–Sat 5:30 am–9 pm | Closed Mon | www.dotsofvermont.com

Dot's is hard to miss as you roll into the picturesque downstate Vermont town of Wilmington. Just look for the only neon sign in town, thanks to a local ordinance that has banned neon signage on businesses. Fortunately, the neon sign over the door at Dot's has been grandfathered in.

Dot's is not a burger joint. It's a classic New England diner that serves comfort food favorites like pancakes, chili, and sandwiches but also happens to serve one of the best burgers in Vermont. Locals and tourists alike frequent Dot's, which sees healthy crowds year round. Nearby Mt. Snow attracts thousands of skiers and snowboarders on winter weekends, many of them looking for burgers.

The name of the restaurant goes back half a century but the actual building dates to 1832, making it the oldest structure in town. For its first seventy years, the building was a post office and in 1900, became a general store. In 1930, the store became a restaurant and had many names over the next few decades. In 1952, a man named Dude Sparrow bought the restaurant for his wife, Dot. When the Sparrows sold the diner to John Reagan in 1980, the name stayed.

The burger at Dot's starts as a hand-formed patty of fresh ground 80/20 Angus chuck. A mayo lid is used for portioning and the six-ounce patty is cooked to temperature over a flame grill with lava rocks. It's served on a toasted, seeded white bun and nothing else but potato chips and a dill pickle spear. "They come plain," Mitch explained, "but we do not shy away from special requests." Cheese selection is american, swiss, pepper jack, and Vermont cheddar and the usual condiments are available, including lettuce, tomato, and sliced red onion.

The burger at Dot's is best chased with a chocolate malt. I asked now-retired waitress of thirty-eight years Shirlee what drink would go best with this juicy burger. She responded with a straight face, "A beer." She's right, and Dot's does have a selection of beer and wine, but I was there at 10:30 a.m. and had just finished my coffee.

In late August 2011, Dot's was pummeled by Hurricane Irene. The restaurant is cantilevered over the Deerfield River and when the storm hit, the river rose an astonishing eight feet in fifteen minutes. The town was caught off guard and Dot's sustained formidable damage. It took almost three years for the restaurant to reopen and involved a massive renovation that included rebuilding the ancient stone foundation. "They had to cut the building in half and lift it out of the way with a crane," waitress Annabelle explained. With the help of a local, grass-roots movement Dot's reopened in 2014 and looks incredible. Period details were used and the historic front porch returned. And of course the famous neon sign was salvaged and is back in use. Dot's was back in business after the renovation and the menu is unchanged. But sadly, in 2017 John passed away and Patti continues to run Dot's.

Even though the Reagan family has owned and run Dot's for almost forty years, people still walk in and ask, "Where is Dot?" The friendly staff gets a kick out of the question and reply by jokingly pointing at longtime manager Mitch Soskin saying, "There's Dot!"

THE WHITE COTTAGE SNACK BAR

863 West Woodstock Rd | Woodstock, VT 05091 | 802-457-3455
Open Daily 11 am–10 pm (May to October) | whitecottagesnackbar.com

"A lot of people come here thinking it's that great rock-and-roll town in New York," former manager Norm Corbin told me. He added with his New England accent and a smile, "Well, it's nawt." This Woodstock is deep in the mountains of Vermont, complete with covered bridges and gentle streams. Downtown is a destination with tour buses dumping happy shoppers onto the quaint main drag all summer long and well into foliage season. White Cottage is not here, though. Head a mile west out of town and you'll find a sixty-one-year-old snack bar that has been making summer better since its opening day in 1957.

"Everything is made in house, the sauces, the coleslaw, everything," manager Scott Noble told me. All of the dairy used at White Cottage is from local farms and the beef for the burgers comes from Vermont cows. A local meatpacker in Burlington supplies the snack bar with fresh six-ounce Angus chuck patties. The burgers are cooked on a flame grill and served on toasted, classic white squishy buns. The bacon cheeseburger is the favorite at White Cottage and the standard call is to order one with "the works": lettuce, tomato, diced onion, pickle, mayo, mustard, and ketchup. This is an amazingly juicy burger so don't let it sit around. Within minutes, the juices will disintegrate the bun. I asked for one medium and it was cooked to temperature perfectly.

To order at White Cottage, step up to one of the windows. Pick up your burgers when your name is called over the loudspeaker. There's a tendency to go back to the window where you paid, but the pickup window is actually around the corner to the right. There's plenty of seating on the porch and out by the river that runs behind White Cottage.

Burgers aren't the only thing on the menu and you'd be a fool to walk away from White Cottage without a side of deep-fried clam bellies. In fact, even though the onion rings are amazing, order a side of these clams with your burger. Scott gets clams from Ipswich, Massachusetts, and they have a legion of fans. "Some people come from Ipswich to have the Ipswich clams here," Scott told me. Ipswich is two-and-a-half hours away. They're that good.

White Cottage suffered a massive blow when Hurricane Irene blew through New England on August 29, 2011. The storm knocked the entire building off its foundation and the business was destroyed. "I ripped the rest down and started over," owner of twenty-nine years John Hurley explained. Fortunately, insurance covered everything and John was able to not only rebuild but upgrade everything. "In a way, the hurricane was actually a good thing—I got the renovation I wanted." Through it all, the menu never changed. "Everything we make is exactly the same," John told me.

White Cottage is a seasonal snack bar and locals look forward to the opening every year. Locals know it's spring when this burger outpost opens the first Friday in May.

Ice cream is king at White Cottage and in the peak of the summer the place is overrun by families looking for one of the snack bar's thirty-three flavors and soft serve. Ice cream is scooped behind a large picture window and kids can watch the action by climbing a two-step platform. Scott explained, "Parents were always lifting the kids up to watch us scoop so I made the steps from some scrap wood." How thoughtful is that?

Of the business John told me, "I love it," but when October rolls around he's ready to shut down the White Cottage for the season. "When Columbus Day comes we are closed up and out of here," John told me. "I'm in Florida four days later."

VIRGINIA

THE CAVALIER STORE

2920 Rivermont Ave | Lynchburg, VA 24503 | 434-845-3837
Mon–Fri 10 am–12 am | Sat 10 am–1 am | Sun 10 am–10 pm

The Cavalier is a sweet, broken-in bar in a residential neighborhood where the bartenders are completely in tune with the regulars. "We know exactly what everyone drinks, and what they eat," the bartender told me as I ate my burger. "This guy right here?" and he pointed down the bar, "I know he wants another Budweiser." And with that the guy said, "Can I get another Bud?" Ahh, the simple pleasures in life . . .

The building is a substantial brick-and-glass block structure that dates back to 1919 with quite a past. It opened as a combination grocery store and auto repair shop, became a pharmacy, which changed its name four times in ten years, then became Cavalier Store in 1938 but as another pharmacy with a lunch counter. Apparently it was the kind of place where women could sneak a drag from their husbands who didn't want them smoking. Then finally, in 1958, the store, which took its name from an apartment complex across the street, became a confectionary which has morphed

over the years from a lunch counter to into a beloved local tavern.

It was current owner of thirty-one years Wells Duffy that is responsible for the tavern feel of Cavalier. "When I bought the place in 1987, they

ceiling is covered with donated license plates and the walls with hundreds of photos, framed articles, and school pennants. You could spend hours looking at it all.

Belly up to the green Formica bar and place your order. There's one burger on the short menu, the Cavalier Burger, and it's buried in a section labled SANDWICHES. The Cavalier is also known for their grilled reuben and even more so for their addictive thick-cut fried spuds with seasoned salt and a house made ranch dressing for dipping. You'll definitely want to order some with your burger.

only sold sandwiches and hot dogs." The Cavalier also still sold some grocery items but Wells got rid of those. "I didn't see any point in it," Wells told me. "Big supermarkets were popping up all over." Wells also made two other major changes to the Cavalier—he added two long bars and added a burger to the menu.

The interior of Cavalier is pure function and looks like it could handle a rowdy crowd. A pool table takes center stage by the front window and the wooden booths are carved up with sixty years of abuse. During the day, the place is illuminated by the large picture windows, and at night lighting is low and is limited to random strings of colored Christmas lights and a huge glowing Cavalier Store sign that likely hung from the storefront years ago. The

The straightforward, honest bar burger at Cavalier is made from six-ounces of fresh ground beef and cooked on a flattop with two slices of american cheese. "The burgers will always taste better on a flattop," Wells pointed out, "because they cook in their own juices." Get yours "all the way" and there will be crunchy fresh lettuce, raw onion, and tomato. And, you guessed it, if you are a fan of ranch dressing go ahead and put that on the burger, too.

In what seems like a throwback to the pharmacy days "candy bars" are actually listed on dessert section of menu. Also, Cavalier is also a package store—you can get beer to go here.

"Only day we are not open is Thanksgiving, and Christmas night we are the busiest,"

Wells told me. They are also open no matter the weather, and regulars know this. The kitchen runs on gas so even if the electricity is out the Cavalier Store is up and running.

At seventy-one Wells has no intention of retiring anytime soon. "I wouldn't know what to do with myself," he told me, "I'm definitely not going to sit home and watch soap operas."

TEXAS TAVERN

114 West Church Ave | Roanoke, VA 24011 | 540-342-4825
Open Daily 24 Hours (Except Christmas) | www.texastavern-Inc.com

"I hope you plan on having a Cheesy Western," were the first words out of Matt Bullington's mouth after I introduced myself. I was thrown because I thought I had come to Texas Tavern for a straightforward burger, possibly a classic thin patty on a tiny white squishy bun. What Matt was selling me was actually the most popular burger at his eighty-six-year-old hamburger stand.

The Cheesy, as the regulars call it, is a glorious combination of hamburger patty, cheese, pickle, onion, relish, and mustard with a gently-scrambled egg on top. Since that first visit years ago, I've consumed more than a handful of Cheesies, and I ask for them a bit differently each time. I think I've hit a sweet spot, with my order consisting of three patties (they are paper thin) and a dollop of the Texas Tavern's hot dog chili (not to be confused with their "chile"—more on that later).

"We sell hundreds of Cheesies a day, especially to the late-night crowd," Matt told me. How late? "We are open all night." In fact, the only time

the Texas Tavern closes is for part of Christmas Eve and Day.

Matt is the great-grandson of Nick Bullington, the man who opened the small hamburger stand in downtown Roanoke in 1930. "He saw Roanoke as a boomtown and decided to build

his restaurant here." Boomtown it most definitely was. Roanoke served as a major railroad hub and the Norfolk & Western Railroad famously employed thousands at their steam locomotive manufacturing plant. Nick, an advance man for the Ringling Brother's Circus, had collected recipes from his extensive travels around the United States. After observing the best ways to make a hamburger, and with a borrowed chile recipe from a hotel in Texas, he felt confident in opening his own place.

The chile at Texas Tavern is not what you are thinking. It's a locally beloved dish made with beans, served in a small bowl as a sort of soup, or side dish while you wait for your burger. For the condiment "chili," ask for the stuff they put on the (excellent) hot dogs. It's so popular that it can be taken away by the gallon.

The grill area is just inside the front window, which was typical of burger joints of the era. The cook's station is a testament to efficient food prep and execution. An impossibly small twelve-by-eighteen-inch griddle serves as the soul of the "kitchen," with two small burners for frying eggs above it. Next to that within reach are containers for burger buns, relish, pickles, and onions. The entire compliment of ingredients and cooking apparatus to prepare everything on the menu occupies a mere six square feet—absolutely amazing.

The Texas Tavern is a rare vestige of a bygone era because nothing has changed since opening day. "Everything is original," Matt told me. The dented steel countertop, impressively

worn footrest bar, and ten lumpy red leather stools are authentic. Some repairs to the griddle in 1975 are the extent of any "renovations," outside of the frequent paint jobs that keep the place looking as fresh and inviting as it likely was in 1930.

All types find themselves at the Texas Tavern counter, and at all times of the day. I've seen college kids at 2 a.m., men in suits at 3 p.m., and quiet old-timers there for breakfast. Matt explained once, "We get all types in here. Whether you are the governor or a hobo, you'll be treated like a millionaire at the Texas Tavern."

CLARK'S RESTAURANT

731 U.S. 101, 6 Miles South of Aberdeen | Cosmopolis, WA 98537 | 360-538-1487
Mon–Thurs 7 am–7 pm | Fri & Sat 6 am–8 pm | Sun 6 am–7 pm
www.clarksrestaurant.com

Every once in a while I get a tip which is not exactly vetted. Most of these tips require more research and hopefully new discoveries are made. But in the case of Clark's Restaurant, I could find nothing. My local experts had only heard of the place and information was sketchy. This is likely because Clark's is not near anything and is two hours southwest of Seattle, deep in the woods. There was only one solution—jump in a car and get out there.

The tiny town of Artic, Washington, was supposed to be "Arctic" but a spelling error one hundred years ago sealed its fate. I was about a mile from my first visit to this outpost in the woods and thought to myself if the burger was crap at least the drive was beautiful. Little did I know I was about to strike the hamburger jackpot.

Clark's plays the part of restaurant/community center well. The cozy country store interior is a mix of tables with green checked tablecloths and a counter with swivel stools. Antiques on the walls and wagon wheel hanging lights complete the scene.

The banter between the owner's daughter, Ranie Creamer, and the regulars is priceless and real. I heard Ranie say to one customer as he was leaving, "Come back when you can't stay too long!" One conversation about Trump became so heated that I slowly moved away from the action.

The menu is enormous at Clark's and the servings are large. The burger options range from a single quarter-pound burger up to a double with thirteen ounces of beef on a six-inch bun. The most popular burger is the Deluxe cheeseburger with bacon, which comes standard with lettuce, pickles, tomato, onion, and Clark's "special sauce," which is really the Northwest's signature mayo/mustard burger sauce called Goop (see recipe, page 380).

Clark's balls fresh beef and presses the balls onto patties with a heavy, custom-made weight. Years ago they ordered fresh, pre-formed patties from their supplier but Rich made the switch to bulk beef when he wasn't getting what he wanted. "When you cook a pre-formed patty it sort of cups up—know what I mean?" The burgers are cooked on a well-seasoned flattop and get a nice griddle crunch with a craggy edge.

At first it was a gas station, open in 1923. The Clark family bought it in 1960 and used it to sell their homemade ice cream, burgers, and more. It was sold again in 1984 to the Lewis family who ran it until 1997 when Rich and Kathy Pacana found the restaurant for sale and in disarray. They bought it and cleaned it up. "We put the whole valley to work!" Kathy remembered. She worked at Clark's years earlier and explained, "I knew what it was, and what it could be again."

Kathy and Rich were high school sweethearts and grew up in the area. Many decades and a few marriages later, they reconnected, married, and now run Clark's with their daughter.

It's not often I find a burger destination this remote that can actually make great burgers. There had to be something behind this place, and sure enough there was . . . and the answer blew my burger mind.

The burger roots run deep at Clark's. Many burgers in Washington contain a dollop of tasty Goop but no one seems to have mastered the regional sauce like Eastside Big Tom, one of my favorite burger joints in America. Rich worked for Bob Eagan at Big Tom in Olympia (so his burger lineage was sound) and everyone knows that their Goop sauce is a trade secret. I was

shocked to find out that the Goop at Clark's is the *exact same recipe*. Turns out Bob Eagan gave them the recipe as a wedding gift! And to make matters even more bizarre, after leaving the burger business Bob became a Unitarian minister and officiated their wedding.

At lunchtime, Clark's is filled to capacity with hungry customers. I'm not sure where they come from because they place is surrounded by nothing but trees. "People come here on the way to the beach," Ranie told me. Beach? Nearby Cohassett Beach on the Pacific is only thirty minutes away. If that's where you are headed, you must make a stop Clark's, coming and going.

DICK'S DRIVE-IN

111 N.E. 45th St | Seattle, WA 98105 | 206-632-5125 | Open Daily 10:30 am–2 am
(Multiple Locations around Seattle) | www.ddir.com

At first glance, Dick's looks like it might be a tired old drive-in serving frozen hockey pucks for burgers. But Dick's is anything but tired, and as the locals know, it's as vibrant as ever, serving excellent fresh beef burgers, addictive fries, and hand-dipped milkshakes. The '50s have come and gone, but Dick's remains over six decades later, proving that simplicity and good food are the keys to longevity.

Dick's is a drive-in. There are multiple locations around town and only one has indoor seating. It's the sort of drive-in where you park your car and walk up to the window to order and pay. General manager Ken Frazier told me, "Dick's has always been a walk-up. Originally there were three separate lines, one for shakes and ice cream, one for burgers and soft drinks, and one for fries." In the '60s, Dick's streamlined the system selling, all products at all windows. At the 45th Street location, there's no seating anywhere and Maria, the longtime manager, told me, "In the summertime, people bring picnic tables and chairs and set up in the parking lot. It's really cute."

The first Dick's was built in 1954 in the Wallingford neighborhood of Seattle just west of the University of Washington. On my first visit to the popular burger stand, I arrived fifteen minutes before opening to find workers inside scurrying to ready the griddle and cook the fries. There was no one in the parking lot. But within five minutes a hungry mob had gathered. When the first window called, "May I take your order?" I counted forty-five people waiting to get their "Dick's Fix," a phrase a regular left me with.

The efficiency of Dick's is mind-boggling. Twenty-four employees, all wearing crisp paper caps and clean aprons, are set to repetitive tasks, such as weighing the fresh ice cream that goes into the shakes or prepping the buns with their secret sauce.

The menu is simple—hamburgers, cheeseburgers, fries, shakes, and soda. The thin patties of fresh beef are delivered to all locations in the chain every morning. The burgers, cooked on a flattop griddle, can be ordered plain or as the preferred Dick's Deluxe. The Deluxe comes with two quarter-pound patties, cheese, lettuce, mayo, and their special chopped pickle and mustard sauce. The sauce, a tangy, sweet, and creamy proprietary blend, should not be missed. All burgers are served on the perfect white squishy bun wrapped in waxed paper.

If you love fries, you'll be in french fry heaven at Dick's. The fries are lightly greasy, thin, and fresh, not frozen. The shakes, also incredible, only come in the three classic flavors of chocolate, vanilla, and strawberry.

If you ask for extra sauce for your burger or ketchup for the fries, you'll get a little serving in a small condiment cup, but expect to pay. Ketchup and other condiments are five cents extra and the reason is mostly environmental, not financial. "We feel that the cup is much nicer to use for dipping than some foil pouch," Ken explained, "and by charging a nominal amount we feel we are minimizing waste." Gotta love a burger joint with a conscience.

The people of Seattle love Dick's. I was hard-pressed to find a carnivore that didn't frequent the place. Bill Gates visits frequently. "Last week he had a Deluxe, fries, and a shake," Maria told me. Even Sir Mix-A-Lot, Grammy Award winner and Seattle native, immortalized the Broadway location in his first hit song. In the lyrics, his posse skips Taco Bell for Dick's. The truth is, if there were more places like Dick's, serving wholesome, fast food, we'd all be avoiding those other corporate burgers.

EASTSIDE BIG TOM

2023 East 4th Ave | Olympia, WA 98506 | 360-357-4852
Mon–Sat 10 am–8 pm | Sun 11 am–6:30 pm | www.eastsidebigtoms.com

When I first found Big Tom fourteen years ago, it could easily be described the most nondescript burger stand in America. Even today, the large BIG TOM is the only added flourish to this historic burger joint. If it were not for the large menu on the street side of the building, you'd think you had arrived at a construction trailer that had been haphazardly dumped in a parking lot. But the long lines of cars on each side of the structure are a hint that something good is happening inside. Indeed there is. Big Tom daily sells over five hundred fresh thin-patty wonders to loyal drive-up customers. But that's not all. Big Tom's trademarked "Goop" is dispensed here, a salad-type dressing that, in varying forms, is a Pacific Northwest mainstay for burgers.

"Goop is essentially mayo, mustard, and pickle relish with a secret salad dressing mixed in," longtime owner Chuck Fritsch told me. "What's the saying? 'If I told you I'd have to kill you'?" he said with a laugh. "It's really not a big secret," he admitted, "But if you are not making it in huge batches it doesn't taste the same." I can see why someone might want to copy the recipe—the taste is addictive. Besides adorning the Big Tom special double-double, Goop is also offered as a dip for the tater tots and fries. What could be more appealing or more American than "Tots 'n' Goop"?

In 1948, Millie and Russ Eagan opened a burger stand east of downtown Olympia and called it (coincidentally) In and Out. Millie took her inspiration for a drive-thru from a popular motor court across the street. For the original stand, the Eagans relocated a minuscule barbershop from another part of town. Since then, the stand has been rebuilt and changed names more than once, but has always been on the same spot. Through the decades the Eagans expanded to nine stands in and around Olympia, but today only one remains.

Big Tom was the son of Millie and Russ Eagan. Overweight and inventive, he was known to help himself at the griddle and created a large burger that was not on the menu. Today, it's a best seller at the burger stand that bears his name, a double meat, double cheeseburger with lettuce, tomato, chopped onion, and the famous Goop. Be prepared for the inevitable dripping Goop as you take your first bite. Chuck told me, "We are known for making a sloppy burger." Chuck buys fresh ground 18 percent fat thin patties for the burgers at Big Tom. They are cooked on a flattop griddle that is usually filled to capacity with the sputtering patties.

The interior of Big Tom, which is all kitchen, is a lesson in functionality. An astounding amount of prep and cooking is done in the 288 square feet that is populated by up to seven employees at peak times. Every square inch is utilized—think submarine galley.

Chuck started working at the tiny burger stand in the '50s when he was fifteen years old peeling potatoes. "It was warm and dry and sitting in a cubicle did not appeal to me," Chuck said about his longevity in the business.

Chuck has retired from day-to-day at Big Tom and has almost completed turning the business over to his son, Michael, who literally grew up in the stand. Chuck once pointed to a small space between the employee bathroom and slop sink. "We had the crib right there." Michael jokingly describes the transition as "indentured servitude," but joking aside has managed to grow the business to almost two times since he took the reins. He told me, "I never thought I'd wrap myself around a hamburger joint," but he seems to enjoy the life.

As an owner, Michael began a transformation of the drive-up business by first adding a small seating area. That area grew, tables have been added as well as a separate ice-cream stand across the parking lot. There's also a curious dinosaur collection building and when I asked Michael why, he changed his voice to that of a child and said, "I want to go to the place with the dinosaurs!" He told me people pose with the enormous triceratops every day. Michael also added color panels to the roof of the burger stand to supply hot water, and was responsible for the new, oversized BIG TOM sign. He said of the sign, "I'm sure we broke some sort of city code." Michael plans to run the burger stand for a long time, or as he put it, "At least until I reach Dad's age."

GOOP SAUCE

Goop is a sauce that has made its way onto many burgers in the Pacific Northwest, especially the older-style classic burgers. All of the Goop I've had tastes pretty much the same, and all are protected by their respective burger institutions and contain highly secret ingredients. But to legitimately call your sauce Goop, you need to be Chuck Fritsch at Eastside Big Tom in Olympia, Washington. That's because Chuck has trademarked the name and arguably makes some of the best Goop in the area.

I can see why he keeps his recipe under wraps—Goop is addictive. It adorns not only the burgers at Big Tom, but the fries and tater tots as well (tots 'n' Goop = heaven). I once asked Chuck for the recipe, and he said, "What's the saying? If I told you I'd have to kill you?" So he didn't give me the recipe. But I've done some testing and I think I've come pretty close. When I wrote this up years ago, I read it back to myself and imagined Chuck laughing.

Makes enough for 12 quarter-pound (125 g) burgers

¼ cup (125 mL) mayonnaise

¼ cup (60 mL) Miracle Whip

2 tablespoons (30 mL) sweet relish

3 tablespoons (45 mL) yellow mustard

1. Whisk mayonnaise, Miracle Whip, relish, and mustard in a bowl and serve on your favorite burgers. The color should resemble a 1971 Curious Yellow Plymouth Barracuda.

2. Tell your friends it's not the real thing but pretty damn close.

RED MILL BURGERS

312 North 67th St | Seattle, WA 98193 | 206-783-6362 | Tues–Sat 11 am–9 am
Sun 12 pm–8 pm | Mon Closed | www.redmillburgers.com

Red Mill is easily one of the most talked about and awarded burger joint in the Seattle area. They were also on *GQ* magazine's now-famous "20 Burgers You Must Eat Before You Die" list way back in 2006. And there's good reason for this—the burgers are amazing. But at Red Mill it's not only about great tasting food. The staff is young, the vibe is totally upbeat and you feel like you are at a party, not just a burger joint. And it's very likely that the Rolling Stones will be turned up loud no matter what time of the day it is. "We are HUMONGOUS Stones fans," general manager and family member Michael Shepherd told me. There's really not much better than big classic burgers and rock music.

But the restaurant has an odd history. The Phinney Ridge location (there are now two others) was not the original. Nor is there any ownership connection to the former business, which shuttered in 1967 and was located miles away near downtown in the Capitol Hill neighborhood. The Red Mill Ice Creamery & Sandwich Shop opened in 1937 and closed thirty years later. Before the diner closed two of the Shepherd sisters were waitresses at the restaurant. Then twenty-seven years after Red Mill shut down siblings John and Babe Shepherd got the idea to reopen the beloved diner. "We were all sick of what we were doing," Michael told me, "so we brought it back." They

obtained permission to use the name from the original owner and Red Mill Burgers reopened on December 20th, 1994, five days before Christmas. "We opened it with fifty bucks in our pockets," Michael told me, "so there were no gifts that year—everyone got T-shirts!"

The tiny kitchen is a model of burger efficiency. It's staffed mostly by energetic teenagers who each have a role—one on the register, one makes shakes, one on the fryer, and so on, and the system works incredibly well. The first time I visited 18-year-old Kate, with her hair dyed a glorious bubble gum pink, barely broke a sweat as she

the Double Bacon Deluxe with Cheese, which gets two patties, two slices of crispy bacon, american cheese, red onion, green leaf lettuce, tomato, pickles, and a housemade secret sauce called Mill Sauce. Although close in profile, the smoky mayo (as a sign under the menu clearly states) is not Thousand Island dressing. And don't miss Babe's Onion Rings, truly amazing, especially when dipped in Mill Sauce.

One of the most notable items at first glance into the kitchen is the impressive tower of bacon sitting on the flattop. Every morning, Red Mill cooks forty-five pounds of bacon for the burgers and BLTs, then the strips are stacked in an orderly, crisscross fashion so that the tower won't topple (think Jenga).

The restaurant is hard to miss if you are driving north on Phinney Ave. The main thoroughfare makes a hard left and a right, as if the road was built around something. In the bend sits Red Mill in a very visible and equally vulnerable location. Recently the Shepherd family had a thick concrete barrier installed in the street and I knew exactly why. "Over twenty-three years we've only been hit ten times," Michael told me, "all by drunks at 2 a.m."

managed the endless amounts of burger orders coming in. Kate would transfer cooked patties from the flame grill to buns that had already been prepped with condiments, which sit on the flattop next to the flame grill. On a busy Saturday Red Mill can move over 600 burgers.

Red Mill uses fresh ground quarter-pound patties that are thin and cook super-fast on the flame grill. It seems the most popular burger is

AMERICAN LEGION POST #67

133 North Main St | Lake Mills, WI 53551
Open Fridays Only, May–Oct, 10 am–8 pm

I had to make a special trip to Lake Mills, Wisconsin, for a hamburger and timing was everything. When I discovered that this eighty-five-year-old burger stand is only open on Fridays in the summer, the planning began. I had only twenty-three Fridays to choose from.

The American Legion Post #67 Hamburger Stand is a gem. It's wedged between two larger buildings in the heart of downtown Lake Mills and has been there since 1950. For twenty-four years before that, the American Legion had a portable stand set up across the street. The stand today is walk-up service only with a severely limited menu, my kinda place. Hamburgers, cheeseburgers, and sodas are all you can spend your money on (with the exception of a must-have T-shirt that depicts a burger, or "slider," midway down a playground slide). Your only option for condiments is with or without onions. Ketchup and mustard are available on an old typewriter table on the sidewalk. "The most popular burger is one 'with,'" stand operator Randy told me, which is a burger with stewed onions. Typical for an old-time stand,

cheese takes a back seat and makes up only a third of all burgers ordered.

I squeezed into the tiny stand while my burger was being made and immediately recognized a cooking method that is rapidly disappearing throughout the Midwest—the deep-fried burger. That's right, the one-fifth-pound burgers at Post #67 are deep-fried in a huge, shallow tank filled with canola oil. The fresh pattied meat comes in every Friday from

Glenn's Market in nearby Watertown and over 2,500 burgers are plopped in the hot oil on a busy day. Not too long ago the tank was filled with rendered lard and for health reasons they have switched to canola. These burgers are great but I can only imagine how sublime a lardburger must have been.

The first went down fast so I ordered another. The hot oil soaks the soft white squishy bun and becomes a condiment to the peppery burger. If you ask for cheese, a slice is placed on the bottom half of the bun so the hot oil from the burger melts it on contact.

The stand is run by a rotating crew of five, members of the American Legion Post #67 just down the street. Most of the crew members are in their seventies and eighties; each is a veteran who served in Korea or Vietnam. They have a great system worked out for delivering hot and tasty burgers to waiting customers. Someone takes your order at the tiny window and writes a code on a paper bag. The bag is passed back to another who shouts out the order. The cook pulls a burger out of the oil and hands it to another vet, who puts it onto a bun and wraps it up. The wrapped burger is then slid to the bag man who matches the wrapped burger to the code on the bag. When things heat up and the orders start pouring in, this system hums like a well-oiled machine (pun intended).

There was an awesome note near the tank of oil and onions that read, "On the first, third, and fifth Fridays take a minimum of fifty burgers to Post 67 for bingo at 7:30 p.m." What a perk for those bingo players!

Everyone seems to have a great time on their shift and no one minds that they are not getting paid. Most of the volunteers are retired military and are compensated in burgers and beer. Not the kind of beer you take home, the kind you enjoy on the job. Intrigued, I asked past Commander Don Hein, "When does the drinking start?" He told me bluntly, "Whenever we start working." I gathered from the other vets hard at work that in most cases they are way too busy bagging burgers to drink themselves into oblivion. And as Don pointed out, "You really can't come down here and get hammered."

ANCHOR BAR

413 Tower Ave | Superior, WI 54880 | 715-394-9747 | Sun–Thurs 11 am–2 am
Fri & Sat 11 am–2:30 am | www.anchorbarandgrill.com

Turn off your cell phone, grab a pitcher of beer, and disappear into the Anchor Bar for a few hours. You'll thank me later.

That's the type of place the Anchor is—a very comfortable, dark bar that is blanketed in the most amazing collection of nautical ephemera that you will find anywhere. The stuff is everywhere. Floor, walls, ceiling. "We have more stuff in the basement but there's no room to put it up," Adam Anderson, part owner and the son of the man that opened the place, told me. "It's like a museum in here." Superior, Wisconsin, is a shipping town and a bar like the Anchor fits right in.

Grab the table just inside the door on the right if you can. "We call that the library," Adam said of the table, which is actually a tiny, semi-private nook lined with books, board games, and more than one globe. Sitting here, separate from the rest of the bar, you actually feel as though you are enjoying the captain's quarters on a tall ship.

The centerpiece of the bar is a lifebuoy from the famous SS *Edmund Fitzgerald*, a Great Lakes freighter that met its demise one cold winter night in 1975. The tragic event was popularized in a song by Gordon Lightfoot, "The Wreck of the *Edmund Fitzgerald*." A violent storm and a failed radar caused the ship to sink taking with it twenty-nine crewmembers who were never found. "There's a group that comes

in every year on the anniversary to toast the dead," Adam told me.

Adam's dad, Tom, worked at the Elk's Club in town and bought the bar when he heard it was for sale. His first move was to add food to the menu and started serving burgers. He and his manager of almost forty years collected from garage sales over the years the many rope nets, ships gauges, running lights, portholes, and shipping photos that make up the decor. That manager, Bean

Pritty, continues to run the Anchor with Tom's sons, Adam and Aaron. Tom passed away in 2008 and Adam decided to move back home and leave his job as a successful sous-chef near Minneapolis to run the Anchor. Thanks to the dedication of Bean Pritty, in Adam's words, "The place kinda runs itself. If I'm here I'm just in her way."

There are more than a few burger options at the Anchor, seventeen to be exact. All start with a griddled, hand-formed, six-ounce patty made from fresh ground 83/17 chuck. The beef comes to the bar from a local butcher and Adam told me, "If I run low during the day, they'll bring us more." Most of the burgers sound pretty wacky but good (like the "Sour Cream and Mushroom" or the "Oliveburger,"

the most popular). I opted for another favorite, the "Cashewburger," topped with swiss cheese and a copious amount of whole, roasted, salted cashews that have been warmed on the griddle. A young grillperson named Tom (who incidentally is named after the former owner and is the son of Tom's best friend) explained, "They get a little softer when you put them on the grill." Naturally, the idea for the Cashewburger was born over beers. According to Adam, "My dad liked cashews so he put them on a burger one day." When a friend asked why, Tom responded, "Don't you like cashews?" The texture of the Cashewburger is unusual but amazing. No other condiments are necessary. The grease from the burger mixes with the chunky nuts and the swiss cheese creating a salty, cheesy, beefy flavor profile. And hey, cashews are good for you! The fries are also really good. There's a french fry press next to the deep fryer and when an order, comes in the grillperson grabs a potato, slams it through the press and tosses the fries in the hot oil. The fries are that fresh.

There are a few easy-drinking beers on tap (like Keystone Light and the local beer, Grain Belt) that can be purchased by the pitcher (three-dollar pitchers all day Monday) but don't miss the Anchor Bar's amazing selection of microbrews. There are over ninety flavors to choose from. "That's our dessert menu," Adam joked, pointing to a box of candy bars behind the bar.

"It's a likable dive," a longtime regular named John told me sitting at the bar. "It doesn't pretend to be anything that it isn't."

BUD WILLMAN'S LUNCH

1901 Washington St | Manitowoc, WI 54220
920-684-0005 | Mon–Sat 7 am–8 pm | Sun 7 am–7 pm

It really looks like nothing more than a plumbing supply store from the outside, even though letters on the side of the building give a major clue as to what is going on inside. But step into this beige box to find a gleaming, functional diner filled with happy regulars, and Jan Willman working hard at the flattop.

It's often quiet at Willman's with customers, spread around the counters, stools, tables, and booths, focused on eating. The only sounds come from the exhaust fan, the burgers sizzling on the flattop and from Jan, who is there holding court with his quick wit.

"People from out of town always ask 'Can I have a plate?'" second-generation owner Jan said of his waxed paper–wrapped burgers that are wrapped whether you are eating in or leaving. "No plate. That's just the way it has always been."

The "small" cheeseburger is like a slider, a three-ounce patty served on a classic, locally made, hand-sliced bun. The large burger is the way to go, where Jan presses two of the three-ounce wads

"My dad always said 'Make 'em like you are making your best one,'" Jan told me. "He never liked to do things half-assed." Jan's father Bud Willman opened his burger restaurant in 1957 after working at the locally favorite (and now shuttered) Trio Lunch. "That's where he learned to squish the onions into the burger." The original location of Bud Willman's was on the corner a bar a block away, but in 1977 he moved to the current location, formerly a gas station.

Written on the side of the building by the front door it says OPEN AM. The space in between is clearly missing a digit and some important information. Jan told me, "A customer walked in one day with the '5' in his hand and said 'You're not open at 5 a.m. anymore.'" True, the days of predawn opening is over and

together and serves it on a larger bun they call a "hard roll" (which is actually very soft and pillowy). The incredible flavor in a Willman's burger in part comes from the thin sliced onion that is pressed into the patty on the flattop, much like the fried onion burgers of Oklahoma. The burger also gets the Wisconsin treatment where the heel of the bun receives a generous slather of local butter before the ketchup, mustard, and pickle go on.

Willman's now opens at the more reasonable hour of 7 a.m.

Jan has been working at Willman's since he was twelve where he started as a dishwasher. In 1988, Bud passed away and Jan became the owner. He told me his dad often imparted wisdom. "He always said it's five percent skill and ninety-five percent bullshit." Well it looks like Jan has got it down, one hundred percent.

Owner Scott Prescher

CHARCOAL INN SOUTH

1313 South 8th St | Sheboygan, WI 53081 | 920-458-6988
Sun & Mon Closed | Tues–Fri 6 am–8 pm | Sat 6 am–7 pm
www.charcoalinn.com

I was on the road in eastern Wisconsin doing research for the next burger book when a fan from Sheboygan messaged me on Instagram. I take all fan recommendations very seriously and pointed my rental car in the direction of Charcoal Inn South, home of a burger that combines a brat with a beef patty.

Sheboygan is known far and wide for bratwurst, not burgers. So much so that for over sixty years Sheboygan has thrown a multiday party for the beloved sausage called Brat Days (which was cancelled for twelve years from 1966 to 1978 for excessive rowdiness). For those not well versed in the excellent foods of Wisconsin, the bratwurst is a thick pork sausage of German decent.

Charcoal Inn started its life as the Tastee Ice Cream Shoppe in 1940. At some point the

essence of a backyard barbecue. It's an aroma that screams comfort food.

The big seller here is the Charcoal Inn Sandwich "works." The grillperson first takes a fresh bratwurst, splits it down the middle and pulls the casing off. It's tossed on the grill next to a burger patty. The two meet a locally made, hand-sliced hard roll (which is actually pillowy soft) which has been toasted on the flame grill. "Works" adds spicy mustard, ketchup pickles, sliced rings of raw onion, and, true to Wisconsin burgers, a big smear of soft butter. You wanted cheese with that? You just waved your tourist flag. No self-respecting Sheboygan native would ever get cheese on a bratwurst. Of course no problem on a burger, which Charcoal Inn sells, too. The brats and fresh beef come in fresh daily from Miesdfeld's Market, an enormous local butcher shop and meat emporium.

The staff at Charcoal Inn is very friendly and I hope you get to meet manager Jori who has been at the restaurant forever. She told me, "When he's not here [Scott] I've been here the longest!" I forgot her name when I was ordering a burger once and that upset her. She twisted up her face and joked, "Would you like your burger cooked or raw?"

I pointed out to Scott once that I was impressed by all of the written accolades on the walls of the dining room, everything from the *Chicago Tribune* to *Gourmet* magazine. He acknowledged, "We have a unique thing going here in Sheboygan," and added, "It's been really good to us, but probably because we haven't changed a thing since we opened."

place became Eddie's Lunch, then Charcoal Inn around 1973. The owner was struggling financially with the place and it ended up in foreclosure. Along came Roger Prescher and his son, Scott, who bought the business in a sheriffs sale on the court house steps in 1984. "We decided to take an adventure," Scott told me. Both quit their full time jobs and never looked back.

Charcoal Inn has a great long counter that offers excellent views of the burgers and brats being cooked. Like Mickey Lu's up in Marinette, Charcoal Inn cooks all of their burgers over a charcoal flame grill in full view behind the counter. Because of the indoor charcoal grill, the burger has the unmistakable smoky

DOTTY DUMPLING'S DOWRY

317 North Frances St | Madison, WI 53703 | 608-259-0000
Tues–Thurs 11 am–11 pm | Fri & Sat 11 am–12 am | Sun & Mon 11 am–10 pm
www.dottydumplingsdowry.com

Dotty's is in its fifth location in over thirty-five years. "Goddamn eminent domain was the reason for the last move," Jeff Stanley mumbled when I asked him about the moves. It seems the latest incarnation of Dotty's is working for him, though. The exterior resembles a working-class Irish pub complete with black paint, small-paned windows, and the bar's name in gold. The interior is impressive—quality-crafted dark wood, large inviting bar, and an astounding collection of model aircraft dangling from the ceiling. There is even an eight-foot scale model of the Hindenburg positioned over the grill area.

Curiously, Dotty's was not born in Madison. And it also was not at first a burger joint. Jeff opened a clothing and jewelry shop called Dotty Dumpling's Dowry in Des Moines, Iowa, in 1969. Within a few years, he turned the gift shop into a burger joint, then made the move to Madison in 1974. The first reincarnation of Dotty's in Madison was a ten-stool burger counter.

Friend and columnist Doug Moe, who once referred to Jeff as "The Hamburger King of Madison" directed me to Dotty's. Jeff's bigger-than-life persona is infectious, and he is a well-liked underdog around town. He is damn proud to hold the title of king and knows his burgers. The first time I walked into Dotty's, Jeff announced without warning, "Hey, everybody! This is the guy who made that hamburger film!" Today, Stanley's daughter, Rachael, runs Dotty's and in keeping with tradition has been dubbed "Hamburger Princess."

"We only use the highest-quality ingredients," Jeff said as I took a big swig from my beer. His burgers are made from six ounces of fresh ground chuck, pattied in-house. They are grilled on an open flame in plain sight of all customers and placed on specially made local buns that have been warmed and buttered. A Dotty's grillman once explained, "Jeff requests that the buns are not cooked fully so they remain soft."

This attention to detail and Jeff's public persona have put Dotty's on the top of local hamburger polls for decades (over thirty "Best Of" accolades locally alone). Being a stone's throw from the University of Wisconsin's Kohl Center and Camp Randall Stadium doesn't hurt either.

The name Dotty Dumpling's Dowry comes from an Arthur Conan Doyle short story, the same writer who brought us Sherlock Holmes. Dotty's menu is extensive, including an ostrich dish and the bar has an impressive twenty-four beers on tap. And skip the fries and make sure to get Dotty's excellent deep-fried cheese curds—they are indeed a necessary evil.

JOE ROUER'S BAR

E1098 Co Rd X | Luxemburg, WI 54217
920-866-2585 | Tues–Sun 11 am–8 pm | Closed Mon

The first thing you smell when you get out of the car at Joe Rouer's Bar is cow manure. "Smells like money!" local burger expert and good friend Todd McIlwee said out loud. The bar/restaurant is at a country crossroads surrounded by miles of dairy farms. The spartan exterior of Joe Rouer's was only the beginning of an unforgettable burger experience and if it weren't for the beer neon in the windows, you wouldn't even know you were walking into a bar.

We had arrived at 5 p.m. to beat the dinner crowd only to walk into the peak of "supper"—the place was packed. Like the exterior, the interior is a lesson in restraint. Ultraclean and organized this place is no broken-in dive. The enormous horseshoe bar sheathed in woodgrain Formica and ringed with substantial barstools is the centerpiece of the restaurant. A sea of other high tops, barstools, and tables fill out the rest of the dining room, and there's even an outdoor patio so you can, as someone at the bar pointed out, "take in the fine Wisconsin dairy breezes."

The bar has been in the same family since 1952 when Joe and Helen Rouer opened a standing-room only bar. "There used to be five bars in Duvall," great-grandson Mike Bultman Jr. told me, and originally Joe's bar was across the street. The place burned to the ground in 1990 and was closed for a year to rebuild at

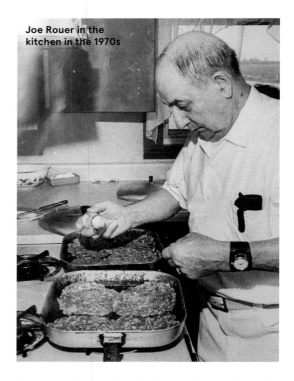

Joe Rouer in the kitchen in the 1970s

the current location. "That was devastating for a lot of people," Mike told me. Today, the bar is owned by Joe's grandson Michael Bultman (Mike's dad), who has owned the place since he was eighteen.

The original location was always closed on Fridays to not compete with the other bars that had Fish Fry Fridays, a very important food tradition all over Wisconsin. Mike explained, Joe and Helen would patronize other places on Fridays.

water to the height of the burger and covered. "That's to melt the cheese," Mike explained, but there's some crazy science going on here where sure, the cheese melts, but the combination of rendered beef fat, water, and seasoned salt definitely creates a sort of beef broth in which the burger marinates.

Mike explained that at Joe Rouer's there's ". . . no lettuce and tomato or anything like that." And there shouldn't be. When you get right down to it a burger should be all about the beef. The burger at Joe Rouer's is moist and exploding with beefy essence with the onions rounding out the intense but simple flavor profile. It is as honest as a burger can and should be, the perfect comfort food.

Former defensive tackle for the Packers Gilbert "The Gravedigger" Brown is a known burger lover and has been spotted at the bar more than once. Mike told me, "He gets a triple, a double, and a single."

This burger blew me away. It may have been the simplicity of elements, it could have been the low expectations after seeing the nondescript exterior of the farmland watering hole, or it could have been because this really is a great burger. I applaud the family that maintains tradition, especially when it's in the form of a truly tasty burger experience that makes its regulars happy.

Joe was always in the kitchen, and Helen was always bartending. Helen is fondly remembered as a true character, and as her grandson pointed out, "She liked her Kessler's [whiskey] and smoked Pall Malls. She was hardcore." Today, menu options have expanded since the early days, but you are here for the burger. "We didn't have anything but burgers and chips for years," Mike Jr told me, "and we didn't even have prices or a menu until the late 1980s." Your burger choices are with or without onions. Get the onions. They are cooked until just translucent and perfect.

It's the method and the beef that make this burger great. Since the beginning, the burgers have been cooked in skillets on a stovetop and nothing has changed. Hand-formed patties that are somewhere around a quarter pound ("leaning toward one-third pound," Mike pointed out) are cooked, flipped then the pan is filled with

KEWPEE SANDWICH SHOP

520 Wisconsin Ave | Racine, WI 53403
262-634-9601 | Mon–Fri 7 am–6 pm | Sat 7 am–5 pm | Closed Sun

At one time, Kewpee Hotel Hamburgs were all over the Upper Midwest. The first Kewpee opened in Flint, Michigan, and was one of the first hamburger chains in America. Like many of the great burger chains of the '30s and '40s, Kewpee downsized during the Great Depression and saw further decline as the owners experimented with franchising. Today, only five Kewpees in three states remain and are all privately owned. The Racine location is the sole surviving Kewpee in the Dairy State.

On my first visit to Kewpee, I sat at one of the low horseshoe counters and was happy to see that at 10 a.m. the griddle was already filled with burgers. The place is huge and could easily seat fifty people. This version of the restaurant is relatively new, but over the last century the building has been replaced three times.

Kewpee does not use a patty machine like its sister restaurant in Lima, Ohio. In fact, there are very few similarities between the two Kewpees. Owner and lead grillperson Rick Buehrens told me, "Here, you'll get a totally different burger than at the Ohio Kewpees." For starters, Rick has eschewed the original Kewpee method of forming square patties in favor of the even more traditional method of smashing balls of beef. He uses an ice-cream scoop to form loose balls of fresh ground beef

and can produce six balls to the pound. In the morning, trays are filled with the balls and kept cold in the back. During a busy rush, Rick will take an entire tray, dump it onto the large flattop griddle, then sort and smash the mess into perfect patties.

An entirely separate flattop nearby is used to toast the buns. Ask for a cheeseburger and watch what happens. Rick does not sully the burger side of the griddle with cheese. Instead he'll toss a cold slice on the left side of the flattop for a few seconds to melt. Like magic, the cheese doesn't stick to the surface (or the spatula) and is transferred smoothly to your cheeseburger.

The burger options at Kewpee are basic—a single or double, with or without cheese, served on locally made, soft white buns. A burger with everything has pickle, chopped onion, mustard, and ketchup. I couldn't help but notice that the ketchup was clearly more prominent than the mustard. "That's based on what customers were telling me," Rick explained. "It seems like I put less mustard on these days."

Rick should know about changing tastes over time. He started working at Kewpee in 1976 as a dishwasher and became the owner after twenty-seven years of sweat equity.

While waiting for your burgers, make sure to check out the enormous display case that contains hundreds of vintage Kewpie dolls of all shapes, sizes, and colors. The inspiration for the restaurant's name came from the popular turn-of-the-century doll. The display lends a touch of history to an otherwise modern diner. Though the space has been updated, the burger has remained faithful to its roots and is made with the freshest ingredients. Sink your teeth into a classic and slip back in time with a Kewpee burger.

MICKEY-LU BAR-B-Q

1710 Marinette Ave | Marinette, WI 54143 | 715-735-7721 | Tues–Thurs 9 am–10 pm
Fri & Sat 9 am–11:30 pm | Sun 11 am–10 pm | Closed Mon

Mickey-Lu is way north in Wisconsin, only minutes from the Michigan Upper Peninsula on Highway 41. All the tourists and trucks have to drive past the restaurant because it's the only road north to Canada. With its enormous signage and red-and-white color scheme it would be impossible not to stop.

Much like walking in to the Apple Pan in LA or Shady Glen in Connecticut, the place seems almost too period-specific in decor to be real. It's an old-school burger counter with boomerang Formica and doo-wop pouring out of the original 1958 Seberg "stereo" juke. It's as if time stopped but the burgers kept coming. Everything here is original from opening day 1942, with the sole exception being the "new" curtains.

Owner Chuck Finnesy

First time I walked into Mickey-Lu, I spotted owner Chuck Finnessy right away and said, "How ya doing?" He quickly responded, "Oh, just trying to look busy!" And busy he was. Chuck runs the show at Mickey-Lu and works the unique indoor charcoal grill just behind the counter. Grab one of the stools directly in front of the flames, a front row seat to the action. Here you can also watch Chuck work at lightning speed to get the burgers out. Watch as Chuck constantly reaches into the grill, flames and all, to retrieve cooked patties. He joked, "I was married for thirty years—my tolerance for pain is *very* high."

Chuck grinds and patties all of his burgers daily at the restaurant. I asked what size the thin patties were and he said, "All I know is that they cook fast." They look to be around one-fifth-pound. The burgers cook fast because they are over

a direct flame from an indoor charcoal grill. Chuck uses the same briquets you might use in your backyard Weber so the flames envelop the patty and cook it in seconds. Because of this Chuck has to keep a constant eye on progress or end up with a grease fire situation. At one point while he was talking with me (my fault), a waitress asked, "Are you burning that?" pointing toward the grill, "No just scorching," Chuck quipped.

The burger arrives at your counter spot on a thin piece of waxed paper and frankly doesn't look like much. A cheeseburger with "The Works" is mustard, ketchup, pickles, onion, and a pat of butter, served on a local, small Zemal roll that has been warmed on the grill. The sloppy mix of flavors and textures, and the smokiness from the grill, is mind-blowing . . . and then the butter hits you. You'll need a second one ASAP.

The all-female staff has all been there for over a decade or more and know just about everyone who walks in. On a busy day the restaurant can serve up to 1,300 burgers, which is amazing because Chuck is only cooking eight burgers at a time on the tiny grill.

The restaurant was opened in 1942 by Mickey Lu Brodinski. "It's a French name," Chuck joked. He is only the third owner in the seventy-six-year history of the restaurant and has been there every day since he bought in 1988. "You don't have to be a genius to run a restaurant," Chuck told me, "you just have to be there."

NITE OWL ICE CREAM PARLOUR & SANDWICH SHOPPE

830 E Layton Ave | Milwaukee, WI 53207 | 414-483-2524
Sun & Mon Closed | Tues–Sat 11 am–6 pm

Inside and out, the Nite Owl feels like an authentic version of Al's Diner in the '70s sitcom *Happy Days*. I almost expected to find Ralph and Potsie in a booth, Fonzie at the juke, and Al sticking his head out of the kitchen. The show was famously set in Milwaukee so I wonder where the inspiration came from . . .

But the Nite Owl predates the plot in *Happy Days* by about a decade and opened in 1948. Ralph Roepke was a butcher and sold beef to a custard stand across the street from the Milwaukee airport called Bob's Airport Custard. He saw the owner struggling with the business and offered to buy the place. He changed the name to Roepke's Airport Custard and then eventually rebuilt the entire restaurant in 1954 and called it Nite Owl. The place was so named because they would stay open until 3 a.m. (Funny side note: Today no one sees the Nite Owl at night because it actually closes before

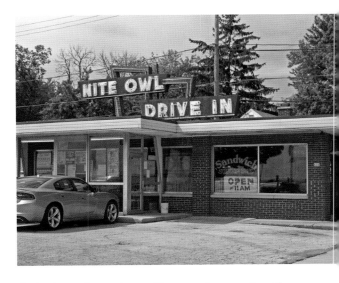

dark. Sometimes they will even close earlier if they run out of beef.)

Ralph's sons, John and William, continued the family burger tradition and took over Nite Owl after him. Today, John still works in the kitchen, firmly planted daily in front of the

griddle, a spot he has occupied for almost sixty years. John's son Chris represents the third generation of the Roepke family at Nite Owl and has worked at the restaurant since he was sixteen. Chris plans to keep the Nite Owl humming for decades to come and told me, "If I work until I'm seventy we will have been open one hundred years—that's my goal."

The restaurant is split in two, with one half used for takeout and the other a dining room with booths, tables, and black-and-white checker linoleum flooring. The tiny kitchen is in the center to service both sides. There's no table service on the dining room side. To place an order, head for the order counter to the left as you walk in the door (look for the menu overhead). Then look for a seat and wait for your order.

The patties at Nite Owl are very large and made from fresh beef Nite Owl gets every day. "The size varies since they are handmade," Chris explained. The patties are supposed to be around one-third of a pound but mine, even after cooking, was closer to a half pound. It was definitively a two-fister that could not be eaten with one hand. Amazingly the tiny diner can go through over six hundred patties on a busy day.

The burger to get is the cheeseburger, works. This includes fried onions, ketchup, mustard, and pickles. It's cooked on a flattop and served on a wide, butter-soaked, toasted bun. It's a truly beefy burger with loads of cheese that is also infused with the unmistakable flavor of decades of onions cooked on a seasoned griddle. Even if you are dining in, the burgers are served wrapped in paper—no plates are offered.

Directly across the street from Nite Owl is the entrance to Milwaukee International Airport's general aviation, i.e. where the private jets land. "We get quite a few pilots pilots that purposely refuel at MKE so they can get a burger," Chis told me. If I were a pilot, I would most definitely plan the same. Arguably one of their most famous fly-in customers was a pre-presidential Donald Trump. "He ate here in the '90s, came over from the terminal," Chris told me, and added, "But he left no tip! We are still a little bitter about that." And his dad offered, from his spot at the griddle, "That's why he's got all that money!"

PETE'S HAMBURGERS

118 Blackhawk Ave | Prairie du Chien, WI 53821 | No Phone
Open Mid-April through Mid-October | Fri & Sat 11 am–9 pm | Sun 11 am–7 pm
Closed Mon–Thurs | www.peteshamburgers.com

"Don't tell Mom we stopped here," I overheard a woman say to her brother. When I asked why, she told me, "We are heading to our family reunion." That's the kind of place Pete's is—a 109-year-old institution that makes you want to stop, even though you shouldn't. The draw is too great, the burgers amazing.

Pete's is a tiny, neat burger stand right in the center of the quaint southwestern Wisconsin town of Prairie du Chien. Little has changed at Pete's in the last century, except for the size of the place, which has gone from very small to small. "In 1909, Pete Gokey started selling burgers from a cart at fairs and circuses," his granddaughter Colleen explained. He then set up a table to sell burgers on a corner only a few feet from where the stand now sits. Colleen is one of many Gokeys that work at Pete's, which is still owned and operated by the Gokey family. The tiny stand is filled with Gokeys. When I was there great-grandson Patrick Gokey was working the griddle.

The burgers at Pete's are not your standard American hamburger. A visit to Pete's is a must because the burgers at Pete's are cooked in a way that I've never seen anywhere else. They are boiled. I know that sounds strange, but local hamburger expert and friend Todd McIlwee told me once, "I like to think of them as 'poached.'" And

poached they are. Most have never had a burger quite like this.

A large, flat, high-lipped griddle or "tank" is filled with about an inch of water and a pile of quarter-pound balls of beef are dumped into the tank. In the center sits a mountain of thinly sliced onion, stewing in the hot water. The beef balls are pressed into patties that bob in the water like little boats and are flipped and ready in fifteen minutes. The griddle can hold up to seventy patties and remains completely silent as the patties boil, bubble, and bob. I can only imagine that if

★ 399 ★

this had been a standard griddle with that many burgers on it and no water, it would be a loud, sizzling mess.

The buns, soft white beauties from a local bakery, are not toasted. If you want onions, the grillperson scoops a bunch from the pile and transfers to a bun taking a moment to drain any remaining water. Cheese? Not at Pete's. In 109 years, a burger has never seen a slice of cheese at Pete's. In fact, a burger with or without onions is your only option.

As you've probably surmised, this burger is not a big, charred grease bomb. Quite the opposite, the burger at Pete's is moist, ridiculously hot, and not greasy. The limp onion, soft bun, and steamy hot beef package is surprisingly tasty. Your options for toppings are ketchup, mustard, and horseradish mustard.

Although Pete's is small, the stand employs a dual window system to service customers. One Gokey makes burger magic at the griddle while two others work the windows, wrap burgers, and make change. The dual window setup makes for an excellent study in line dynamics. Most of the time both lines have an equal number of patient customers. But every once in a while, a line grows with over twenty-five tourists and newbies that don't realize there's a second window. Without fail, a regular spots the imbalance and goes for the empty window. When I saw a regular named Ernie Moon briskly approach the empty window I asked why. "If they want to stand in line," he said, gesturing to the opposite window, "that's fine with me!" He then explained, "I guess that's what

you'd call having 'experience.' I've been coming here for sixty years." The reality is that the lines move very quickly. Assuming the griddle is full of burgers ready to go, you can step up to place your order and be walking away in thirty seconds with a steaming bag full of hamburger history.

Rumor has it that years ago a Chicagoan passing through town asked Pete what he was cooking his amazing tasting burgers in and Pete told him, "Hamburger oil." He then proceeded to sell him a gallon of water.

Don't make the mistake of showing up in Prairie du Chien in the cold months looking for a burger at Pete's. The tiny stand is seasonal and only open for six months of the year. And even during that time they are only open three days a week, Friday, Saturday, and Sunday.

"This stand put all the grandkids through college," Mary told me, which numbered fifteen. "I think my grandfather would be amazed that it's still here." And how fortunate we all are that Pete's thrives.

THE PLAZA TAVERN

319 North Henry St | Madison, WI 53703 | 608-255-6592 | Mon–Thurs 11 am–2 am
Fri & Sat 11 am–2:30 am | Closed Sun | www.theplazatavern.com

The sauce is the draw and its ingredients are most definitely kept secret. Only a handful of insiders know the fifty-plus-year-old recipe. "A bunch of restaurants claim they serve a Plaza Burger but they don't," grillman Mick once told me with assurance. "Hey, I don't even know the recipe!" Which is a little strange for a guy who probably made over a thousand of the thin patty wonders that week alone.

Owner Dean Hetue sequesters himself in a locked room in the kitchen to concoct the creamy white tangy sauce the Plaza has been putting on their burgers since the mid-1960s. "All I can tell you," Mick went on, "is that it's a sour cream and mayo-based sauce, and the rest is a secret." Whatever it is, this unique topping is good. Very, very good.

The Plaza is a tavern first, so the burgers at this popular watering hole seem like an afterthought. Regardless of the Plaza's standard collegiate look and feel, the burger is anything but standard. Cooked on a tiny griddle next to the long rows of hard booze, the unique arrangement of elements suggests that this is more than just another bar burger. Fresh, thin quarter-pound patties are grilled in plain sight of bar patrons, placed on incredibly soft half-wheat buns, and served with a dollop of the famously addictive sauce. The presence of a wheat bun actually makes it feel like you could have one or two more, guilt-free.

The Tavern has the look of an enormous romper room for adults, complete with endless diversions for the buzz-addled, ranging from darts to pool and with pinball and video games for the solo drinkers. There are TVs everywhere and the Plaza's sheer size suggests that large, boisterous crowds can fill the place (with the University of Wisconsin around the corner that's not difficult to imagine, and it's been rumored that Joan Cusack was once tossed from the bar). But the few times I've been there (during lunch), I pretty much had the place to myself.

The Plaza has been a bar for over a century, with a stint as a speakeasy during Prohibition. In 1963, Mary and Harold Huss bought the bar and introduced their burger. Mary concocted the now-famous sauce and placed her burger on a half-wheat bun that is still used today.

Dean started working at the Plaza in 1980 in hopes that one day he might own the place. "I figured that if I stuck around long enough . . ." His patience paid off, and in 2003 the second generation of the Huss family sold Dean the tavern—and the recipe for the secret sauce. "I have a great photo of me handing Tom Huss the check and he's handing me the recipe," Dean told me, laughing. "It almost looks like we are in a tug-of-war." That recipe now rests in a safe deposit box, and in Dean's head. "My wife knew the recipe, but it's been years since she's made the sauce. I'll bet she forgot."

The menu at the Plaza is limited to things you might eat while drinking, i.e. "bar food."

Hot dogs and a fishwich are available, but you'd be wise to indulge in a few Plaza Burgers. They also serve one of my favorite sides, a not-to-be-missed treat of the upper Midwest, the fried cheese curd. Imagine a rustic, homespun version of the processed mozzarella stick, and you'll get the picture. Impossibly good, these deep-fried, random-sized wads of breaded fresh cheese are worth every calorie.

The Plaza sits on a bizarre little street near the state's capitol building and among the bustling stores catering to Madison's large student population. "There's so little parking out front," Dean mused, "so it's amazing that so many people find their way here." Dean has noticed, in his nearly four decades at the tavern, students turn into alumni and continue to patronize the Plaza. "It's the sauce that brings them back."

SOLLY'S GRILLE

4629 North Port Washington Road | Milwaukee, WI 53212 | 414-332-8808
Mon 10 am–8 pm | Tues–Sat 6:30 am–8 pm | Sun 8 am–4 pm | www.sollysgrille.com

For the burger purist and lover of the things that make America unique, a visit to Solly's is imperative. Pure and simple, Solly's serves one of the last real butter burgers in the nation. When I say "real" I'm referring to the copious amounts of creamy Wisconsin butter that is used on their burgers, as opposed to what their surrounding competition calls a butter burger. To everyone else who peddles this great Wisconsin

treat, the burger bun is coated with a thin swipe of butter, much in the way you might butter your toast if you were on a diet. Solly's dramatically bends the rules and treats the butter as a condiment. In other words, you actually won't believe how much butter goes on the burger. The first time I visited Solly's, I stood and watched that which I had only heard about from disbelieving past patrons. Could they really use upward of two to three tablespoons of butter on one smallish cheeseburger? Oh yes, they do, and have been for over seventy years.

I kid you not when I say that a butter burger at Solly's, as gross as it may sound, is an absolutely sublime experience in the gastronomic fabric of America and should be experienced by all. You may also catch yourself doing what I did subconsciously on my first visit—dipping the last bite of your burger back into the pool of butter on your plate. You quickly discover that whatever guilt you harbored while taking your first bite has dissolved by your last.

In 1936, Kenneth Solomon bought Bay Lunch in Milwaukee a clean sixteen-stool diner that served coffee, hamburgers, and bratwurst, and changed the name to his own. In 1971, he relocated Solly's Coffee Shop a few miles north to the Milwaukee suburb of Glendale. He left the restaurant to his second wife, Sylvia, and she in turn sold the business to her son and current owner, Glenn Fieber.

The cheery and cherubic Glenn, fresh from a successful construction business, was faced with an unusual dilemma early in his ownership— move or perish. In 2000, the city government actually assisted Glenn in moving the entire restaurant a few hundred yards south to make way for, of all things, an outpatient heart clinic.

The interior of Solly's is a comfortable blend of yellow Formica horseshoe counters, swivel stools, and wood paneling. As they have been for decades, the burgers, fries, and shakes are all prepared in view of the counter patrons.

The fresh ground three-ounce thin patties show up at Solly's daily and are cooked on a large flattop griddle. The toasted buns are standard white squishy, but a soft "pillow" bun is also offered. There are many burger combinations and sizes (like the impressive two-patty "Cheese Head" that an ex-Navy Seal friend of mine devours with ease), but I suggest doing what my good friend and butter burger devotee Rick Cohler has been doing for almost sixty years at Solly's—just order a butter burger.

Rick introduced me to Solly's. On our first visit together, he begged me to try a burger "without" which is a burger on a bun with butter only, no onions. I obliged and immediately understood what all the fuss was about. As you bite into a freshly built butter burger, you actually have the opportunity to experience the texture of soft butter before it melts into a pool on your plate. Unlike Rick, my "usual" at

Solly's is a burger with onions. The stewed onions at Solly's are like none other I have experienced. They are both sweet and salty, and full of flavor. I could eat a bowl of them with a spoon.

Glenn is one of my truest allies in the burger world. He understands his place in American history and his duty to supply hungry burger lovers with a treat as unique as the butter burger. And I've been to Solly's so many times that Glenn finally gave me my very own spot at the counter, identified by a plaque. Needless to say, I'm honored to be a part of Solly's hamburger history.

VILLAGE BAR

3801 Mineral Point Rd | Madison, WI 53705
608-233-9956 | Mon–Sat 11 am–2 am | Sun 12 pm–7 pm

"As a little kid I helped restock the liquor shelves and chip racks here," Mark Kampa told me. "I was eleven, and I always wanted to be in the bar business." Mark is the fifth owner in the bar's long history, which started in 1928 when Theodore Herling opened a grocery store at the intersection of three busy streets in Madison, directly across from a public golf course that had opened a year earlier. Following Prohibition, Herling converted the grocery store into a bar, most likely to pick up business from the golfers because the course had no halfway house.

Mark's dad was friends with the previous owners and would stop in weekly for a burger and a few beers. When Mark was at University of Wisconsin, only a mile away, he started bartending the Village Bar, which became a full-time job after college. "I was working in corrections during the day and bartending at night, and eventually saved enough for the downpayment," he told me recently. And after twelve years bartending

bought the iconic bar in 1999, which means Mark has spent most of his life at the bar.

The Village Bar is known for their burgers, or should say, burger. That's right, for half a century this joint has sold only one burger, two ways—with or without cheese. And it's served on a classic white squishy bun, on a Styrofoam plate, with pickles on the side. "You can also get onions fried or raw," Mark told me, "but that's it." Don't ask for lettuce or tomato, not here. It's a bar burger, and simply one of the best.

The cheese arguably steals the show here. If you ask for the Brick Burger, prepare to be cheesed. Mark buys only the best Wisconsin Wunderbar brick cheddar and slices it thick for the burgers. Brick is a creamy mild cheddar that melts like American but has a very unique taste that is more complex.

The burgers are cooked on a flattop just inside the front door. Mark gets his fresh 85/15 chuck patties from a local grocer and can make up to 250 on a busy Friday or Saturday (which is impressive for a bar that is only eight hundred square feet). The patties get a sprinkling of Lawry's seasoned salt before hitting the griddle, and watch what happens when the Brick cheese goes on—Mark covers the burger with a lid but tosses a handful of bar ice under the lid to create instant steam. The Brick cheese melts in seconds.

The best seats are at one of the fourteen bar stools. At some point in the 1960s large picture windows were installed where there would normally be rows of booze. The view out the window, only fifty feet away, is of the first tee and ninth green of the golf course and the action is endlessly entertaining. "We see a lot of bad putts from here," Mark told me, laughing. And anyone who has teed off from the first tee box anywhere does not want a crowd watching. At this course, you get the regulars at Village Bar.

Village Bar is a real sports bar with all local teams represented. You'll be surrounded by local team pride, and if you show up on game day (like I did the first time there) wear some red or be the odd one out. Check out the glass-topped tables— they are actually curio tables filled with all sorts of local ephemera and school pride. Just don't get distracted by the game and slam your beer down.

WEDL'S HAMBURGER STAND AND ICE CREAM PARLOR

200 East Racine St | Jefferson, WI 53549 | 920-674-3637
Mon–Thurs & Sun 10:30 am–9 pm | Fri & Sat 10:30 am–10 pm

Somewhere south of Route 94 on a lonely stretch of highway between Madison and Milwaukee sits a gem of a burger stand. I was tipped off to Wedl's by good friend and burger icon himself, Glenn Fieber of Solly's Grille in Milwaukee, Wisconsin. He told me, "Ya gotta go out there, they are making a great little burger."

The stand at Wedl's is actually eight-by-eight feet, which is sixty-five square feet—small for a place that can move up to six hundred burgers on a busy day. When I asked former owner Bill Peterson the size of the minuscule, nearly century-old stand, he went inside the larger adjacent ice cream

larger ice cream parlor but I knew the answer. "The people of Jefferson won't allow me to change anything. I can't break tradition."

In 2007, Eric and Rosie Wedl became the eighth owners of the burger stand and ice cream parlor after buying the business from the Petersons. As Bill was looking to sell, he asked his faithful twenty-year-old burger flipper Bert Wedl if he was interested in buying the place. Bert in turn talked his parents into it, and in doing so he secured his own job and possibly the future of the historic burger stand. And he told me recently, "I hope to take over one day."

The burger at Wedl's is a classic one-sixth-pound patty griddled and served on a white squishy bun. Bert grinds chuck steaks in the basement of the parlor, throws in some "secret seasonings" (tastes peppery) and rolls the grind into small golf ball–sized balls. The balls are smashed thin on the ninety-year-old griddle and cooked until the edges are crispy.

Bert is barely thirty now and has flipped burgers at the tiny stand since he was fifteen. I couldn't help but notice that when things got slow behind the grill he would step out of the stand and sit on the steps of the ice cream parlor. Do you think Bert was subconsciously trying to avoid being the next victim of a hit and run? I do.

parlor and produced a tape measure. The parlor, formerly a grocery store and at one time a hat shop, is over eight hundred square feet larger than the separate stand that sits proudly on the corner. In 1999, the stand was leveled by a reckless drunk driver while two kids were inside flipping patties. Miraculously, the employees survived with only grease burns but parts of the stand were scattered for blocks. The original griddle, a perfectly seasoned, low-sided, cast-iron skillet was recovered from the debris two blocks away. A small hole was patched and it was put back into service. After much cajoling the stand was rebuilt on the same spot. I asked former owner Bill Peterson why he wouldn't just move the burger operation into the

ZWIEG'S

904 East Main St | Watertown, WI 53094 | 920-261-1922
Mon–Thurs 5:30 am–8 Pm | Fri 5:30 am–9 pm | Sat 5:30 am–7 pm | Sun 7 am–2 pm

The first time I visited Zwieg's, the McDonald's down the street had just suffered a bad fire. "I swear I didn't do it!" Mary Zwieg joked. Mary is married to Glenn Zwieg and Glenn's parents opened this local favorite burger counter in a defunct Bartles-Maguire filling station. It is positioned perfectly at the east end of town and still looks a lot like a vintage gas station, minus the pumps.

Grover and Helen Zwieg (pronounced like "twig") saw opportunity in converting the station into a hamburger joint to feed the late-night revelers when the bars let out at 1 a.m. "We used to be open until two thirty in the morning, though I don't know if they remember eating here." Glenn told me. "Every Sunday night, there was a polka fest in town and they'd all end up here afterward, still polka-ing!" In the 1950s, Glenn's parents added a dining room to the twelve-stool counter and pretty much nothing has changed since. "We did replace the griddle in 1998," Mary pointed out, but it had been in use for fifty years, since the

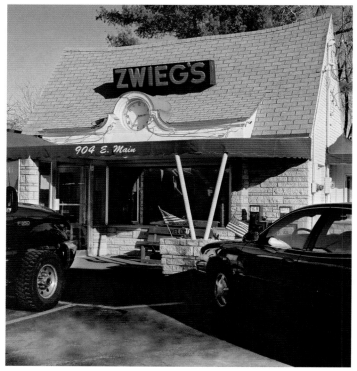

burger (and the best beef-to-bun ratio) is the double with cheese. Many are ordered with pickles and ketchup, but everyone gets theirs with onions.

The burger has been on the menu since the beginning. "That's ALL that was on the menu!" Glenn joked. Today, Zwieg's actually has an extensive menu with soups, sandwiches, and fish-fry Fridays. "I have forty-five sandwiches on the menu but most people order the burgers," Mary told me. One tasty curiosity is the hamburger soup, which is basically a chicken soup with browned hamburger meat in it.

Glenn, now seventy-five, started working at his parent's restaurant when he was in seventh grade. "I used to run down, empty the dishwasher, and eat," he told me. From that point on he has always worked at Zwieg's. He bought it in 1976, and has dedicated his entire life to the restaurant. He told me, "This is what I know."

Thank God there are still places like Zwieg's around. It's a comfortable, happy place where a counter full of regulars are really just friends waiting to be met. I'll never forget walking into Zwieg's the first time. By the time I left I knew everyone. That kind of hospitality is what makes great burgers taste even better.

beginning. It was such a big deal that the replacing of the griddle made the local newspaper.

The Zwiegs are not big on change and their customers are happy about that. They've been using the same butcher for their patties forever and Mary told me, "If they go out of business I don't know what we'll do." The burger starts as a thin one-fifth-pound patty that is cooked on the flattop in full view of the counter patrons. Sliced onion is placed on the patty. When the burger is flipped, the onion is grilled between the griddle and the patty. The patty, with its onion, is transferred to a soft white bun that has been toasted with butter on the griddle. The most popular

MY EXPERT BURGER TASTERS

After the first edition of *Hamburger America*, a small group of dedicated burger fanatics emerged hailing from every corner of the country. Some wrote e-mails saying they would do anything to have my job and, not surprisingly, they all wanted to help with future research. Most were already established food bloggers and local burger experts in their respective cities.

I continue to find this new network of friends to be indispensable and see them as first responders to new discoveries. It may sound silly, but they became my EBTs, or Expert Burger Tasters, a job they all took very seriously. After the second edition hit stores, my EBT roster quadrupled. The group was no longer small, and today, they are even more dedicated to the mission.

EBTs thanklessly enter questionable dumps, long forgotten drive-ins, and sometimes drive for hours to sample burgers and gather information. Their advance work makes my research easier and more focused. In the old days, I wasted hours blundering into a town eating all of the wrong burgers. In the process, I also made great new friends and burger allies, most of whom joined me on the road when I showed up at their favorite burger joints. When we filmed *Burger Land* for the Travel Channel, EBTs from the cities and towns we visited were on the show as local experts and burger confidantes. Life is good.

BurgerBeast in Miami; Charlie S. in Minneapolis; Seth A. and Teddy G. in Memphis; Jason C. in Seattle; Rob in Des Moines; David H.S. and Wayne G. in Dallas; Brad S. in LA; Travis Z. in Sheboygan; Jim E. in Ohio; Joe P. in Tulsa; BillysBurgers in Atlanta; The Rev in NYC; Clay D. and Todd Q. in the Midwest; Titus in Chicago; and the list goes on and on . . .

But one EBT continues to stand out: Todd McIlwee from Waunakee, Wisconsin. His dedication is beyond comprehension. He has driven hundreds of miles in pursuit of hamburger knowledge and our recent journey into Northern Wisconsin was epic.

There are others that have led me to the burgers of my dreams and I'm indebted to you all. Thank you for reminding me that I'm not alone out there in my search for greasy goodness and passion for American food history.

THANKS

This is my 4th book about hamburgers, and every single note during 2 years of research was jotted down on yellow legal pads with stolen hotel pens.

Thank you to my burger obsession enablers. I'm not alone in my nearly two decade burger quest. I have amassed an absurd amount of hamburger knowledge and owe an enormous debt of gratitude to dedicated food experts, fans and friends in many parts of the country for pointing me in the right direction and filling my brain and belly with unforgettable burger experiences. If I attempted to make a list it would go on for pages.

The first edition of this book never would have seen the light of day had it not been for my agent, Laura Dail, who saw the rejection letters piling up and persisted to find the book a home. That home, Running Press, has been patient with flexible deadlines for which I'm very grateful. Thanks to my editor of over a decade Jennifer Kasius, designer Jason Kayser, copyeditor Susan Hom, and everyone else at Running Press.

Writing an accurate guidebook with a soul is very complicated. Getting the family histories right is just as important as addresses and phone numbers. With now over 200 burger joints included this version is more detailed than ever. Huge thanks to the ultra-organized and indispensable Sydney Rey for making it all make sense (and attempting to keep me on schedule).

Walking into a familiar burger spot and being treated like a regular could very well be one of the greatest feelings in the world. Thank you to all the restaurants involved for sharing your stories and getting personal with me. Your cooperation has made writing this book a pleasure.

Enormous thanks is due as well to my close friends and family who have supported me and my burger mission from the beginning. I don't think any of you imagined my obsession would endure and neither did I. And after traveling tens of thousands of miles and writing about everyone else's family, it's great to come home to my own two, burger-loving children, Ruby and Mac.

INDEX